D0765286

NEXT LEVEL SUPPLY MANAGEMENT EXCELLENCE

YOUR STRAIGHT TO THE
BOTTOM LINE® ROADMAP

ROBERT A. RUDZKI • ROBERT J. TRENT

J.ROSS
PUBLISHING

Read the Reviews

"*Next Level Supply Management Excellence* provides a refreshing, strategic perspective on many complex aspects of supply management. The concise, straightforward approach to the multiple dimensions of supply management excellence should make it easy for you to apply the principles. This is a must-read for progressive supply management executives!"

Ernest G. Gabbard, CPSM, C.P.M., CPCM,
Senior Director, Corporate Strategic Sourcing,
Allegheny Technologies Incorporated

"Rudzki and Trent present a compelling case that a 'next level' for supply management is clearly attainable, and lay out the steps to get there. The key factors that will open this door are leadership and vision, but both must be shared and articulated broadly by the C-Suite. There is a large pot of gold at the end of this rainbow."

Brad Holcomb CPSM, CPSD, SVP & CPO, Dean Foods Company

"Executives are often looking for the secret to success, the fast and easy way to elevate their companies above the competition. If you are serious about SCM and want to drive the 'how' in addition to the 'what', Rudzki and Trent provide us with the answers:

- Identify and analyze key benefits by embracing truly strategic supply chain management for your organization.
- Garner genuine and continued support and involvement from both top management and internal customers across the organization.
- There are no shortcuts. Stake out the roadmap and then follow it diligently keeping the end goal in mind.
- Communicate successes and shortcomings consistently and frequently to all the stakeholders in the organization.
- You are only as good as your weakest supplier.

I had the pleasure of hiring Bob Rudzki and his team to conduct the work at CMC."

Matt Kramer, President, Kramer Global Advisory
Former EVP, Commercial Metals Company

"Having led the corporate procurement function and a significant transformation in a previous role, I feel this book is a must read for anyone undergoing or trying to understand the strategic transformation process and potential payoff. It's a great complement to *Straight to the Bottom Line®*."

John D. Smith, SVP, GM, Caesars Entertainment Corporation

"*Next Level Supply Management Excellence* is a terrific book. It applies equally to the CPO who wants to take their procurement organization to an even higher performing organization, as well as the CPO who is just beginning a transformation process. It covers a broad range of topics, with deep dives into leadership, talent, client relationships, and risk management. These are areas that MUST be focus areas for ANY sustainable transformation of procurement. I wish I had this 'guidebook' 10 years ago when I began to devise our purchasing journey!"

> **Rick Hughes**
> **Chief Purchasing Officer**
> **The Procter & Gamble Company**

"Leading analysts and practitioners have recognized for a while now that supply management practices and methodologies must be taken to the 'next level' if supply management is going to continue to deliver the returns the organization expects. But most professionals have had no idea how to accomplish this as there have been no manuals or guidebooks . . . until now. *Next Level Supply Management Excellence* is the first book to not only define the foundations of a 'next level' supply management organization, but to also provide a transformation roadmap that an organization can use to make the transition."

From advanced collaboration and negotiations management through idealized design and energy management to a detailed discussion of risk management and complexity, this is the first book that will help you understand where the untapped opportunities are, how to tackle them, and how to realize sustainable savings while identifying and managing risk from a bottom-line perspective. The discussions of idealized design and complexity alone will have you looking at your supply chain in a whole new light.

So, don't just read this book, devour it!"

Michael G. Lamoureux, Ph.D., Editor-in-Chief, Sourcing Innovation

"The title of the Rudzki and Trent book, *Next Level Supply Management Excellence*, is an apt description of the contents. A collaboration of an academic and an advisor, both with decades of actual senior leadership experience in supply management, create a how-to guide of advanced practices that is full of this-is-how-it-is-done insights.

What is great about the book is the relevance of the topics. I regularly poll CPOs about supply management topics that are important to them. It is uncanny how closely the contents of the book matches up with the projects that supply management executives are currently undertaking. Risk management, talent management, lean procurement, export compliance, and contributing to the company's growth, for example, are leading front burner issues."

Dan Meckstroth, Chief Economist, Council Director, Manufacturers Alliance

"With *Next Level Supply Management Excellence: Your Straight to the Bottom Line® Roadmap*, Robert Rudzki and Dr. Robert Trent have authored and collected a set of outstanding essays and contributions that truly provide a 'next level' contribution to their earlier books in the same area. From the intersection of working capital management and procurement strategy to global trade, supply risk and operations/lean initiatives, this volume expertly covers a range of essential topics in enough depth to keep even an expert practitioner actively engaged and taking mental notes throughout.

For organizations looking to teach their next generation of procurement, finance, and supply chain leaders about the supply management topics that will shape their efforts for decades to come—or for those looking to get a leg up on a range of emerging subjects on their own—I can't think of a better reference that covers so much ground and provides an actual roadmap of how to affect change and put advanced supply management topics to work. It's already taken a place at the front of my desk (not even my bookshelf) and I suspect it will be there for a long time to come."

Jason Busch, Director and Editor, www.spendmatters.com

"If you could pick only one book on sourcing and supply management, this would be the one. Regardless of your title or experience, the authors challenge the status quo of sourcing and supply management and encourage you to think strategically. Whether you have led, or are thinking about leading a transformation within your organization, this book will give you the confidence and tools necessary to get started and take your organization to a higher level of performance."

Daniel H. Kaufman, CPSM, Vice President Sourcing, International Specialty Products

"This is an inspiring, thought-provoking, and educational read on the future road map that best in class companies should take. The authors offer a well thought out and structured approach with numerous real-life examples on how to drive profit straight to the bottom line. I especially found the understanding and discussion on the importance of total cost of ownership and life cycle management well done. In particular, the evolution of the concept from landed total cost to include specification, operation, and disposal was exceptional. These are areas that can have the biggest impact on a company's bottom line.

"I highly recommend this book not only to members of the supply management profession but also to the C level of any organization that truly wants to take the right costs out and have those dollars materialize on the bottom line."

Todd Snelgrove, Global Manager: Value, SKF USA Inc.

"*Next Level Supply Management Excellence* is an important book for senior executives and leaders of procurement and supply chain departments. Written by knowledgeable experts, the book is a definitive work on turning your supply management organization into a strategic driver for improving top-line and bottom-line performance.

I found the emphasis on talent management to be refreshing. All too often, senior executives tend to focus more on the measurable KPIs and less on the selection/development of our employees. This book puts all of the transformation dimensions into proper perspective."

Randall S. Dearth, President and CEO, LANXESS Corporation

"Bob Rudzki and Robert Trent provide valuable insight into initiating and sustaining procurement transformation results, including developing staff, gaining leadership support for the new role of procurement in the organization, and linking procurement's activities to business strategy and financial objectives. *Next Level Supply Management Excellence* is the procurement executive's practicum for transformation, with critical insights into migration from tactical buying to strategic procurement."

Quave Danielle Burton, Vice President, Procurement Services, Collective Brands, Inc.

"*Next Level Supply Management Excellence* is an excellent sequel to *Straight to the Bottom Line®*. The book is straight to the point with real-world examples and no nonsense guidance. It includes excellent insights on supply management transformation, speaking the language of finance, and even the use of purchasing consultants. As a CPO across diverse industries for over ten years, I believe that this is the most comprehensive and up-to-date roadmap that all CPOs need to be versed in to take their organizations to the next level. Actually, this book's principles are applicable whether you are buying for a manufacturing or a service firm or whether you are a small or big business.

This is a must-read not only for supply chain professionals, but for any business leader who wants to supercharge their critical supply chain initiatives."

Howard Levy, Chief Procurement Officer, Biomet, Inc.

Copyright ©2011 by Robert A. Rudzki and Robert J. Trent

ISBN: 978-1-60427-059-4

Printed and bound in the U.S.A. Printed on acid-free paper.

10 9 8 7 6 5 4 3 2 1

Library of Congress Cataloging-in-Publication Data

Rudzki, Robert A., 1953-
Next level supply management excellence : your straight to the bottom line
roadmap / by Robert A. Rudzki, Robert J. Trent.
   p. cm.
  Includes bibliographical references and index.
  ISBN 978-1-60427-059-4 (hardcover : alk. paper)
1. Business logistics. I. Trent, Robert J. II. Title.
  HD38.5.R83 2011
  658.7—dc22

                                            2011015504

Phone: (954) 727-9333
Fax: (561) 892-0700
Web: www.jrosspub.com

Contents

Foreword

As a supply management professional have you ever felt a sense of frustration over the pace of progress in your organization? Have you championed a particular initiative that you *know* will improve both operational and cost performance, only to see it wither on the bureaucratic vine? Are incremental improvements in the supply management process the best you've been able to pull off?

If the answer to all or most of these questions is yes, you need to take your actions and attitude to the next level. This book by Robert Rudzki and Robert Trent will help you do that. It lays out the tactics and strategies you can put in place to unlock the potential of supply management excellence in your business. The authors speak authoritatively not just about the existing state of supply management practices, but more importantly about the emerging practices that lead to that next level.

Rudzki and Trent are well qualified and well positioned to tell this story. Together, they bring a background of front-line practitioner expertise, consulting engagements across a range of industries, and an academic rigor to the research that informs the messages conveyed in these pages. Yes, many of the approaches they advocate are challenging and demand an intellectual and operational stretch. But in all cases they are grounded in solid principles that have been tried and tested in the real world.

To get to the next level of proficiency, supply management people need to understand accepted best practices at the current level. That's a great feature of this book—it lays out the details of techniques like strategic sourcing, supplier collaboration, and risk assessment to ensure a basic understanding of these concepts. Then it offers practical steps for elevating performance across each of these best-practice areas to move on to the next, higher level of excellence. That's a rare quality among business books these days.

A great example of this is the discussion around procurement's early involvement in capital expenditure projects. While most managers probably recognize the value of early involvement, relatively few organizations do this successfully and in a structured manner. The authors fill that gap by explaining how it's done—and as a bonus offer an insightful case study on how Alcoa fully integrates its procurement function into the capital expenditure process. The results posted by the industry leader were truly amazing, as you will learn.

In fact, solid case examples add context, color, and depth of understanding throughout the book. These are top-flight companies whose mastery of the art and science of procurement is a model to anyone in an industry. Consider Colgate's successful attack on product complexity throughout its global supply network, or Boston Scientific's supplier-oriented approach to risk management. Just as valuable are the authors' anecdotes and personal experiences drawn from their deep and diverse background.

Next Level Supply Management Excellence can, in fact, get you and your organization to the next level. It has all the information, insights, and instruction needed. But there's one more important element: You, the reader. Achieving the kinds of breakthroughs promised in these pages calls for a certain amount of boldness, courage, and a willingness to persevere. And importantly, real progress depends on breaking out of the comfort zone of doing the same things the same way.

Let's restate this a little more simply: achieving the next level of supply management excellence is all about personal leadership. Bottom line, that's the powerful underlying message of this book.

—Frank J. Quinn, Editorial Director, *Supply Chain Management Review*

Preface

In 2005 Robert A. Rudzki led an effort that resulted in a book titled *Straight to the Bottom Line®—An Executive's Roadmap to World Class Supply Management*. This book argued persuasively that the actions taken by progressive supply organizations will work their way, as the title suggests, straight to the bottom line. This book was immediately embraced by practitioners as they pushed forward into a brave, new, and oftentimes uncharted world. The book continues to sell well as more and more supply leaders recognize the need for their procurement groups to become strategic contributors. After *Straight to the Bottom Line®* Bob Rudzki authored two more books—*On Demand Supply Management: World Class Strategies, Practices and Technology* and the general leadership book *Beat the Odds: Avoid Corporate Death and Build a Resilient Enterprise*.

About a year after the introduction of *Straight to the Bottom Line®*, Robert Trent introduced a book titled *Strategic Supply Management—Creating the Next Source of Competitive Advantage*. This book detailed what purchasing groups needed to do to become strategic supply management organizations. He then published two more books—*End-to-End Lean Management: A Guide to Complete Supply Chain Improvement* and *Managing Global Supply and Risk: Best Practices, Concepts, and Strategies*.

These six books provide a solid picture of what procurement and supply organizations (as well as supply chain organizations) should look like today. The problem comes whenever we use the word "today." The word becomes obsolete as another word called "tomorrow" replaces it. Soon, a whole bunch of tomorrows come and go, so much so that it eventually becomes time to define the next level of knowledge and understanding. And that is exactly what we do here. Welcome to the next level of supply management excellence.

What is Unique About this Book?

A number of unique themes and features underlie this book. They combine to create a final product that we think differentiates itself from other procurement and supply management resources. These themes and features include the concept of the next level; a focus on leadership and transformation; a set of new and expanded topics; the inevitable merger between supply management and finance; and the power of collective wisdom.

Defining the Next-level

This book is about something we have termed the "next level." Every discipline has a body of knowledge that defines what we know or what defines excellence today. This knowledge changes, sometimes dramatically, as we discover new and better ways of doing things. Today's standard of excellence becomes tomorrow's average performance. If knowledge does not advance the inevitable result is stagnant economic growth and lower standards of living.

Next-level supply organizations have the capability to look at where they have been, understand the current state of knowledge, and project what they need to do to be successful over the next five years. They can visualize what that next level of knowledge and expertise looks like. It was not that long ago when supply base reduction and crafting longer-term supply agreements, for example, were new, exciting, and even a bit frightening to most supply managers. Now, these practices barely elicit a yawn. But what comes after that? And instead of a strict focus on material cost reductions, why not think about revenue enhancement and better management of capital projects? Instead of thinking about direct materials, why not think about how to manage every good and service that an organization requires? As supply organizations take a broader view of their domain, entirely new areas of opportunity and growth begin to take shape. This broad-based thinking begins to define areas that require next-level thinking, something that is a major focus of this book.

A Focus on Leadership and Transformation

It is not enough to present next-level activities and approaches and assume they magically happen. Equally important is a need to provide a framework for getting from "here" to "there," or what we refer to as the transformation process. We view transformation as the process of fundamentally altering organizational capabilities to improve the achievement of results. And let's not underestimate the central relationship between leadership and successful transformation. An emphasis on leadership and transformation appear throughout this book. In fact, the first section of the book, titled *Leading Supply Management Transformation*, includes six chapters that deal primarily with leadership and transformation.

New and Expanded Topics

One of the more enjoyable parts of crafting this book involved identifying the procurement and supply management topics that have not received serious attention from other sources. This book is not about reiterating what others have already done. New topics appear that are not addressed well in other supply management books, making this a valuable resource. Some of these topics include:

- an in-depth treatment of supply chain complexity, one of today's hot business topics

- applying Lean thinking and techniques to supplier development
- a comprehensive framework for sourcing and energy management
- combining Lean Six Sigma and supply management
- achieving enhanced sourcing through idealized design
- appreciating what happens when the worlds of sales and procurement collide
- import and export issues affecting international trade
- toolkits for strategic sourcing success
- an enhanced set of supply management performance measures
- five chapters that relate to the important connection between supply management and finance, including working capital and capital project management

Topics that are more familiar to readers are enhanced to include next-level thinking. In one of our earlier books we addressed early procurement involvement during new product development, primarily to achieve product cost reductions. We extend this topic in this book to feature collaborating early and often with suppliers, including during new product *and* technology development, to achieve top-line, revenue growth. A narrow focus on cost reduction, while still important today is becoming passé.

In the organizational governance realm we define what a future supply organization should look like as well as introduce some important ideas related to virtual teams. Within talent management we think about something called talent analytics as well as how to manage external talent resources, not just internal resources. We also extend our thinking about strategic sourcing, negotiations management, and supply risk management beyond today's commonly accepted body of knowledge. A focus on the next level drives some new thinking across a variety of areas.

Regarding supply management technology, we make the point that technology is a key "enabler" of the overall supply management plan or program. This key enabler continues to undergo rapid evolution in capabilities, service models and providers. As a result, we decided to create an out-of-book supplement on technology—a resource that can be easily updated as appropriate. Readers are invited to visit the book's website (www.NextLevelSupply.com) and periodically check the Technology section for supplemental materials.

Stressing the Inevitable Merger between Supply Management and Finance

We are of the strong belief that next-level supply leaders must understand and speak the functional language of finance. That language, perhaps more than any other captures the attention of corporate leaders, shareholders, and Wall Street analysts.

A number of chapters in this book relate to financial topics, something we do not see in other supply management resources. Chapter 4 addresses speaking like a CFO and getting senior management's attention; Chapter 7 is about collaborating with suppliers to achieve revenue growth; Chapter 10 deals with comprehensive energy management; Chapter 15 focuses on procurement's central role in managing working capital; and Chapter 16 is about early procurement and supplier involvement in capital projects. Whether we like it or not the next level of supply management excellence will feature strong linkages between procurement, finance, and financial thinking. Don't worry—this book has you covered when it comes to the inevitable merger of supply management and finance.

The Power of Collective Wisdom

This book includes the contributions and insights of several dozen procurement and supply management leaders. These individuals have generously contributed in various ways—some authored or coauthored entire chapters; others provided in-depth interviews that became end-of-chapter cases or value-added content within a chapter; some provided relevant research and data from their companies, and still others reviewed our completed chapters for accuracy, completeness, and content. When you read this book you are benefitting from the wisdom of procurement and supply leaders who have hundreds of years of collective experience. This book taps into some really good minds.

Organization of the Book

This book, which is for anyone interested in understanding what a more advanced state of procurement and supply management will look like over the next five years, is divided into three major parts. Part One, *Leading Supply Management Transformation*, includes six chapters that build the foundation and provide the framework for moving to the next level of supply management. In particular, leadership, transformation, organization, and talent management all play a predominant role in Part One.

Part Two, *Critical Topics in Supply Management Transformation*, includes ten chapters that provide significant detail about areas that essentially define a next-level supply organization. And finally, Part Three, *Additional Key Topics in Next-Level Supply Management*, presents a variety of topics that will add value to the reader's knowledge base and next-level professional agenda.

Most readers will find that some of the ideas presented in this book require some appreciable changes that take them out of their comfort zone. The journey that results from these changes will bring higher-level visibility, accountability, risk, and hopefully reward. But no matter how far we travel, or how much we change, there will always be another destination beyond the one we just arrived at. The next level of supply management presented here will eventually be replaced with a new next level. As Zig Ziglar once said, "Go as far as you can see and when you get there, you will always be able to see farther." It is time to see and go farther, keeping in mind that continuous change is inevitable.

Acknowledgments

In the Preface, the authors note the important role played by the Contributors in the development and refinement of this book. The extensive experience of the Contributors was valuable and appreciated by the authors, and we hope, by the readers as well. All of the Contributors are well-known by one or both of the authors. They represent peers, past and current colleagues, as well as individuals with whom we collaborate on consulting and advisory work. Perhaps more importantly, the Contributors are also known to many as leading supply management leaders.

The authors also wish to acknowledge the following individuals and associations for their support of this book:

- Andrew Reese, Editor, *Supply and Demand Chain Executive* magazine, for his permission to reprint his case study regarding the supply chain transformation at Commercial Metals Company—which appears as Chapter 17; and also for his support of the survey behind the chapter on sales and procurement perceptions of each other—Chapter 20.
- Lori Freifeld, Editor, *Sales & Marketing Management* magazine; Cam Mackey, Director and Dan Meckstroth, Ph.D. and Director, Manufacturers Alliance/MAPI; for their support of the survey behind the chapter on sales and procurement perceptions of each other—Chapter 20.
- Andrew Bartolini, Managing Director of Ardent Partners, and former Vice President of Aberdeen.
- Jason Hekl, Vice President of Coupa, Inc.
- Kevin Potts, Vice President of Emptoris, Inc.

Finally, the authors acknowledge the encouragement received from past and current students (Trent), and past and current colleagues and clients (Rudzki), to share their perspectives about Next Level Supply Management Excellence.

About the Authors

Robert A. Rudzki

 Robert A. Rudzki, a former corporate financial and procurement executive, is President of Greybeard Advisors LLC (www.GreybeardAdvisors.com). Since its formation, Greybeard has become a leading provider of advisory services for procurement transformation, strategic sourcing and supply chain management. Mr. Rudzki has personally been an advisor to some of the leading companies in major industry sectors. He, and his colleagues at Greybeard, help companies do what is described in this book.

Prior to founding Greybeard Advisors in 2004, Mr. Rudzki served as Senior Vice President for Bayer Corp., the North American subsidiary of Bayer AG. At Bayer, he led a nationally-recognized transformation that generated significant improvements in costs and working capital, and was a finalist for *Purchasing* Magazine's Medal of Excellence. Prior to Bayer, he was an executive at Bethlehem Steel Corp., where he oversaw Bethlehem's global procurement and logistics activities. During his tenure, Bethlehem's procurement organization was recognized as "top quartile" in a global benchmarking study conducted by A.T. Kearney, and was also twice recognized by *Purchasing* Magazine as a "Best Place to Work."

A frequent speaker at conferences, Mr. Rudzki is co-author of the supply management best seller *Straight to the Bottom Line*®, and is co-author of *On-Demand Supply Management*. He is also the author of the leadership book *Beat the Odds: Avoid Corporate Death and Build a Resilient Enterprise*, and authors a blog on the website of Supply Chain Management Review magazine.

Mr. Rudzki graduated Summa Cum Laude from Lehigh University, with a BS degree in industrial engineering, and earned an MBA in finance from The Wharton School. Bob can be reached at Rudzki@GreybeardAdvisors.com.

Robert J. Trent, PhD

Dr. Robert Trent is the supply chain management program director and the George N. Beckwith professor of management at Lehigh University, where he teaches at the undergraduate and graduate levels. He holds a B.S. degree in materials logistics management from Michigan State University, an MBA from Wayne State University, and a PhD in purchasing/operations management from Michigan State University.

Prior to his return to academia, Bob worked for the Chrysler Corporation. His industrial experience includes assignments in production scheduling, packaging engineering with responsibility for new part packaging set-up and the purchase of nonproductive materials, distribution planning, and operations management at the Boston regional parts distribution facility. He has also worked on numerous special industry projects. Bob stays active with industry members through research projects, consulting, and training services. He has consulted with or provided training services to 40 government agencies and corporations and worked directly with companies on dozens of research visits.

Bob has authored or co-authored dozens of articles appearing in business publications. He has also made presentations at numerous conferences and seminars. His co-authored study on cross-functional sourcing team effectiveness was published through the *CAPS Research* in 1993; a co-authored research report on purchasing/sourcing trends was published through CAPS in 1995; a third CAPS project that investigated how organizations reduce the effort and transactions required to purchase low value goods and services was published in 1999; and a co-authored *CAPS Research* study on global sourcing was published in 2006. He is also the co-author of a textbook titled *Purchasing and Supply Chain Management* and the author of the book *Strategic Supply Management: Creating the Next Source of Competitive Advantage*. His book, *End-to-End Lean Management: A Guide to Complete Supply Chain Improvement* was published in 2008. Another book, *Managing Global Supply and Risk: Best Practices, Concepts, and Strategies*, was published in 2009. He and his family reside in Lopatcong Township, New Jersey. Bob can be reached at rjt2@Lehigh.edu.

About the Contributors

James M. Baehr

Jim has been a Senior Advisor with the independent advisory firm Greybeard Advisors LLC since 2005. His most recent corporate role was as vice president of Global Information Technology Procurement for Reed Elsevier, a New York based publisher/information provider. Prior to that, as Director of Technical and Services Procurement for Bayer Corporation at its U.S. Headquarters in Pittsburgh, he led IT sourcing teams in NAFTA and globally. Jim also has extensive experience in IT Management and a successful career in IT sales.

He's conceived and successfully implemented both corporate and international sourcing strategies for indirect materials and services to manage and reduce total cost of ownership. Other achievements in procurement include developing and institutionalizing an international contracting process and associated negotiations training. His client engagements include overseeing and assisting numerous sourcing teams ranging from fleet management, to all aspects of IT, to marketing, as well as being a Strategic Sourcing & Negotiations Management (SSNM) trainer and coach.

Jim has served on several industry association advisory boards and community associations in various capacities including the Institute for Supply Management, the Society of Information Managers, the Board of Governors of the Joint Chemical Group of Pittsburgh, and the Executive Committee of the Chemical Association of Pittsburgh, Chemical Processor Directors—Information Technology Subgroup. Some of his speaking engagements include Marcus Evans, the Institute for Supply Management, IACCM, the Center for Business Intelligence and the Pharmaceuticals Technology Congress.

Jim can be reached at Baehr@GreybeardAdvisors.com.

Mark S. Berlin

Mark began his professional career as an engineering designer for Ford Motor Company, transitioning to global procurement. Serving in a variety of procurement management positions, that included integrating Ford Asia-Pacific procurement, into Ford's global procurement activities.

Utilizing the concepts of Lean, Mark has a track record of delivering bottom line value through supplier and cross-functional collaboration and sustainable low cost country (LCC) solutions. He has held vice president roles in the construction equipment and automotive industries. He is recognized for developing high performing procurement and supply chain teams in automotive, airline, construction equipment, lighting, heating and cooling, and technology industries. These teams evaluate current state operations and transform processes for sustainable cost and revenue improvements, leading and influencing across company matrices, cultures, and time zones.

Mr. Berlin holds a bachelor's degree in business administration from Madonna University and an MBA with a concentration in international business from the University of Detroit-Mercy. He is a member of the Institute for Supply Management and the Council of Supply Chain Management Professionals. He also is a frequent speaker at business conferences, where he discusses supply chain management, working capital improvement and similar topics. Most recently, he was interviewed by Gartner for an article on the perils and pitfalls of sourcing in China. In addition, Mark is one of Greybeard's senior advisors.

Mark can be reached at Berlin@GreybeardAdvisors.com.

Gregg Brandyberry

A recognized pioneer in procurement and sourcing technology, Gregg Brandyberry is CEO of Wildfire Commerce, and, senior advisor for A.T. Kearney Procurement and Analytic Solutions organization. Mr. Brandyberry was most recently the vice president of Procurement of Global Systems and Operations at Fortune 150 pharmaceutical giant GlaxoSmithKline. Mr. Brandyberry has over 30 years experience in a variety of industries including automotive, textile, manufactured goods, electronics, and healthcare. He has experience in laboratory, quality, manufacturing, IT systems, operations, procurement and supply chain having held senior management roles in each discipline.

In 2003, under Gregg's leadership, GlaxoSmithKline was awarded the prestigious Charter Institute of Procurement and Supply award for "Best Use of Technology by a Procurement Organization". Additionally in 2005, A.T. Kearney identified GlaxoSmithKline as having deployed a global best practice portfolio of electronic procurement tools (2005 Assessment for Excellence in Procurement). In 2008, Mr. Brandyberry was named as one of the Top 25 Supply Chain Executives by Supply Chain and Logistics magazine. He was also recognized as one of the Top 100 Most Inspirational Pharmaceuticals Executives by PharmaVoice100 (the first supply chain executive to achieve this award).

Mr. Brandyberry sits on many advisory boards and is a past trustee for the Center for Strategic Sourcing Leadership (CSSL).

Gregg can be reached at: greggbrandyberry@wildfirecommerce.com.

Christine S. (Christie) Breves

Christine S. (Christie) Breves is Chief Procurement Officer for Alcoa, responsible for the company's global procurement of goods and services, including strategic materials, indirect materials and services, and capital. Prior to her current position, she was vice president of procurement within Alcoa's Global Business Services organization. Ms. Breves was named to her present position in December 2004.

Ms. Breves joined Alcoa in 1998 as director of procurement, following Alcoa's acquisition of Alumax Inc., the aluminum producer. During her career at Alumax, she held a series of management positions in accounting, maintenance, strategic planning, materials management, and purchasing. Earlier, Ms. Breves held positions at Exxon and Raybestos Manhattan.

Ms. Breves obtained a bachelor's degree in business administration with an accounting emphasis from the College of Charleston and an MBA degree from The Citadel, both located in Charleston, South Carolina. She currently serves as vice chairman of the CAPS Board of Trustees. She is a member and past chairperson of the Purchasing Round Table. She served on the Board of Directors of Quadrem, an e-marketplace serving the mining and metals industry, from 2002–2007 and is a past member of Purchasing Magazine's Editorial Advisory Board. Ms. Breves is a Certified Purchasing Manager and served on the ISM (*Institute for Supply Management*) Board of Directors from 2001–2007.

David Butler

David Butler is currently the Senior Director of Global Sourcing for Philips-Respironics, a leading global provider of solutions for the Home Healthcare marketplace. In his 14 years with Philips-Respironics, David has held roles in supplier quality engineering, quality control and the past nine years as the leader of the global sourcing organization. During his tenure, David has led the transformation of the sourcing organization from a tactical buying group to a strategic global purchasing organization which today manages $500M in direct material spend. David's organization has become known for their ability to team with the new product development function to optimize supplied material and service solutions that meet the needs of the home health care customer. His work in this area was chronicled in the book *The Incredible Payback* written by Dave Nelson, Jonathan Stegner and Patricia Moody.

Prior to joining Respironics, David was employed as a quality manager for Rock Tenn Company, a statistics consultant for companies in the steel industry and as a production team leader for the Pepsi-Cola Company. David holds BSIE and MSIE degrees from the University of Pittsburgh and has been certified as a Quality Engineer, Auditor, and Reliability Engineer.

David is currently serving on the Editorial Advisory Board for the recently established My Purchasing Center on-line magazine.

He can be reached at dbutler4665@yahoo.com.

Ronald D. Casbon

Ron has been a senior advisor with Greybeard Advisors since 2008. Prior to joining Greybeard, he served as Head of Indirect Materials and Services Procurement at Bayer Corporation's U.S. Headquarters in Pittsburgh, Pa.

Ron has more than forty years of experience in Purchasing and Materials Management at both the corporate and business unit levels. Prior to joining Bayer, Ron completed a successful career in the steel industry holding positions of General Manager of Transportation and Logistics and General Manager of Capital and MRO Procurement. Areas of purchasing and materials management experience include: business planning, strategic sourcing, consortium buying, inventory management, surplus asset liquidation and disposal, transportation and logistics and project expediting.

Ron is a Certified Purchasing Manager (C.P.M.), an active member of the Institute for Supply Management-Pittsburgh Chapter, and is a past president and director of national affairs for the Lehigh Valley Chapter of ISM.

Ron can be reached at Casbon@GreybeardAdvisors.com.

Mark Donovan

Mark Donovan, has a BA in economics from Wilfrid Laurier University and a Lean Six Sigma Black Belt, is a retail/supply chain veteran, established the collaboration with Washburn University, the Topeka Chamber of Commerce, and with Doug Von Feldt created the Lean Six Sigma program at Washburn University in January of 2009. He has taught the Lean Six Sigma course in the US as well as in China and Latin America.

Mr. Donovan has served in a number of senior level positions including his current role of Director of Continuous Improvement at Collective Brands Inc. (Payless ShoeSource), with the responsibility of building and driving the Corporate Continuous Improvement program across CBI's global operations. Previous to that he was with Freidman's Jewelers as vice president of Merchandise Planning, Distribution & Operations Finance and spent fifteen years with Blockbuster Entertainment where he served in a number of senior roles, including Assistant Corporate Controller and SR Director of Supply Chain Finance, where he led the Lean Six Sigma initiative.

Mr. Donovan has served on a number of boards including on the University of Texas-Dallas, C4ISN Advisory Board, which he currently services, the North Central Texas Workforce Board, The McKinney Education Foundation,

The McKinney Community Development Corporation, the Canadian Motion Picture Foundation, and the De La Salle College Board of Trustees.

Mark can be reached at markadonovan@yahoo.com.

Theodore L. Eichenlaub

As a senior energy advisor at Greybeard Advisors LLC, Ted takes pride in assisting energy end-users in developing cost effective and insightful solutions to their commercial, technical and regulatory energy management issues.

Ted's extensive experience was gained from diversified responsibilities within the energy intensive steel industry. He has worked in various engineering, purchasing, and management capacities at Bethlehem Steel Corporation with special emphasis on fuels, utilities, and energy related processes. Among his assignments, Ted directed an instrumentation and control engineering group, managed a technical services department of 120 hourly and salaried employees, and managed corporate level energy procurement activities for natural gas and other fuels with an annual spend of several $100 million. He consulted to the corporation's various plants on energy related matters.

A successful leader and team player, Ted has participated in the justification, engineering, installation, and operation of capital projects ranging into tens of millions of dollars. He directed QA practices to assure efficient fuel and power operations, implementation of innovative labor practices, as well as the strategic purchasing of supply chain components for natural gas, fuel oil, and propane. He has achieved millions of dollars in energy related cost reductions through strategic supplier selection, contract negotiation, bypass initiatives, risk management, and regulatory intervention. His combined plant and corporate level experience lend a well-rounded understanding and customer focus to problem solving and opportunity development.

Ted can be reached at Eichenlaub@GreybeardAdvisors.com.

Peter Franolic

As leader of the energy practice for Greybeard Advisors LLC, Peter leads efforts to assist clients to achieve best practices in comprehensive energy management and reduce their overall energy cost. He provides experience and knowledge in developing energy management practices that fully incorporate the tools and opportunities available in today's turbulent market environment.

Prior to joining Greybeard Advisors, Peter was Director, Corporate Energy Affairs, for Bethlehem Steel Corp., one of the largest industrial consumers of energy in the U.S. In that position, he was directly responsible for the overall annual energy budget exceeding $500 million. He managed all aspects of energy procurement including natural gas, electricity, fuel oils, and prepared gases like oxygen and nitrogen. He led efforts to develop price/risk management strategies for the energy commodities, energy project development, and coordinated both state and federal regulatory and legislative activity impacting on energy.

During his career, Peter led or was a key participant in many teams that developed and executed many energy cost reduction opportunities resulting in millions of dollars per year in cost benefit. These benefits were accomplished through negotiating special contracts, developing unique rate structures for utility service, aggressive participation in utility rate proceedings, leading edge participation in evolving market opportunities, innovative hedging strategies for natural gas, implementing energy efficiency projects, etc.

Peter has developed in-depth experience in most aspects of the energy industry and has used this experience to produce significant benefits for clients in a variety of industries.

Peter can be reached at Franolic@GreybeardAdvisors.com.

Jonathan P. Gilbert

Jon has been a senior advisor with Greybeard Advisors LLC since 2008. An expert in supply chain management, logistics, sourcing, and planning, he has over 21 years of experience in improving service, reducing cost, increasing efficiency, and integrating new technologies for clients in the manufacturing, distribution, and services sectors.

Jon specializes in strategic sourcing, building departmental capabilities, improving processes, designing and optimizing logistics networks, and developing strategies for transportation and logistics. He has recently completed projects for Commercial Metals Company, United Technologies, Celanese Corporation, Tenneco, DTE Energy, and other Fortune 500 companies.

Jon has consistently developed and successfully implemented sourcing strategies for transportation, logistics, and supporting services that reduce total cost of ownership for his clients.

Before starting his consulting career, Jon served as Vice President, Logistics and Planning for NuCO2 of Stuart, Florida. He has also held significant leadership positions at MF Electronics as Director of Operations, and at BOC Group where he managed supply chain planning and software development teams. Jon started his career in national account sales and marketing at Pyle Corporation, a Pennsylvania-based trucking company and 3PL provider.

He is a CSCMP member and a former vice president of the New Jersey/New York Chapter of the American Society of Transportation and Logistics.

Jon can be reached at Gilbert@GreybeardAdvisors.com.

Stephen R. Johnsen

Stephen R. Johnsen is President of Bayer International Trade Services Corporation (BITS). BITS is an Interest Charge-Domestic International Sales

Corporation (IC-DISC) that provides trade and compliance services to the roughly $13 billion in U.S. business of Bayer AG. In this position, Steve is responsible for all aspects of trade policy and compliance for the Bayer U.S. operations' nearly $5 billion in annual international transactions. Steve administers the international trade compliance policies and procedures and is responsible for administration of customs business activities and export controls for all of the U.S. Bayer operating companies (MaterialScience, HealthCare and CropScience).

Steve developed Bayer's Tier III C-TPAT program and oversees free trade agreement, tariff suspension, duty drawback and foreign trade zone programs. Steve serves on the Executive Committee and Board of Governors and is currently Chair Elect of the American Association of Exporters and Importers (AAEI). Steve serves on the boards of several other non-profit organizations including Aliquippa Impact, Inc. He is an active member in AAEI's Chemicals and Bulk Commodities Committee, the American Chemistry Council's Subteam on the Chemical Weapons Convention and Export Controls, and the American Chemistry Society.

Steve is co-author of *Global Sourcing & Purchasing Post 9/11: New Logistics Compliance Requirements and Best Practices*, which was released in October 2005 and highlights customs compliance and supply chain security requirements. He is the program lead of Bayer's North American strategic initiative to embed compliance as a fundamental business operating principle and serves as the secretary of Bayer Corporation's Compliance, Audit and Risk Management Committee. He has extensive experience in creating corporate compliance programs, crafting effective internal controls and developing auditing programs. Steve has a Bachelors of Science degree in chemistry from Grove City College and is a licensed customs broker. Prior to joining Bayer, Steve was a chemist and technical service engineer for the Quaker State Corporation.

Steve can be reached at johnsen.s@comcast.net.

Richard D. Kelly

Richard D. Kelly is President of Worldwide Sourcing Advisors, LLC (WSA). WSA is an advisory firm that provides procurement, supply chain, and business development expertise. Prior to founding WSA, Richard was Vice President of Purchasing at Altria Group and Philip Morris USA.

Under his leadership, Altria received numerous Supplier Diversity awards and established innovation partnerships. Richard was co-sponsor of the Altria Worldwide Sourcing team with his colleague from Philip Morris International prior to its divesture. His career at Altria involved synergy activities in cost savings initiatives, supplier programs and strategic sourcing with Kraft Foods, Miller Brewing, and St. Michelle Winery. After Altria's acquisition of UST, Inc. and John Middleton, Inc., he consolidated and streamlined purchasing activities by establishing the Altria Client Services Purchasing Center that supported all the operating companies and corporate functions for Altria Group.

He served as an expert witness to the Virginia State General Assembly on the value of manufacturing and its supply base to the overall economy. The Mayor of Richmond, VA appointed him to a Procurement Taskforce for the City which provided recommendations for process improvements and cost savings. He is a frequent speaker on the value of free enterprise and partnerships for Junior Achievement and ISM chapters.

Richard collaborates with Greybeard Associates LLC in conducting procurement transformations and promoting professional procurement development. He has an MBA from the Fuqua School of Business at Duke University and a BS in public health with Honors from the University of North Carolina at Chapel Hill.

Contact Richard at rkelly@WorldwideSourcingAdvisors.com.

Jason Magidson

Jason is co-founder of Wildfire Commerce, a procurement consultancy and software development company, where he led the design and implementation of the online reverse auction site, SourcingFactory.com. At Wildfire Commerce, Jason has led a number of collaborative innovation projects that have produced breakthroughs in sourcing and IT, among other areas.

Jason honed his procurement innovation skills over 11 years at GlaxoSmithKline (GSK), where he contributed hundreds of millions of dollars to the bottom line (in both expense reductions and incremental sales). As Director of Global Procurement Systems and Processes, Jason created a suite of world-class procurement systems. His team won several awards including the *Baseline ROI Magazine* award for the IT project with the highest ROI (> 5,000%). In a specially created role as Director of Innovation Processes, Jason worked across the company to streamline and transform processes.

Prior to joining GSK, Jason spent ten years in the strategic management consulting firm, INTERACT, co-founded by legendary Wharton Professor Russell Ackoff. There, he gained broad experience working with numerous Fortune 500 companies.

Jason has been published in *Harvard Business Review* and *The PDMA Toolbook 2 for New Product Development*. He also co-authored the book, *Idealized Design*.

Jason holds a BS from the Wharton School of the University of Pennsylvania and a PhD from The Union Institute & University.

Jason can be reached at productwishes@yahoo.com.

Pierre Mitchell

Mr. Mitchell is responsible for leading the development of research and other intellectual property within Hackett's Procurement Research and Advisory services, where he also serves as an adjunct business advisor. He has over 20 years of industry and consulting experience in procurement, supply chain and information technology. Previously, he was vice president of supply management research at AMR Research and a manager at Arthur D. Little, where he led numerous supply chain and procurement transformations at Fortune 500 companies. Other industry positions include manufacturing project manager at The Timberland Company, materials manager at the Krupp Companies, and engineer at EG&G. He has been named by Demand and Supply Chain Executive magazine as one of the top 50 practitioner "pros to know" in supply management, and is a frequent speaker and author on procurement trends and best practices. He holds an engineering degree from Southern Methodist University and an MBA from the University of Chicago.

Pierre can be reached at pmitchell@thehackettgroup.com.

Doug von Feldt

Doug Von Feldt has over 20 years of experience in manufacturing, distribution, and retail and is currently a deployment leader in Continuous Improvement at Collective Brands Inc. (Payless ShoeSource). Previous to that he was the IT director at O'Sullivan Industries and was the CIO and assistant GM at Earp Distribution where he was responsible for the day-to-day operations of the company. He helped start the Lean Six Sigma program at Washburn University where he created the training curriculum and material. As a part-time instructor at Washburn, he provides instruction in Lean Six Sigma and related topics and has taught over 1000 professionals in over 75 companies.

He has led hundreds of information technology and process improvement/Lean Six Sigma projects in over 15 countries throughout his career. He has helped dozens of companies implement Lean Six Sigma and other quality initiatives over his career.

He is a Lean Six Sigma Master Black Belt and a Project Management Professional (PMP) from the Project Management Institute. He also completed the Phillip Crosby Quality College course and is a senior member of the American Society of Quality.

Doug can be reached at doug@crimsoncorporation.com.

Dedication

In the past 10 years, approximately 600,000 businesses have failed in North America. Countless other companies are among the "walking wounded;" lacking intervention those businesses will inevitably die as well.

Taking the practice of supply management to the next level is an important ingredient in ensuring the success of any enterprise. Of course, supply management is not the only reason that a business might succeed or fail. However, supply management is a critical component for success. Without "next level" supply management, a company cannot hope to excel in addressing the tough issues and exacting performance expectations of tomorrow's challenging business environment.

At a professional level this book is dedicated to the executives and supply management professionals who are constantly striving to make their organizations successful, and are willing to take the initiative—as leaders—to boldly take their organizations to the place where the future is found: the next level.

At a personal level this book is dedicated to our families, who constantly help us to personally reach the "next level."

This book has free material available for download from the
Web Added Value™ resource center at *www.jrosspub.com*

At J. Ross Publishing we are committed to providing today's professional with practical, hands-on tools that enhance the learning experience and give readers an opportunity to apply what they have learned. That is why we offer free ancillary materials available for download on this book and all participating Web Added Value™ publications. These online resources may include interactive versions of material that appears in the book or supplemental templates, worksheets, models, plans, case studies, proposals, spreadsheets and assessment tools, among other things. Whenever you see the WAV™ symbol in any of our publications, it means bonus materials accompany the book and are available from the Web Added Value Download Resource Center at www.jrosspub.com.

Downloads available for *Next Level Supply Management Excellence: Your Straight to the Bottom Line® Roadmap* include supplemental information about opportunity assessments, international trade and compliance, transformation roadmaps, comprehensive energy management, strategic sourcing & negotiations management training and mentoring, and supplier surveys.

Part One

Leading Supply Management Transformation

1

The Next Level—an Overview for the C-Suite and Supply Management Leaders

---

One of our favorite questions to ask an audience is this: "Please raise your hand if you believe that most senior executives around the world understand the enormous potential of modern supply management." At best, 10% of the audience raises their hands. The follow-up question takes the next logical step: "Keep your hands raised if you believe that those same executives understand how to achieve that enormous potential—how to build the transformation roadmap." Typically, no hands remain raised.

Is this an indictment of most senior executives? Or is it an indictment of supply management leadership for failing to create executive awareness and develop the business case for what is possible? Or is it both?

This chapter addresses these tough questions. It offers real-world ideas on getting top management's attention to the potential of supply management by highlighting the bottom-line implications. That's followed by the overview of a set of guidelines, or *dimensions*, for transforming supply management from a transaction-based, reactive function to a powerful strategic force. Included in this discussion is practical advice on selecting the right organizational design to support the transformation effort as well as a discussion if *good is enough* is really good enough.

What Is Meant by Transformation?

It seems that every conference speaker, and every company, is touting *transformation*. It has become such an overused word that it is beginning to lose its

3

meaning. Let's start the discussion with a brief review of two fundamentally different definitions.

Webster's defines the word *transform* as a change in composition, structure, character, or condition, "to change the outward form or appearance." That strikes us as a superficial, skin-deep definition. Now consider this alternative perspective. To transform means to fundamentally alter the capabilities and improve the achievement of sustainable results. That seems to us to be more in line with what organizations really should want to achieve. It is the latter definition that we employ throughout this book.

Figure 1.1 provides some depth to what we want to transform *from* and what we want to transform *to*. At a broad level, this transformation can be best described as moving from a tactical perspective to one that is strategic. Transformation is a complex construct with many dimensions.

Speaking the Language

Senior executives might stay awake at night for any number of work-related reasons. Based on our own experiences, the top sleep disrupters typically revolve around these issues:

- Can the company meet or exceed earnings and performance expectations?
- Can we grow revenues and earnings year-over-year?

Role	Tactical	Strategic
Organizational level	Back office, transactional	Executive–Seat at the Table
Metrics of success	Meeting headcount objectives, transactional efficiencies	Revenue enhancement, cost reduction, working capital, ...
Skills	Paper processing, clerical, ...	Leadership, cross-functional, cross-cultural, strategic, analytical, ...
Career path	Lifetime	Candidates for high-potential job rotations throughout the company
Job content	Boring, repetitive	Creative, substantial impact, fun
Other	Lone ranger	Team player, strategic business partner

Figure 1.1 A key question: Transform to what?
Source: Greybeard Advisors LLC. Copyright 2009–2011. All rights reserved.

- Are we able to reduce risk and volatility in revenues and earnings?
- How can we continually improve return on invested capital (ROIC) or return on equity?
- How can we create a unique business model, one that is difficult for competitors to copy?

The surprising fact is that a successful supply management transformation can favorably impact all five of the performance areas imbedded in these questions. As a corporate function, it is uniquely positioned—more so than most functions—to have a broad and sustainable impact on the business. The sad fact, though, is that most senior executives are unaware of this potential. A big reason for this lack of awareness is that no one has communicated the opportunity in his or her language. Awareness doesn't just happen by itself. The central challenge for supply management professionals, then, is to take a leadership role in helping their senior management understand.

Toward this end, every chief supply chain officer (CSCO) or chief procurement officer (CPO) needs to be conversant with the performance improvement framework shown in Figure 1.2. This is one of our favorite charts and is the essence of relating supply management to improved corporate performance. Let's walk through this framework briefly—a more involved discussion appears in Chapter 4.

Two important measures of corporate performance are ROIC and cash flow. ROIC is calculated by taking the annual earnings of a business and dividing it by the total capital invested in that business (long-term debt and stockholder's equity). ROIC is important because it is an indicator of the current health of a business. For a business to deliver value to its shareholders, ROIC needs to exceed the corporate cost of capital. A company that operates where its ROIC is lower than its cost of capital is essentially liquidating itself.

Improving profits helps to improve both ROIC and cash flow. Reducing the capital intensity of your business also helps to improve ROIC and cash flow. Improving profits while also reducing the capital needed to run the business has a powerful compounding effect on ROIC and cash flow.

So how do we go about improving profits? There are two fundamental ways: revenue enhancements and cost reductions. Supply management can—and should—play an important role in each of those areas, as indicated with examples shown in Figure 1.2. Supply management should, for example, take a leadership role in creating a more responsive supply chain, thereby helping the company to win more business (and increase revenues) from customers. Supply management should also take the lead applying good processes to better manage all areas of spending, not just those typically assigned to procurement.

So far so good, but how do we reduce capital intensity? Again, there are two ways: working capital improvements and capital expenditure improvements. Once again, supply management can play an important role in each of

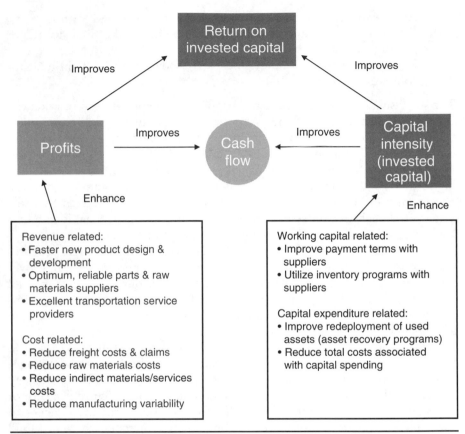

Figure 1.2   World-class supply management drives performance
Source: Greybeard Advisors LLC. Copyright 2005–2011. All rights reserved.

those areas. In many companies, for example, there is no clear responsibility for analyzing and coordinating supplier payment terms. This area is ideally suited for supply management to take a lead role, as is pointed out in a later chapter on working capital. With regard to capital expenditures, experience demonstrates that the sooner procurement is involved in new projects (even at the concept stage), the better the overall project economics and ramp-up time will be.

A thorough opportunity assessment for supply management requires a careful evaluation of the improvement opportunities in each of the four categories shown on the exhibit. Then, to tie it together for the executive audience, you relate those improvement opportunities to the company's income statement and balance sheet. Going that extra step allows you to demonstrate the impact of supply management on net income, earnings per share, ROIC and cash flow—all key areas of interest for senior executives. It's a powerful way to communicate the enormous potential of a transformed supply management organization in the language of senior executives and in a manner relevant to your company.

Each situation is unique. However, in our experience it's not unusual for a well-done opportunity assessment to demonstrate that a company's ROIC has the potential to double or triple from its pre-transformation levels. The next logical question is, "If that's the case, why aren't there many 20% ROIC super-performers in the business world?" The answer is painfully simple. Achieving that step-change in performance doesn't just happen by itself. It takes leadership and a well-designed, well-planned transformation roadmap.

Dimensions of a Successful Transformation

Supply management transformation refers to the successful conversion or metamorphosis of supply management from a transaction-based, reactive function to a pro-active, strategic driver of business performance—whose input is regularly sought by other areas of the company.

Companies that have successfully transformed their supply management activities into world-class performers have paid attention to six key dimensions of transformation. As shown in Figure 1.3, those dimensions are procurement's role, objectives, leadership, organization, best practices, and innovation

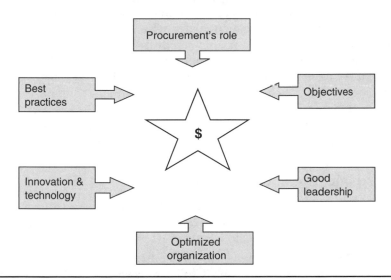

Figure 1.3   Six dimensions of successful transformation

Source: Robert A. Rudzki, Douglas Smock, Michael Katzorke, and Shelley Stewart Jr., *Straight to the Bottom Line*. Fort Lauderdale, FL: J. Ross Publishing, 2005.

and technology. Underlying these six dimensions are more than 30 specific initiatives that ultimately comprise a comprehensive transformation plan. (A more detailed discussion of the *star chart* transformation framework appears in Chapter 3.)

Before you even start thinking about which initiatives to focus on, you need a strong leader in place to sponsor the transformation process. The logical place to look is the head of procurement or supply chain management. If that person is not comfortable in a leadership role, then you'll need to look elsewhere. It's a sad fact that not enough people are comfortable in leadership roles. (Lee Iacocca's book, *Where Have All the Leaders Gone?*, is a great read on this subject.)

Simply stated, the transformation leader has to be willing to advocate change, which often means putting his or her neck on the line. Here's what we mean. First, he or she will need to develop a bold vision with stretch objectives that relate to the interests of senior management. And again, these objectives must be communicated in the language of the executive suite. The transformation leader must also be willing to lay out a specific transformation plan and roadmap, with concrete milestones that feature achievements rather than just activities.

Perhaps most importantly, the transformation leader must be willing to construct a business case that offers a performance commitment (that is, $X million of new cost reductions to the bottom line in each of the next few years) in exchange for the executive support (budget, people, outside support, tools, and systems) needed to make it happen. Without that show of confidence and commitment by the transformation leader, why would the rest of the executive team be willing to commit people and budget to the effort?

When one of the authors of this book was a corporate CPO, he did exactly what we're describing—and it made a huge difference to bottom line results. This approach helped create the excitement and commitment within the organization needed to energize the transformation. Believe it or not, once you're willing to go down this path, and once you are comfortable with the leadership imperative, the rest is easier than it might seem.

The Organizational Chart Diversion

One dimension of the transformation effort, organizational governance and design, demands special attention because of its potential to make or break the effort. Let's take a closer look, drawing on material from *Beat the Odds: Avoid Corporate Death and Build a Resilient Enterprise.*

To set the stage, consider the following scenario, which you may have actually experienced yourself. A company is experiencing overall performance problems that just don't seem to go away. The senior management team decides that the organization structure is at fault, and that a corporate reorganization will give the necessary boost to performance. Soon, the consultants arrive, and they draw up a whole new organization chart. New divisions are created on paper, management councils are designed, reporting relationships are changed, and job descriptions are re-written. Much time and money are spent on correcting things that may not have been broken in the first place. Management breathes a sigh of relief, thinking that the performance problems are about to be solved.

Yet performance does not measurably improve. In fact, it worsens. Employees become disenchanted with senior management for not fixing things and start losing their focus. Although a poor organizational design can impede success, organizational design is rarely a driver of success. Furthermore, the temptation to apply the *organizational chart fix* to an enterprise ignores an important reality: the informal relationships and networks inside an organization are often more important than the formal reporting structures and charts. Moreover, these informal ties are guided more by the organization's purpose, values, and vision than they are by the consultants' new chart. This holds true whether we're talking about the overall corporate organization or the supply management function specifically.

The message in all of this should be clear: Before redrawing the supply management organization chart, it is much more productive to first address the role, objectives, leadership, and best practices dimensions. Build your transformation game plan for each of these critical dimensions before tackling the organizational issue and the specific enabling technology.

With the right role, objectives, leadership and best practices in place, or at least planned, the foundation is created for success. You now can view organizational design in terms of your corporate culture and what you want to achieve through supply management. Put another way, you can view organizational design in a strategic, transformation context.

Thinking about this subject, author Rudzki distinctly remembers attending a CPO peer group meeting a few years ago when the discussion turned to organization. One of the attendees offered this solution to the various challenges being raised by the audience: "Procurement should be centralized, and all other corporate functions should also report into us." As you can imagine, that idea drew quite a round of laughter (even though some of the CPOs at the meeting would have liked to give it a try). But that bold suggestion did bring up some important questions: Can a centralized procurement function work well in a decentralized corporate culture? Can a decentralized procurement function ever be as effective as a centralized one? Who should procurement report to in the corporate hierarchy? These are all good questions.

At a broad level, what is the ideal organization design for supply management? There is no single answer, contrary to what many hope and expect. Yet the classic options basically boil down to three: centralized or centrally-led, hybrid, or decentralized. (Figure 1.4 lists the advantages and issues of each

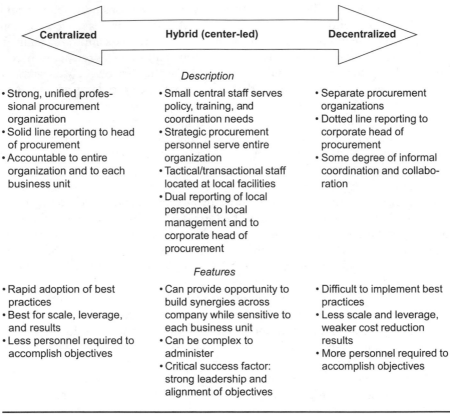

Centralized	Hybrid (center-led)	Decentralized
Description		
• Strong, unified professional procurement organization • Solid line reporting to head of procurement • Accountable to entire organization and to each business unit	• Small central staff serves policy, training, and coordination needs • Strategic procurement personnel serve entire organization • Tactical/transactional staff located at local facilities • Dual reporting of local personnel to local management and to corporate head of procurement	• Separate procurement organizations • Dotted line reporting to corporate head of procurement • Some degree of informal coordination and collaboration
Features		
• Rapid adoption of best practices • Best for scale, leverage, and results • Less personnel required to accomplish objectives	• Can provide opportunity to build synergies across company while sensitive to each business unit • Can be complex to administer • Critical success factor: strong leadership and alignment of objectives	• Difficult to implement best practices • Less scale and leverage, weaker cost reduction results • More personnel required to accomplish objectives

Figure 1.4   Main organization types

Source: Robert A. Rudzki, Douglas Smock, Michael Katzorke, and Shelley Stewart Jr., *Straight to the Bottom Line*. Fort Lauderdale, FL: J. Ross Publishing, 2005.

approach.) In general, a truly decentralized supply management organization has difficulty delivering world-class results in an efficient manner. Enterprise-wide leverage and coordination is more difficult, and often more resources are deployed across more locations than would otherwise be necessary.

That's the reality. But believe it or not, some companies may not care. We've talked with CPOs who work for profitable companies. Their executive teams aren't showing much interest in optimizing supply management performance through strategic consolidation of key activities. Eventually, they will change their perspective if business conditions change.

A fully centralized supply management organization can present some challenges too, depending on internal corporate culture. Even if the overall corporate structure favors centralization, a centralized supply management function still must be responsive to the needs of the individual businesses. The satisfaction of your internal clients (your executives, business unit leaders, and other key internal stakeholders) is paramount—whatever structure is selected.

Hybrid structures are popular because they allow you to build and coordinate synergies across the company while being sensitive to each business unit's unique needs. This is often accomplished by co-locating procurement personnel both at corporate headquarters and at the business operations. In many cases, these individuals have dual reporting responsibility to the local operations or finance head and to the corporate CPO.

Regardless of which option ultimately proves to be the best for your situation, consider applying these two proven techniques: creation of an executive steering committee and a procurement council. The steering committee is typically comprised of senior executives, who represent corporate functions and business units. The committee provides high level oversight and support of the transformation initiative. In the best of all worlds, members of the steering committee also act as sponsors of individual sourcing teams. Their involvement can send a powerful message of commitment, both internally and to suppliers.

The procurement council typically is comprised of the CPO and his or her direct reports in the supply management organization. It can be a valuable forum for driving change, sharing best practices, assuring alignment, and spurring results. We have witnessed procurement councils achieve these very goals, greatly advancing the overall transformation effort.

One last question should be asked with regard to organizational design. Should supply management report directly to the CEO? Direct reporting is really a two-edged sword. On the one hand, the CPO has direct access to the top executive in the organization. But on the other, this reporting relationship could result in a diminution of focus on the supply management ball.

Consider what happened to one CPO who was made a direct report to the CEO. He started getting invited to many staff meetings unrelated to his job. Most of the discussion at those meetings, he felt, was a waste of his time and a distraction from his core responsibilities. The key to supply management success is not the lines on the corporate organization chart. The real key is access. The CPO should have regular and easy access to the executive suite and to the heads of the business divisions. Chapter 5 takes the organizational design discussion to the next level.

Skin in the Game

One last ingredient of a successful supply management transformation is what we call *skin in the game*. This refers to the importance of having the interests of key stakeholders and participants linked to the objectives of the transformation process. You might think of skin in the game as the mechanism to increase the likelihood that all the pieces—and all the players—work smoothly together.

Skin in the game can be manifested at different levels. At a minimum, it starts with incorporating objectives of the transformation plan into the annual, written performance objectives of relevant employees. By relevant employees, we mean everyone from the CEO to the entry-level buyer—from procurement professionals to internal clients. Anyone who can influence the success of the transformation process should have some skin in the game.

The next step is the linking of personal objectives to meaningful financial incentives and consequences. One company we have worked with ties a significant percentage of its annual bonus program to the success of the procurement transformation plan. The program sets annual milestones on key dimensions of the plan, including quantifiable cost reductions.

Meaningful incentives can be effective in encouraging superior performance and achieving objectives. However, what about the individual *blocker* who just won't participate, or worse, actively works against the transformation? We have encountered such troubling situations a few times during our careers. When the particulars of one specific instance were discussed with a top executive at the company, his response was straightforward: "That's why we have flagpoles. Not just to rally the troops for a good cause but, if necessary, to hoist the recalcitrant party up in the air so everyone can see the example." Though this response is a little harsh, the point is well made.

The underlying message is that you need to address problems quickly and publicly. A reluctance to deal with noncompliance is a big reason why transformation efforts get derailed. That's not to say that you look for people to serve up as examples. First, try to understand why the individual appears to be blocking the transformation effort by having a conversation with him or her. Second, determine what's driving the behavior. Make absolutely certain that the individual has all the necessary facts at his or her disposal. You may discover that their reluctance to comply is based on some fundamental misunderstanding or a perception that they're being left out.

Traditional purchasing:
- Potential of 0–3% price reductions

World-class supply management:
- Potential of 5–10% total cost reductions for direct spend
- Potential of 10–40% total cost reductions for indirect spend
- Revenue enhancements—better able to compete for sales with a more responsive supply chain
- Improved cycle time for new product/service development
- Working capital improvements
- Improved market knowledge for company-wide benefit
- Better risk management and enhanced business planning
- Improved ROIC/ROE, cash flow, and EPS

Figure 1.5 Supply management transformation offers big benefits

In the final analysis, you don't want reluctant compliance. You want active commitment. And that really is the litmus test of supply management transformation. Genuine transformation produces significant, sustainable results both near-term and long-term, as shown in Figure 1.5. Moreover, it does so by creating an enormous amount of positive energy and commitment from all areas of an organization. Without that, you might be stuck with a few *quick wins* that eventually disappear, along with you and your company's credibility.

Is *Good Enough* Good Enough?

The title of this section derives from a theme that arose initially in the technology world: is *good enough* good enough? In one application of this idea, it has been suggested that software developers deliberately leave bugs in the code so as to shorten the schedule for product delivery (recognizing, of course, that the bugs can be corrected in the next product release). Others define it as providing the minimum quality that you can get away with.[1]

Some would say that the Mars Rover program was a positive example of this philosophy at work. Rather than design the ultimate Rover research vehicle at untold cost, NASA focused on the key functionality that it needed to accomplish mission objectives and spent much less money by having an 85% solution, rather than a 110% solution.

This section looks at the *good enough* topic from more than a *purchase of software* perspective, consistent with the six dimensions of supply management transformation described in this book.

Why Is There an Issue?

In our experience, too many executives seem to take an approach toward procurement and supply management that is equivalent to adopting a satisfactory or good enough approach. Commonly, this manifests itself as an organization in which supply management demonstrates some or all of these characteristics:

- Has a tactical or operational role
- Has informal and soft objectives with no profit and loss relevance
- Utilizes traditional day-to-day purchasing tactics as opposed to strategic practices such as strategic sourcing
- Tends to be consumed with tactical activities and is unable to devote sufficient time and attention to strategic initiatives
- Is micromanaged rather than led
- Lacks cross-functional involvement and support
- Has relatively few modern processes, skills, tools, and systems to enable its evolution into a sustainable value creator

Organizations that fit this description leave considerable value on the table, leave themselves open to competitive threats from others in their industry that *get it*, and ultimately fail to meet their obligations to their various constituents, including stockholders.

The First Question

As discussed earlier, the most fundamental question to be answered is: What is the desired role for supply management in your company? Related to that, what is the desired role for suppliers in supporting your company's strategy and objectives?

Supply management organizations have three fundamental options they can pursue. The first option, a strategic one, is to become a competitive asset for their company. In this role, supply management takes a leadership role in business performance improvement across all drivers of ROIC and cash flow (see Figure 1.2). They contribute to revenue enhancement, drive improvements in total cost, lead thoughtful enhancements to working capital, and partner with their internal clients and with suppliers to enhance capital expenditure programs. In short, they migrate from a primarily administrative function to become a competitive differentiator for their company. How to achieve the strategic option is the purpose of this book.

A second option is much more tactical. In this option, the supply management organization remains an *internal utility* for the company. In this role, it has a tactical and operational focus and is valued mainly for its process efficiencies and for making sure everything arrives on time. Organizations that place supply management in this role tend to be heavily focused on such administrative crutches as internal service level agreements and the cost of processing transactions. They often have not yet realized the ROIC potential associated with next level supply management. The prospect of *investing* in supply management is like speaking a foreign language to their executives.

A third option is to transfer some of the supply management function to an outsourced service provider. This may make sense if there is minimal in-house expertise, insufficient scale, or a desire for further improvements in process or costs after achieving a first round of accomplishments in house. But in this scenario, the company is essentially saying that it sees no contribution from suppliers other than cost. Supplier innovation is difficult to capture in an outsourced model.

Which choice is best for your company? We're not aware of any company that has won the competitive battle by relegating its supply management organization to either an outsourced option or an internal utility option. Companies that have become the leaders in this function have adopted a strategic role for supply management, encompassing all aspects of attention to ROIC, cash flow, and innovation, while their competitors take a more tactical view.

To phrase it another way, revenues, costs, working capital, and capital expenditures are, without exception, important for any business. As a result, supply management—which can influence each of these areas—should, for all of these reasons, be a corporate priority.

Is Best in Class Really Worth the Journey (and the Investment)?

In the blogosphere, there has been an on-again off-again debate regarding *best in class*. In one particular blog, Procurement Leaders, writer Steve Hall argues that seeking to become best in class in everything is impractical, a mistake, and an indulgence. He argues that it would be more appropriate to set and chase achievable goals that are in line with the business.[2]

In the blog "Good Enough, Best, or Next—Which Do You Choose?" Sourcing Innovation blogger Michael Lamoureux points out that "because you only have so much time and so many resources at your disposal . . . you have to prioritize to get the most bang for your buck." Later, he punctuates his comments by reminding the reader that "business is about returns, which is necessary for sustainability of the business."[3]

An important take away is that best in class or *next level* supply management must be evaluated with a critical business oriented perspective, rather than a theoretical *perfection* objective. After all, we are competing with other corporate priorities, each of which is seeking a share of limited corporate resources in terms of personnel and dollars. The question becomes how does the supply management agenda compare? Do your CEO, CFO, and your internal business unit clients see a compelling case to support a supply management transformation?

One way to approach this challenge is to use publicly available conclusions from a variety of research firms. Results from A. T. Kearney's "Assessment of Excellence in Procurement" study and the Hackett Group's research on world-class performers directionally confirm the value of striving for world-class supply management performance. In one revealing chart (see Figure 1.6), the performance advantage of becoming world class is indisputable.

Industry studies and research results are great for suggesting the potential, but they often aren't sufficient for obtaining senior management buy-in and resources. What is most useful is to develop a candid, facts-based, current state assessment, a desired future state, and a transformation roadmap and business case that is specific to your company (Chapter 3 addresses this topic further). Without these measures, the initiative will likely be viewed as a technology-based project, and ownership will go to the chief information officer. A properly conducted review and plan can shift the situation from battling for a small piece of your CIO's current IT budget pie to successfully obtaining an entirely new budget allocation to support a well-thought-out, comprehensive transformation plan owned by supply management (with technology as one component of that plan).

For the most part, the investments organizations make in procurement continue to pay off in a traditional sense...

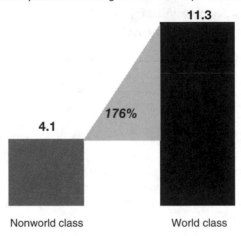

Return on investment
Ratio of total spend cost savings to the cost of procurement, 2010

Figure 1.6   It generally pays to invest in procurement
Source: The Hackett Group. Reprinted with permission

In fact, as a technology-related initiative, a key issue becomes: who has the larger voice or control—IT or procurement? As Andrew Bartolini, chief research officer at research firm Ardent Partners and former vice president at Aberdeen Group, put it, "Technology is an enabler; a means to an end—a literal solution to a problem. Unfortunately, this often gets lost in the solution selection and deployment processes. Successful technology deployments are driven by functional and technical leaders who keep their eyes on the prize and a sharp focus on extracting the greatest business value out of a solution." If you allow this debate to be characterized narrowly as a technology or IT-focused matter, then the outcome is problematic. That's one reason you should cast the discussion in terms of total opportunity and transformation necessary across multiple dimensions, rather than just a request to fund new tools or software.

In general, the journey to next level or best in class supply management—when done correctly—is worth the investment. However, the specific actions, opportunities, and investments are unique to each company and must be identified before a final recommendation can be made.

Two Case Studies: Technology Budget-

Centric vs. Opportunity-Centric

Two recent cases will help to demonstrate the difference in outcomes that is possible. Company A made a top-down decision to implement a company-wide enterprise resource planning (ERP) platform. As part of the justification for the large ERP project, each functional area of the company was asked to estimate benefits. These benefits, mostly assumed to be efficiency improvements from the implementation of ERP, were aggregated into an overall business case for approval of the total ERP project.

The projected benefits in the supply management area were in the millions of dollars, which satisfied the business case process. The systems integrator confirmed for the company that these were reasonable assumptions for ERP benefits for supply management.

As part of Company A's approach to this ERP project, it established teams to critically evaluate current processes as well as organization design. The executive in charge took this role seriously and engaged an outside, independent advisory firm. The firm performed the candid assessment and developed a tailored transformation roadmap described in this book. The outcome surprised this company: by shifting from a technology-centric approach to an opportunity-centric supply management transformation, the projected annual cost structure improvement could be 20 times higher! For this company, that was real money. Needless to say, this company's executive team approved pursuing the supply management transformation roadmap, eventually becoming extremely satisfied with the results.

Company B eventually came to the same conclusion as Company A but through a different path. An ultra-lean company, its supply management personnel were totally consumed with day-to-day tactical buying. The concept of strategic procurement was a distant wish. With the help of a technology vendor and a mega consulting firm, Company B developed and presented a business case for a best-of-breed eSourcing suite. The business case was compelling: invest X (one-time) and obtain an annual benefit of two to three times the investment. Of course, the request for capital was approved.

There was only one catch: the supply management department had acknowledged in its budget request the need for a still-to-be-defined *change management* program to support the new technology tools and warned of the substantial risks if this was not done. Company B wanted a fresh perspective on this subject before it began implementing the technology, so it engaged an outside, independent advisory firm. The outcome was similar to what happened with Company A. By shifting from a technology-centric project view to an opportunity-centric approach with a supply management transformation roadmap, the projected annual cost structure improvement was projected to be much higher—about 10 times higher!

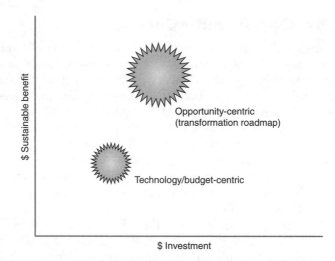

Figure 1.7   The view affects the outcome (start with the opportunity rather than the tools)

The point of these cases is illustrated in Figure 1.7. If you view the world through a technology lens, you restrict your understanding of the size of the opportunity, as well as underestimate all that is required to accomplish sustainable change. Technology alone will not suffice since it is really a strategy enabler.

Are There Some Areas Where Good Enough Is Okay?

Bringing about successful supply management transformation involves balancing and prioritizing a wide array of initiatives. Is it possible to shortcut some areas without significantly impacting the capability of the supply management organization to achieve best-in-class results? The short answer is no.

There will be significant adverse impact if you shortchange any of the six transformation dimensions. Figure 1.8 identifies what is likely to happen if any one of the six dimensions is missing or seriously shortchanged. If two or more are shortchanged, the effect is likely to be compounded. Note that we are talking about shortchanging a dimension for a protracted period. This is different from the need to prioritize the many elements of the transformation plan. A well-constructed transformation roadmap, as described in Chapter 3, will often sequence the entire menu of specific initiatives over an 18- to 36-month timeframe.

It is not an accident that strategic role, objectives, and leadership are listed in the first three positions on the chart, followed by optimized organization and best practices, and wrapping up with enabling technology. Note in particular that the

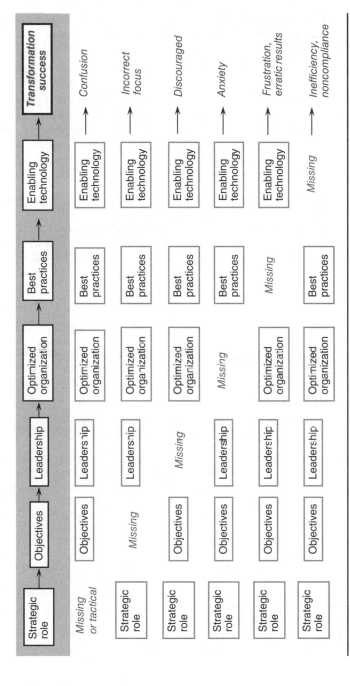

Figure 1.8 Leading supply management transformation

optimized organization dimension, which includes the professional resources that we talk about in Chapter 5 on Talent Management, comes before technology.

Andrew Bartolini of Ardent Partners highlighted that point in an interview with one of the authors when he said, "Great processes and technology can only get you so far. Best-in-Class performance within a procurement department begins and ends with its people." In another interview, Jason Hekl, vice president of eProcurement leader Coupa, noted that "Software does not do anything on its own. It's only as good as its users." Adds Kevin Potts, vice president of eSourcing leader Emptoris, "To be world class in supply management, I can't imagine how you could do that without world class people."

The business landscape continues to evolve at a fast pace. That creates a climate of uncertainty, volatility, and risk. In that environment, business leaders are looking for capabilities to deliver sustainable results at a reasonable cost of investment, combined with flexibility or minimal switching costs. New software models, such as SaaS and cloud-based subscriptions pioneering by Coupa in the eProcurement realm, make it possible to test out and utilize leading-edge technology while reducing the upfront investment and sharing the risk with the software vendor.

With that said, technology alone is not the answer and can prove to be an under-adopted and underutilized asset. It needs to be understood that technology is an enabler and not a fix. Too many senior executives perceive technology as a painkiller—a medicine that produces a quick fix for what ails their supply management function. The long-term health of supply management though requires

---

What's a BHAG (and why is it important)?

In the classic leadership book *Built to Last* (James C. Collins and Jerry I. Porras), the concept of BHAG was introduced. A BHAG (big hairy audacious goal) is a common element among long-lasting, successful companies and organizations. What is so powerful about a BHAG? A BHAG engages people. It is tangible, energizing, and highly focused. People *get it* right away since it takes little or no explanation. President Kennedy's pronouncement that "We will land a man on the moon . . . " is a famous example of a BHAG that captured the minds and hearts of an entire nation.

On a similar note, management guru C.K. Prahalad (who passed away in 2010) always told executives to think big. "Set ambitious goals and then figure out how to mobilize the resources to achieve them—rather than the other way around. Most companies limit themselves because they focus primarily on what they believe they can afford."

Do you have a BHAG for your supply management organization? If not, you should think about developing one. It's a valuable component of an overall transformation plan.

a regimen—the six elements described earlier—where technology is only one treatment. Otherwise, achieving the next level is compromised by *good enough*.

Concluding Thoughts

Business is about returns and results. Perform the current state assessment candidly and make sure that the opportunity assessment and transformation roadmap are done comprehensively. You then have the ability to understand—and communicate—the business impact from embarking on the transformation journey across all relevant dimensions. That is an important prerequisite for sustainable executive support and resources.

Chapter Notes

A portion of this chapter is based on the following article by one of the authors, with permission of Supply Chain Management Review: Robert A. Rudzki, "A Leader's Guide to Supply Management Transformation," *Supply Chain Management Review*, March 2008, 12–21.

1. James Bach. "Good Enough Quality: Beyond the Buzzword." *Computer Magazine*. August 1997, 96–98.
2. Steve Hall. "The Big Debate: Best in Class in an Indulgence." *Procurement Leaders* (blog). September 3, 2010.
3. Michael Lamoureux. "Good Enough, Best or Next—Which Do You Choose?" *Sourcing Innovation* (blog). July 25, 2010.

2

Leadership as a Principle of Lasting Success

"Leaders must challenge the process precisely because any system will unconsciously conspire to maintain the status quo and prevent change."
Kouzes & Posner

The Leadership Challenge

The following is a true story. Not that many years ago, a major corporation conducted an executive search for a new chief procurement officer (CPO). The search was successful, and the new CPO reported for duty at his new company. Beyond the normal human resources duties a new employee needs to complete on the first day, the CPO also had the opportunity for an expansive discussion with his new boss.

One of the topics the CPO raised related to specific expectations the boss had for him in this role. One aspect of the response surprised the CPO: the boss indicated that in his opinion, a significant number of employees would need to be replaced in the organization the CPO was inheriting. The boss indicated that he had come to that conclusion because he was disappointed with the results generated by the employees. When asked what magnitude of employee turnover might be appropriate, the boss said "at least 25%." This figure and comment astonished the CPO for three reasons:

1. During the interview process, no indication was given that the staff might be so poor; on the contrary, the situation was characterized positively.
2. The 25% figure equated to more than 50 people.
3. The boss indicated that he would support firing, and then hiring, that many people (i.e., this was not a budget-cutting move).

The CPO faced a challenge and an opportunity. How he handled it is a revealing anecdote about leadership.

Keep in mind that the described conversation occurred on the first day the CPO was on board as a new employee. He listened, asked relevant questions of his boss, and then went about the normal process any executive would do in a new job: he gathered data and made observations. He spoke with internal clients throughout the organization, at all levels. He interviewed, in depth, more than one third of his own employees within the first 60 days. In effect, he conducted an assessment of the organization he inherited—and he did that assessment across a number of dimensions. This was much like the assessment process described in this book.

The conclusion he reached: the disappointing results were not caused by poor employees. On the contrary, the employees were solid. What was missing were good leadership, clear roles and responsibilities, explicit objectives, upgraded training, good business processes, and a number of the other transformation fundamentals described in this book.

The CPO designed and implemented a transformation roadmap. A year later, the organization was performing at a high level, results were better than anticipated, and less than five employees needed to be changed out.

The lesson here is that anybody can fire and hire employees—it takes no particular leadership talent. The effective leader makes the effort to understand root cause issues, designs a transformation plan to address gaps, and takes action to implement that plan no matter what the politics may be. Speaking from personal experience in the corporate world, the authors can attest that it is much more gratifying doing the right thing than taking the easy way out and doing the politically expedient thing.

This chapter is devoted to the subject of leadership—a vitally important ingredient in the journey to achieving and sustaining the next level in supply management.

Leadership as a Fundamental Principle[1]

Albert Einstein once said that insanity is doing the same thing over and over and expecting different results. This quip gets grim smiles of recognition from nearly every smart businessperson we've come across.

Managers are just as guilty of doing the same things over and over again as line workers are—more so, in fact, since the consequences of their unthinking repetition are far greater. They're also guilty by omission—meaning that if they fail to lead in inspiring others to do things differently, nothing will ever change.

In the leadership book *Beat the Odds*, a nine-principle leadership framework is presented that helps explain why some organizations sustain their success over the long term, while most organizations ultimately fail. While the *Beat the Odds* framework is often used in a total-enterprise perspective, it applies equally well to ensuring the success of major functions within an enterprise, such as supply management.

Leadership is the fourth of nine principles. Establishing the foundation for leadership and vision are three necessary preceding conditions: the purpose of the organization, the core values, and the ideas for creating the future (see Figure 2.1).

Building upon those three foundation principles, it is critical to articulate an inspiring vision internally so that employees can understand and become excited about where an organization is heading. It is also important to communicate that vision externally—at the right time—to gain the confidence and support of external constituents as well. This is not just a job for the CEO and the top team. It is necessary for the vision to cascade down from leader to leader, right down to the line supervisors.

Conveying a company's or a supply organization's future direction with vigor and passion is an area in which many companies fall down. We can think of a company where executives, managers, and analysts would engage in *chart wars*—devoting considerable time to drafting, redrafting, and refining presentations, memoranda, and other forms of communication. Tellingly, however, if you asked employees to explain the substance of what the company was

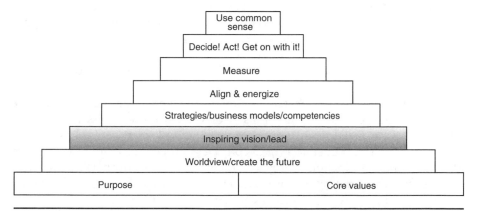

Figure 2.1 Nine principles to beat the odds

trying to achieve, what its vision was, and what its strategy was, most would pause significantly and then, in a monotone that suggested lack of enthusiasm, deliver an incomplete recitation of some boilerplate language developed years previously by executive management.

The message did not fail for want of time spent drafting the company's vision, objectives, and strategy. This was an example of failing to articulate an inspiring vision, one that employees could take to heart and mind and that would excite and guide employee actions. Facing considerable internal and external challenges, the company was further constrained by employees who were neither effective nor energized in helping to achieve management's vision.

How do you communicate a vision? And whose job is it? Let us emphasize an earlier comment that it is the job of all leaders in the organization to evangelize about the vision. If it isn't built into their performance reviews, it should be. The methods can and should be many, including a regular CEO letter in the employee newsletter or a motivating speech from the stage at the annual executive forum. It may well include communication through *management by walking around*—something that Randy Dearth, CEO of Lanxess Corporation, is good at and which employees appreciate (for a case study on Lanxess' leadership practices, see the book *Beat the Odds: Avoid Corporate Death*). In addition, it may involve formal but friendly special reports published on the corporate website and in hard copy, to be disseminated to employees, clients, and suppliers alike.

The point is that there is no set formula for how to articulate a vision. It does not always have to be scheduled or scripted, and it does not have to be long. But it will happen best if it is conveyed through a variety of channels and media, and if it is expressed with some zest. Above all, it absolutely must be consistent and credible. In other words, the vision will not gain traction if a middle manager puts a very different spin on it than the CEO (or the CPO in the case of the supply management vision) has done. And it simply won't take at all if managers' actions don't align with their words. The alignment refers to other core leadership traits beyond great communication. An executive can be as eloquent and persuasive as the day is long, but if he or she is not perceived to be a good leader in other ways, the impact of the message will be diluted.

From an employee perspective, understanding and being motivated by the vision is critical because it underpins efforts to act on other essential principles. First, it can build significant energy and help to align the workforce with the new direction (Principle #6). Second, it is crucial for employees to have the *big picture* information if they are to contribute effectively (Principle #5). Employees who don't *get* the vision also run the risk of focusing on the wrong activities and the wrong performance metrics (Principle #7).

The Dilbert comic strip sometimes aims its arrows at the way in which companies fail to convey their strategic vision. A favorite episode involves an exchange between Dilbert and his boss about strategy. The narrative goes like this:

> Dilbert: How much budget do I have for my project?
> Boss: I can't tell you. If you knew what your budget was, you'd spend it all.
> Dilbert: Can you at least tell me what our company strategy is?
> Boss: No, I don't want you to lose hope.

So what constitutes an inspiring vision versus a regular vision? It immediately captures your heart as well as your mind. It engages you, grabs your attention. It's exciting and provocative. You want to sign up to be part of the effort. You're willing to make a substantial personal and professional commitment to the inspiring vision.

One of the most inspiring visions ever presented was President Kennedy's call for America to put a man on the moon by the end of the 1960s. It captured the hearts and minds of an entire nation. Early in the last century, Anglo-Irish explorer Sir Ernest Shackleton provided a classic example of outstanding leadership when he managed to keep his icebound crew alive and healthy during their 18-month ordeal in Antarctica. His success has been credited to outstanding leadership skills, including optimism, communication, courage, planning, discipline, and flexibility. Anyone who has read the account of the odds against Shackleton's expedition understands that he inspired his crew to do the impossible.

Obviously, a new corporate direction lacks the life-or-death urgency that helped Shackleton's messages get through. In addition, clearly, it lacks the drama and deep reservoirs of national pride that helped Kennedy inspire the Apollo landing. Pronouncements from corporate executives have another strike against them: even the most passionate, energizing business leaders engender suspicion, mistrust, and sometimes outright disbelief if their words are known for not often matching their actions. Employees are rightly wary of management's latest announcements on the *strategy du jour*.

That said, many companies do succeed in conveying clear visions. Which ones do you find to be inspiring? Which ones do you think most employees would find inspiring?

- "To experience the sheer joy that comes from the advancement, application, and innovation of technology that benefits the general public." Sony
- "Become #1 or #2 in every market we serve and revolutionize this company to have the speed and agility of a small enterprise." GE
- "To build a motor car for the great multitude . . . It will be so low in price that no man making a good salary will be unable to own one . . ." Ford

Do you have a simple yet inspiring vision for your supply management function? One of the authors, as a CPO, took his procurement council through a vision-building exercise that created a fresh, bold supply management vision related to the corporate strategy. He then boiled down his company's new supply management vision to a three-point statement and memorialized it for his organization in a number of ways, including coffee cups and attractive paperweights that prominently displayed the vision and the corporate logo.

Articulating an inspiring vision is one element of a broader subject: leadership practices. Leadership is not a subject for CEOs only. One of the greatest mistakes a company can make is to assume that only the CEO *leads*. Even executive recruiters can fall into the trap of thinking about *leaders* as chief executives only. In a keynote presentation at a Chief Learning Officer (CLO) Symposium, Len Sherman, then head of the learning practice at the global consulting firm Accenture, shared this anecdote with the audience:

> A few months ago, an executive recruiter called to ask me if I had any ideas on who might be suited for a Fortune 500 CLO opening he was trying to fill. I asked him to tell me the job specs for the position, and he shared with me a number of characteristics primarily associated with the technical aspects of a senior education officer. The job spec included experience in individual and organization needs assessment, competency modeling, all aspects of training and development, performance technology, executive group facilitation, action learning, team and organization effectiveness, process engineering, consulting practices, and change management. In short, it included all the relevant professional learning skills.
>
> Now don't get me wrong. These are all necessary and important skills. But they are far from sufficient to succeed as a CLO of a large organization in today's challenging business environment. So I told my recruiter friend that I thought his client might be better served by a CLO who also . . . demonstrated [an] understanding of the key business drivers and profit levers of the corporation, a truly global mindset, proven experience with delivering business results, an established track record in running a business entity, strong executive presence, communication skills, an ability to influence key stakeholders inside and outside the corporation, and exceptionally strong leadership qualities.
>
> My executive recruiter friend replied that I must have misunderstood . . . he was looking for a CLO, not a CEO, who he thought would better fit the job characteristics I had just described. No, I replied. In my view, many of the attributes of both jobs are similar. Without strong management and leadership skills, neither a CLO nor a CEO is likely to succeed in their mission.[2]

Leadership vs. Management

Let's be clear what we mean by leadership. There is a meaningful difference between management and leadership (see Table 2.1). Good managers successfully cope with complexity. But good leaders successfully guide and cope with change. Both skills are important to your organization. Not many individuals, however, possess both sets of skills.

Prior to 2001, Xerox Corporation certainly didn't demonstrate much in the way of real corporate leadership. Its spectacular successes in commercializing photocopying technology and creating an entire industry in the mid-to-late 20th century were subsequently offset by a series of leadership blunders that saw several outstanding Xerox technology innovations commercialized by others. Several of the key features of today's personal computer, for example, originated in Xerox's Palo Alto research center but were not adopted by Xerox into its own product portfolio.

The story was similar at Kmart before its merger with Sears—and before the retailer entered Chapter XI proceedings. Management failed to keep up with changes in the retailing business and with the changing expectations of its customers. After the company emerged from bankruptcy in May of 2003, it still lacked a clearly articulated vision of what it would be and how it would distinguish itself from its chief competitors, such as Wal-Mart (everyday low prices) and Target (cheap chic). Even the merger of Kmart and Sears, orchestrated by major Kmart stockholder Edward S. Lambert's ESL Investments, has not yet changed the picture. Without a clearly defined and articulated vision and strategy that is well led, the combined retailer's ultimate success as an operating retail business will remain problematic. That is an observation separate from the expectation that the merger—from a strictly financial and tax perspective—may serve as a useful platform for additional retail acquisitions.

Earlier, at Sunbeam, CEO Al Dunlap attacked costs so savagely that he cut into company muscle—and damaged Sunbeam's ability to deliver on its promises to customers and Wall Street analysts. *Chainsaw Al*, as he became

Table 2.1 Leadership versus management: an important distinction

Leadership	Management
• Create change	• Control complexity
• Set new direction	• Develop plans
• Create strategy	• Allocate resources
• Align people	• Organize and staff
• Promote positive outcomes	• Prevent negative outcomes
• Empower people and processes	• Control people and processes

Source: Based on materials from John Kotter, Harvard University and Carol and Jack Weber, University of Virginia Darden School of Business.

Table 2.2 Leadership's five essentials

1. Challenge the process
a. Search for opportunities
b. Experiment and take risks
2. Inspire a shared vision
a. Envision the future
b. Enlist others
3. Enable others to act
a. Foster collaboration
b. Strengthen others
4. Model the way
a. Set the example
b. Plan small wins
5. Encourage the heart
a. Recognize contributions
b. Celebrate accomplishments

Source: *The Leadership Challenge*, Kouzes and Posner.

known, repeatedly cut staff ranks and allegedly employed aggressive sales accounting tactics. At the same time, he failed miserably to excite Sunbeam's management ranks with any coherent vision of the company's future. These fundamental failures, combined with a personal leadership style that was characterized as *bullying*, created a destructive environment at Sunbeam.[3]

Since leadership is fundamentally about creating change, let's take an executive tour through the subject of leadership and change. Many books have explored this subject. A classic is *The Leadership Challenge* by James M. Kouzes and Barry Z. Posner. The authors develop a five-stage process (five key practices), as shown in Table 2.2.

The purpose in *challenging the process* is to establish the belief that challenging the status quo is not only acceptable—it is desirable. The idea behind *inspiring a shared vision* is to develop excitement about where the organization is heading and what management is trying to accomplish. *Enabling others to act* is about providing the support mechanisms that enable employees at all levels to succeed. The idea of *modeling the way* is to illustrate, through appropriate examples and small wins, the behaviors and results desired. And *encouraging the heart* refers to reinforcing the right behaviors and results and demonstrating positive consequences on a personal level.

Resistance to Change

Successfully articulating a vision requires one additional insight: not all people in the organization are equally receptive to change. Researchers and marketers divide populations into six significant segments: from the innovators—that tiny percentage eager to be on the bleeding edge of change and new ideas—through the early adopters, the early majority, and finally, to the late majority, the laggards, and the fraction who will never buy in.

Many managers, when trying to initiate breakthrough change, make the mistake of trying to convince those who simply won't be convinced. Their outreach would be far more productive if they started by identifying the innovators and early adopters in their organizations and got them on board. Most of the rest tend to follow in due course.

With a well-articulated, inspiring vision—plus the appropriate leadership practices at all levels of the organization—your employees will be committed to the chosen vision, rather than merely complying with requests and procedures. They will also have sufficient information and guidance on how they can contribute to the development of supporting strategies and tactics, business models, and competencies.

Providing Feedback

An essential element in building an organization of leaders is to provide feedback on leadership behavior and practices. The systematic practice of gathering feedback from direct reports, colleagues, and superiors, so-called *360-degree feedback*, is invaluable for assessing the initial state of a leader's aptitude. Used periodically (annually or biannually), it can measure progress, or lack of progress, across key leadership practices and provide constructive input for improvements.

Equally important, a 360 can provide senior executives with a fact base upon which to make promotion and career planning decisions for aspiring professionals at all levels. Companies that are serious about building their leadership talent should build 360s into their annual performance review and succession planning processes. Simply stated, they must remove the hit-or-miss approach from their efforts to develop leadership talent (see Box: The 360 That Never Was at the end of this chapter).

Who Leads with Real Vision?

We have no hesitation in putting the following companies on the honor roll for their embrace of this principle at the corporate level:

Allied Signal/Honeywell

Allied Signal/Honeywell under Larry Bossidy was a classic example of effective leadership. From his early commitment and personal leadership on Six Sigma to his determination to instill a culture of action and execution, Bossidy exemplified some of the best characteristics of a leader.

Bob Rudzki had the opportunity some years ago to see the videotape of Larry Bossidy's management meeting at Allied Signal relating to Six Sigma. In that kickoff meeting, he clearly discussed the need for Six Sigma throughout Allied Signal, the training that would be made available to all members of management and ultimately all employees, and the leadership role he expected his managers to play. He wrapped up by plainly stating that anyone who did not make a commitment to the program after the need was explained and the training was provided would not be part of the Allied Signal team. The presentation was highly effective, not because it was intimidating, but because the logic was inescapable.

Siemens

A different example of leadership was on display during the tenure of Heinrich von Pierer, CEO of electronics giant Siemens. In the mid-1990s, Siemens was exhibiting dismal bottom-line performance due to high costs, slow decision-making (not atypical of some German companies), products designed by engineers rather than for customers, and other factors. Von Pierer recognized that generating breakout performance at Siemens would require, among other changes, adopting a more American-like business culture. Among his initiatives were adopting clear goals for management, introducing a strong link between pay and performance, placing importance on speed of decision making, making innovation a priority, and forcing product development efforts to deliver products pleasing to the customer. Von Pierer even adopted a few tricks from the Jack Welch playbook, including quarterly meetings in which business unit leaders met with him for an intense grilling.[4]

Continental Airlines

Continental (now part of United Airlines) is a testimonial to our belief that leadership can make a difference even in a *structurally defective industry* (to borrow the term used in the book *Confronting Reality* by Larry Bossidy and Ram Charan). CEO Gordon Bethune took Continental from the brink of disaster in the mid-1990s to the status of one of the few successful airlines, despite Continental's *hub-and-spoke* system design that conventional wisdom said could not compete with low-cost airlines.

Leadership and Vision Checklist

How do you think your organization's executive team is doing in terms of articulating an inspiring vision and leading at all levels? Does your supply management leadership team do a good job leading? Try answering these questions (and try them on your colleagues too):

- Do we regularly articulate an inspiring vision of our organization to our employees?
- How excited are our employees about where we are heading?
- Are our employees willing to make substantial personal and professional commitments to our vision, or do they simply seem to be complying?
- Does our organization understand the distinction between leadership and management?
- Do we have the right balance between leadership and management in our organization?
- Do we utilize BHAGs that engage and energize the organization?
- Do we select, develop, and promote those who are recognized as leaders by their peers, subordinates, and superiors?

One Indicator of an Effective Leader

There are a number of reliable *litmus tests* to gauge whether you are (or work for) an effective leader. The one we will describe here can be boiled down to a simple metric: does the leader know what to do with each additional full-time equivalent resource? To say it another way, if given a few extra personnel, what does the leader do with them?

Why is this a useful indicator? Leaders or managers who have given real thought to their strategic objectives and who have developed a detailed transformation roadmap (and associated business case) will know EXACTLY what to do with each new resource (and it won't be issuing purchase orders).

In fact, as is described in Chapters 1 and 3, by going through an assessment and roadmapping process, you'll have done the homework to communicate to senior management the business case for supply management transformation—and created an awareness of the payback from *investing* in people and capabilities.

The flip side is the overworked, tactical manager who is literally too busy to even think about how to deploy new personnel for strategic benefit. Does this sound familiar?

Correcting a Leadership Error

Many organizations view selection of leaders as a risky undertaking. The thinking seems to be: "Yes, leadership is important, but if we make a mistake selecting a particular leader, as a practical matter it is difficult to correct that mistake promptly." Many more have only rudimentary leadership development programs—if they have such programs at all. Additionally, many leadership development programs often gloss over one of the most critical skills needed for successful leadership: how to make decisions.

It is not easy to offload poorly performing business leaders. But that problem can exist at any level, from the selection of a CEO down to the choice of a first-line supervisor. One answer: 360-degree feedback can help mitigate the risks of a mistake being made in the first place (see Box: The 360 That Never Was).

However, what if the mistake has been made? That depends on who you are. If you're the supervisor of the incorrect choice, then you must face up to the error. The sooner you do so, the easier it will be. In fact, delaying the action will only cause additional damage to the job's responsibilities, yourself, and the company. In other words, things will probably get worse with time. As Mike Krzyzewski, Duke University basketball coach, said in his book *Leading from the Heart*: "When a leader makes a mistake and doesn't admit it, he is seen as arrogant and untrustworthy. And 'untrustworthy' is the last thing a leader wants to be."

The next step is to gather facts and observations. Arrange for a 360-degree survey for the purpose of diagnosis. A 360 can be done promptly, and the results known within a short period. If you prefer, you can conduct some informal *skip-level interviews* with people who report to the person in question and with others who are his or her peers. Then approach the person with your facts and observations. You might be surprised to find they welcome the opportunity to talk about a situation that they may feel is not working out as intended.

Now let's say you're a subordinate of the substandard leader, and your boss's boss doesn't see the problem with the person you now report to. The situation is more difficult, but it's not impossible. How you approach it will depend on your company's internal workings, but the basic idea is the same: the person who made the selection needs the information and insight that you possess. Often, the human resource department can be a good sounding board and ally. Sometimes it is possible to approach the decision maker directly or through a mutual friend. As a last resort, write an anonymous letter and send it directly to the decision maker. If you feel that is the appropriate avenue, then you'll need to provide facts, not opinions, to have a credible communication.

A Final Thought about Successful Leaders

An old saying summarizes what we all know implicitly but often forget. In its short form, the message is simple and relevant to achieving the next level of supply management performance:

Visions are good
Objectives are good
Strategies and plans are good
Teams are good

Studies are good
Consensus is good
Skills and competencies are very good
Thinking is also very good
But, only doing the right things creates value

As a leader, you not only have the opportunity—but also the obligation—to ensure that your resources are focused on the most value-creating activities (many of which are described in this book). If you need more strategic resources—follow the recommendations in this book and obtain them!

Concluding Thoughts

In a world of increasing complexity, the difference between being a world-class company in your industry versus being a *follower* or even *roadkill* can often be attributed to a set of nine *beat the odds* principles. Leadership is one of those nine principles for long-term corporate success, and leadership is equally important for the success of major corporate functions such as supply management. With effective, inspiring, and bold leadership, it is possible to achieve the next level of supply management in a reasonable time frame. Without good leadership, the goal is out of reach.

The 360 That Never Was[5]

Not long ago, a Fortune 500 CEO needed to replace his company's outgoing head of procurement. He proceeded to select a manager who talked a great story, in spite of past concerns about the manager's leadership skills. No professional assessment was conducted to confirm the manager's strengths or weaknesses. The CEO just *went with his feel* based on his personal rapport with the candidate.

One of the first acts by the new procurement chief was to meet with each of the new employees recruited on college campuses during the previous CPO's tenure. The message was simple, direct, and puzzling at first: you needed to spend at least four years in your entry-level buying job *to master the details* before you could be considered for a new assignment. Every one of the new hires immediately began to look outside the company for new jobs. Half did leave within 12 months, and word spread that the new CPO was working to reduce headcount—cheaply—by encouraging employees to depart.

Trust in the new CPO was not enhanced by this approach to employees, and his effectiveness was further diminished by other actions that raised doubts about his understanding of procurement's role. Finally, in an effort to address the worsening results from the increasingly ineffective procurement organization, the CPO suggested that procurement be formally centralized.

continues

continued

The CEO agreed, despite the fact that the company's organization structure favored strong business units. The result was a further disconnect between procurement and its internal clients, and a belief by the business-unit heads that this CPO had a personal agenda that was inconsistent with their objectives.

In less than two years, a well-functioning procurement organization had been reduced to a tactical mess that was no longer contributing to the success of the company.

What is the message? Selecting the right leader cannot be done casually. It must be done with an understanding of the functional skills needed—and using hard facts to identify which candidates truly possess the critical leadership abilities.

Chapter Notes

1. Robert A. Rudzki. *Beat the Odds: Avoid Corporate Death & Build a Resilient Enterprise*. Fort Lauderdale, FL: J. Ross Publishing, 2007.
2. Len Sherman. (keynote presentation, CLO Symposium Keynote Presentation, February 16, 2004).
3. "Chainsaw." *Business Week*. October 18, 1999.
4. "For Siemens, Move into U.S. Causes Waves Back Home." *The Wall Street Journal*, September 8, 2003; "Game, Set, Match." *The Wall Street Journal*. February 2, 2001; "Siemens Climbs Back." *Business Week*, June 5, 2000.
5. Robert A. Rudzki, Douglas Smock, Michael Katzorke, and Shelley Stewart Jr., *Straight to the Bottom Line*. Fort Lauderdale, FL: J. Ross Publishing, 2005.

3

You Have a Choice to Make: True Transformation or Evaporating Results

---

"Without real procurement transformation, only 60% of the value of procurement initiatives is retained by year two. This value drops by 10% for each subsequent year."

Institute for Supply Management

When one of the authors was a Fortune 500 chief procurement officer, he came to know several senior partners at consulting firms very well. In a moment of relaxed conversation, he asked one of the partners whom he trusted to describe what distinguishes a successful consulting engagement from a failure. The answer surprised him.

The consulting firm partner drew the bottom curve on Figure 3.1 and proceeded to explain the shape as follows: When a project starts up and is adequately resourced, there are some quick wins, and early momentum is established, which is the rising portion of the lower line in the chart. As the project matures and consulting resources depart, the line flattens out and eventually begins to turn downward. This explanation strongly implies that the presence of consultants, or lack of, was the determining factor in the direction of the line—which seemed to be a self-serving rationale. The consultant's explanation was further accentuated by his own observation that over 95% of all consulting projects turn out to be like the lower line on the chart! As it turns out, that explanation is both correct and incomplete.

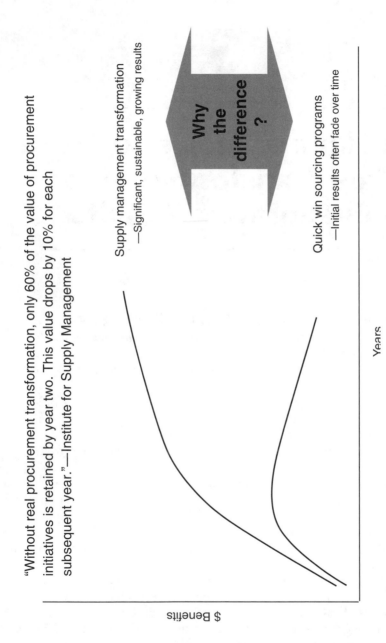

"Without real procurement transformation, only 60% of the value of procurement initiatives is retained by year two. This value drops by 10% for each subsequent year."—Institute for Supply Management

Supply management transformation
—Significant, sustainable, growing results

Why the difference?

Quick win sourcing programs
—Initial results often fade over time

$ Benefits

Years

Figure 3.1 Conventional *sourcing programs* alone often fail to sustain their initial results

It is correct in the sense that the vast majority of consulting projects or transformation efforts seem to have great difficulty generating results that are sustainable. Examples abound, including a multibillion dollar U.S.-based company that subsequently engaged Greybeard Advisors for transformation assistance—several years after a big-firm consulting project—because it "had nothing to show for the original project" according to its head of *indirect* procurement (see Where's the Beef? later in this chapter). The explanation is incomplete in the sense that the presence or departure of consultants is typically not the sole determinant of sustainable process and results.

As introduced in Chapter 1, companies that have successfully transformed their supply management activities into world-class performers pay attention to six key dimensions of transformation. As shown in Figure 3.2, those dimensions are (1) procurement's role, (2) objectives, (3) leadership, (4) organization, (5) best practices, and (6) innovation and technology. Underlying these six dimensions are more than 30 specific initiatives that ultimately comprise a comprehensive transformation plan.

For most companies, it's impractical to try to advance across all 30-plus initiatives from the very beginning of a transformation effort. You need a carefully thought-out roadmap that takes into account your current position (the so-called *as is* state) and establishes a logical sequence of initiatives that build on each other. From personal experience and work in guiding clients, we can say with certainty that this task involves both art and science.

True Transformation Rather Than Evaporating Results

You might wonder, why not keep it simple and focus on just one initiative, such as strategic sourcing? Some companies have done that, focusing on that singular theme as their path to glory. Yet often, after an initial flurry of quick wins, those companies see their gains evaporate as the program falters. The reason: such single-focus programs lack the necessary pillars of support for a successful, sustainable transformation—those six dimensions or pillars shown in Figure 3.2.

To say it another way, you really have a choice to make—true transformation or evaporating results. There is not much in between—even though countless companies seem to aim for a half-hearted, *good enough* approach (Chapter 1). Lacking the supporting pillars of a transformation roadmap, such half-hearted attempts inevitably turn into evaporating results.

Successful transformation takes tremendous leadership, a well thought-out transformation plan, best practices introduced in the right sequence, effective and enabling technology, and a few other key ingredients. That's one of the reasons the original book *Straight to the Bottom Line: An Executive's Roadmap*

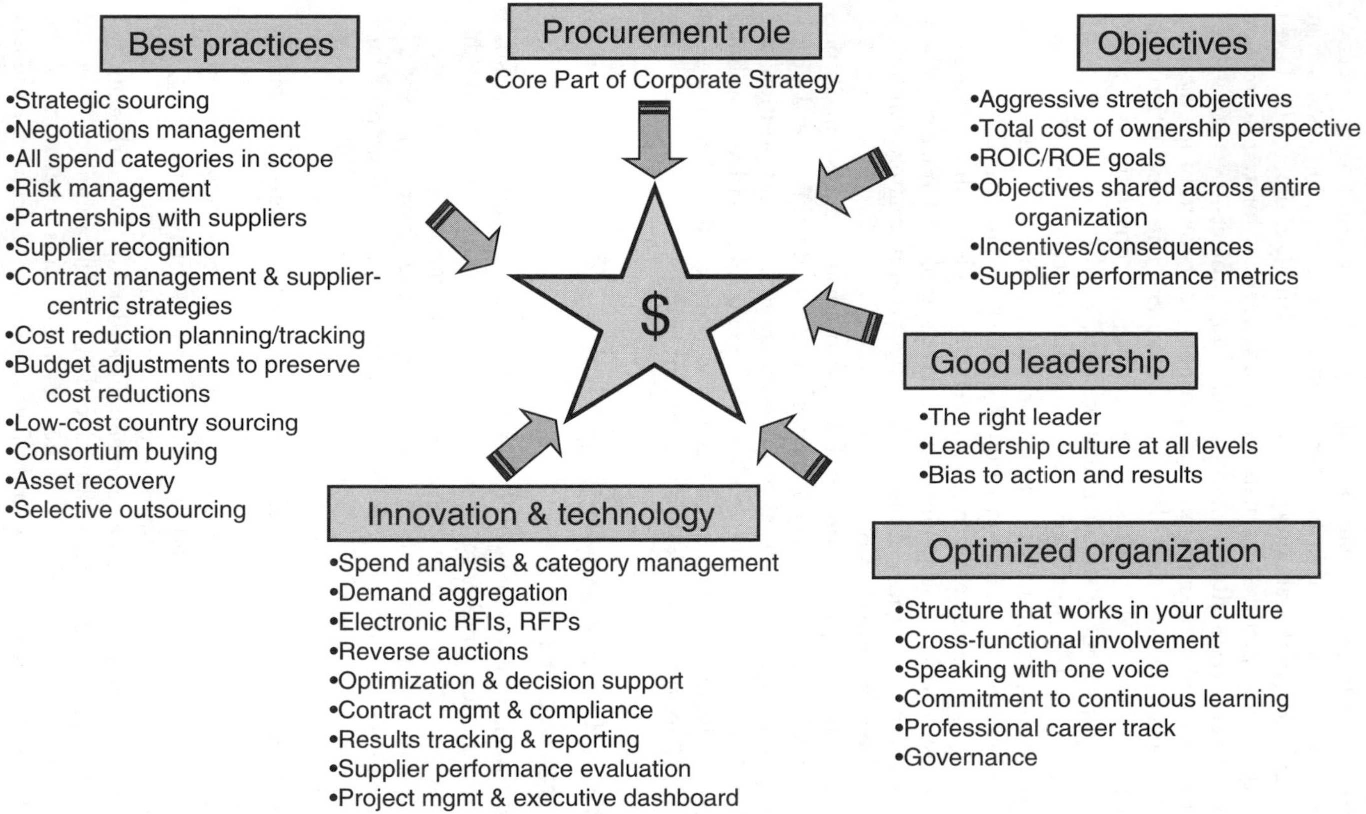

Objectives
- Aggressive stretch objectives
- Total cost of ownership perspective
- ROIC/ROE goals
- Objectives shared across entire organization
- Incentives/consequences
- Supplier performance metrics

Good leadership
- The right leader
- Leadership culture at all levels
- Bias to action and results

Optimized organization
- Structure that works in your culture
- Cross-functional involvement
- Speaking with one voice
- Commitment to continuous learning
- Professional career track
- Governance

Procurement role
- Core Part of Corporate Strategy

$

Innovation & technology
- Spend analysis & category management
- Demand aggregation
- Electronic RFIs, RFPs
- Reverse auctions
- Optimization & decision support
- Contract mgmt & compliance
- Results tracking & reporting
- Supplier performance evaluation
- Project mgmt & executive dashboard

Best practices
- Strategic sourcing
- Negotiations management
- All spend categories in scope
- Risk management
- Partnerships with suppliers
- Supplier recognition
- Contract management & supplier-centric strategies
- Cost reduction planning/tracking
- Budget adjustments to preserve cost reductions
- Low-cost country sourcing
- Consortium buying
- Asset recovery
- Selective outsourcing

Figure 3.2   Achieving world-class sustainable results requires attention to transformation initiatives across six key dimensions

Source: Robert A. Rudzki, Douglas Smock, Michael Katzorke, and Shelley Stewart Jr., *Straight to the Bottom Line*. Fort Lauderdale, FL: J. Ross Publishing, 2005.

to World-Class Supply Management was written. When the authors first met to frame out that book, they looked for common success factors in the eight procurement transformations they led in their careers. One of the ways they summarized their framework for success is what appears in Figure 3.2.

The first critical element of success or potential failure relates to the role that procurement has in your organization. Companies that make procurement and supply management a core part of their corporate strategy are more likely to have great results and success.

The next area of attention relates to objectives. It's important to have stretch objectives, such as a total cost of ownership perspective and return on invested capital (ROIC) goals that are shared across the entire organization. To say it another way, if procurement's objectives are not shared by operations and other key functions, and if procurement's objectives are not linked to broad corporate metrics such as ROIC and earnings per share, the chances of success are diminished.

Regarding an optimized organization, it's important to have a structure that works well in your culture. That can mean centralized or a center-led hybrid structure. It might even mean decentralized if you have a decentralized corporate structure, though the internal politics of a decentralized corporate structure can be successfully addressed if you design a center-led approach properly. Cross-functional involvement is also critical for success, as is having the entire organization speak with one voice in any contact with suppliers. Chapter 5 covers organizational design issues in-depth.

Good leadership involves having the right senior person in a position of authority who can be an advocate for the necessary changes required for a successful transformation. It also involves encouraging and developing a leadership culture at all levels of the organization. Furthermore, it involves creating an organizational bias toward action and results. Chapter 6 on talent management explores this topic further.

Best practices are critical to a successful transformation. Heading the list are strategic sourcing and negotiations management, the *next level* of which is covered at length in Chapters 8 and 9.

A key transformation enabler is innovation and technology. The sub-functions shown in Figure 3.2 can provide significant value to your activities. Better yet, solutions available today are proven and well-integrated to ensure that the savings negotiated upfront by procurement actually makes it to the bottom line. One of the historical challenges facing procurement managers has been that many of the technology tools that supported procurement were separate, stand-alone applications or only available via consultants, making it difficult (and expensive) to use them broadly enough to have any kind of impact. This has changed dramatically in recent years.

Classic Pitfalls to Avoid

Before discussing the importance of a transformation roadmap, it's worthwhile to spend a little time identifying and reviewing some of the classic pitfalls relating to procurement transformation.

Focusing on the wrong first priority is a common mistake. Organizational charts and reporting relationships are important subjects but should not be the first priority in designing a transformation roadmap. Similarly, revising job titles and addressing salary issues can often generate more organizational problems than solutions. Software by itself is also not an appropriate first priority, since software and systems are properly viewed as enablers of something else. Similarly, strategic sourcing by itself will not sustain a supply management transformation.

Another common pitfall is hiring a consulting firm that specializes in strategic sourcing programs as a stand-alone initiative without the supporting pillars of transformation or one that pushes the more recent fad of *risk-free cost reduction programs*. These topics are discussed as part of Chapter 6 regarding how to use external resources effectively in transforming to the next level.

Finally, a classic pitfall is failing to build interest and commitment from your internal clients and from the executive team and, associated with that, failing to make this a cross-functional journey. To say it another way, supply management can only accomplish so much on its own; executive support and cross-functional involvement are key to achieving maximum success.

Constructing the Transformation Roadmap

The star chart of Figure 3.2 can serve as the foundation for an assessment of your current state and the framework for developing a relevant transformation roadmap for your company. The first step is to arrange for a candid and comprehensive comparison of your company's current state compared to supply management and procurement best practices across a number of dimensions. The resulting gap analysis helps to identify and quantify opportunities and prioritize initiatives.

It is important to sequence the roadmap elements so that they build on each other. In our experience, that is part art and part science. Performed well, the roadmap will create sustainable results and momentum while building organizational capabilities and support that drive superior performance. Performed poorly, it can be the reason for the evaporating results depicted in Figure 3.1

The star chart dimensions should be evaluated by an independent authority, either internally or externally, who interviews supply management personnel and internal clients using a structured but flexible interview process and who reviews policies, processes, spend data, contracts, skills, and a variety of other revealing information. This evaluation process ensures that all relevant perspectives and facts are uncovered, leading to the ability to paint an accurate picture of the *current state* and offering a relevant and informed perspective on the transformation journey.

The process just described is preferred to the more mechanical *rate yourself* approach for a few simple reasons: it uncovers more information and enables deeper insights through the live interview process, it relies on an independent party to evaluate and assess the current state and the readiness of the organization for change, it takes a holistic view of the transformation challenge, and it creates a relevant transformation roadmap and business case based on practical experience.

Concluding Thoughts

Becoming world class in supply management is much more than mastering one business process (e.g., strategic sourcing) or implementing the latest technology tools. Companies that have created sustainable transformation results have focused on many initiatives, spanning six key dimensions.

Transformation is a journey. The length of the journey can be shortened by developing a roadmap for change that is based on the learnings of other companies that have succeeded (or failed) on that journey.

Where's the Beef?

Early in his post-corporate career as an advisor, Bob Rudzki was invited to meet with the head of indirect procurement for a large company. During that meeting, the director of indirect procurement casually mentioned that five or six years previously, his company had engaged one of the big consulting firms for *a strategic sourcing program*. Bob was puzzled. "Why, then," Bob asked, "do you want to talk with us?" "Simple," was the reply. "In spite of the touted success of that sourcing program at that time, we have nothing to show for it today. No embedded process, no upgraded skills, no strategic role, zilch." As Bob was to later learn, this company is not alone. Too many *sourcing programs* were simply not approached from the perspective of change management and sustainable transformation.

 Web Added Value™

This book has free material available for download from the Web Added Value™ resource center at *www.jrosspub.com*

4

Speaking Like a CFO and Gaining Senior Management's Support

Too many companies have already taken a fatal bullet but don't yet realize they are dying. In the last 10 years, a meaningful number of Fortune 500 companies have gone out of business or otherwise fallen from the top 500 rankings. That's just one indicator that something is amiss. But consider this fact: in that same 10-year period, over 600,000 American businesses of all sizes filed for bankruptcy. All of these companies were *walking wounded* at some point but failed to take effective action to staunch the bleeding of poor performance before it was too late.

In this chapter, we'll show you how to determine if your firm may already be among the walking wounded, and we'll set the stage for next level supply strategies that are much more than a Band-Aid approach to regaining and sustaining corporate financial health.

Concerns of C-Level Executives

In Chapter 1, we described some of the principal interests and concerns of senior executives. To recap, *C-level* executives tend to agree that their top priorities include:

- Meet or exceed the earnings expectations of Wall Street and their investors
- Achieve growth in revenues and earnings and sustain that growth year-over-year

- Reduce the volatility in revenues and earnings and thus reduce surprises and risk
- Improve return on invested capital (ROIC) and thereby reduce the amount of capital needed to fuel the growth of the business
- Create a business model that is difficult for competitors to copy

One of the best-kept secrets in the business world is that advanced procurement and supply management can impact all of these senior management objectives—simultaneously.

Procter & Gamble (P&G) and United Technologies (UTC) are two companies that are performing exceptionally well in their industries, and they are widely regarded as among the best managed companies in the world. Their stories highlight the role that procurement and supply management can have in turbo charging the performance of companies. P&G and UTC are examples of exceptional corporate performance due, in part, to elevating supply management to a strategic role.

Let's assume that your firm is like most companies and is not performing at the level of a P&G. How would you know if your company is already in trouble, and—more importantly—what could you do to dramatically improve your financial performance regardless of your current level of business performance? How do you take your company to the next level?

ROIC as an Indicator of Health or Trouble

In classic financial management courses, professors will tell you that to enhance shareholder value you must achieve returns on invested capital greater than your company's cost of capital. The best-performing companies and the best stocks over time tend to be those that have ROIC greater than their corporate cost of capital.

The flip side of the equation is more sobering. When your ROIC is less than your cost of capital, the lifeblood of your firm is draining away—you are among the walking wounded. How fast your firm dies will depend on how much of a shortfall exists between ROIC and cost of capital, and how much you have in financial reserves to fund that shortfall. In the absence of ROIC improving, the firm inevitably disappears.

ROIC is typically defined as earnings of the business, divided by the capital invested in the business, as indicated in Figure 4.1. When you increase profits, that improves ROIC as well as cash flow. An improvement in capital utilization also improves ROIC and cash flow. Moreover, when you improve both profits and capital utilization, you create a powerful compounding effect on both ROIC and cash flow.

Obviously, then, ROIC is dependent on the profits of a business, in relation to the assets invested in the business. As we'll see shortly, advanced supply

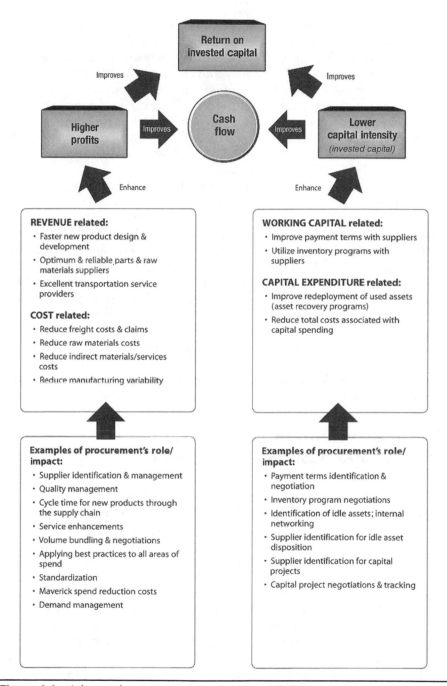

Figure 4.1 Advanced procurement can improve ROIC in many ways

management can have an enormous positive impact on each element of the ROIC equation. Few corporate groups can make that claim.

With regard to the top line of the income statement—the revenue line— success with customers is often heavily influenced by the effectiveness of your supply chain. How well do your suppliers work in tandem with your own organization? Getting the supply side in good shape can help to grow revenues and change the competitive dynamics in your favor. Just imagine the impact on your business if you could make it to market with new products months— if not years—ahead of your competition, and with a lower cost structure. Chapter 7 will cover this topic in detail.

With regard to costs, in most companies, more than 50% of the cost structure relates to procurement and supply chain costs. In spite of that importance, most senior executives don't know where to start to dramatically reduce those costs and improve their bottom line on a sustainable basis. With regard to the assets invested in the business, advanced procurement and supply management—working with the supply base—can have a significant impact on working capital levels and on capital projects, thereby favorably impacting ROIC.

There are many strategies to address each of these important drivers of ROIC. In this chapter, we'll look at each component strategy and then show you the magnitude of what is possible. Then, we'll address the specific topic of how you can put it all together into a successful transformation plan that can turbo charge your ROIC—and make the difference in your company's future. Part Two of this book builds on the ROIC model and has chapters devoted to each of the four drivers of ROIC and cash flow.

Procurement Strategies That Can Impact Total Business Performance

In the last 20 years, world-class procurement departments have adopted new processes and tools to unlock and create new shareholder value, to accelerate change, and to create powerful supply chains with which their competitors are now trying to catch up. So, what are the key strategies that you need to know in order to add value to your bottom line?

When it comes to improving margins and profits (lower left, Figure 4.1), procurement can have an impact through initiatives that favorably impact revenues and other initiatives that directly target costs of the business. On the revenue enhancement side, more companies are beginning to realize the value of working collaboratively with suppliers on innovation and on reducing the cycle time from product concept through delivering that new product to the marketplace.

With regard to costs, world-class companies view all areas of spend as being within the scope of modern procurement practices (i.e., no category of spend is too *strategic* or off-limits), and they pay particular attention to reducing maverick spend and ensuring compliance with negotiated contracts.

When it comes to improving the capital intensity of the business (lower right, Figure 4.1), procurement can have an impact through initiatives that favorably impact working capital and through initiatives that impact the total investment in capital assets. For example, payment terms offer enormous opportunity to add value and financial flexibility by negotiating longer net terms, plus attractive discount options if you elect to pay early. Similarly, inventory programs offer the opportunity to free up significant working capital, and so-called *asset recovery* initiatives offer a disciplined approach to realizing value from underutilized or idle plant and equipment.

To summarize the framework we have discussed so far, advanced procurement—if given the right role, the right tools, and adequate resources—can directly impact all four strategic drivers of ROIC and cash flow.

What Is the Potential Impact on My Business?

Let's now take a closer look at the degree of impact that procurement and supply management can have in several key areas.

First, what is possible in revenue support and enhancement? Consider the subject of new product development cycle time. Would reducing the time from product concept to shipping improve your competitive standing and win new sales? If you could reduce that cycle time by 50% and beat competitors to market, while also reducing total sourcing and manufacturing costs, would that be a plus for your business? For most companies, that would have a huge, positive impact. Supply management, working closely with key suppliers, can help make this happen, a topic covered in Chapter 7.

Next, with regard to costs, the conventional wisdom is that procurement should focus principally on the *big ticket* areas of spend, such as raw materials and energy. You certainly should devote attention to raw materials and energy—not just to reduce costs but also to reduce volatility through better risk management. However, if you focus only on the big ticket spend categories, you'll miss out on the enormous opportunities presented by all other, indirect areas of spend. It is often possible to achieve double-digit reductions in costs for those indirect spend categories (see Figure 4.2). In fact, in our experience, the so-called *indirects* offer one of the biggest single areas of opportunity—if approached properly. The bottom line is this: focus on both direct and indirect spending. Doing so can have a powerful effect on corporate performance.

A few years ago, Bob Rudzki was interviewing the president of a major business regarding his impressions of the company's procurement activities. He offered some specific advice: "Bob," he said, "we need to spend more time and effort on raw materials costs." Bob asked him why he said that. The answer was simple: "Because it's the biggest part of my cost structure. We

Category	Benchmarks
Raw materials	2 to 5% & better risk mgmt.
Packaging	10 to 20%
Indirect materials and services	10 to 20%
Information technology	15 to 30%
Professional services	8 to 15%
Logistics/transportation	7 to 15%
Media, marketing, promotional items	10 to 20%
Other indirects	5 to 15%
Capital projects	7 to 15%

Figure 4.2   What is possible in cost reduction?
Source: Robert A. Rudzki, Douglas Smock, Michael Katzorke, and Shelley Stewart Jr., *Straight to the Bottom Line*. Fort Lauderdale, FL: J. Ross Publishing, 2005.

spend $1 billion per year on raw materials and only $500 million on all of the rest—the indirects." He then suggested that he would be happy with a 2-3% reduction in raw materials costs, given his tight gross margins.

Bob then told him that for the so-called indirect spends (those things that don't become part of the physical product), it is often possible to achieve 15 to 20% cost reduction or more, if approached properly. The business unit president quickly did the math in his head and saw that the bottom line opportunity from focusing on the indirects was actually greater than by focusing on just the direct spend. He quickly supported focusing on both areas of spend, simultaneously. The subject of *next level* approaches and best practices for cost management and cost reduction is covered in Part Two of this book.

With regard to working capital initiatives, modern procurement departments are including payment terms in their requests for proposals and are often pleasantly surprised by the responses. This can have a meaningful impact on your business. For example, for each $1 billion of purchases, moving from net 30 days to 1%/10 with net 45 days offers the option of taking the payment discount and improving earnings by some $10 million/year (minus the interest earnings on the cash used to pay early) or the ability to grow accounts payable and cash by about $40 million, by paying in 45 days. Chapter 15 addresses the subject of payment terms more comprehensively.

Similarly, including inventory terms in the RFP can offer suppliers the opportunity to show their creativity as well. Inventory programs with suppliers can free up tens of millions of dollars in capital for other purposes.

For capital projects, there is a direct correlation between the total costs associated with that project and the moment that procurement is involved. The message here is simple: involve procurement *and suppliers* at an early stage to optimize the total costs of any capital project. You've perhaps seen it happen too many times. Well-intentioned engineers and plant operators go running down the path of conceptualizing the project, and designing the equipment, before seeking any input from their professional procurement colleagues.

Getting procurement and suppliers involved early in the process, even at the concept stage, makes it more likely that the best ideas are considered before it is too late and that the commercial foundation for success is established before too many *technical details* are locked in. This subject is covered extensively in Chapter 16.

An Illustration of What Is Possible

We've been describing some of the impacts that advanced procurement and supply management can have in particular areas relating to improving profits and improving the capital intensity of your business. Let's pull it all together with an illustration of an income statement and a balance sheet.

In Figure 4.3, you'll see a simplified income statement for our hypothetical manufacturing company. This company has $800 million net income—not bad, you might say. Whether it is good or bad requires some additional information. In the next figure, you'll see a simplified balance sheet for the same company—consistent with the size and profitability shown on the prior chart. The ROIC for this company—pretransformation—is calculated by taking the net income and dividing it by the total sum of long-term debt and stockholders equity. In this example, the company has an ROIC of 7.8%, as shown in Figure 4.4. We need one more piece of information to complete

	Pretransformation
Net sales	25.00 billion
Purchased goods/svc	15.00
Other cost of goods sold	5.50
Gross profit	4.50
SG&A Expenses	3.00
Depreciation & amortization	0.50
Income before taxes	1.00
Provision for income taxes	0.20
Net income	$ 0.80
EPS	$2.00 per share

Figure 4.3   Turbo charge your ROIC—income statement (pretransformation)

	Pretransformation
Cash & equivalents	$ 2.00 Billion
Accounts receivable	4.00
Inventories	3.00
Property, plant, & equip	4.00
Other assets	7.00
Total assets	20.00
Accounts payable	1.25
Other current liabilities	5.50
Long-term debt	4.00
Other long-term liabilities	3.00
Total liabilities	13.75
Total equity	6.25
Total liab. & equity	$ 20.00 Billion

ROIC =

$$\text{ROIC} = \$800 / (4{,}000 + 6{,}250) = 7.8\% \text{ Pretransformation}$$

Figure 4.4   Turbo charge your ROIC—balance sheet (pretransformation)

our pretransformation assessment—this company's weighted average cost of capital is about 10%.

This company's ROIC is less than its cost of capital. *It is among the walking wounded.* Whether that condition proves fatal will depend on the actions that its management takes to significantly improve ROIC.

Now comes the enjoyable part. The changes that are possible—based on what we've described so far and elaborate on in Part Two of this book, are indicated in Figure 4.5. Revenues are shown to increase 3%, purchased goods and services costs (as a percentage of revenues) are reduced from 60% to 55%, and SG&A expenses as a percentage of revenues are reduced by 1%. Those three improvements—which, by the way, are achievable based on what we've covered so far—have a large cumulative impact on net income and earnings per share.

	Pretransformation	Posttransformation
Net sales	$ 25.00 billion	$ 25.75 billion
Purchased goods/svc	15.00	14.16
Other cost of goods sold	5.50	5.67
Gross profit	4.50	5.92
SG&A expenses	3.00	2.83
Depreciation & amortization	0.50	0.50
Income before taxes	1.00	2.59
Provision for inc. taxes	0.20	0.60
Net income	**$ 0.8 billion**	**$ 1.99 billion**
EPS	*$2.00 per share*	*$4.98 per share*

Figure 4.5   Turbo charge your ROIC—income statement (posttransformation)

The balance sheet changes are shown in Figure 4.6. The revenue growth causes accounts receivable to grow slightly. Inventory levels are reduced slightly because of the lower level of purchased goods costs plus a modest 2% reduction from inventory consignment programs. Accounts payable grow because the company has renegotiated payment terms from net 30 days to net 45 days. In addition, the reduction in capital intensity due to the improvements in accounts payable and inventories (less the growth in accounts receivable), allows for a pay-down of long-term debt.

The compound effect of better profits and better capital intensity has an enormous impact on ROIC—going from 7.8% pretransformation to over 20% posttransformation.

That's real change, and it's not fantasy. Each of the changes described here is very doable. Next level supply organizations will firmly have their sights set on this kind of ROIC improvement.

What's Needed for Success?

You might ask, why aren't lots of companies performing at 20+% ROIC? There are two reasons. One, there may be other adverse trends in their business that are partially or completely offsetting the good impacts from advanced supply management—for example, weakening product selling prices or skyrocketing labor and health care costs. But setting those factors aside for the moment, the main reason you don't see many companies with 20+% ROIC is that these improvements don't just happen by themselves. It takes tremendous leadership, a well thought-out transformation plan, the right best practices in the right sequence,

	Pretransformation	Posttransformation
Cash & equivalents	$ 2.00 billion	$ 2.00 billion
Accounts receivable	4.00	4.12
Inventories	3.00	2.77
Property, plant, & equip	4.00	4.00
Other assets	7.00	7.00
Total assets	20.00	19.89
Accounts payable	1.25	1.88
Other current liabilities	5.50	5.50
Long-term debt	4.00	3.27
Other long-term liabilities	3.00	3.00
Total liabilities	13.75	13.64
Total equity	6.25	6.25
Net Income	$ 20.00 billion	$ 19.98 billion
EPS	*$2.00 per share*	*$4.98 per share*

ROIC: from 7.8% to 20.9%

Figure 4.6   Turbo charge your ROIC—balance sheet (posttransformation)

effective and enabling technology, and a few other key ingredients. That's one of the reasons the original book *Straight to the Bottom Line* was written.

When the authors first met to frame out that book, we looked for common success factors in the eight procurement transformations we have led in our careers. One of the ways we summarized our framework for success is shown in Figure 1.3 in Chapter 1—which highlights six key areas of attention. This framework was discussed in Chapters 1 and 3, so we won't say much about it here other than to reinforce its relevance to sustainable transformation.

Tracking and Measuring Results Credibly

In 1994, when Bob Rudzki was offered the opportunity to step outside his financial career track and run the global procurement and transportation operation of Bethlehem Steel, he had a memorable meeting with his new boss, the president and COO of the company. He offered Bob an observation that guided Bob's early plans. "Purchasing keeps telling me they're saving this company millions, but I can't find it on our income statement."

Perhaps the single most important distinction you need to make is to separate cost reduction from cost avoidance. Why do we say that? It's simple. Cost reduction in operating expenses can, generally, be tracked to changes in operating costs on the income statement. Cost avoidance doesn't have the same ability. So, if you try to add cost avoidance to cost reduction and then report your total *savings*, you've just created a misleading figure that has no relevance

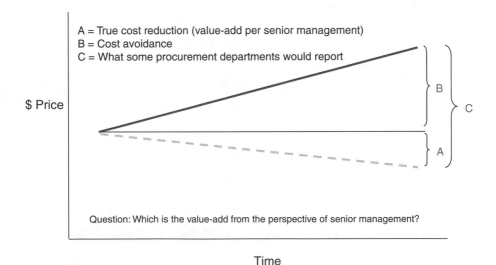

Figure 4.7   Danger, Will Robinson, danger!

to the profit and loss (P&L) statement that your internal clients look at on a monthly basis (see Figure 4.7).

That's not to say that you should not track cost avoidance. We encourage companies to have a robust system that tracks operating cost reductions, capital cost reductions, and cost avoidance (and other metrics). Just never add them together, or you will lose P&L relevance.

The importance of P&L relevance cannot be overstated. If you report procurement results that can't be found on the income statement, your credibility will suffer greatly. In fact, we recommend banning the word *savings* from your practice. Either a result is cost reduction or it is cost avoidance. But do not label it by the vague term savings.

To have the best chance of credibility with your internal clients, you need to build a framework and tracking system that is P&L relevant—and that means tracking and reporting only cost reduction from operating costs (see Figure 4.8). This framework is one of the foundations for a credible approach to reporting the results from the efforts of your teams.

One of the important design choices in building a credible cost reduction tracking system is what cost reductions should be measured against. There are some basic choices:

- Costs of a baseline year (e.g., the year just before your efforts began)
- Prior year costs (so-called *year-over-year reporting*)
- Business plan (budget) for the current year
- Market

	P & L impact from
• Initiatives (sourcing efforts)	
– Price	XXX
– Nonprice	XXX
– Total	XXX
• Volume fluctuations	XXX
• Marketplace factors (inflation)	XXX
• Net change in operating costs	XXX

Only cost reduction counts. Cost avoidance, if tracked, is not added to the cost reduction figures. It is useful to track not only the impact of initiatives, but also the impact of volume and inflation. It is also important to track capital categories separately from expense categories. Done properly, the net change (operating costs) should come close to agreeing with the accounting system figure for P & L impact.

Figure 4.8   Cost reduction tracking framework
Source: Greybeard Advisors LLC. Copyright 2005–2011. All rights reserved.

In the most advanced organizations, capabilities exist to measure against all of these. What's right for you will depend mainly on your company's financial office and your internal clients.

Another useful technique is to track progress on individual projects from the initial *identified opportunity* through *on the table* (initial offers) to *final negotiated* results to *realized benefits* (see Figure 4.9). You can use your tracking system to create interest and build momentum for your results.

The concepts of *identified, on the table, negotiated,* and *realized* results can be thought of as milestones that are directly related to different phases of strategic sourcing. Identified results are the outcome of doing the homework on a sourcing category—they represent the potential cost reductions possible for all efforts currently underway. On the table results reflect the current status of RFP discussions that are in progress but unfinished. You can think of this as work-in-progress. Negotiated results are the annualized results from completed negotiations. Realized results reflect the implemented results flowing to the bottom line. Figure 4.10 shows one approach for displaying that information in a format suitable for senior management.

Tracking and Measuring Results

A simple and powerful best practice is to obtain stakeholder signoff regarding the sourcing strategy as well as the methodology for calculating results. If you've kept your stakeholders informed and involved throughout your sourcing process, this should be a relatively simple task.

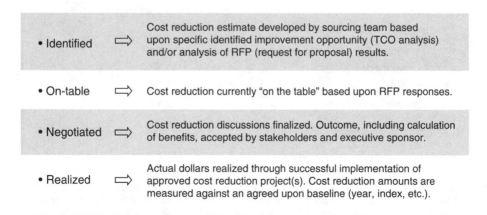

- Identified ⇒ Cost reduction estimate developed by sourcing team based upon specific identified improvement opportunity (TCO analysis) and/or analysis of RFP (request for proposal) results.

- On-table ⇒ Cost reduction currently "on the table" based upon RFP responses.

- Negotiated ⇒ Cost reduction discussions finalized. Outcome, including calculation of benefits, accepted by stakeholders and executive sponsor.

- Realized ⇒ Actual dollars realized through successful implementation of approved cost reduction project(s). Cost reduction amounts are measured against an agreed upon baseline (year, index, etc.).

Figure 4.9   Definition of key cost reduction terms

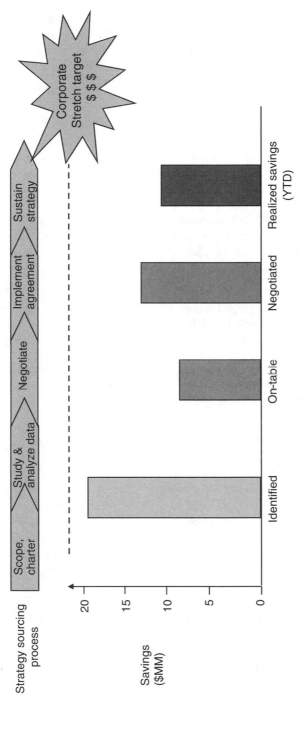

Figure 4.10 Cost reduction—total program progress reporting

The specific practice that we share with companies involves summarizing all key information on one page. As a result, your internal clients/stakeholders can quickly see and understand such things as:

- Sourcing category
- Baseline annual spend
- Team leader
- Team members
- Sourcing strategy
- Selected supplier(s)
- Inception date and term of new contract
- Key provisions
- Estimated cost reduction by business division
- Other quantifiable and nonquantifiable benefits
- Method of calculating benefits, with an example
- Investments needed (if any)
- Team leader signature and sign-off block for the stakeholders

These elements can be built into a one-page format that serves as a template for all of your sourcing teams. Importantly, once you have the signoff in hand, it can serve as a reminder to make budget adjustments to preserve the negotiated results—and ensure that they make it *straight to the bottom line*.

Compliance, Results, and the Role of the Financial Office

There are numerous reasons why savings reported by the procurement department fail to hit the bottom line. One of the principal culprits is maverick spend.

In Figure 4.11, you'll see a table that we refer to as the strategic sourcing—compliance multiplier. The matrix shows different levels of negotiated cost reduction for a new contract (5%, 10%, 15%, or more), and different levels of compliance with that contract (from 25% up to 95%). The table shows the amount of benefit that actually makes it to the bottom line based on each combination of negotiated cost reduction and actual compliance. Just to make the illustration easy to follow, we are assuming a $10 million amount of spend that could be directed to that new contract.

A fairly typical result, for example, might be to negotiate a 5 to 10% cost reduction with your supply base. That sounds good until you realize that in many companies, the initial compliance with that new contract might only be 25 to 50%. So what you are looking at are true, bottom-line results in the boxed area in the top-left portion of the figure. For the procurement group to

% Cost reduction	Compliance with new contract				
	25%	50%	75%	85%	95%
05	$125,000	$250,000	$375,000	$425,000	$475,000
10	$250,000	$500,000	$750,000	$850,000	$950,000
15	$375,000	$750,000	$1,125,000	$1,275,000	$1,425,000
20	$500,000	$1,000,000	$1,500,000	$1,700,000	$1,900,000
25	$625,000	$1,250,000	$1,875,000	$2,125,000	$2,375,000
30	$750,000	$1,500,000	$2,250,000	$2,550,000	$2,850,000

($ to the bottom line for each $10 million of spend)

Best practices + good compliance = $ to the bottom line

Figure 4.11 Strategic sourcing/compliance multiplier

really add value, it needs to utilize best practices to identify the best suppliers, negotiate world-class contracts, and then ensure a high level of compliance.

On the chart you can see the impact of negotiating a 10 to 15% cost reduction, combined with an 85 to 95% level of compliance. To really make sure it gets to the bottom line, it's critical to communicate the new contracts and relevant spend to your controllers. Furthermore, ask them to adjust budgets so that the favorable variances created by your sourcing successes are not automatically spent on other things. What we are looking at in the boxed area to the right are significantly higher numbers hitting the bottom line.

Compliance

All too often, after a long and productive sourcing initiative, the team celebrates success when the new contract is finalized. The best efforts don't end there. They continue with a well-developed implementation plan. That plan includes— among a long list of actions—involving the finance and accounting staff in ensuring that negotiated benefits make it to the bottom line.

Without a pro-active approach on budget adjustments, this is what typically happens: the new contract creates favorable variances at the cost center level, and the individual cost center manager has the freedom to spend that favorable variance on other things. As a result, no one can *find* the benefits from the new contract on the bottom line. This is especially true with indirect materials and services.

Most companies do not regularly adjust budgets for new contracts. If your company is in that category, you can improve your value-add, and your credibility, by starting now. Involve your finance and accounting partners—they have as much at stake as you do.

A Word of Caution

One of the persistent challenges facing procurement and supply management is that of compliance. Unfortunately, the effort to improve compliance is often focused on after-the-fact enforcement. It can be much more productive to understand the fundamental reasons that people choose to use—or ignore—new contracts. Often, these reasons are related to the approach used by the supply management organization.

Compliance typically refers to the percentage of a new supply contract that is being utilized by internal users. So, 100% compliance means that everyone that could be using a new contract is doing so (i.e., there is no *maverick spend*).

A next level supply perspective is that compliance is not just an enforcement metric—it also reflects the *effectiveness of the process used to understand internal needs, engage the supply marketplace, and select and negotiate with suppliers*. Compliance has the best chance of being maximized when:

- A true, robust strategic sourcing process is utilized.
- Stakeholders are identified and asked for input.
- Stakeholders are involved throughout the sourcing process.
- Local needs are explicitly considered.
- A total cost of ownership perspective is used.
- All options are on the table (no preconceived notions).
- Internal clients can see the benefits of proceeding with the recommended sourcing strategy and ultimately using the contract.
- Your sourcing efforts are part of a well-designed transformation roadmap.

When all of these are present, compliance generally is high—right from the onset of a new contract.

Concluding Thoughts

In summary, the key components of attracting and holding senior management's attention are:

- Speaking their language
- Developing a vision with bold objectives that directly relate to senior management's interests (EPS, ROIC, cash flow, risk management, etc.)
- Laying out your transformation plan and roadmap
- Viewing technology as an *enabler* of your transformation plan and stretch objectives
- Building your business case (what you expect to deliver in exchange for resources and budget, speaking with one voice discipline)
- Willing to make a commitment to gain top management's commitment
- Leading and making it happen

It is important to keep in mind that becoming world class in supply management is much more than mastering one business process (e.g., strategic sourcing) or implementing the latest technology tools. Companies that have created sustainable transformation results and capabilities have focused on many initiatives spanning the six key dimensions of transformation.

Transformation is a journey. The length of the journey can be shortened by developing a roadmap for change that is based on the learnings of other companies that have succeeded (or failed) on this journey.

5

Creating the Next Level Supply Organization

A review of any company that has attained supply leadership will usually show that careful consideration has been given to the organizational design and governance structure. While its importance appears over and over, one of the least exciting topics within supply management involves organizational design. The topic simply does not generate the same excitement as some other supply management topics. Ignoring the importance of organizational design, however, can have serious consequences when a misalignment occurs between your strategic objectives and the design and governance structure that is supposed to help attain those objectives. Trying to act as one supply voice when organizational authority is spread across different operating units will lead to some interesting outcomes, to say the least.

This chapter approaches organizational design and governance from various perspectives. First, we define what is meant by these terms. Next, five trends that have greatly affected supply designs are presented followed by a more in-depth analysis regarding the shift toward center-led supply management. Specific design features that support next level supply organizations follow with a discussion of the widespread use of teams, including virtual teams. The chapter concludes with the organizational characteristics of a next level supply organization.

Understanding Organizational Design

Organizational design is a primary enabler that provides the foundation for which supply excellence is built. For that reason alone, it is important to pay attention to this topic.

What, then, is organizational design? Organizational design is a broad concept that refers to the process of assessing and selecting the structure and formal system of communication, division of labor, coordination, control, authority, and responsibility required to achieve an organization's goals.[1] One way to think about an organization's design is that it often resembles a complex web reflecting the pattern of interactions and coordination that links technology, tasks, and human components.[2] The formal design of an organization is far more complex than what an organizational chart can ever show. The design also helps define an organization's governance structure. The governance structure refers to how an organization is governed, including how control is exhibited and authority is distributed.

The objectives that a firm hopes to achieve will influence its design. If supply managers want to pursue increased coordination and integration across the supply chain, then design features may offer opportunities to enhance coordination and integration. A variety of design features support three kinds of integration—cross-functional, cross-locational, and cross-organizational. If better supplier selection decisions are a sought after objective, then cross-functional commodity teams will likely be part of the design mix. If it is important for supply personnel to work closely with internal customers, then a collocation model will become attractive. The need to have a presence in emerging sourcing markets will likely result in the establishment of international purchasing offices (IPOs). We think you get the idea here. Clarify the role of your supply management department, next identify your key supply objectives, and then establish the design that supports achieving those objectives.

Trends Affecting Organizational Design and Governance

Some well-defined trends are affecting the design of supply organizations. Hopefully, the design that an organization puts in place is not the result of random occurrences. It should be the result of careful consideration given to what supply leaders are trying to achieve. It is also the result of some macro changes and trends that affect the practice of supply management.

Trend 1: Moving toward Center-led Supply Management

We have witnessed a steady shift along the decentralized-centralized authority continuum over the last 20 years. One driver behind a shift toward greater centralization is the realization that a failure to leverage purchase volumes results in lost opportunities to achieve double-digit cost savings. Decentralized authority structures are not good at coordinating activities beyond the site or local level. Another driver is the higher expectations that executive leaders have regarding the contribution of the supply function. Achieving these expectations requires an organizational design that elevates the visibility and authority of supply management. This has resulted in the development of design features that elevate the supply management group within the corporate hierarchy while providing centralized authority to develop company-wide contracts and processes. This trend is so important that the next section discusses it in-depth.

Trend 2: A Growing Reliance on Teams

A growing reliance on organizational work teams over the last 20 years, particularly cross-functional teams, represents several shifts in thinking. The first is a realization that higher level supply management, unlike traditional purchasing, is not a functional pursuit. Strategic supply management is organizational rather than functional in scope and benefits from the support and active involvement of various functions, including finance and engineering. A second realization is that teams offer the potential for better, more effective decision making. These two realizations have resulted in teams becoming a primary design feature within most supply organizations. A reliance on teams is not going to change anytime soon.

Trend 3: Moving Away from Materials Management

It has become increasingly evident that supply organizations have shifted away from responsibilities that are part of a traditional materials management group. This is not to say that materials management activities have disappeared. They simply have been automated or became the responsibility of other groups once supply leaders decided this was not the best place to commit their energy. Supply organizations have removed themselves from the day-to-day management of materials and transactions by separating strategic and tactical responsibilities within their organizational design.

Trend 4: Taking a Global Perspective

Even after most supply organizations recognized the need to shift from a decentralized to centrally led supply model, this shift reached only as far as the regional level. A common model involved creating a supply organization that assumed a regional perspective, such as North America, Europe, or Asia. It is only over the last decade or so that supply organizations have recognized a regional model is inadequate when suppliers and operating sites are worldwide. If leveraging purchase volumes and supply practices was a good idea at the regional level, won't global integration offer new opportunities? Design features that stress communication, coordination, and consistency across worldwide sites and suppliers are tangible outcomes from this trend.

Trend 5: Spanning across Boundaries

Almost by definition, higher level supply management requires supply professionals to work cross-functionally and cross-organizationally. Greater internal and external boundary spanning is now an accepted part of the job. Certain design features explicitly promote boundary spanning, including product development teams with supply and supplier involvement, buyer-supplier councils, and collocation of supply personnel with internal customers. The days of operating within the same four walls are over.

Center-led Supply Management—A Next Level Mandate

Throughout purchasing history, we have witnessed a back and forth movement (the proverbial pendulum swing) between centralized and decentralized placement of authority. Supply managers are now witnessing a shift toward central control and coordination that is not likely to reverse soon, at least for certain decisions and activities.

What is unique about this shift compared with previous historical periods is the intense pressure to reduce costs brought about by global competition. An inability to raise prices demands the coordination of supply activities and the consolidation of purchase volumes in an effort to minimize supply chain costs. The challenge becomes one of knowing what to manage from a center-led level while remaining responsive to the needs of business units and operating sites.

Research reveals that a positive relationship exists between firms that indicate their current design and governance structure promotes the attainment of supply objectives and centrally coordinated decision-making authority. In other words, centralized or center-led supply organizations are more likely to say their design promotes the attainment of supply objectives than less centralized firms.

An emphasis on centrally led or centralized governance, coordination, and decision making within supply management is clearly evident from research. Consider the following, which shows the emphasis that firms place on center-led or centralized authority and governance:[3]

- Over 70% of research respondents say their decision-making authority within supply management is centralized or highly centralized.
- Almost 60% of respondents say their overall business unit is structured and governed centrally, 39% say their business unit is decentralized with some coordination, and only 2% indicate their business unit is decentralized.
- Over 50% say their business unit's strategy decisions are now made from a worldwide perspective while 33% take a regional perspective.

- Almost 75% of respondents indicate their most important purchases are coordinated from a center-led or headquarters group.

Whether we like it or not, supply management is a process that is best managed from a centrally led level and that means the presence of strong executive leadership. The terms centrally coordinated or centrally led do not necessarily refer to the presence of a large corporate procurement staff. In fact, the presence of a large central staff sometimes concerns lower level units as they think about a loss of control, longer decision-making times, and a bureaucracy that is far removed from day-to-day realities. Central coordination can occur across regions, business units, sites, and other functional groups through various design features that have little to do with a massive physical presence of people residing in a central location.

Supply leaders should consider design features that support a continued movement toward centrally led or centrally coordinated supply management. This includes the use of centrally coordinated commodity teams, formal positions that separate strategic and tactical supply responsibilities, lead buyers to manage noncentrally coordinated items, strategy review and coordination sessions between functional groups and locations, and a higher level chief procurement officer (CPO). A later section describes some of these features in greater detail.

Planning and execution levels are often different within a centrally led supply model. Talking about a strong centrally led effort is only half of the story here. We also know that site-based control of operational activities is also important. A model that is becoming increasingly common is to separate strategic activities, which are often associated with planning, from tactical activities, which involve day-to-day decisions or tasks. A later section discusses the separation of these activities.

Not everyone is comfortable with a centrally led approach to sourcing, and others are not comfortable with the concept of centralization. As mentioned, centralization may imply bureaucracy and a lack of responsiveness to operational needs, and these concerns are often justified. When this is the case, executive managers should use their organizational design as a way to coordinate global activities without having to group purchasing professionals in a central location. These companies will maintain some supply activities at a decentralized level, particularly those involved with day-to-day materials management, while creating organizational models that feature coordinated discussions between business units or operating locations. Another model might feature supply professionals assigned to specific business units in a matrix structure. These individuals will have a dual reporting relationship to the management of the business unit and the center-led leadership. Whatever model is pursued, rest assured that the findings regarding the linkage between centrally led decision making and supply management success are clear.

Next Level Organizational Design Features

As mentioned, the organizational design and governance features that are put in place should directly support the attainment of strategic objectives. Within the supply domain, this means creating an organization that achieves far more than simply cost reductions. The next level supply organization must be capable of supporting strategic objectives at the corporate level. The following presents a set of organizational design features that support a governance structure that supports supply management excellence.

A Chief Procurement Officer

It should go without saying (although we will say it anyway) that if supply organizations pursue a strong center-led governance structure, a higher level procurement officer is critical to success. We know that a positive relationship exists between firms that believe their current design promotes the attainment of supply objectives and the reporting level of the highest supply officer.

Research evidence as well as anecdotal experience is clear regarding the importance of a CPO. We also know that an essential part of the CPO position involves making regular strategy and performance review presentations to the president, CEO, and board of directors. An earlier study found that having the CPO make regular strategy and performance presentations to the president or CEO correlates highly with an organizational design that helps companies achieve their supply objectives.[4] This is accountability at the highest level.

The visibility and resources that come with having a position in the corporate hierarchy that is on par with other functional executives is critical. Of course, every functional group can argue they should have an executive position that reports well up the corporate hierarchy. Supply executives must make the business case why they should have a senior executive who is on par with other functional executives.

No clear consensus has emerged regarding the ideal placement of the highest supply executive. One school of thought argues for having the CPO report directly to the CEO. After all, how much more visibility can you get than being a direct report to the CEO? A second school of thought argues for reporting one level below the CEO. Proponents of this argument say the CEO has far too many issues to worry about and that supply management will not receive the visibility it deserves. This position argues that reporting to an individual who still has major organizational authority, such as an executive vice president, is a better way to go. The placement of the CPO will often be a function of a company's size and complexity.

It's hard to imagine achieving a demanding set of supply objectives without an executive leader who has the skill, authority, and resources to translate a global vision into reality. Companies that expect advantages from their organizational design must never discount the importance of a higher level procurement officer, as well as the reporting level of that position. When we visit companies, one of the first questions we ask concerns the reporting level of the highest supply officer. The answer to that question is often quite revealing regarding the importance of the supply organization.

Executive Steering Committee

Just as it is hard to imagine a leading supply organization without a higher level supply officer in charge, it is hard to imagine the absence of an executive steering committee or advisory board to provide strategic guidance. These boards or councils, usually comprised of internal executives from various functional and operating groups, are much more than cosmetic. They are accountable for some serious work. The following are the responsibilities of a supply leadership council for a major global company:

- Establish the strategic direction for purchase commodities
- Charter and staff strategy development teams
- Search *outside the box* for new sourcing methods
- Coordinate strategy development with other groups
- Pursue consistent supply policies, procedures, and processes worldwide
- Establish company-wide improvement targets
- Ensure compliance to corporate agreements

Just as leading supply organizations feature a higher level supply executive, next level supply designs are also supported by a visible steering committee or council.

Customer Advisory Boards

A rarely used design feature is something we call customer advisory boards. These high level entities attempt to link key tier-one suppliers, the OEM, and the OEM's primary customer, forging an integrated supply chain at the strategic, rather than operational, level. This design feature is clearly not for every company. However, our expectation is that those companies that successfully create customer advisory boards are operating at a level that is way beyond most competitors.

Figure 5.1 identifies the variety of benefits that could accrue from introducing your key suppliers to your primary customers. At a high level, these boards facilitate trust and communication. Although this may sound counterintuitive, one of the goals of these boards is for suppliers to look beyond their immediate customer (i.e., the OEM) to the primary customer. After all, the fruits of the suppliers' labors are going to end up with the primary customer. Why not streamline the communication process?

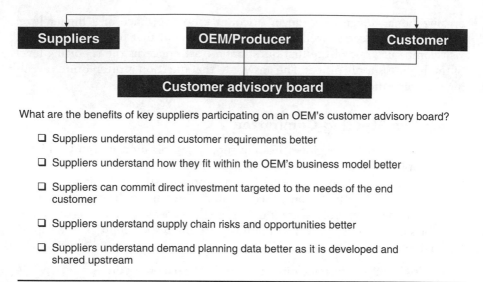

What are the benefits of key suppliers participating on an OEM's customer advisory board?

❑ Suppliers understand end customer requirements better

❑ Suppliers understand how they fit within the OEM's business model better

❑ Suppliers can commit direct investment targeted to the needs of the end customer

❑ Suppliers understand supply chain risks and opportunities better

❑ Suppliers understand demand planning data better as it is developed and shared upstream

Figure 5.1   Customer advisory boards

Let's provide an example where a customer advisory board would be applicable. Suppose that a major aerospace company is designing a new fighter for the U.S. Air Force. Given that product development within the aerospace industry features extensive outsourcing of design and production, it is in everyone's interests for the primary supply chain players to get together early and often. The supplier(s) who are responsible for designing electronic systems will come to realize that a primary customer objective is to have the aircraft ready to perform its mission, or what is called *uptime*. Since electronics make up a large part of why aircraft are not mission ready, a design effort that does not feature rapid electronic serviceability will likely lead to excessive downtime. Suppliers will soon realize that to meet the end customer's requirements, electronic modules that quickly pop in and out of the aircraft are likely needed to support rapid service turnaround. And rapid service turnaround directly supports the aircraft uptime objective. The possibilities presented by customer advisory boards are intriguing and largely unrealized at this time.

Buyer-Supplier Councils

Buyer-supplier councils feature executive-to-executive interaction between a supply organization and its key suppliers. Generally, the council does not exceed around 12 noncompeting suppliers. Many companies choose to rotate their membership over preestablished time periods.

The creation of a buyer-supplier council is a clear indication that a supply organization is thinking strategically. The council provides an ideal forum

❑ Share future product development plans

❑ Develop joint measures of supply chain success

❑ Create a co-destiny and trust between supply chain members

❑ Align long-range goals and technology development plans

❑ Develop updates regarding business strategy and outlook

❑ Brainstorm ways to add value to the ultimate customer

❑ Involves 7-12 key noncompeting suppliers

❑ Membership rotates among suppliers

❑ Meets on a regular basis

❑ Provides a forum for discussion between senior supplier executives and the executive team of the customer organization

❑ Enhance the supply base's feeling of being part of the team

Objectives

Characteristics

Figure 5.2 Buyer-Supplier councils

for exchanging information. The frequency of contact that results helps build higher trust across the supply chain. Figure 5.2 summarizes the objectives and characteristics of a buyer-supplier council at a leading producer of transportation equipment. At the highest supply levels, we expect to see a CPO position, an executive steering committee, and a buyer-supplier council.

Separation of Strategic and Tactical Responsibilities

A shift toward a center-led supply model almost demands the separation of strategic and tactical responsibilities. Physically separating strategic and tactical groups within the organizational structure makes sense for several reasons. Few people can operate comfortably in a strategic and tactical environment or switch easily between the two. Furthermore, in a decentralized model, operational or tactical activities must be satisfied first, leaving less time for longer-term planning and strategy development. Decentralized models also feature minimal coordination, duplication of effort, and often the sub-optimization of strategies, procedures, and operating best practices across worldwide locations.

While research reveals that a majority of supply organizations are highly centralized in their governance, not all tasks or responsibilities are managed at a central level. This separation between centralized and decentralized decision making, particularly as it relates to execution, helps maintain responsiveness to internal customer requirements at lower organizational levels. Research reveals that certain activities are largely coordinated or managed at a centrally led or centralized level for the most important purchases while other activities remain the responsibility of sites or operating units. Activities such as developing category or commodity purchase family strategies, negotiating and establishing company-wide contracts, evaluating and selecting suppliers, locating potential supply sources, managing critical supplier relationships, and managing supplier development activities typically fall under the strategic activities umbrella.

Research also reveals that certain responsibilities usually remain part of a decentralized governance structure. Examples of these responsibilities include executing schedules and inventory plans, expediting goods and services, issuing releases or purchase orders, planning inventory levels, developing requirements schedules, and routine communication and follow up with suppliers. Other activities such as resolving supplier performance problems and providing supplier performance feedback are somewhat more evenly distributed between centralized and decentralized responsibilities.

Few individuals can manage strategic and tactical or operational duties at the same time. In fact, when pressure is on, the operational duties usually take precedence over the strategic responsibilities. After this reality became apparent, the separation of responsibilities became an attractive design option. Separation literally means maintaining separate groups to manage different kinds of work. This makes sense for a number of reasons:

- The processes are quite different (e.g., compare strategic sourcing with all of its components to processing requisitions)
- The performance metrics are different
- The skill sets required for success are different
- It ensures dedicated resources for each activity

A side benefit of proceeding in this fashion is that your personnel—once aligned with the activity that best suits their capabilities and interests—are often less stressed and more productive. Figure 5.3 provides further detail regarding the separation of strategic and tactical personnel and responsibilities. Figure 5.4 highlights the different kinds of measures that populate each level.

Collocation with Internal Customers

Collocation of supply personnel should be an important part of organizational design models. The logic behind a collocation model is fairly straightforward. Referring to Michael Porter's original value chain model, supply management (called purchasing in his model) is a support function. By definition, support functions have internal customers who have requirements that need to be understood and supported. A collocation model provides supply managers with a better understanding of internal customers and their requirements. This model also helps internal customers gain a better understanding of the role that sup-

Strategic and tactical separation

– Strategic –		– Tactical –
■ Shared services or executive team	← **Organization level** →	■ Plant and/or business division
■ CPO, VP, General Manager, Procurement Director, Procurement Manager, Commodity Manager, Strategic Sourcing Manager, Senior Strategic Sourcing Specialist, Strategic Sourcing Specialist	← **Job titles** →	■ Purchasing Manager, Stores Manager, Plant Buyer, Purchasing Specialist, Purchasing Assistant, Materials Hourly, Stores Hourly
■ Leveraging SSNM process and spend; acquire and utilize market knowledge for company-wide benefit	← **Responsibility** →	■ Order requisition to receipt
■ Lead commodity team, negotiate contract, manage agreement	← **Commodity team role** →	■ Team member, selection input, implementation, performance management, understands plant requirements
■ Strategy formulation & implementation, strategic planning, supplier analysis, supplier negotiation, supplier relationship management, supply chain management	← **Skill sets** →	■ Procurement transaction processing, supplier relationship management, quick response to operations issues

Figure 5.3   Strategic and tactical separation

ply management plays while building trust between supply representatives and those they support directly.

Figure 5.5 highlights some key features of a collocation model. Collocation with operations, an important internal customer, can provide insight into supplier performance; awareness of supply requirements in terms of cost, quality, delivery, and cycle time; and an understanding of external capacity, material, and service needs. Collocation with technical personnel allows purchasing to gain insight into material specifications, product and process technology requirements, and new product requirements.

While collocation has not progressed as rapidly with the demand side of the supply chain, collocation with marketing supports the integration of demand and supply planning. Collocation with marketing may also offer early insight into new product ideas as well as planned demand shifts due to product promotions or price changes. One major company assigns a supply representative to marketing to help negotiate printing, promotion, and trade show contracts.

Tailored metrics for strategic and tactical personnel

Strategic personnel	Tactical personnel
Demonstrated adoption and leadership of strategic sourcing & negotiations management for assigned areas of spend	Responsiveness to operational issues
% of spend covered by written sourcing strategies	Effectiveness in resolving operational issues
Market/commodity knowledge summaries completed and approved; contract summaries written and approved	Efficiency in processing reqs, P/Os, etc.
$ benefits achieved vs. baseline	Accuracy in processing reqs, P/Os, etc.
Number of strategic relationships designed & implemented	Meeting invoice audit objectives
Supplier performance vs. established KPIs	Mastery of new system(s)
Innovative ideas contributed by suppliers	Participation and support of strategic sourcing projects
Supplier development success (new qualified suppliers; diverse suppliers)	Pitching in to assist other team members
Annual internal client feedback results	Annual internal client feedback results
Adherence to ethical standards	Adherence to ethical standards

Figure 5.4   Tailored metrics for strategic and tactical personnel

In fact, with supply management support, the marketing group has decreased the number of print suppliers it uses from 600 to 5.

Supply executives must consider a number of issues related to collocation. First, collocation is not about simply working in the physical presence of other groups. Rather, it is about embedding the supply professional into the planning systems of that group. Second, supply managers must determine the amount of time to allocate to collocation. Will supply professionals be collocated on a full-time or part-time basis? Finally, what reporting relationship best supports collocation? In a typical collocation model, the supply professional maintains a dotted-line reporting relationship to the collocation group with a solid-line reporting relationship to the supply organization.

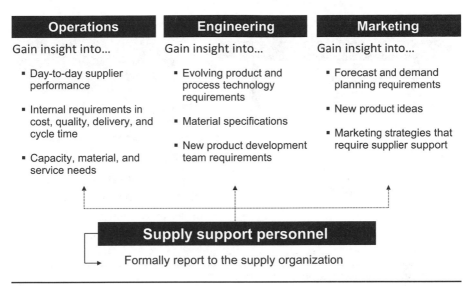

Operations	Engineering	Marketing
Gain insight into...	Gain insight into...	Gain insight into...

Operations — Gain insight into...
- Day-to-day supplier performance
- Internal requirements in cost, quality, delivery, and cycle time
- Capacity, material, and service needs

Engineering — Gain insight into...
- Evolving product and process technology requirements
- Material specifications
- New product development team requirements

Marketing — Gain insight into...
- Forecast and demand planning requirements
- New product ideas
- Marketing strategies that require supplier support

Supply support personnel

Formally report to the supply organization

Figure 5.5 Supply collocation with internal customers

Organizing around Critical Processes

A process orientation features an organization designed around critical processes, such as supplier evaluation and selection, new product development, demand and supply planning, and customer order fulfillment. When organizing around processes, cross-functional participants work concurrently in an environment featuring the horizontal (i.e., cross-functional) flow of information across the supply chain. Figure 5.6 illustrates a process orientation.

Over the last ten years, dozens of books and countless articles have been published that address some aspect of business process management.[5] Research evidence suggests that an often-predicted movement away from strict functional alignments is in fact occurring. One study revealed a clear link between organizations that are structured around major processes and the ability to attain their supply chain objectives.[6] This study also concluded that process-centered design features, such as the use of cross-functional teams and executive positions responsible for overseeing processes rather than narrower functional tasks, should show large increases in usage compared with more traditional design features.

An increase in the use of cross-functional teams, especially those that rely on full-time rather than part-time members, reveals a growing process focus. Various studies have concluded that over three-fourths of companies now rely on cross-functional teams to support their product development efforts. Other research has revealed a consistent increase in the use of teams to support other

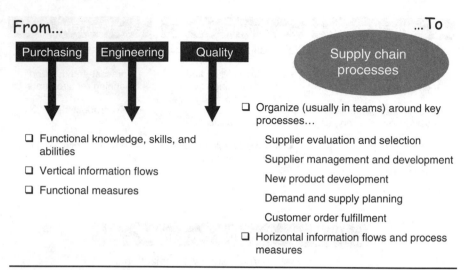

Figure 5.6   Organizing around processes

value-chain objectives, particularly over the last ten years. The use of teams is discussed later in the chapter.

While evidence suggests a shift toward process-centric thinking, it is unlikely that corporations will ever disband their functional structures. Spreading expertise across full-time process teams would dilute the functional knowledge required to operate a business. The need to maintain a critical mass of functional knowledge ensures that some functional structure, albeit a diminished one, will remain in place. The dramatic changes in design, measurement, and information that surround a shift from a functional to a process-centered organization also ensure that any changes will be gradual. Rest assured, however, that a shift toward the process-centric organization is underway.

Early Involvement on New Product Development Teams

New product development teams are a critical part of most organizational designs. Increasingly, these teams include supply representatives as full-fledged members. An expected shift toward a process orientation, as well as collocation of purchasing with technical personnel, promotes increased supply involvement with new product development teams. Many companies are discovering that, when it comes to product design and development, linkages between engineering, supply management, manufacturing, and suppliers help strengthen the design and development process. When used effectively, development teams can rely on supply representatives to identify suppliers for early design involvement or for production needs, monitor supply markets and trends, question specifications, and help the producer meet its target costs.

The level beyond supply involvement in new product development involves supplier involvement. While supplier involvement sounds easy, widespread implementation can be a different matter. Protecting confidential information will always remain a primary concern to most buying organizations. Other barriers include not knowing how to pursue early involvement, maintaining too many suppliers for a given commodity, or relationships that are adversarial rather than cooperative. The importance of new product teams that include suppliers requires some thought about how to overcome these barriers. The trend toward greater early involvement is unquestionable in most industries.

Research findings are persuasive about the value of including suppliers as part of a buying organization's teams, including new product development teams. We know that teams that rely on supplier input and involvement when the task warrants involvement are more effective, on average, than teams that do not involve suppliers. Furthermore, compared with teams that do not include qualified suppliers as participants, teams that include suppliers as participants report some important outcomes that any supply leader would welcome. These outcomes include greater satisfaction regarding the quality of information exchange between the team and key suppliers, higher reliance on suppliers to support directly the team's goals, fewer problems coordinating work activity between the team and key suppliers, and greater effort put forth on team assignments. But let's not stop there. Teams that include suppliers as participants report supplier contributions across many performance areas, including cost reduction ideas; quality improvement ideas; ways to improve material delivery; material ordering lead time reductions; and process technology suggestions. What's not to like here? A later chapter explores the idea of early involvement in greater detail.

International Purchasing Offices (IPOs)

Most supply managers recognize their limited ability to manage activities that happen thousands of miles away. An important design feature that does not receive much attention, particularly as it relates to managing risk in emerging markets, is the use of international purchasing offices. At some point, companies realize that constantly traveling from the home market or relying on third parties to represent their interests in a sourcing region just doesn't do the job. Establishing IPOs is a natural progression as supply organizations become more sophisticated with international purchasing.

IPOs are often a formal part of a company's organizational design and will increase in importance as global supply management expands. Research reveals that half of larger companies (those with sales greater than a billion dollars a year) have at least one formally established IPO somewhere in the world. This figure declines rapidly as company size decreases. Large companies not only have the purchase volumes to justify international offices, they usually have the resources to support them.

It is incorrect to conclude that IPOs are located only in emerging countries, although Eastern Europe and China are well represented as locations. An IPO provides a company with a day-to-day presence in any supply market or region where it intends to buy. European companies, for example, often have buying offices located within the United States.

A Center for Advanced Purchasing Studies investigation revealed that overwhelming consensus exists regarding the importance of IPOs.[7] Over 85% of companies with IPOs say these offices are extremely important to their international success while 10% say IPOs are moderately important. Only 5% say IPOs are less than moderately important with no company indicating these offices have limited importance. Approximately half of all companies that maintain at least one foreign buying office say their IPOs are more than meeting or exceeding expectations while one-third indicate their IPOs are meeting expectations. No consensus exists regarding the number of IPOs that a company should maintain around the world.

The kinds of services that an IPO provides are important and varied. At least 70% or more of companies with at least one IPO say these offices identify suppliers and evaluate their capabilities, negotiate and execute contracts with suppliers, resolve quality and delivery problems directly with suppliers, develop supplier capabilities, measure supplier performance, evaluate product and service designs and samples, facilitate import and export activities, and perform logistical coordination. The use of IPOs should only increase as supply organizations search the globe for buying opportunities.

Lead Buyers

Leading supply organizations know they have to continuously review their purchase requirements to determine at what level those requirements are best managed. Some categories or commodities are obvious candidates for center-led leadership and will be managed from a company-wide perspective. Other items are unique to an operating location and will be managed locally. For complex organizations, there are often in-between items that are used by multiple locations but do not justify a commodity management approach. A supply organization should designate a single location or buyer to take the lead for managing these in-between items. The individual who assumes this role is expected to demonstrate leadership when sourcing these items much the same way that commodity teams demonstrate leadership.

We did not provide an exhaustive presentation of potential organizational design features. For organizations that expect to operate at the next level of supply management, however, most, if not all, of these described features will be parts of the supply model. This is the A list when it comes to organizational design. Table 5.1 presents a fuller array of organizational design options that supply leaders have at their disposal. Remember that organizational design is much more than boxes and lines on a chart.

Table 5.1 Potential supply management organization design features

✓ Cross-functional teams that manage some part of the supply process
✓ Physical collocation between procurement and marketing, operations, and/or engineering
✓ A corporate level steering committee that oversees company-wide supply initiatives
✓ Formal supply strategy coordination and review sessions between business units or divisions
✓ Formal strategy coordination and review sessions between supply management and other functional groups
✓ Centrally coordinated commodity teams that develop and implement company-wide supply strategies
✓ An executive buyer-supplier council or committee that coordinates supply chain activities with key suppliers
✓ International procurement offices that support international purchasing
✓ Specific individuals assigned responsibility for managing supplier relationships
✓ Lead buyers or site-based experts designated to manage noncentrally coordinated items
✓ Regular presentations by the chief procurement officer to the CEO and Board of Directors
✓ A formal group or team responsible for demand and supply planning
✓ An executive position responsible for coordinating supply chain activities from supplier through customer
✓ A shared services model that provides support to business units or locations
✓ On-site suppliers to perform activities such as ordering, replenishment, and inventory control
✓ A customer advisory board that includes the company, key customers, and key suppliers
✓ A formal separation of strategic and tactical procurement and supply responsibilities, personnel, positions, and structure
✓ A higher-level executive officer who has a supply-related title
✓ A matrix reporting structure that features supply professionals reporting to more than one business, region, or manager
✓ An organization designed around supply processes rather than functions
✓ Formal value analysis or value engineering groups with supply involvement
✓ Product development teams that formally include supply professionals
✓ Product development teams that formally include suppliers
✓ Membership with a recognized purchase consortium
✓ A virtual organizational design featuring individuals, groups, and/or departments linked by IT systems
✓ Project teams that work on specific procurement and supply tasks rather than continuous assignments

Using Teams to Support Supply Objectives

The use of organizational work teams will remain a popular and even growing part of organizational designs. Our estimates are that at least 80% of companies use teams in some capacity. While a reliance on teams will remain popular, relatively few research studies have established a clear connection between teaming and higher performance, although a wealth of anecdotal evidence exists showing that cross-functional teams offer huge benefits when pursuing sourcing projects. The exception here involves teams for developing new products. Their effectiveness is well documented.

Over 50 years ago, a leading behavioral scientist wrote that groups and teams can accomplish much that is good, or they can do great harm. He noted there is nothing implicitly good or bad, weak or strong, about teams, regardless of where an organization uses them.[8] There is no reason to doubt that this belief is less valid today. Anyone who has been a member or leader of an organizational work team knows that teams can have a less than desirable side. They can waste the time and energy of members, enforce lower rather than higher performance norms, create patterns of destructive conflict within and between groups, and make notoriously bad decisions. Groups can also exploit, stress, and frustrate members—sometimes all at the same time.[9] They also consume massive amounts of organizational resources. While hopefully more effective in terms of the decisions they make, teams are not necessarily known for being efficient.

As we look toward the future, supply managers should use teams selectively. Major hurdles or barriers exist that can affect how well teams are used, including within supply management. Three notable barriers include extensive reliance on part-time teams that create conflicts with regular job responsibilities, measurement systems that fail to recognize or reward team or member contribution and performance, and a national culture, at least in the United States, that is inherently individualistic. Americans sometimes feel uncomfortable working within a design model that is clearly collective. As a result, it is often necessary to provide *team training* at the start of strategic sourcing projects.

Any downside to using teams has not deterred their widespread use. The following is a sampling of where we see teams and groups within supply management. Each represents a formal part of an organization's design:

- Cross-functional teams that manage some or all of the procurement and supply process (e.g., strategic sourcing and negotiations management)
- A corporate level steering committee that oversees company-wide supply initiatives
- Centrally coordinated commodity teams that develop and implement supply strategies

- An executive buyer-supplier council or committee that coordinates activities between your firm and your key suppliers
- A formal cross-functional group or team responsible for demand and supply planning
- A customer advisory board that includes your company, your key customers, and your key suppliers
- Product development teams that formally include supply representatives and suppliers
- Project teams that work on specific supply tasks (rather than teams with continuous assignments)
- Supplier development teams

Most corporations are enamored with the use of teams. Nothing is on the horizon that indicates a shift away from organizational work teams will occur. Fortunately, we know a great deal about their use.

Managing Virtual Teams

Adding to any complexity surrounding the use of teams is the growth in virtual teams. The defining characteristic of a virtual team is they have members who are not located in close proximity, making face-to-face meetings a rare occurrence. Supply leaders increasingly see virtual teams as a way to coordinate many supply locations and personnel around the world. The bottom line is that virtual teams have become a fact at many supply organizations, particularly those that have worldwide buying, engineering, and manufacturing centers. We should know how to benefit from their use.

Virtual teams present some unique challenges. Most research has concluded that even small physical dispersion between members can adversely affect team efficiency and effectiveness. Performance typically declines rapidly as the geographic dispersion moves across countries and continents.[10] When asked to rank the importance of various factors related to the success of their global business teams, team members said cultivating trust among team members and overcoming communication barriers were the two most important. Unfortunately, these team members also rated these two factors as the most difficult to overcome.[11] Of course, this is not the only set of challenges that virtual teams face.

Various research projects have helped identify certain practices that characterize successful virtual teams. While some of these practices apply to any type of team, they are especially relevant when team members are located around the world.[12]

Make state-of-the-art communication tools available: Virtual teams will likely fail without access to communication tools, particularly when teams operate virtually. Managing virtual teams requires state-of-the-art communication tools that allow real-time information sharing, collaboration, and the coordination of worldwide team activities. Real-time communication tools include web-based meeting software, instant messaging tools, electronic mail, audio and video conferencing technology, and wikis. The link between state-of-the-art communication tools and a set of desirable outcomes means that supply leaders must not ignore this important issue. In a perfect world, every team member would have access to technology such as Cisco's Telepresence. However, we do not live in a perfect world.

Provide an online resource where members get to know one another: These resources are similar to online social networking sites where members can communicate and share information. They are designed to help members get to know one another, appreciate what each member brings to the team, and accelerate the development of intra-team trust, something that takes longer to develop compared with teams that feature collocated members. Supply executives should also consider face-to-face meetings among members.

Make sure boundary spanners make up at least 15% of team membership: A boundary spanner is an individual that crosses team, functional, and even organizational borders. This ability allows these individuals to make many connections that can provide useful external resources. An earlier study of cross-functional teams revealed that access to expertise and resources outside of a team was a key factor that affected team success. Boundary spanning members are especially useful for knowing where these resources reside. Do not discount the importance of this role.

Select at least some members who already know each other: Research reveals that virtual teams are more productive when at least some of the members have a previous working relationship, something that is called a heritage relationship. No magic formula exists that tells us what the ratio of familiar to unfamiliar team members should be. We do know that it is often better to not start from scratch in terms of member familiarity.

Assign challenging tasks: This is sound advice for any team, virtual or otherwise. Research conducted many years ago found that team members respond positively by demonstrating higher commitment and effort when given a challenging assignment. Research also shows that team effort is a primary predictor of team success. There is every reason to believe that virtual teams, even those with members from different cultures, will respond favorably to interesting and challenging assignments.

Related to challenging tasks are meaningful tasks that affect a corporation as a whole. Meaningful tasks inspire a shared sense of mission as well as convey the importance of the team's work. They also tend to energize members while aligning them with a common mission that each member understands. While the members of a virtual team may be very different geographically and demographically, the one thing they hopefully all share is a commitment to a meaningful task.

Divide work into modules that can be transferred between members: An attractive feature of virtual teams is that the team, at least theoretically, can work across time zones 24 hours a day. While some team members sleep, others are working away on their part of an assignment or project. Work should be seamlessly transferred from one group to another. Probably the best teams to study to see how this is mastered are software development teams.

It might also be a good idea, whenever possible, to divide work into discrete tasks that can be pursued somewhat independently. This helps prevent a team from being held up because their work was delayed by a member located at a different site.

Require virtual teams to establish goals with regular updates: The link between effective goals and team effectiveness is well accepted among researchers. Compelling evidence suggests that team effort and performance are higher when teams develop and accept challenging goals. We also know that teams with goals usually perform at a higher level than teams that are asked to do their best without explicit goals. There is no reason to believe that the importance of goal setting does not hold across cultures.

Part of the time that virtual teams spend when communicating as a group should be to update their progress toward established goals. These goals should be posted in a way that provides the appropriate level of transparency within and outside the team. Organizations should develop a process for goal setting and reporting that creates consistency across teams, including the use of goal setting templates that identify team goals and member accountability.

Next level supply organizations will have mastered, or at least be competent, in the use of virtual teams. Their growth is predictable given the trend toward the coordination of supply management activities on a worldwide basis.

Supply Management's New Look

As we look toward the future, we expect supply organizations to transform themselves into something that looks dramatically different than earlier designs. Figure 5.7 summarizes some of the features that will define supply management's new look. Minimal involvement with day-to-day operations or transactions will mean a smaller professional staff that if not located in a central location, will report to a central location. A clear delineation between the placement of planning and execution authority will also occur.

The kinds of activities that next level supply organizations manage will be best described as strategic. A primary focus when creating the right structure will be on developing (including negotiating) worldwide, rather than regional, supply strategies that support a clear set of sourcing requirements. The supply group will be responsible for managing nontraditional items and services, increasingly in a virtual setting. These teams will move beyond direct items and manage anything that involves significant expenditures,

❑ Smaller, but more highly qualified professional staff

❑ Minimal involvement with day-to-day operations or transactions

❑ Act as an internal consultant and problem solver

❑ Responsible for managing alliances and other critical relationships

❑ Take greater responsibility for nontraditional purchasing

❑ Involvement with cross-enterprise negotiations

❑ Manage value-creating activities across the organization and with suppliers

❑ Become process managers who oversee strategic responsibilities

❑ Responsible for developing strategies that match sourcing requirements

Figure 5.7   The supply organization's new look

particularly items that can be neatly placed within a commodity management structure. Acquiring or developing the expertise required for managing such a large portfolio of goods and services worldwide will continue to be a human resources challenge.

Next level supply organizations will also be responsible for managing a set of truly strategic internal and external relationships. Accomplishing this will require supply organizations to be boundary spanning by design, particularly across external boundaries. Specific features will be established that promote these boundary spanning requirements.

We also expect to see widespread use of matrix organizational designs as supply management increasingly assumes a global perspective. Supply management resources will often be allocated across an organization with tight control and coordination from a strong central leadership. Movement toward a center-led model should continue as supply organizations work to coordinate their processes and activities from a global perspective.

Concluding Thoughts

An effective organizational design does not simply happen, although most of us probably take our organization's design and our involvement within it for granted. Over time, a major debate has arisen concerning organizational design. Does strategy follow structure or does structure follow strategy? In other words, does a company pursue activities because it has the organizational capabilities to do so (strategy follows structure) or does a company identify what needs to be accomplished and then create the organization that is needed (structure follows strategy)? In reality, both scenarios occur depending on the situation.

As it relates to supply management, it is probably best for structure to follow strategy simply because most supply organizations have been limited in their organizational capabilities. When a supply organization resembles something just beyond a traditional purchasing department, any ideas about becoming a strategic contributor are going to be limited. The dream of becoming a next level supply organization will remain just a dream without design features that align with next level thinking.

Chapter Notes

1. G. Hamel and C. K. Pralahad. *Competing for the Future.* (Cambridge, MA: Harvard Business School Press, 1994), as referenced in D. Hellriegel, J. W. Slocum, and R. W. Woodman, *Organizational Behavior.* (Cincinnati, OH: South-Western College Publishing, 2001), 474.
2. G. T. Silvestri. "Occupational Employment Projections to 2006." *Monthly Labor Review* 120 (1997): 39–57.
3. Robert M. Monczka, Robert J. Trent, and Kenneth J. Petersen. "Effective Global Sourcing and Supply for Superior Results." *Center for Advanced Purchasing Studies,* 2006. www.capsresearch.org.
4. Robert J. Trent. "The Use of Organizational Design Features in Purchasing and Supply Management." *Journal of Supply Chain Management* 40, no. 3 (Summer 2004): 4.
5. Douglas M. Lambert. "The Eight Essential Supply Chain Management Processes." *Supply Chain Management Review* 8, no. 6 (September 2004): 18; David Mackay, Umit Bititci, Catherine Maguire, and Aylin Ates. "Delivering Sustained Performance through a Structured Business Process Approach to Management." *Measuring Business Excellence* 12, no. 4 (2008): 22; John Jeston and Johan Nelis. *Business Process Management: Practical Guidelines to Successful Implementation.* (Butterworth-Heinemann, 2008).
6. Robert J. Trent. "The Use of Organizational Design Features in Purchasing and Supply Management." *Journal of Supply Chain Management* 40, no. 3 (Summer 2004): 4.
7. Monczka, Trent, and Petersen.
8. R. Likert. *New Patterns of Management.* (New York: McGraw-Hill, 1961), 162.
9. J. R. Hackman. "The Design of Work Teams." chapter 20 in *Handbook of Organizational Behavior.* (Englewood Cliffs, NJ: Prentice Hall, 1987), 315–342.
10. Frank Siebdrat, Martin Hoegl, and Holger Ernst. "How to Manage Virtual Teams." *Sloan Management Review* 50, no. 4 (Summer 2009), 66.

11. Vijay Govindarajan and Anil K. Gupta. "Building an Effective Global Business Team." *Sloan Management Review* 42, no. 4 (Summer 2001), 64.
12. Lynda Gratton. "Working Together . . . When Apart." *Wall Street Journal*, June 16–17, 2007, R4.

6

Internal and External Talent Management

Every eight seconds, something interesting happens in the United States. A member of the 76-million baby boomer generation turns 65. What this means is that over the next five to ten years, a record number of people will be leaving the workforce—and taking with them years of wisdom and experience that is not easily replaced. And let's not forget that the next generation has 11% fewer members to replace those who are departing.[1] If you are not worried about the impact of that much talent walking out the door, you should be.

To appreciate the impact that departing talent can have on an organization, we only have to look at a major consumer products company located in the Eastern U.S. Its portfolio of products include some of the best-known products in over-the-counter health care. Its brands are built on an implicit trust with consumers that safety and quality can be taken for granted. Unfortunately, the consumer's trust may have been misplaced. Over the last several years, this unit has suffered quality lapses and product safety problems that have attracted the unwelcome attention of the U.S. government, consumers, and the press.[2]

A number of factors are behind the affairs affecting this company, including a cultural change that stressed output and cost cutting, sometimes at the expense of product quality. While the company did not pursue large-scale layoffs in its quality control unit, over time, its analytic testing laboratory saw its experienced, full-time scientists replaced by lower cost, inexperienced employees and contract workers. Eventually, the Food and Drug Administration issued a report that cited incomplete investigations, poor sampling practices, and inadequate record keeping at the company. The company eventually closed an entire facility for an extended period, costing the company hundreds of millions of dollars of revenue. Having people available for a job is not always the same as having the talent available for a job.

This chapter approaches one of the most important parts of the supply management process—the talent management process. The first part of the chapter defines what is meant by talent management. Then we identify the important reasons why supply organizations should be concerned about making talent management one of their most important processes. This is followed by a discussion of personnel assessment and training. The next section presents approaches for acquiring, developing, and retaining human resources. The chapter concludes with a discussion of managing external talent.

What Is Talent Management?

Interestingly, there is no real consensus about what talent management is or precisely how to define the concept. Lewis and Heckman conducted an extensive review of the academic literature and professional press and concluded that a clear lack of clarity or consensus exists regarding this term. From their extensive review, they were able to identify three main perspectives related to talent management.

The first perspective says that talent management is comprised of the usual practices associated with human resource management, including employee recruiting, development, and retention. From this perspective, talent management is nothing more than a trendy term that will change once a more fashionable term becomes available. The second perspective focuses on modeling the flow of personnel throughout an organization based on factors such as skill development, growth, attrition, and the supply and demand for human resources. A third perspective stresses the sourcing, development, and rewarding of human talent. This perspective argues for the differential treatment of employees based on their knowledge, skills, and expertise. Certain employees, this perspective argues, have the ability to make significant contribution and difference to the performance of an organization.[3] These three perspectives reveal that talent management is a broad construct.

At a broad level, talent management is the process through which employers anticipate and meet their needs for human capital.[4] For our purposes, we view talent management as a continuous process that involves six primary activities— identifying, recruiting, redeploying, developing, rotating, and retaining human resources across an organization. First, talent management involves identifying the knowledge and skills that a supply organization requires, both currently and in the future. This identification occurs at the tactical and strategic level. Supply leaders then seek to identify current and projected gaps between what a supply organization has available to it and what it will require in the future.

Second, talent management involves the active recruitment of qualified personnel into a business. We could easily argue that human resource recruitment is one of the most important endeavors that a supply organization undertakes. After all, supply management is a knowledge business. The decisions made during recruitment will have long lasting consequences. A later section presents various approaches for recruiting talent into a supply organization.

Next, talent management involves redeploying human resources in order to find the right professional fit for each employee. This entails matching tasks and jobs to employees. Talent management also involves actively developing talent within the supply organization. Development includes formal training, coaching and mentoring, assigning leadership roles to individuals, and encouraging employees to seek college degrees and professional certifications. It is a key part of an organization's continuous improvement process that is covered later in the chapter.

In addition, talent management involves rotating personnel into and out of the supply organization. This is especially important since it is not unusual for supply personnel, including senior supply leadership, to come from other functional groups, particularly finance, engineering, and operations. Finally, talent management involves the ever-important efforts at retaining those employees who are central to effective supply management. This means recognizing and rewarding superior individuals. It can also mean not eliminating positions at the first sign of economic trouble.

Some observers will include the concept of engagement when discussing talent management. A thorough perspective of engagement comes from Hewitt and Associates, who argue that engagement is a measure of energy and passion that employees have for their organization. Engaged employees are individuals who take action to improve business results. They say positive things about their workplace and strive to go above and beyond to deliver extraordinary work.[5] A study by Towers and Perrin found that over 65% of highly engaged employees expected to remain with their employer while only 12% of disengaged employees planned on staying.[6]

The alternative to talent management is having the supply function outsourced to an external supplier. For most supply professionals that is not an appealing option. A Delphi futures study predicted that the ability to integrate and manage strategic suppliers will be considered a core competency and will not be outsourced. Achieving this prediction, however, requires people who understand how to manage critical supplier relationships. Nearly anything of significance that happens with supply management requires the right people rather than simply the right technology.

Why Be Concerned with Talent Management?

As highlighted in the opening of this chapter, we can probably conclude that some good reasons exist for wanting to pay attention to talent management. Within the procurement space, we have witnessed a shift from lower-level, tactical purchasing to longer-term, strategic sourcing and supplier management. The need to better manage the level of talent within the supply organization has never been greater. Consider, however, some recent statements from supply executives about how they perceive their procurement organization:[7]

- I don't think the people we have in purchasing currently have the ability to be strategic
- We see a lot of order entry—not buying
- We are after best price, best price, best price
- There is no process for strategic sourcing
- We are running on expired contracts
- Everybody is a function within their own silo
- We can't afford to continue paying professionals to perform clerical work such as order processing
- There's no accountability because there is no visibility

An increasing body of research is emerging that links talent management practices with a powerful set of performance results. One study, for example, found that the leadership quality of employees accounted for as much as 45% of organizational performance.[8] In supply management, this figure could be even higher given the knowledge, rather than manual, requirements of the discipline. A review of studies conducted throughout the 1990s reveals a strong correlation between the quality of human resource management systems and practices and some important organizational measures, including employee turnover, sales per employee, and market value.[9] Within supply management, make procurement a desired position, and it will raise the caliber of the outcome.

Here we present some specific reasons why talent management must be emphasized within procurement and supply. These reasons include a wider skill set that supply management requires, demographic changes leading to the loss of deep smarts, and the expanding role of supply management involvement into new areas. Even if these reasons are immaterial, the simple fact remains that supply management is a knowledge business that requires smart individuals. That alone makes talent management a concern.

Wider Scope of Supply Management

Depending on how detailed we become, we could identify hundreds of areas that could conceivably be part of the supply management knowledge and skill set. One thing we know for certain is the knowledge and skills that support a strategic supply perspective are vastly different than those that support a traditional or tactical perspective. This makes talent management that much more important.

Consider the knowledge required to manage costs. A strategic supply model requires an understanding not only of price management but also of cost management. Price analysis refers to the process of comparing one price against another, against external price benchmarks, or against other available information without in-depth knowledge about underlying costs. Cost analytic techniques focus primarily on the cost elements (labor, materials, overhead, etc.) and drivers that are aggregated to create a price. Extending this further, supply managers must understand any factors that affect total cost. They must also understand any pricing strategies that suppliers are using, such as price skimming, cost-plus pricing, or market penetration. By better managing and reducing the cost elements, drivers, and external factors that make up a price and eventually a total cost, a supply organization should see lower purchase prices compared with prices where cost management did not occur. Cost management is exponentially more complex than price management. We could write an entire book on cost management techniques.

Besides cost management, other knowledge and skill areas where supply organizations should retain a competency include an ability to understand how to develop strategies that support a firm's competitive business model. This means that supply managers must have the ability to understand that model. Supply personnel must also be able to take a holistic or integrated view of the business, which means they understand how the different elements of a value chain combine to create value.

A strong knowledge of process rather than functional management is also required. Because processes create the output that creates value, supply managers must be able to visualize those value-creating processes, articulate their objectives, and understand their role within a process. And without question, having personnel with an ability to manage critical supplier relationships will become even more important in the future. An understanding of electronic business systems, the ability to perform statistical analyses and make fact-based decisions, and the ability to seamlessly work across boundaries are also part of today's supply management knowledge and skill set. Boundary crossing refers to working across functional boundaries, enterprise boundaries, geographic boundaries, and cultural boundaries. Expanding scope makes talent management an important part of the supply management process.

Demographic Changes and the Loss of Deep Smarts

Any growth in the U.S. population over the next 15 years is expected to occur primarily through immigration, making the need to manage a culturally diverse workforce a key part of the talent management process. Furthermore, the percentage of males relative to females in U.S. colleges has been decreasing, further changing the complexion of the supply management profession.

An issue that will confront nearly all developed countries over the next 10 to 15 years involves an aging population in developed countries. The period of the most rapid growth in the ratio of seniors (age 65 and older) to the working-age population will occur in the 2010s and 2020s, creating strains on benefits programs and retirement systems. This mass migration out of the workforce also highlights the degree to which talent will exit the workforce. In 2010, there was one senior for every four working-age people in the developed world. By 2025, this ratio is projected to be one to three.[10]

As the opening to this chapter suggested, the loss of experienced talent, whether through retirement or cost cutting, should be a concern. And this concern relates to something called *deep smarts*. Deep smarts represent experienced-based wisdom, and when the deep smarts walk out the door, the wisdom IQ of an entire organization falls. In their book *Deep Smarts*, Dorothy Leonard and Walter Swap write:

> Throughout your organization are people whose intuition, judgment, and knowledge, both explicit and tacit, are stored in their heads and—depending on the task—in their hands. Their knowledge is essential. They are, relative to others, expert. These are the people with Deep Smarts, and it is not an exaggeration to say that they form the basis of your organizational viability.

Deep Smarts address a special form of experience-based expertise that is critical for managers to understand and appreciate—for their own benefit as well as that of their organizations. Deep Smarts are a potent form of expertise based on first-hand life experiences, providing insights drawn from tacit knowledge, and shaped by beliefs and social forces.

Deep Smarts are as close as we get to wisdom. They are based on know-how more than know-what. It involves the ability to comprehend complex, interactive relationships and make swift, expert decisions based on that system level comprehension but also the ability, when necessary, to dive into component parts of that system and understand the details. Deep Smarts cannot be attained through formal education alone—but they can be deliberately nourished and grown and, with dedication, transferred or recreated.

Although the sheer amount of practice and experience is not a powerful predictor of expertise, the combination of an extended period of concentrated effort coupled with self-reflection has been shown to build expertise in a wide variety of domains. Most evidence suggests that it takes at least ten years of concentrated study and practice to become experts as opposed to being merely competent.

The issue here is not whether there are people to replace those who are departing. Your organization will always receive applications, sometimes hundreds, for open positions. The issue is the loss of institutional knowledge that might never return. Perhaps the lesson here is to respect our elders, particularly since demographic changes reveal they are heading for the door.

The Expanding Domain of Supply Management

The reality today is that supply organizations are involved (or should be involved) with just about every important purchase that a company makes. And when purchases are too small to involve supply personnel directly, the supply organization should be responsible for developing the systems that allow internal users to obtain what they need. This can include establishing blanket purchase orders, providing procurement cards, and setting up online ordering systems.

Instead of sourcing only direct materials, today's supply organization is involved with buying indirect items, services of all kinds, and capital equipment and structures. Instead of simply buying components, supply managers are responsible for sourcing assemblies, systems, and even finished goods. In addition, let's not forget the role that supply managers provide as they support the activities of other groups, including marketing, engineering (especially during new product development), finance, and operations. The expanding involvement of supply personnel demands personnel who do more than buy direct items from the comfort of their office.

We could list other reasons for the growing importance of talent management within supply management. The ones discussed here, however, give us a good idea about the important relationship between talent management and supply management success. The bottom line is that procurement and supply management require the best people available. It is not a production environment with automated equipment and robots.

In the final analysis, the primary reason for pursuing talent management is to make a significant contribution to the bottom line. Performed correctly, talent management enables a supply organization to maximize its impact by maximizing its talent. Talent management is all about:

- Assigning the right people with the right skill set to the right positions
- Knowing the difference between strategic and tactical responsibilities
- Recognizing the differences between skills and competencies
- Understanding how to maximize the advantage that comes with *deep smarts*
- Providing the opportunity for people to succeed
- Making procurement a desirable career choice
- Realizing the value of procurement
- Achieving the next level of supply management excellence

Professional Assessment and Development

For decades, organizations have attempted to identify the kinds of knowledge, skills, and competencies required to perform at superior levels. A major focus of most talent management efforts has been to identify the kinds of skills, knowledge, and competencies required to perform a certain task or job and to develop a plan to mitigate any weaknesses. At times, competency assessments are specific, which is often the case within supply and supply chain management. We may want to evaluate, for example, an individual's knowledge of contract law or familiarity with analytic cost management techniques. At other times, assessments evaluate more generic areas, such as communication skills, problem solving abilities, and conflict management skills that apply to nearly any organizational setting. The bottom line is that assessment is not a new phenomenon.

Defining Knowledge, Skills, and Competencies

Knowledge, skill, and competency assessment has a role in each part of the talent management process. So, what do we mean by these terms? Knowledge relates to knowing something with familiarity gained through experience, learning, or association. We often speak of a body of knowledge as it relates to different professional areas. Obviously, we expect supply professionals to master a body of knowledge, which is often evidenced through academic degrees and professional certifications (discussed later). Anyone who has ever attended school (which is practically everyone in the developed world) has had assessments of his or her knowledge conducted on a regular and sometimes painful basis. This assessment consists of exams and grades.

Skills represent the ability to use one's knowledge effectively and readily during the execution of performance. For example, most of us had to take a road test (nervously) with a state examiner sitting in the passenger seat. The road test demanded performance through the effective use of our knowledge of road safety and driving. It is important to recognize that two broad types of skills exist.[11] Basic skills, the first type, typically are acquired by workers prior to entering the labor force. They consist of literacy, problem-solving, numerical reasoning, and written communication. The second type includes occupational or job-related skills required by employees to perform a specific job or function. Figure 6.1 shows how one company divides its basic and job-related skills within the supply management domain.

Taking this discussion to a higher level, competencies involve a measurable pattern of behavior and knowledge that cause or predict superior performance in a given role or set of defined responsibilities. They allow us to solve problems by developing solutions that prevent their recurrence with a minimum utilization of energy.[12] Like skills, we can divide competencies into two broad categories—business and functional competencies. Business competencies, which are essential for individuals who expect to move into executive management, involve the recognition of business requirements and, when needed, proactive application of correct business practices. Functional competencies involve the understanding of technical systems, processes, and principles and how they influence company functions, products, or strategy.

Tier 1 skills–fundamental	Tier 2 skills–intermediate	Tier 3 skills–advanced
• Typing • Basic computer systems (e.g., MS Office) • Basic mathematics • Editing and preparing documents for approval (e.g., requisition to PO) • Order placement and expediting • Maintaining files and records of materials, prices, inventories, and deliveries	• Knowledge of business law • Contract language • Contract management • Economics • Negotiating • Finance • Cost/price analysis • Value analysis • Developing and using standard costs • Sourcing • Preparing and presenting the business case • Materials requirements planning	• Working capital management techniques • Demand and supply planning • Production processes/planning (internal and at supplier) • Supply markets impacting assigned products • Short- and long-range planning • Total cost of ownership evaluation • Managing critical supplier relationships • Global sourcing

Figure 6.1   Skills—Basic and job-related

Figure 6.2 presents a hierarchy of knowledge and competencies across four levels—market and functional, cross-functional, cross-cultural, and *soft side*. Figure 6.3 reveals that the mix of these four levels shifts as personnel progress toward higher levels of responsibility. Figure 6.4 notes that experience requirements also tend to increase as positional authority increases.

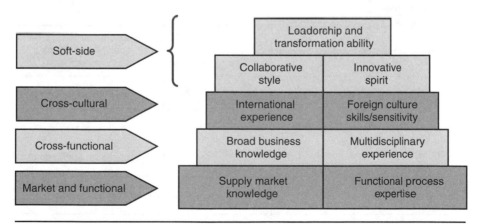

Figure 6.2   Building knowledge and competencies
Source: Adapted from Center for Advanced Purchasing Studies, Institute for Supply Management.

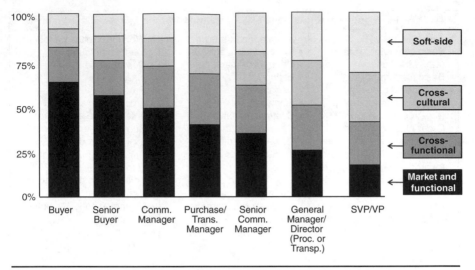

Figure 6.3 Relative distribution for each level of career progression

Position	Skills	Experience and/or education
Category Manager/Forecasting	Advanced	8–10 years procurement experience, other business experience, operations experience, and/or advanced degree
Sr. Buyer/Sr. Analyst/Sr. Svc Representative	Advanced	8–10 years procurement experience, other business experience, operations experience, and/or degree
Financial/Systems/Inventory Analyst	Intermediate	3–5 years finance experience, other business experience, operations experience, and/or degree
Buyer/Service Representative	Intermediate	3–5 years procurement experience, operations experience, and/or degree
Assistant Buyer	Fundamental	General business experience, operations experience, and/or degree
Clerk/Administrator	Fundamental	General business experience

Figure 6.4 Experience requirements by position

Gap Analysis

Assessment, formally and informally, can occur that addresses the knowledge, skills, and competencies required of individuals, departments, and even entire organizations. Exams, job-performance reviews, professional certification tests, and self-administered or third-party assessments are all part of the process of evaluating strengths and weaknesses against predetermined criteria. It is not enough for an assessment to reveal strengths or weaknesses. This information, which is the beginning of the improvement process, forms the foundation for building an action plan for further development. The development of personal goals and plans should be an integral part of the assessment process.

Gap analysis must be a large part of any assessment process. A gap is the distance between where we want or need to be in terms of performance compared with where we actually operate. Where an individual operates is the output from the assessment process. Gap analysis has two primary objectives. The first is to identify and rank those areas with the most critical gaps. The second objective is to develop plans that will help close the performance gap.

The knowledge, skills, and competencies that an individual requires often differ from position to position, industry to industry, and across organizational levels. Within supply management, these competencies may also divide along tactical and strategic levels. Something we know is that no standard or agreed-upon set of knowledge, skills, and competencies exist within supply management. Ask 10 people for their listing of the knowledge and skills required for successful supply management, and the chances are good that 10 different lists will emerge. In reality, we have yet to see any consensus about the knowledge and skill set that comprises procurement and supply management.

Assessing Strengths rather than Weaknesses

Most assessments focus on improving an individual's weaknesses. A different approach is called *StrengthsFinder*, which, through an online assessment that relies on something called strengths psychology, identifies an individual's 5 top strengths out of 34 potential strengths. This approach includes strengths that are not specific to any one functional group or organizational area. The strengths are more generic than specific. Samples of some of the strengths assessed include achiever, analytical, strategic, futuristic, and learner.

The logic behind this approach is that superior performance, even greatness, comes from building on strengths rather than on those areas where an individual is inherently weak. Instead of investing time and resources trying to change weaknesses (which might result in only a marginal payback), this approach argues that time and energy are best spent on those areas that offer the greatest payback. A person who struggles with numbers, for example, is unlikely to become a great accountant or statistician, no matter how hard he or she tries.

As the author of *StrengthsFinder* states, "Even the legendary Michael Jordan, who embodied the power of raw talent on a basketball court, could not become the 'Michael Jordan' of golf or basketball, no matter how hard he tried."[13] The point here is to maximize your strengths while managing your weaknesses.

Once an individual completes the strengths assessment, he or she receives a Strengths Discovery and Action-Planning Guide that includes the top five strengths report; 50 Ideas for Action tailored to your individual strengths based on thousands of best-practices; a Strengths Discovery Interview that helps an individual think about how his or her experience, skills, and knowledge can help further build strengths; and a Strengths-Based Action Plan for setting specific goals for growing and applying personal strengths in the next week, month, and year.

At the organizational level, we see a focus on strengths while managing weaknesses all the time. It is common today for organizations to stress internally their core capabilities while managing through outsourcing those areas where they offer nothing unique. The same logic applies as individuals grow their strengths while taking steps to manage their weaknesses, such as attaining a basic level of competency in weak areas.

Professional Certifications

Various professional associations have developed bodies of knowledge and self-assessments for use by their members. Within the supply chain space, for example, APICS has developed the operations management body of knowledge (OMBOK). The purpose of the OMBOK is to outline the areas of knowledge required to successfully manage the processes for producing and delivering products and services.[14] It is also the most developed of the bodies of knowledge within supply and supply chain management. For that reason, it is mentioned here.

Organizations use resources like OMBOK to identify the kinds of knowledge their operations and supply chain professionals should possess. While originally developed for manufacturing companies, OMBOK also identifies the specific knowledge areas that apply within the distribution, health care, retail, utility, and hospitality industries. It also identifies the knowledge areas that are applicable to the most common supply chain and supply management job titles. APICS groups its body of knowledge into the following categories:

- Strategy
- Supply Chain
- Processes
- Planning and Control
- Scheduling
- Project Management
- Advanced Manufacturing and Service Technology
- Emerging Operations Technologies

APICS also awards two professional certifications that reflect the mastery of a body of knowledge—an individual can earn the designation certified in production and inventory management (CPIM) and the designation certified supply chain professional.

The Institute for Supply Management (ISM) also offers professional certifications. These include the certified professional in supply management (CPSM), the certified purchasing manager (CPM), and the accredited purchasing practitioner (APP). Professional certifications are evidence that an individual has mastered a professional body of knowledge.

These certifications, like all professional certifications, require exams that represent a body of knowledge. The CPSM certification, for example, requires an individual to take three exams. The first exam, foundation of supply management, includes contracting and negotiations, cost and finance, international, social responsibility, sourcing, and supplier relationship management. The second exam, effective supply management performance, includes forecasting, logistics, materials and inventory management, organization and department assessment, planning, product development, project management, and quality. The third exam, leadership in supply management, includes leadership, risk and compliance, and strategic sourcing. These exams provide some insight into what makes up the body of knowledge within supply management.

Next level supply organizations understand the importance of employee assessment within the talent management process. While some organizations develop their own assessments of knowledge and skills, others rely on third parties to administer assessments and interpret their findings. If done effectively, assessment with development plans and goals should lead to better organizational performance. If done poorly, organizational consultants are guaranteed future business.

Next Level Talent Acquisition Strategies

A study by Deloitte involving nearly 1400 human resource practitioners from over 60 countries revealed that the ability to attract new talent and the ability to retain human talent were perceived as the two most critical human management issues facing organizations.[15] Different ways exist for gaining access to the human resources required for next level supply management. The purpose of each approach is to gain access to personnel and leaders that are the source of future procurement and supply leaders.[16]

Develop Closer Relationship with a Select Group of Colleges

Similar to suppliers of direct materials, progressive companies develop close relationships with a select group of colleges and universities. These companies extensively recruit interns, co-op students, and recent college graduates from these institutions. A host of benefits may be available through close industry-university relationships. In fact, recruiting companies may even receive preferential *customer* treatment. Is any supply organization against preferential treatment?

At the university where an author of this book is employed, companies that have a close relationship with the undergraduate supply chain management program can expect certain recruiting advantages that are not available to every company. Companies that treat the university as a *preferred supplier* can expect treatment as a *preferred customer*. This includes:

- A personal introduction to the head of career services at the university
- Interview meeting space in a private conference room instead of a common student interview area
- Access to students in other majors to broaden the pool of qualified candidates
- Early access to the supply chain management resume book
- Counseling and timeline guidance on university recruiting strategies and milestones
- Rapid transmittal of internship and job opportunities to potential students through an electronic mailing list
- Special help with the administrative aspects of posting job opportunities and attending the university career fair
- Special *meet and greet* information sessions sponsored by the supply chain management club
- An opportunity to have students work on projects that benefit the sponsoring company directly
- Introductions to the appropriate staff in the graduate program

Based on extensive experience, those companies that have developed a special relationship with the university more often than not are successful in recruiting the better students from the talent pool.

Recruit Management Consultants

Another option for acquiring supply management talent involves hiring consultants who are leaving the consulting industry. Again, based on personal experience, consulting firms hire some exceptional people who take on demanding supply management projects for their clients. This is especially true at the top-tier consulting firms. While at first glance, the consulting profession may appear glamorous, after several years, the travel and hours associated with consulting projects begins to take a toll, particularly if the consultant has a family. At that point, these talented individuals often begin to search for a different career option. Next level supply organizations will readily tap into the recruiting pipeline that features consultants who are exiting the profession.

Recruit External Talent

Like many professional sports teams, some companies go to the marketplace and *buy* the talent they need. This approach requires a willingness to make attractive offers that will entice supply leaders to join a company. It may make sense to team up with a first-rate executive search firm to coordinate recruiting efforts if this is a preferred option for obtaining supply management talent.

Recruit from Other Functional Groups

Supply organizations often recruit talent from other functional groups for a variety of reasons. First, purchasing has evolved into supply management, an evolution that clearly benefits from personnel with a broad range of knowledge and skills. Second, the talent pipeline within purchasing is sparse at many companies, forcing supply leaders to recruit from outside the purchasing domain. Finally, supply management has become an attractive career option that appeals to professionals from other functional groups.

It is increasingly common to see individuals with engineering or finance backgrounds working in supply management. At many companies, supply management is now viewed as a promising career path offering exciting opportunities. A word of caution is in order here. When recruiting from other functional groups, it is important to not be perceived as stealing talent from other internal groups, particularly when those groups are needed to support various supply management objectives.

Recruit Honorably Discharged Military Personnel

Companies such as Boeing, Raytheon, Air Products, and General Electric regularly tap into a talent pipeline that provides access to highly skilled and highly motivated individuals. This pipeline includes enlisted personnel and officers who are honorably discharged from the military. Airlines have known for years that the military is a primary source for highly experienced pilots. Why would other job classifications be different? Besides receiving training that is highly sophisticated, these individuals have usually worked under demanding conditions that require a high degree of teamwork. This is a talent pipeline that supply organizations should pursue more aggressively.

Next Level Talent Retention and Development Strategies

All the talent acquisition efforts in the world are diminished if a supply organization experiences high turnover. While talent acquisition is important, the talent management process does not stop at that point. The emphasis must shift from acquiring human resource talent to retaining and developing that talent. An appropriate comparison involves supplier selection. Few supply leaders would argue that selection represents the end of the supplier management process. Once a supplier is selected, the emphasis should shift to management and development. Employees are much the same way. The following offers some approaches that next level supply organizations will rely on to retain and develop their supply personnel.

Team Leadership Assignments

Extensive experience with supply management work teams has convinced us that team leadership assignments offer an ideal training ground for developing future supply leaders. Besides the challenge of managing people from different functional disciplines and often different geographic locations and cultures, the team leadership role is one of the most demanding today. As noted in Chapter 5, teams are an integral part of the supply management process whose use is increasing rather than decreasing. A baseball analogy is appropriate here. In some respects, team leadership roles are like a minor league assignment before being called to the major league. Effective team leaders are prime candidates for future supply leadership positions.

Mentoring Programs

Many companies have created mentoring programs to develop their promising supply leaders. With these programs, a senior supply leader works directly with junior personnel to provide guidance and to share knowledge and experience. The mentors meet with the junior personnel on a regular basis, introduce him or her to other executives, and include these individuals in any experiences that would further develop their leadership ability, such as participating in buyer-supplier executive meetings.

Not all mentoring occurs at the executive level. Given the importance of teams, it makes sense for team leaders to mentor team members who will eventually assume formal leadership roles. It also makes sense to assign a mentor to new college hires. This approach assumes the mentors are qualified to assume that role and will be diligent in their responsibilities. Various research studies have found that mentoring programs have not consistently resulted in the development or advancement of those being mentored. Mentoring is another one of those activities that must lead to accomplishment.

Knowledge Transfer Programs

One increasingly popular method to deal with the ongoing need for talent development is to work with advisory firms who specialize in providing subject matter experts (SMEs) or deep smarts. These deep-experienced advisors are literally engaged for the purpose of transferring their extensive, relevant knowledge to the client's teams. This is a fundamentally different approach than a conventional consulting model; they can be characterized by flexible arrangements including providing coaching and advice on an as-needed basis. Knowledge transfer programs are often used to supplement other professional development initiatives.

Job Rotational Programs for High Potential Hires

Rotational programs involve assigning promising new employees to work in different areas over a period of a year or two. Progressive firms identify their most promising recruits, often during the college recruiting process, and then place them in a job rotational program. At the end of the development program, these individuals have a solid understanding regarding how the supply organization works, not to mention a knowledge base that often far exceeds employees who were not part of a rotational program. These individuals are also highly visible as they move through their job assignments.

Although these programs are expensive to operate, their use is considered a best practice for developing future leaders. An analysis by *Businessweek* revealed that over 30 of the top 50 companies rated as the best places for college graduates to work offer formal management training programs. These programs satisfy a variety of objectives, including exposing the employee to many areas of a business while enhancing their knowledge and skill base. Some of these programs feature international assignments.

Leadership Development Programs

An American Management Association commissioned study found a significant relationship between the presence of leadership development programs and improved market performance.[17] Leadership development involves a broad category of activities with the specific objective of developing leadership capabilities. General Mills, for example, conducts a program called Building Great Leaders. As part of this program, groups of the company's 500 top managers sit down individually with human resource managers to review the results of 360-degree feedback and two personality assessments. These managers also attend a session conducted by a senior vice president that addresses leadership issues.[18]

The percentage of companies that have developed formal leadership programs is hard to determine because these programs come in all shapes and sizes. Those that develop these programs usually focus on the knowledge and skills they think managers will need as they progress through their careers. With that said, some companies have experienced a disappointing attrition rate after employees complete a leadership development program, certainly an unintended consequence by anyone's measure. Oftentimes younger managers, whose higher potential was a major factor in being selected for a development program in the first place, find they are quite marketable after their program is complete. Talented employees just became even more talented.

A Pennsylvania company found that over half of the managers who completed its advanced management program left the company within a year or two of program completion. This rate is much higher than the rate for managers who have not participated in the program. The leadership development program may actually be counter-productive.[19]

Continuous Training Courses

As companies shift toward strategic supply management, they nearly always find they need to retool their workforce. More often than not, this retooling takes the form of continuous training programs. Rest assured from earlier in the chapter that the knowledge and skills required for tactical procurement are not the same as those required for strategic supply management. If you are looking for an apple to orange comparison, tactical versus strategic is probably it. This is not to say that tactical competencies are unimportant. They are simply different than what is required to support a strategic perspective. World-class supply management encompasses both strategic and tactical competencies, which Chapter 5 illustrated.

Another approach for developing the workforce includes offering shorter courses that relate to supply management. These courses, which can be developed internally or by third parties, usually cover topics such as quality management, lean thinking, team building, and negotiation. Most companies develop a generic menu of courses and then offer them to employees on a regular basis. Best practice companies carefully assess the knowledge and skill needs of their future supply leaders and then craft training programs that are customized to that employee's unique developmental needs. An employee who is assuming the role of a commodity team leader, for example, might benefit from team leadership and negotiation training. Another employee who is being assigned to a supplier development team would likely benefit from lean supply or six-sigma quality training. Ideally, these training modules are available for on-demand viewing asynchronously through web-based systems.

Personnel Skill Advancement Rewards

Another development approach focuses on rewarding personnel for advancing their skills and knowledge through formal education. This includes earning degrees or certificates in supply management, which were discussed earlier. Each year the ISM publishes a listing of colleges and universities that offer degree and certificate programs related to procurement and supply management. Even many colleges and universities that do not have formal supply programs offer courses related to supply management. Supporting continuing education through tuition reimbursement will further encourage the development of your company's human resource capabilities.

Career Ladders

Progressive companies provide some perspective of the path that supply professionals might follow as they progress through their careers. These perspectives, called career ladders, are valuable when recruiting new talent into the supply organization. Figure 6.5 provides some insight into career ladders. This figure illustrates the different levels where a supply career can progress while showing various supply tracks. Employees usually appreciate a graphical representation of how their careers might advance.

Career ladders are important because most organizations have *de-layered* the number of levels they maintain from the top to the bottom of the organization. In an earlier era, younger professionals could easily see their career progression through well-defined steps. These levels have given way to broader groupings of positions within a band rather than discrete steps. Career moves that were previously vertical, which meant a promotion, now often appear as lateral or horizontal moves. As a result, career ladders are an important tool for retaining talent within the supply organization as they help employees visualize their growth.

Talent Analytics

A body of knowledge is emerging about something called talent analytics and how organizations use analytic data to support their talent management processes. Talent analytics, which represent the state of the art in talent management, involves adopting sophisticated methods of analyzing employee data to ensure the highest productivity, engagement, and retention of top talent.[20] Six kinds of detailed statistical analytics help companies answer important human talent questions. While some of the analytics are more likely to be applied with direct labor, for example, taken as a whole, they support the overall objective of better managing a labor pool. These six analytic approaches include:

1. *Talent supply chain analytics* address how workforce needs should adapt to changes in the business environment.
2. *Talent value model analytics* analyze why employees choose to stay with or leave an organization.
3. *Workforce forecasts analytics* help identify when to increase or reduce staffing levels.
4. *Human-capital analysis analytics* provide insight into which actions have the greatest impact on the workforce and the business.

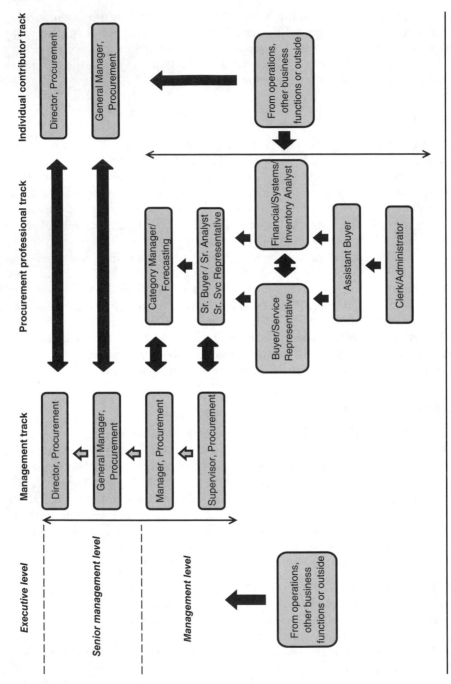

Figure 6.5 Supply management/procurement career ladder

5. *Analytical human resources* help identify which departments or individuals need attention.
6. *Human-capital facts analytics* help identify the key human-related indicators that link to organizational performance.

Talent analytics explicitly recognizes the link between applying the right data and tools to human processes and enhanced corporate performance. Employees are a rich source of collective data that managers can use to make better human resource decisions.

Managing External Talent

The original *Straight to the Bottom Line*® book has a chapter with a provocative title: "Consultants: To Use or Not to Use—That is the Question." When the authors wrote that book they were speaking as corporate practitioners, having led successful procurement transformations, including extensive experience using consulting firms. We are going to build on that original perspective and share some additional perspectives that chief procurement officers have revealed to us, as well as observations from recent experiences working with various companies as consultants and advisors. A table and explanation that appears in that original chapter concerning when to use external talent is worth repeating here (Table 6.1).

Table 6.1 When to use external talent

Unnecessary to use external talent	Consider using external talent
Benchmarks confirm that your internal processes/results are best-in-class	You lack benchmarks and are uncertain how good your processes and staff are
Company is able to make ongoing investments (people, systems) to achieve and remain best-in-class	Not able to invest as needed
Best-in-class category/market expertise	No particular internal strength
No urgency to achieve significant cost reductions	Time is of the essence for achieving improvements
Best-in-class currently and still reaping new benefits each year	Not generating significant new benefits each year
Internal staff able to effectively deal with internal politics	Internal politics constrain achievement of cost reduction objectives; a *third party* might have credibility
Your organization lacks a leader, and you hope that the consulting firm can fill that gap	You want to supplement your internal talent for a defined time period

Source: Robert A. Rudzki, Douglas Smock, Michael Katzorke, and Shelley Stewart Jr., *Straight to the Bottom Line.* Fort Lauderdale, FL: J. Ross Publishing, 2005.

Why Use External Talent?

The classic reasons for using consultants include a desire to jump-start change and improvement, a need to introduce and embed new best-in-class business processes, and a need to acquire expertise that is lacking within your organization. Additional reasons include a desire to leverage the prior experiences of the consulting firm and a need to supplement internal resources with the talented resources that a qualified firm can quickly muster for a major engagement.

The classic, worst reason to use consultants is that your organization lacks a leader in a functional area. The consultant becomes a way to compensate for this lack of leadership. An unwillingness to make a change to introduce true leadership is replaced with the hope that the consulting firm will fill this void. We advise never letting consultants run a project or run a part of your business. This ignores the responsibility for identifying the right internal leader and opens the door to the likelihood of countless, run-on consulting assignments. In fact, this encourages something we call the *trail of bread crumbs* approach that limits the sharing of ideas to a thin stream of mini-morsels, which keeps the client always wanting a little more (and keeps them engaged far longer than they should be). This is in stark contrast to the approach where the advisory firm creates a detailed master plan of transformation initiatives.

Next Level Perspectives

Over the last six years, one of the authors of this book and his colleagues have worked extensively with large- and medium-size companies across most industry segments (manufacturing, process, health care, services, retail). These individuals have witnessed some excellent practices relating to using consultants (or advisors) intelligently while also coming across far too many poor practices. In one case, for example, a *post mortem* review of a consulting project by a large firm revealed fundamental errors by the client and the consulting firm. Some of the key learnings appear in Table 6.2. Take a minute or two to review this table. You should notice that using consultants intelligently requires mindset and behavior changes by both the client company as well as the consulting firm.

A Fundamental Choice: Teaching How to Fish

One of the fundamental choices to consider when pursing external talent is whether to retain a consultant or an advisor. The distinction is not just semantics: it is core to what you are trying to achieve. Do you want someone to perform some work and then depart, leaving little process knowledge or category experience behind? This might be an appropriate approach if your company is on a burning platform (i.e., it is hemorrhaging badly).

Table 6.2 Actively managing consultants

What typically happens	Leading edge practice
Top-down directive that procurement department will work with a specific consulting firm.	Procurement leader takes the initiative and sends a request for information to a broad range of potential service providers (large and small firms; consulting vs. advisory firms); short list invited to respond to a request for proposal (RFP).
Selection criteria unknown beyond assumed personal relationships at the executive level.	Selection criteria established as part of the RFP process are consistent with the needs/desires of the procurement organization and the company.
Consulting firm uses "A" team to manage the executive relationship but sends "B" team of inexperienced junior consultants to learn on the job and do the project.	Firm is selected only after ironclad assurances that A team of experienced advisors will be assigned; resumes of advisors are provided; client encouraged to interview each advisor.
Consulting agreement is rigid and aggressive, requiring steadfast commitment to large number of full-time consultants for defined timeframe (often 6 to 12 months or more).	Agreement is flexible, reflecting the client's workplace realities, needs, and timing.
Consulting firm disrupts everyone's regular job in bid to ensure that its project is everyone's priority and is a success.	Firm works with the reality of client's workplace and schedule and is careful not to be a disruptive force.
After consulting firm leaves, reported savings start to evaporate or can't be found.	Firm has embedded processes and capabilities into client organization, which now can create more successes on its own.

Alternatively, do you want an advisory approach in which process knowledge (e.g., specific best practices such as strategic sourcing and negotiations management [SSNM]) and commodity knowledge are transferred to your organization in a planned and deliberate manner? To use a familiar analogy: do you want someone to hand your team an already-prepared fish dinner, or do you want your team to learn how to be successful fishermen themselves?

Optimize by Examining the Pieces

In addition to the fundamental choice previously noted, better decisions regarding how to use external resources are possible when a proposed project is disaggregated into its components (i.e., what you are trying to accomplish) with a candid assessment of your internal ability to achieve those objectives on your own. If internal capability is lacking, identify options to supplement your internal staff. It all boils down to deliverables and timing (regardless of who does the work), access to the needed amount of the right talent to do the specified work, and the leadership of change.

Figure 6.6 shows the major components of a procurement transformation initiative leading to the use of strategic sourcing teams. Phase I is comprised of a current state assessment compared to best practices in supply management; an opportunity assessment of the financial impact possible by adopting best practices; and the construction of a tailored roadmap and business case. Phase II is comprised of transformation and change management guidance; strategic sourcing training accompanied by process coaching through one or more waves of projects; providing category experts for the areas of spend targeted in the various waves of projects; and providing analytic support for the sourcing teams.

The ideal consulting project—from the perspective of the consulting firm—is one that requires a client to commit to Phases I and II. Yet, from the customer's perspective, there is little good reason to commit to both phases at the same time. If the consulting/advisory firm has confidence in its abilities to deliver real value, it should be willing to provide the Phase I deliverables prior to the client committing to the Phase II project. There is no good reason to give an entire project to one firm unless they have proven themselves to have a full range of required expertise.

One of the biggest opportunities to optimize results regarding the use of external resources relates to the final column on the right side of the chart: analytic support. Never agree to a *blended rate* proposal from a consulting firm; such a blended rate will mask the excessive fees charged for right-out-of-school analysts. You can save a great deal of money on projects that require analytic work by utilizing in-house analysts or hiring analytic talent directly.

Caution: Risk-Free Savings Programs Are Costly

So-called *risk free cost savings programs* have become a popular marketing ploy of some consulting firms. These programs are designed to give the consulting firm—as risk taker—a much higher total compensation than the much simpler time and materials based consulting structure. In fact, these arrangements are designed to provide the consulting firm with a payout of two to four times the compensation that a time and materials approach would entail. In addition, they conceal the daily rates used. Table 6.3 provides additional comments about the three fundamental options for compensating consultants or advisors.

It All Starts with Executive Awareness

One of the best reasons to utilize external advisors is to provide an independent and candid perspective, something that internal personnel may find difficult to do due to a lack of expertise or because of pressure from internal

	Current state assessment vs. best practices	$ Opportunity assessment	Transformation roadmap & business case	Transformation & change management guidance	Strategic sourcing training & process coaching/ advisors	Category experts (SMEs for different areas of spend)	Analytic talent to support sourcing teams
Internal personnel							
Large consulting firm							
Advisory firm							

Figure 6.6 Procurement transformation project components

Source: Greybeard Advisors LLC. Copyright 2009–2010. All rights reserved.

Table 6.3 Potential compensation arrangements

Basic consulting compensation options:
A. Professional time and expenses
B. Hybrid (combination of A and C)
C. Pure success fee
Comments:
A. This option is, by far, the lowest total cost to the client. It also has the advantage of not creating misalignments between client and consulting firm interests.
B. This option is typically constructed by reducing the professional fees by some degree (e.g., 10 to 30%), and adding a *variable* portion based on delivery of program objectives. Problems that can arise are basically similar to those of Option C.
C. This option is typically based on a significant *shared savings* rate—often 30 to 35% of the annualized benefits will go to the consulting firm. For a situation with significant opportunity, this would likely mean an enormous payout. Beyond the substantial cost of this option, major challenges/drawbacks include:
a. Potential misalignment of interests between client and consulting firm (client wants not just cost reduction, but fundamental transformation and capability building; consulting firms in a pure success fee arrangement are incented to drive quickly for savings only and then depart)
b. Administrative and practical complexities of agreeing on savings calculations, and the potential of disputes regarding payments due
c. Unpredictable, and potentially unproductive, behaviors from client employees if the existence of the shared savings arrangement became known

politics. Performing this first step (the assessment) correctly is vitally important because it sets the stage for everything else that follows, especially creating executive awareness.

Here are two examples from completely different industries. Each company made a commitment to transformation during the economic downturn, a time when it was easy to defer such investments. Company A followed the advice and assessment methodology of its external advisors, created executive awareness and support, and added more than 20 new strategic personnel to its supply chain function, more than doubling its human resource commitment. Simultaneously, it committed to a program of SSNM training for its procurement employees, supported by experienced SSNM coaches who ensured the teams learned and applied the process effectively. The resulting performance improvements more than offset the amount committed to the transformation—by a substantial margin.

A second company also followed the advice of its external advisors and made a decision to add approximately 50% to its current base of strategic resources, with a similar commitment to training and team coaching. Again, the resulting improvements more than offset the amount committed to the transformation—by a huge margin.

Concluding Thoughts

Every corporate group has a need for an active talent management process. In that regard, much of what we discussed applies to other functional areas. Simply change the phrase *procurement* or *supply management* to any organizational group. One thing is certain, however. Strategic supply management involves knowledge areas that require leaders with intelligence and foresight. It is not something we can automate.

Why do some companies commit to building organizational capabilities in supply management, year after year, while others do not? Based on our experience, there is a straightforward link between executive awareness of the value of strategic supply management and top management's willingness to invest in supply management capabilities, including human capabilities. The road to success in achieving an organizational commitment to all aspects of talent management starts with creating executive awareness across a number of areas:

- Awareness of the current state of supply management practices at your company compared with supply management best practices
- Awareness of the opportunity possible by transforming the current state into something closer to world-class practices and capabilities
- Awareness of how to create a comprehensive roadmap for transformation that involves the right internal and external human resources

As discussed elsewhere this is not easy to do. But, if done well, it will help create the foundation for next level supply management.

Chapter Notes

1. Steve Minter. "Identifying Your Future Leaders." *Industry Week* 259, no. 9 (September 2010): 24.
2. This example is adapted from Mina Kimes. "Why J&J's Headache Won't Go Away." *Fortune*, September 6, 2010, 104.
3. Julia Christensen Hughes and Evelina Rog. "Talent Management: A Strategy for Improving Employee Recruitment, Retention and Engagement within Hospitality Organizations." *International Journal of Contemporary Hospitality Management* 20, no. 7 (2008): 743–757, citing R.E. Lewis and R.J. Heckman, "Talent Management: A Critical Review," *Human Resources Management Review* 16 (2006):139–154.
4. Peter Cappelli. "Balance Your Talent Requirements." *Inside Supply Management* 21, no. 10 (October/November 2010): 28.
5. Hughes and Rog, 749, citing Hewitt Associates. "What Makes a Best Employer?" *Insights and Findings from Hewitt's Global Best Employer's Study*. Hewitt Associates, 1–38.

6. Hughes and Rog, 750, citing Towers Perrin. *The 2003 Towers Perrin Talent Report: Working Today: Understanding What Drives Employee Engagement* (Stamford, CT: Towers Perrin, 2003).

7. These comments come from client engagements with Greybeard Advisors.

8. Hughes and Rog, 750, citing L. Morton. *Talent Management Value Imperatives: Strategies for Successful Execution*. R-1360-05-RR (Conference Board, 2005).

9. Hughes and Rog, 750, citing B. E. Becker, M. A. Huselid, and D. Ulrich. *The HR Scorecard: Linking People, Strategy, and Performance* (Boston: Harvard Business School Press, 2001).

10. *Global Trends 2025: A Transformed World* (New York: National Intelligence Council, Cosimo Reports, 2008), 21.

11. Richard M. Cyert and David C. Mowery, ed. *Technology and Employment: Innovation and Growth in the U.S. Economy* (Washington, D.C.: National Academy Press, 1987).

12. Chris Argyris. *Integrating the Individual and the Organization* (New Brunswick, NJ: Transaction Publishers, 1990).

13. Tom Rath *StrengthsFinders 2.0* (New York: Gallup Press, 2007), 7.

14. This information is obtained from www.apics.org/ombok.

15. Hughes and Rog, 747 citing Deloitte. "Becoming a Magnet for Talent: Global Talent Pulse Survey Results." 2005.
www.deloitte.com/dtt/research/0,1015,cid%253D103148,00.html.

16. These approaches are adapted from Robert J. Trent. *Strategic Supply Management: Creating the Next Source of Competitive Advantage* (Ft. Lauderdale, FL: J. Ross Publishing, 2007), 97–100.

17. Minter, 24.

18. Minter, 24.

19. The company in this example compensated its employees at the industry average. After completing the development program, talented managers found the program helped them command a higher salary at peer companies that compensated their employees above the industry average.

20. The material in this section is adapted from Thomas H. Davenport, Jeanne Harris, and Jeremy Shapiro. "Competing on Talent Analytics." *Harvard Business Review* (October 2010): 52–58.

Part Two

Critical Topics in Supply Management Transformation

7

Revenue Growth through Supplier Collaboration

A decade ago, Boeing and General Electric entered into an agreement to develop something truly special. The two companies partnered to develop a new series of 777 extended-range and long-range aircraft that would fly further than any other commercial aircraft in the world. For the first time, nonstop flights from New York to China became routine, saving time by flying over a polar route rather than longer east-west routes that required refueling at an intermediary airport. These planes allow airlines to reduce their fuel consumption, landing fees, and labor costs while getting passengers to their ultimate destination more quickly. The extended-range 777 even set a world record for distance traveled without refueling, making just about any two points in the world within reach of a single flight.

In exchange for being the sole provider of engines for the new 777, General Electric committed $1 billion toward the development of the new aircraft, making this one of the largest-scale examples of supplier-buyer risk and reward sharing. It is also a clear example of how a buying company can draw upon the expertise of suppliers to create a product that generates billions of dollars in new revenue for both companies. To date, Boeing has sold close to 1000 of the long-range and extended-range 777s at over $200 million per plane. GE has sold several thousand very expensive engines that require a steady stream of maintenance over the next 25 years. While the magnitude of this partnership makes it unusual, it highlights the opportunities that are possible when progressive companies work with innovative suppliers. The benefits derived from the supplier-provided engines are a large reason why airlines buy this plane.

This chapter presents revenue growth as the next frontier of supply management and supplier contribution. The chapter first addresses the important linkage between supply management, supplier collaboration, and revenue enhancement. We then define the concept of supplier collaboration followed by the importance of becoming a supplier's customer of choice. The next section talks about how to benefit from supplier innovation during product and technology development. The chapter concludes with case examples of how leading companies leverage supplier capabilities to achieve revenue growth.

Revenue Growth—the Next Frontier of Supply Management Contribution

Figure 7.1 identifies three primary drivers of corporate performance—cost management, asset management, and revenue growth. We are well aware of the need for supply organizations to manage costs. This topic is covered extensively in other books, so there is no need to duplicate that knowledge here. The effective management of capital assets and working capital, a second driver identified in Figure 7.1, is something that next level supply organizations are pursuing aggressively. The third driver, responsibility for revenue growth, represents a new frontier for supply leaders. We view revenue enhancement as a desired outcome from collaborating with innovative suppliers, often during product development. Progressive companies understand the need to work with suppliers that provide game-changing technology and ideas that support product differentiation and market growth.

Many paths exist between supplier support and revenue enhancement. Some of these paths have a direct link to revenue growth, such as incorporating a supplier technology that leads directly to new sales, while other paths

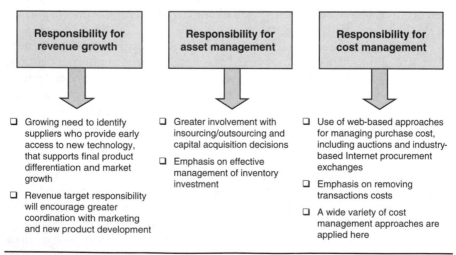

Figure 7.1   Drivers of corporate performance

work their way indirectly. Quality improvements or cost reductions resulting from supplier contributions, for example, can cause the marketplace to take a favorable look at a product, which could lead to new sales. Our focus here is to think about developing direct linkages between supplier collaboration and revenue growth. These traditional or indirect paths are well discussed in other publications.

Being held accountable for revenue growth targets, as well as other corporate indicators, is hard for most supply managers to grasp, particularly those who have spent their careers in a traditional procurement environment. The reason for this is obvious. These individuals have focused their efforts on the cost rather than revenue side of the supply chain. Isn't talking about revenue enhancement, and even being held accountable for achieving revenue targets, something that applies to the marketing side of the business? Isn't any talk about differentiating product technology more applicable to engineering? Involving suppliers at a level that contributes to revenue growth is uncharted territory at most supply organizations. This brave new world is a frightening one to many supply leaders. However, achieving a high level of supplier integration is not going to happen unless there is a supply organization in place that knows how to manage the process.

Whether we like it or not, for some very good reasons the time has come to engage in the revenue enhancement conversation. First, the ability to develop unique advantages from a single-minded focus on cost reduction diminishes fairly quickly over time. Second, an increasing amount of value-add and innovation that differentiates products and services, often in the form of product features, comes from external sources. While we are at the stage where tapping into supplier capabilities still offers the possibility of providing significant competitive advantage, it won't be long before laggard companies are forced to pursue supplier collaboration simply to avoid a competitive disadvantage.

We only have to think about a product that we all understand to appreciate the link between suppliers and revenue growth. Automobiles are purchased today as much for their features as for their performance and design. Satellite-ready radios, in-car communication systems such as Ford's Sync or GM's On-Star, anti-lock brake systems that enhance vehicle safety, surround airbags, and high-performance tires all come from external suppliers. These features support a product package that can differentiate one vehicle from another in the consumers' mind.

In the aerospace world, the revenue benefits that Airbus and Boeing derive from supplier-provided innovations and technology are too numerous to mention. At Gulfstream, a leading provider of business jets, engineers worked closely with a group of critical suppliers when developing the next generation of business jet. Suppliers developed technologies that ensure Gulfstream sustains its reputation as the technological leader in the aerospace world. Honeywell provided major advancements in cockpit avionics, Kollsman created state-of-the-art poor weather and night visioning systems for pilots, Rolls-Royce created a new, more powerful engine, and Vought developed new wing structures. Gulfstream understands clearly the linkage between supplier collaboration and market success.

Identifying the precise effect of a specific supplier engagement and enhanced revenue growth is not easy. In complex organizations, it is always a challenge to partition causality. Determining the impact that supplier innovation and involvement have on revenue growth can be especially challenging. There is no question that finance will need to take an active role in any attempt to validate the impact of supplier involvement on corporate-level performance indicators. While next level supply organizations are acutely aware of their need to connect cause (supplier collaboration) and effect (improved corporate performance), at some point we may also have to take it as an article of faith that well-executed supplier involvement strategies offer something that is good.

Understanding Supplier Collaboration

It is important to agree on something as it relates to supplier contribution to revenue growth. Almost by definition, the kinds of buyer-supplier relationships that will lead to a buying company's revenue growth are collaborative. Unfortunately, this word has become so overused that it has practically become meaningless. In reality, few relationships within the supply chain space are truly collaborative. Collaborative relationships are intensive to manage, requiring executive-to-executive engagement, joint measures of success, and shared risk and reward projects. Supply chain alliances, for example, are collaborative by design. If anyone reading this book does not believe that true alliances are challenging to manage, then they do not understand alliances.

When most practitioners refer to a collaborative relationship, they are really referring to a cooperative relationship. Longer-term contracts, for example, are cooperative by design. They feature open sharing of data and information between the parties. Even the dictionary provides some degree of differentiation between the terms, saying that cooperation means to act or work with another or others while collaboration means to work jointly with others, especially in an intellectual endeavor.[1] Figure 7.2 presents a relationship continuum featuring words that begin with the letter C. While cooperative and collaborative relationships are both placed on the win-win side of the spectrum, collaboration takes the buyer-seller relationship to an entirely new level.

Collaborative relationships usually involve a smaller set of suppliers that provide technology, items, or services that are essential or unique to a firm's success. A willingness to work jointly to identify better ways to operate or to compete in the marketplace is characteristic of a collaborative relationship. These relationships are one of the most intensive relationships possible

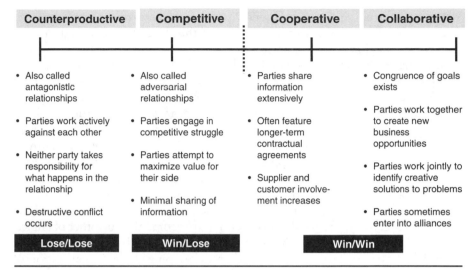

Counterproductive	Competitive	Cooperative	Collaborative
• Also called antagonistic relationships	• Also called adversarial relationships	• Parties share information extensively	• Congruence of goals exists
• Parties work actively against each other	• Parties engage in competitive struggle	• Often feature longer-term contractual agreements	• Parties work together to create new business opportunities
• Neither party takes responsibility for what happens in the relationship	• Parties attempt to maximize value for their side	• Supplier and customer involvement increases	• Parties work jointly to identify creative solutions to problems
• Destructive conflict occurs	• Minimal sharing of information		• Parties sometimes enter into alliances
Lose/Lose	**Win/Lose**	**Win/Win**	

Figure 7.2   Continuum of relationships

between supply chain members. In a collaborative environment, the parties ideally share congruent goals between them and recognize that the value they receive would be far less than if the collaborative relationship did not exist. The opening example to this chapter highlights this point explicitly.

The bottom line is that a buyer-seller relationship that links directly to new revenue is nearly always going to be collaborative by design. Otherwise, these relationships will usually feature a more traditional emphasis on cost reduction.

Becoming the Customer of Choice

Creating a clear connection between supplier collaboration and enhanced revenue growth does not happen by chance. In fact, it is the result of progressive supply management practices that recognize the importance of looking beyond cost reduction when framing the buyer-seller relationship. An objective of any next level supply organization must be to become the customer of choice to its most important suppliers. Nearly every supplier would like to be the supplier of choice (i.e., the preferred supplier) to their customers. Conversely, most buyers should strive to become the customer of choice (i.e., the preferred customer) to their suppliers, especially when these suppliers sell to a variety of different industries.

Preferred customers are first in line when a supplier develops new technologies, first in line to receive innovative ideas that originate with suppliers, and, when market demand exceeds supply, first in line when a supplier's limited output is distributed. It is not hard conceptually to draw a direct line between being a preferred customer and receiving preferred treatment that is special and unique. It is often this special treatment that leads to market advantages that result in enhanced revenue growth.

It is also not hard to find examples where a buyer has clearly benefitted from being the customer of choice to a supplier. Over the last several years, Ford and Toyota have been working to be leaders in hybrid vehicles. At one point, the demand for hybrid transmission systems began to outstrip the supply of transmissions, making supply allocation a reality. Ford executives complained publicly that Aisin Seiki, a Japanese supplier that produced hybrid transmissions, favored Toyota when supplying scarce transmission systems. What Ford should have realized (and probably did privately) is that access to supply is one of the tangible benefits of being a preferred customer. In all likelihood, Ford was not the preferred customer here. If you do not like being on the short end of the allocation spectrum, you need to take actions to become the customer of choice.

In a high stakes game worth billions of dollars, Airbus has publicly accused General Electric of favoring Boeing when developing the next generation of jet engines. Part of the problem is that the new Airbus A350 has a version that will be a direct competitor of the long-range 777, the plane featured at the beginning of this chapter. Airbus's chief operating officer and top salesman says, "The problem we have with GE is they go to Boeing in Seattle and say, 'What kind of engine should we design for your airframe?' Then they come to Airbus in Toulouse and say, 'Here is the kind of airframe you need to build to fit our engine.'"[2] This quote clearly suggests that Airbus sees Boeing as General Electric's preferred customer.

An interesting example of preferential treatment in the retail segment involves JC Penney and its Asian supplier of dress shirts. In a radical departure from a traditional supply chain that features multiple levels of intermediaries within a distribution channel, the Asian supplier uploads point-of-sale data each morning from every JC Penney store. This information tells the supplier exactly what styles, colors, and sizes of shirts that customers purchased the previous day. This allows the supplier to quickly replenish these shirts by shipping them directly to JC Penney stores, thereby avoiding the cost and time required to move inventory through the normal distribution channel. The supplier not only assumes responsibility for placing orders to itself, it has taken on responsibility for forecasting, the design of new shirts, and market testing. Instead of shirts being ordered months ahead of time in anticipation of demand, which is the norm in a traditional retail channel, the supplier quickly responds to demand changes at the store level. The supplier designed this system that provides Penney's with a competitive edge.

The system has not always performed flawlessly, but even when problems occur, Penney's status as a preferred customer helps mitigate any risk. In one instance when the Asian supplier underestimated Penney's needs, a spokeswoman at the supplier said the factory "sacrificed other customers" to complete Penney's needs. The supplier then shipped the shirts via air freight at its own expense. While air freight costs 10 times more than ocean shipping, the spokeswoman stated that "sometimes you have to decide which customers you're going to take care of."[3] Statements like this one are a clear indication that Penney is feeling this supplier's love.

Receiving Tangible Benefits

One of the outcomes from being a preferred customer should be a willingness by suppliers to provide preferential treatment that benefits the buying company. The premise here is that preferential treatment received from suppliers can lead to market advantages that your final customer values. What should a buying company actually expect to receive if it is a preferred customer? The list is varied and probably more extensive than first realized.

The results of being a preferred customer, or the customer of choice, generally fall into three categories. The first category includes various direct investments made by the supplier for the benefit of the preferred customer. We call these investments relationship-specific investments. A partial listing of relationship-specific investments includes providing supplier personnel to work directly at your facilities, providing supplier engineers to support your product design teams, equipment or work cells dedicated to your demand requirements, or holding inventory to support your production needs. Each of these represents a financial commitment made by a supplier on your behalf that should lead to some positive outcomes.

The second category includes a diverse set of items that represent supplier-provided favorable treatment. While these items do not represent direct financial investments by a supplier, they offer the possibility of realizing positive outcomes that are worthwhile. Examples of supplier-provided favorable treatment include:

- Shorter quoted lead times
- Preferential scheduling of orders
- More favorable payment terms
- Performance improvement ideas
- More frequent deliveries
- Access to supply market information
- Better pricing
- First allocation when supply is constrained

The third category includes access to supplier-developed innovation before your competitors have access to that innovation. This innovation could involve physical process innovations, supply chain and other operating innovations, materials and product innovations, and technology innovations. The domain of potential supplier-provided innovation is broad.

How to Become the Customer of Choice

Being the customer of choice places a buying organization in a position to receive preferential treatment that translates directly into top and bottom line improvements. It is not enough to say that your company's objective is to become the customer of choice to suppliers. It takes tangible actions to earn that status. Old school thinking would say that the buyer is king (or queen) and that suppliers serve the buyer. What is all this talk about having to take action to please suppliers?

The reality is that suppliers are becoming more rather than less important to buying organizations. Furthermore, many suppliers have choices about where they will direct their investment dollars and to whom they will provide preferential treatment. While suppliers may sell to you, how anxious are they to serve you? Thousands of suppliers sell to General Motors, but over the last 20 years, few have felt all that committed toward the company, as evidenced by supplier surveys. In reality, General Motors can use all the help it can get.

What are the kinds of things a buying company can do position itself as the customer of choice? One way is to ask suppliers how they view your company as a customer. Table 7.1 presents a tool that a company can use to survey suppliers regarding their perception of the buying company against their perception of an ideal customer. The items in this scale are not the product of an overly active imagination. They are the result of research and focus groups that identified the characteristics of an ideal industrial customer. This tool captures objectively how suppliers feel about a particular customer.

Table 7.1 can easily be extended to add even more value to the assessment process. One of the shortfalls of Table 7.1 is that it implies that all items in the table are equally important to a supplier, which is probably not the case. With a simple modification to the descriptors of this table, a buying company can ask how important each item is to a supplier by making a score of 6 = Very Important, 3 = Somewhat Important, and 0 = Not Important. Next, the difference between an item's importance score and the comparison score to an ideal customer represents a gap. Items with the largest numeric gaps offer the greatest improvement opportunities.

This scale is part of a broader tool called a supplier satisfaction survey. In addition to the comparison against an ideal customer, a full survey should examine the buying company's ability to meet or exceed a supplier's perception in areas such as:

- The customer's ability to communicate quality and performance requirements
- Information sharing and transaction efficiency
- Business-to-business relationships
- Negotiation and contracting practices

Table 7.1 Comparison to an ideal customer

This survey asks you to think about how this customer compares to what you consider to be a best or ideal customer. Compared with what you consider to be an ideal or best customer, how does this customer compare across the following areas?

How does this customer compare to the ideal customer for . . . ?	Much worse than the ideal		Somewhat less than the ideal			Equal to the ideal
Sharing relevant supply chain information	0	1	2	3	4	5	6
Providing a fair financial return on your investment	0	1	2	3	4	5	6
Providing adequate lead times for planning	0	1	2	3	4	5	6
Providing accurate forecasts	0	1	2	3	4	5	6
Sharing of cost savings from improvement ideas	0	1	2	3	4	5	6
Providing correct and clear material specifications	0	1	2	3	4	5	6
Providing smoothly timed order releases	0	1	2	3	4	5	6
Protecting proprietary information and technology	0	1	2	3	4	5	6
Exhibiting ethical and respectful behavior	0	1	2	3	4	5	6
Providing objective performance feedback	0	1	2	3	4	5	6
Providing payment in a reasonable time	0	1	2	3	4	5	6
Minimizing last minute product and order changes	0	1	2	3	4	5	6
Pursuing efficient negotiating and contracting practices	0	1	2	3	4	5	6
Offering longer-term business opportunities	0	1	2	3	4	5	6
Providing opportunities for early involvement during this customer's new product development	0	1	2	3	4	5	6
Designing parts to match your process capabilities	0	1	2	3	4	5	6
Responding to your inquiries in a timely manner	0	1	2	3	4	5	6

(continues)

Table 7.1 *(continued)*

How does this customer compare to the ideal customer for . . . ?	Much worse than the ideal			Somewhat less than the ideal			Equal to the ideal
Providing clear channels of communication	0	1	2	3	4	5	6
Using electronic systems to facilitate transactions	0	1	2	3	4	5	6
Being receptive to your improvement ideas	0	1	2	3	4	5	6
Being knowledgeable about your business and industry	0	1	2	3	4	5	6
Being committed to continuous improvement	0	1	2	3	4	5	6
Developing effective buyer-seller relationships	0	1	2	3	4	5	6
Providing tangible support if problems arise	0	1	2	3	4	5	6
Being clear regarding performance expectations	0	1	2	3	4	5	6

- Ethical and business conduct
- Business opportunities and payment terms
- Responsiveness to supplier concerns or questions

We recommend using a third party to administer supplier surveys to ensure an unbiased response from suppliers. Customers often lack the objective perspective needed to conduct an effective survey. Third-party surveys also provide an environment in which suppliers can provide detailed feedback without fear of reprisal (the third party protects the identity of individual suppliers). It is critical that a buying organization collect objective data with the purpose of improving the buyer-seller relationship rather than trying to identify responses from specific suppliers, especially for punitive reasons.

Revenue Growth from Supplier Innovation

It is well accepted that innovation, which is the act or process of inventing or introducing something new, is essential to longer-term success. The commercialization of new ideas provides the foundation for economic growth, both at the macroeconomic level and at the firm level. As it relates to products and services, a failure to innovate creates the likelihood that a firm's products or services will migrate toward a dark, depressing world where business is won or lost based on price. It is not a fun place to reside.

For an increasing number of companies, a major source of innovation, and therefore a major source of revenue growth, is outside their own four walls. Here we discuss supplier collaboration within the product development process and within the technology development process.

Supplier Collaboration during Product Development

One of the most powerful and likely ways to link collaboration and revenue growth is through early supplier involvement during product development. The reasons for endorsing a product development model that features supplier collaboration are clear. First, the need for continuous improvement demands new ways of doing business. For most firms, collaborating with critical suppliers during product development represents a new way of doing business. A second reason is simply due to the fact that competent suppliers usually have something of value to offer their customers, including insights about market requirements and changes, access to new technology, potentially better ways to manage cost and quality, design capabilities and engineering talent, or problem solving skills.

Third, the need to develop new products faster, better, and smarter is a trend affecting just about every industry. Achieving dramatic reductions in cycle times requires new and creative ways of doing business, including supplier collaboration and early involvement. Next, a continuing focus on outsourcing forces us to think about supplier collaboration during product development. Supplier collaboration becomes a necessity when so much of a buying company's value-add in product designs originates with external suppliers.

We must also appreciate that as product development progresses, the flexibility to make design changes decreases almost exponentially. We know that design changes become more complex and costly as a new product moves through the product development stages. Supplier involvement at early stages of development can bring competent suppliers to the design table early so that better designs emerge. Design decisions made early in the process lock in a large portion of total product costs, so it is important to get the right design. The reasons for involving suppliers early during product development are compelling.

Identifying early involvement supplier candidates: The decision about which suppliers to involve is a crucial one. A number of questions should be asked, including during supplier evaluation and selection, when there is a possibility of involving a supplier during product development. What are the supplier's design and engineering capabilities? Is the supplier's design software and platform compatible with your systems? Does the supplier have experience taking on design responsibilities? Is the supplier willing to commit resources specific to your development needs? Will the supplier safeguard proprietary information? While this is not a complete list of questions, we think you get the idea.

Levels of supplier design involvement: Supplier design support during product development is best viewed along a continuum rather than as a yes or no kind of activity—yes it occurs or no it does not. Four levels of design involvement can occur during product development. These levels include:

1. No design involvement—the supplier adheres to buyer-provided design specifications with no supplier input into the design.
2. White box design involvement—the buyer informally consults with the supplier about design issues.
3. Gray box design involvement—the supplier assumes greater design responsibility, frequently working jointly with members of a buyer's product development team.
4. Black box design involvement—the supplier has total responsibility for specific parts of a product's design.

Research findings are clear that supplier involvement that occurs earlier rather than later in the development process translates into better performance results and that development projects that rely on suppliers for a greater role, such as required for gray and black box design, achieve greater performance outcomes compared with limited design responsibility.

Next level practices: We have known for some time that certain practices correlate highly with effective supplier involvement during product development. Successful firms follow a formalized process to identify purchased items that would benefit from supplier involvement. They also rely more extensively on cross-functional teams for supplier selection as well as the planning of involvement efforts while using the same suppliers for design and full volume production.

More successful companies also make suppliers formal project team members, emphasize more extensive cross-functional and inter-company communication during projects, and are more likely to collocate supplier personnel with buying company personnel during the development project. Finally, companies that successfully collaborate with suppliers during product development are more likely to pursue formal trust development efforts with suppliers, share technology, and conduct joint education and training. Understanding the practices that separate the best from the rest will help supply managers achieve the kinds of outcomes that support enhanced revenue growth.

Current state of procurement and supplier involvement in product development: The Hackett Group recently conducted a research project called the Procurement Value Contribution Measurement Study. Many of the findings from this study explain the state of affairs related to early procurement and supplier involvement with new product development. The following summarizes the key findings from the Hackett study:

- Nearly 60% of firms have no or low supplier involvement during new product development, indicating opportunities for future growth. Only 15% of firms feature high supplier involvement (high involvement is defined as suppliers involved in greater than 75% of all new product introductions).
- The percentage of total annual revenue attributable to early involvement is 20% for firms that involve suppliers during development.
- Nearly half of all firms have no metrics related to procurement or supplier involvement during product development.
- Cost savings achieved during product development is the most measured procurement and supplier involvement contribution area when measurement occurs. Less than 10% of firms measure the incremental revenue derived from procurement and supplier involvement during product development.
- Procurement groups are attempting to elevate their value proposition as it relates to harnessing supply markets for competitive advantage. On the negative side, the study found that most companies are struggling to develop the capabilities to achieve that level of value contribution.
- Around half of all firms have only an informal or ad hoc process for involving key stakeholders, including suppliers, during product development.
- Nearly half of all firms have no initiative in place to foster, capture, and capitalize on supply market innovation. Of those firms with no

initiative currently in place or underway, 70% plan to launch an initiative within the next three years.

- Procurement groups that are successful innovation supporters have relevant metrics, center-led organizational structures, and cross-functional processes in place.
- A lack of supplier priority to support innovation is due mainly to a lack of innovation metrics on supplier scorecards.

These results suggest that tremendous opportunities still exist for tapping into supplier innovation during product development.

Supplier Collaboration during Technology Development

The logic behind collaborating with suppliers during product development is convincing. Why wouldn't the same logic apply even before formal product development takes place? The following presents four ways to collaborate with suppliers during the development of technology that precedes new product development. (Technology is the practical application of knowledge within a particular area.) These four ways include supplier participation within a formal advanced technology development process, collaborating with suppliers when developing technology roadmaps, technology demonstration days, and supplier suggestion programs.

Advanced technology development process: It is well accepted that engaging suppliers during product development can be an effective way to capitalize on supplier innovation. Moving beyond product development, progressive firms are leveraging their supplier capabilities during the development of technology that precedes product development.

Figure 7.3 presents the advanced technology development process at a leading tier-one supplier to equipment OEMs. This company, which in many ways is more progressive than its OEM customers, recognizes clearly that technology innovation, like product development, can benefit from a defined process that builds in opportunities for supplier engagement. This company must constantly provide its customers with products that incorporate the latest and greatest features available in the marketplace. Leveraging supplier innovation is not simply a good idea at this company. It is a necessary part of the strategic planning process. Involving suppliers during the assessment phase of technology development, which occurs in advance of product development, begins to push the boundaries of supplier engagement.

Technology roadmaps: Technology roadmaps with suppliers can be a powerful way to influence the development of technology that provides future market advantages. The development of roadmaps involves sharing future product plans with the objective of encouraging supplier innovations that align with the buyer's longer-term plans. The end result is a visual map that

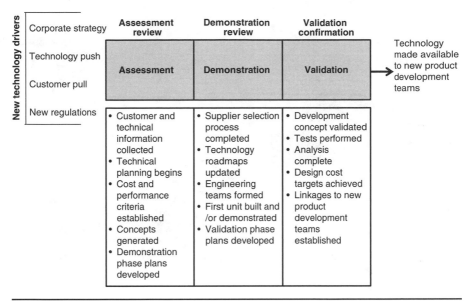

Figure 7.3   Technology development process

links supplier technology development and future product development plans. The process provides an opportunity to influence a supplier's technology investment. Figure 7.4 illustrates the idea of a technology roadmap.

While many professionals understand the concept of technology roadmaps, the reality is they are usually created on an ad hoc basis rather than as part of a strategic planning process. In our experience, roadmaps are usually developed in high-tech industries. In reality, roadmaps have applications to just about any industry that could benefit from supplier-developed innovation and technology.

Technology demonstration days: As companies reduce the size of their supply base and negotiate longer-term agreements with this smaller set, an unintended consequence sometimes emerges. This consequence becomes even more pronounced as supply organizations enter into strategic alliances with select suppliers. What is that unintended consequence? Nonincumbent suppliers, seeing their competitors essentially *lock up* a buyer's business with longer-term contracts, begin to promote their innovations elsewhere. The possibility that supplier-developed innovations bypass a company completely becomes very real.

Progressive companies respond quickly when this risk emerges. One action is to avoid single sourcing of an item unless forced to do so. This maintains some competitive tension between suppliers. A second action involves something called technology demonstration days. (One leading company calls this

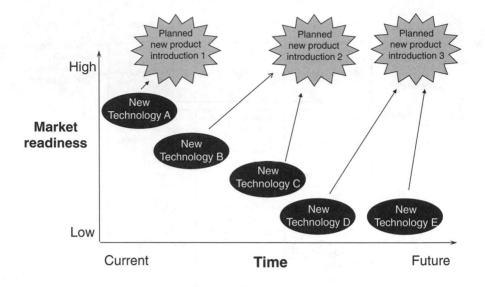

Figure 7.4   Technology roadmap

Source: Adapted from Robert J. Trent and Lew Roberts. *Managing Global Supply and Risk*, Ft. Lauderdale, FL: J. Ross Publishing, 2010.

its supplier showcase). Demonstration days represent a low-cost way to keep the door open for nonincumbent suppliers to showcase their ideas within a particular area. On a regular basis, typically quarterly, a buying organization invites suppliers to make presentations about their advancements within a particular area. This could include, for example, presentations highlighting the development of composite materials or advanced engine technology. The process allows suppliers to get into the mindspace of engineers and others who are involved with making product decisions, including future supplier selection decisions. Similar to roadmaps, this approach is used most often in industries that feature rapid rates of technological change. This does not have to be the case, however. It is a logical approach for opening the door to supplier innovation.

Supplier challenges: Another approach involves identifying specific opportunities where the buying company is looking for innovation, problem solving, or simply continuous improvement. A group of suppliers are introduced to a specific challenge and then asked to respond with a proposed solution. A company that uses this technique regularly had a need, for example, to improve its packaging process. It assembled five suppliers and issued a specific packaging

Table 7.2 Supplier suggestion program best practices

Supplier suggestion program best practices
• Supplier suggestions are submitted using web-based technology and receive a tracking number. • The buying company shows a willingness to commit resources to evaluate supplier suggestions, including appointing a program manager or steering committee to oversee the process. • Engineering resources are available to evaluate the technical merits of suggestions. • Next-level supply organizations link supplier suggestions and the sharing of rewards, leading to greater involvement with the program. • Finance validates savings realized from suggestions. • Supply organizations track the suggestions they receive from suppliers, respond to suggestions in an agreed-upon time frame, and report to executive managers any savings achieved through the system. • The supplier suggestion system serves as a central repository for all ideas received from suppliers.

challenge. The opportunity to win new business usually drives the competitive spirit of suppliers.

Supplier suggestion programs: Few supply organizations have a supplier suggestion program in place. This is surprising since these programs can be one of the most effective ways to be the benefactor of supplier ideas, many of which relate directly to technological innovation that leads to revenue enhancement. The time has come for most firms to put a supplier suggestion program in place. Table 7.2 summarizes a set of best practices that relate to supplier suggestion programs.

Linking Supplier Collaboration and Revenue Growth

The remainder of this chapter presents details about how two leading companies are creating direct linkages between supplier collaboration and revenue growth.

Supplier Collaboration Helps Respironics Breathe Easier[4]

Respironics is a billion dollar medical devices company located outside Pittsburgh. The company, founded in 1976 and purchased by Philips in late 2007, has a product mix that includes devices for the diagnosis and treatment of sleep apnea, including continuous positive airway pressure (CPAP) and bi-level machines; oxygen concentrators for patients requiring supplemental oxygen; apnea monitors for infants at risk of SIDS; asthma treatment solutions;

and hospital ventilators. Innovation and a strong new product pipeline are critical for continued market success since 30 to 50% of revenue at Respironics comes from what the company classifies as new products.

After the purchase of a major competitor, executive leaders concluded the time had arrived to transform purchasing into a strategic contributor. The legacy model of procurement at Respironics resembled what we see at most companies—tactically and transaction-focused activities, not a highly regarded group, and a reactive participant during product development. A senior procurement leader was tasked with transforming purchasing into a strategic sourcing organization. As part of his strategic review, he determined that procurement and tier-one suppliers needed to play an active role during product development.

Market forces were at work that supported the need for a different approach to supply management. Not surprisingly, product life cycles were shortening, which is a critical issue at a company where revenue growth is a function of new product success. The time between the introduction of next-generation CPAP products, for example, declined from five to three years. Other product lines experienced similar declines, making time compression a major driver behind the push for new ways to deliver value to the company. And let's not forget about the continuous need for cost reductions and quality improvements. An evolving set of competitive challenges demand new ways of doing business.

A new sourcing organization emerges: Suppliers provide a great deal of value-add to Respironics products, yet the company historically failed to leverage their capabilities. It became evident the company needed a sourcing organization that was fully integrated with suppliers and the product development process. Achieving this integration required two important elements—suppliers with a willingness to engage early in the product development process and supply professionals who understood technical issues and how to work collaboratively with suppliers. While the first element was readily available, the right people were not.

Respironics created a technical procurement group and staffed it with engineers recruited from suppliers that were not part of the company's supply base. (Chapter 6 addresses talent acquisition strategies.) The new strategic sourcing group, staffed with just over 50 professionals, includes technical people who arrived at Respironics with minimal commercial experience. They are physically located with product development groups. While this was happening, tactical purchasing responsibilities were being shifted to the manufacturing group, creating a separation of strategic and tactical responsibilities. (Chapter 5 discussed this important topic.)

It was essential to place the right people into the supply organization, which required more time than first anticipated. It was also essential to create an organization that could act as the interface between suppliers and development personnel. Building, staffing, and training this organization required about five years to arrive at a point where the strategic sourcing model reached a steady state.

Getting this organization up and running required an extensive selling effort to convince internal participants that the sourcing group could add value to the product development process. Not surprisingly, the legacy of the purchasing group created barriers to early involvement. This is a common theme as procurement groups shift from a focus on functional excellence to becoming a contributor at the highest organizational levels. This shift is often a gradual one.

Collaborating with suppliers during product development: Respironics pursued many of the things that are common to most supply transformations. A supplier reduction initiative resulted in 30 suppliers, for example, receiving nearly 85% of the company's direct purchase dollars of $500 million annually. Supplier switching has become much less common as the remaining suppliers become longer-term members of the supply base. While the company dual sources some of its requirements, this is more for risk management purposes than creating competitive tension between suppliers.

Like most leading companies, Respironics has a product commercialization process with stage or phase gates. At any given time, four to six suppliers are actively involved with a product development project. Once a project proceeds past the concept phase, the sourcing group and suppliers become actively involved (Phase II of development). While supplier involvement during product development has become commonplace, involvement with technology development is not. The sourcing group does create sourcing plans that identify the kinds of technology a design team will need.

Respironics now relies on open-book costing with suppliers during product development, which has eliminated the need for competitive contract bidding. The company focuses on collaboratively managing cost drivers with suppliers rather than relying on negotiations to arrive at a price. Product cost goals are conveyed to suppliers at the start of a development project.

The involvement process has certain important characteristics. First, design support is part of the supplier's cost to serve Respironics. Second, suppliers that provide design support are also responsible for providing items during full-scale production, although Respironics has at times used suppliers that provide only design support. Third, contractual provisions are in place to share savings on a 50/50 basis if a supplier has made an investment that results in direct cost savings. Fourth, strategic suppliers (and they are identified as such) cannot work with competitors, providing Respironics with some level of exclusivity.

Linking supplier collaboration to market success: Sourcing leaders are adamant that supplier involvement has helped improve and differentiate Respironics products in the marketplace. Take, for example, the CPAP product line, which is a major product platform with six variations. A product like CPAP has around 25-30 items sourced from tier-one suppliers. This is misleading since a single item, such as a printed circuit board, may have 75 unique parts. Many suppliers provide assemblies and subsystems rather than single components.

Besides shorter product life cycles, CPAP products are migrating toward the greater use of electronic controls and software, areas that are not part of the company's core capabilities. By working with suppliers on the current generation of CPAP products, Respironics created a product design with 20% fewer parts compared with previous models. This has contributed to a 20% product cost reduction and higher quality levels. Let's not ever discount the importance of quality in medical devices equipment.

The majority of the CPAP part count reduction came out of mechanical areas, such as the humidifier, and plastics. Collaboration with suppliers was instrumental in reducing the part count. A key supplier, working closely with Respironics engineers, helped create a better humidifier design by providing specific ideas that affected the new design. The same is true of the primary CPAP plastics supplier.

CPAP product development cycle time has declined by nearly 12 months compared with earlier development projects. Collaborating with suppliers during product development is cited as a major contribution to this decline. Early involvement has made this important product category more competitive in the marketplace.

Future directions: Reaching a mature state does not mean reaching an end state. Supply leaders recognize that continuous improvement opportunities are always present, and improvements with supplier collaboration are no exception. This includes:

- Seeing even more supplier innovation working its way into product designs
- Sharing of information increases with suppliers compared with what occurs today
- Developing technology roadmaps collaboratively with suppliers, which is something that does not yet happen routinely
- Formalizing total cost models
- Increasing supplier collaboration in new business units where early involvement is not mature or in those units that do not launch many new products

Supplier involvement during product development is largely an institutionalized process at Respironics. In fact, sourcing leaders say it is difficult to tell the difference between internal company designers and supplier personnel when they work onsite. What started as a vision has become a reality that contributes directly to company success. Achieving this vision did not come easily, and it did not come quickly. But through hard work, a commitment of resources, and a strong dose of executive support, it did become a reality.

Growing Revenue through a Collaborative Supply Model

Whenever we write about major supply initiatives that involve serious transformations, we mention the important role that executive leaders play. This statement is so obvious that when we make it, we deserve an eye roll similar to the ones you might receive from your teenagers. Does anyone really doubt that any higher level initiatives, including those that link supply management to revenue growth, can succeed without executive support and leadership? These are not grass roots initiatives that rise up from the depths of an organization. They are the result of a well-thought out strategic plan.

This case highlights a Fortune 500 consumer products company whose supply leadership, as well as its CEO, came to recognize something very important.[5] In order to support the corporate objective of growing top-line revenues, including growth through the faster introduction of new products, drastic changes would be required regarding how this company worked with its suppliers. A supply model that stresses cost reductions would not support early supplier involvement and revenue growth. This case explains the work required to achieve a major transformation that features a collaborative buyer-seller model characterized by open sharing of information and resources. This new model, while not necessarily technical or complicated, did require a major mindset change.

As mentioned, the need to grow top-line revenue forced a discussion about how to better leverage supplier capabilities. Another factor that caused a review of the supply model was a need to accelerate product development cycle times, something that is common to most companies. Finally, a move into a product line away from this company's core business caused a rethink of the product development and supplier involvement process. Fortunately, the vice president of purchasing (we will refer to him as the chief procurement officer [CPO] in this case) was a member of this company's new products committee, a position that allowed him to gain product insights at the concept stage of product development.

A transformation takes shape: Besides the corporate drivers that caused a rethinking of this company's supply management model, several other factors supported a change. First, new personnel began to work for the company, which supported new ways of thinking. Second, senior leadership was impressed by the open architecture approach taken at Procter & Gamble (P&G). The transformation at P&G, including an extensive reliance on suppliers as a source of innovation, received a great deal of press.

Transforming this company's supply culture required more than encouraging words from the CPO. The CPO engaged the head of research and development (R&D) to identify ways to improve the innovation process. The conversation quickly centered on involving suppliers early and extensively during the innovation process. Based on insight and experience, the CPO and the head of R&D identified five suppliers they believed would be critical to the development of an innovative new product. The decision was made to work with existing suppliers since they were more likely to collaborate with the company compared with new suppliers. The selected set of suppliers included a packaging supplier, three components suppliers, and a supplier who was expert in the creative product development process.

The process to identify these suppliers took less than two weeks. This is the advantage of maintaining a supply base that is relatively stable and not excessively large. Do not underestimate the value of having a deep understanding of supplier capabilities, something that is difficult to do when a supply organization maintains 5000 suppliers.

It became obvious that changing a supply model that existed for many years would require intensive selling with suppliers. The CPO and the head of R&D concluded it would be necessary to visit senior executives and explain face-to-face the benefits of a more collaborative buyer-seller relationship. As the CPO maintains, "When senior executives get involved, the focus on a project intensifies." The head of R&D and the CPO traveled to each supplier and met with the CEO. At these meetings, it became clear these executives were anxious to become involved with a new supply model and a product development project that showed growth potential.

A key difference that needed to be explained to supplier executives involved the degree of information sharing that would now occur. In the past, the CPO was not allowed to share market research and product information with suppliers. Open sharing of information would become the norm rather than the exception, including proprietary market research data that was rarely shared in the past.

An important part of this executive-to-executive process involved the development of guiding principles along with the identification of strategic initiatives that would *move the needle* at each company. There was also a need to develop a solid understanding of day-to-day requirements. While strategy is great, execution is crucial. Cross-functional teams that included representatives from procurement and R&D developed a cross-company, stage-gate process that would be followed during product development. The team presented this process to the buying company's CEO and CPO for approval. In fact, the CEO received regular progress updates during the development of the initial product developed under this new approach.

The CPO of the buying company explains the new process this way:

> When purchasing and R&D sit together in front of a supplier,
> the supplier is much more willing to commit their own research

resources to a project. They see that if they are successful with another company's R&D then they will be rewarded with business. Their success is tied to a tangible product and not the changing whims of a buyer. When you add top executives into the fray, both companies get focused on the top priorities, and execution improves. If you are investing, then I will invest too. Let's make this happen, so both companies grow and profit. Let's also disengage quickly if the product is not successful and minimize costs.

The buying company was asking suppliers to make investments that possibly would not show a positive return. Shared investment, shared risk, and shared reward formed the basis of this new model.

The supplier's view: Suppliers can be skeptical when dealing with their customers. They rightfully question if what they have been asked to work on is still an active or hot project for a company. Buyers want to keep suppliers working on things because the project may start up again, and their responsibility is to have the supply base ready. This skepticism begins to change when a supplier's executives understand each party's involvement and risks. Procurement's role is to facilitate these discussions efficiently with the right information and with the right people. Central to success is talking openly with suppliers and building trust. There has to be a belief that collaboration has real value.

During the face-to-face meetings, all five suppliers agreed with the idea of pursuing a collaborative supply model. When offered the opportunity to see marketing concepts, product concepts, and consumer research in early stages, they quickly accepted the offer. One of the suppliers even placed its R&D people on-site at the buying company. These suppliers understand the need to add value to their customers and to pursue partnerships with leading brand owners. They also saw an opportunity to learn more about how a major consumer products company goes to market while gaining insight into how to better serve a key customer. Making the business case for a collaborative model with suppliers was relatively easy.

Key features of a collaborative approach: This new, collaborative approach with suppliers is characterized by certain features, including:

- Executive-to-executive engagement between senior leaders of both companies
- A commitment to invest in new and profitable business opportunities with project portfolios approved by the leaders of both companies
- Shared risk and reward during product development—the parties must be willing to accept project failures with the expectation of being rewarded for appropriate risk-taking when projects succeed
- A sharing of resources, including working in each others' laboratories
- A point-to-point communications model featuring direct linkages between functional groups across the two companies—better ways to

communicate accelerate decision making time and streamline the product development process.

- A simplified product development process that coincided with the supply transformation
- Joint setting of project priorities between companies
- Product development efforts that focus on a few rather than many projects simultaneously
- A commitment by the parties to meet physically to review progress with locations shifting between the supplier and the customer—this helped drive a cultural change away from *not invented here*
- A supplier recognition program that includes a new metric that relates to supplier innovation
- A commitment to share new concepts and business opportunities in defined product categories with each other first (the parties have the right of first refusal)
- Conducting one to two new business meetings per year to continue to fill the project pipeline

Lessons and benefits: A major lesson learned is not to underestimate the time and resources required to transform a relationship model with key suppliers. Transformation does not happen overnight, and many supply organizations must overcome decades of legacy behavior.

The advantages of this new supply model are varied, including the development of a common language within a company and with key suppliers. Furthermore, this new model enables the best use of corporate resources, resulting in higher margins, reduced time to market, and reduced costs due to leveraging R&D capabilities. Another benefit is that product development personnel are more likely to rely on procurement to locate external expertise. This in itself often requires a major internal transformation that can take years at many companies.

The first outcome: If the reader were asked to predict the outcome from the first try at supplier collaboration, he or she would probably predict that the new product exceeded even the most optimistic market estimates. That, however, would be incorrect. This product, for reasons that have nothing to do with supplier collaboration, was not introduced to the market. Does this mean the efforts to transform to a supply model that features supplier collaboration, engagement, and sharing of information was a waste of time?

When it became obvious the product would not be launched, the CPO and the head of R&D went to each supplier to explain the situation. This helped build a foundation of trust for future collaborative efforts. While the suppliers were naturally disappointed, they also understood that not all higher level innovations make it to the marketplace.

Marketing people have a term for learning from a failure in a way that increases the probability that future projects are successful. This term is called *failing forward*. While the product did not meet its commercial objectives, the pursuit of a supply model built on open communication and trust paved the way for future projects. In the words of the head of R&D, "A collaborative approach like one featured here *electrifies* people." The foundation for collaborative relationships that will support revenue growth had been built.

Concluding Thoughts

The days of being measured by traditional performance measures are coming to an end. In reality, it is not only new revenue streams that suppliers can support. We fully expect to see supply organizations being held accountable for their ability to affect a wide range of corporate indicators, including sales and net profit, cash flow and working capital improvements, return on net assets, market share, and return on invested capital. Looking back at Figure 7.1, few groups have the potential to affect as many corporate levers as the supply group. It is time to work those many levers, particularly those that drive revenue enhancement.

Chapter Notes

1. From www.merriam-webster.com.
2. Daniel Michaels and Kathryn Kranhold. "Engine Spat Could Slow Airbus." The Wall Street Journal, July 10, 2007, A10.
3. This example is adapted from Gabriel Kahn, "Invisible Supplier Has Penney's Shirts All Buttoned Up." The Wall Street Journal, September 11, 2003, A1.
4. The authors would like to thank David Butler for his generous support during the development of this case. Mr. Butler continues to lead the sourcing transformation at Respironics.
5. The authors would like to thank Richard Kelly for his generous support during the development of this case as well as his support during the development of this chapter.

This book has free material available for download from the
Web Added Value™ resource center at *www.jrosspub.com*

8

Strategic Sourcing

The business world is populated with an overabundance of buzzwords. Some have their fleeting 15 minutes of fame while others seem to endure as overused or misused terms. Perhaps one of the most overused and misused terms in business today—and it has enjoyed that status for quite some time—is the word *strategic*. As it relates to supply management and procurement, strategic is misused in at least two respects:

1. Form over substance: Simply adding a few bells and whistles to conventional purchasing and then slapping the word strategic onto the process or the department name is not the same thing as adopting the strategic sourcing process as it is intended. (This point is made strongly in the original book *Straight to the Bottom Line®*, Rudzki et al.)

2. Dumbing down the process: Equally concerning are the companies that at one time employed a genuine strategic sourcing process but have *dumbed down* their process to be a nonstrategic, tactical ghost of what it used to be.

The second situation may in some cases be due to the temptation of quick wins that is described later in this chapter and, in other cases, due to a change of leadership that loses sight of the value of a strategic perspective.

Whom are we trying to fool? The reality is compelling: there is a huge difference in performance between world-class organizations employing strategic processes and companies stuck in conventional purchasing practices. Research studies by a variety of research and consulting firms, as noted in Chapter 1, offer quantitative proof that it not only pays to make the transformation to strategic processes, but it pays to maintain that commitment over the long-term.

This chapter approaches strategic sourcing from various perspectives. We first discuss what strategic sourcing is and what it isn't. Next, we present the success factors and pitfalls that are characteristic of the strategic sourcing process. This is followed by a discussion of some special topics that are relevant to next level strategic sourcing. We also present what a supply professional can do to sustain the discipline and commitment of strategic sourcing when under extreme pressure to deliver *quick wins*. The chapter concludes with a recap of the steps necessary for achieving the next level of strategic sourcing.

Strategic Sourcing: What It Is, What It Isn't

When presenting at conferences, one of the authors usually takes the opportunity to poll the audience on various fundamental questions, including whether they are using strategic sourcing in their companies. On a few occasions, he has had the opportunity to ask that question at two different points in the presentation: (1) early in the presentation, before strategic sourcing was defined and described, and (2) later in the presentation after a thorough description of strategic sourcing was provided.

Generally, 40 to 50% of the audience will raise their hands to the first question, indicating that they believe they are using strategic sourcing today. Less than 20% of the audience raises their hands after hearing a thorough description of strategic sourcing. Is strategic sourcing something that we think we know when we see it, but in reality we do not fully understand the concept?

Another relevant anecdote comes out of a recent conversation with a senior executive. In a revealing admission, the executive indicated that "a few months ago we didn't even realize that such a thing as strategic sourcing existed." These examples, and other examples from our collective experience, drive us to offer the following observations:

- Years after the birth of strategic sourcing, many companies of all sizes still are not aware of *true* strategic sourcing.
- A surprising number of companies believe they are using strategic sourcing but in fact are not (*form over substance* as noted earlier).
- Some companies who previously used a true strategic sourcing process have since *dumbed down* their process into a tactical ghost of what it used to be.

Trying to introduce and embed strategic sourcing without the supporting pillars of a transformation roadmap is likely to generate only short-lived benefits (see Figure 3.1).

Leading-edge companies introduce strategic sourcing as one element of a comprehensive transformation roadmap. These companies are the ones most likely to be using true strategic sourcing (and other best practices) over an extended timeframe, yielding substantial and sustainable value.

Strategic Sourcing—a Review[1]

Strategic sourcing is a fact-based, rigorous process that involves substantial internal data gathering and evaluation, as well as extensive external data gathering and interactions, in order to select the most appropriate supply strategy, identify an appropriate negotiations approach, and ultimately select the right supplier. It transforms conventional purchasing into a strategic process involving all appropriate stakeholders in a company. Properly implemented, the process can add significant value by reducing total costs relating to purchased goods and services. In our experience, the concept has expanded beyond adding value to a company's earnings via cost and revenue initiatives to include adding value in other factors affecting return on assets or return on invested capital. This can be done through improvements in payment terms and inventory programs and through enhancements in capital spending procurement and deployment. To put strategic sourcing into perspective, it is one of three critically important elements in modern procurement, which Figure 8.1 depicts.

On a daily basis, there is a need for accurate and efficient transactional execution (often now referred to as just *purchasing*). Here, the focus is on easy and cost-efficient order placement with suppliers, order follow-through and expediting (if needed), order receiving, and order payment. In a state-of-the-art company, the end user (not a purchasing professional) places the order into a system that is populated with approved suppliers and approved materials/prices using master agreements or contracts, and that system communicates directly through electronic media with the approved supplier. As opposed to

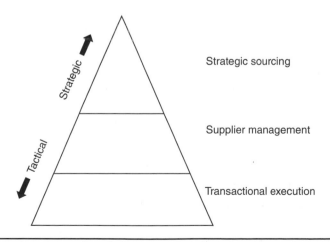

Figure 8.1   Three interrelated elements of modern procurement

Source: Robert A. Rudzki, Douglas Smock, Michael Katzorke, and Shelley Stewart Jr., *Straight to the Bottom Line*. Fort Lauderdale, FL: J. Ross Publishing, 2005.

traditional purchasing, in which the end user communicates his or her needs to someone in purchasing (phone, fax, email), and then that purchasing person communicates with the suppliers, state-of-the-art purchasing involves the direct involvement of the end user while minimizing the nonvalue-added involvement of purchasing.

On a continuous basis, there is a need for supplier management, which involves the continuous and active supervision of the supply base. This includes evaluating supplier performance against criteria agreed-to during the sourcing process's negotiations phase, discussing opportunities for mutual process improvement, and resolving conflicts. Some of these ongoing activities are tactical in nature; others are strategic.

On a periodic basis, there is a need to undertake strategic sourcing initiatives. Intensive strategic sourcing efforts often occur every three to five years for a specific spend category, with active monitoring of the supply market—and internal needs—in between those sourcing projects.

The primary objective of strategic sourcing is to make supply management a competitive differentiator for the business. This is accomplished by employing a multi-stage process to understand supply markets, understand internal needs, identify qualified suppliers interested in your business, structure the right type of relationship, negotiate an agreement, and implement and monitor that agreement. Furthermore, strategic sourcing involves leveraging the corporate spend and working closely with a small, preferred supplier base capable of achieving continuous (year-over-year) improvements in cost, quality, delivery, cycle time, technology, and service.

Traditional product standardization/substitution and volume leveraging will contribute to strategic sourcing cost reduction. However, the larger cost reduction opportunities come from a more strategic focus on opportunities to change or optimize cost components involved in satisfying the requirements. Some building blocks to identify the strategic opportunities include:

- Developing in-depth market knowledge to determine what is possible
- Obtaining end user input regarding current supply and product performance requirements
- Understanding the supplier's cost structure
- Evaluating product and/or process change options
- Optimizing freight, handling, and inventory costs
- Optimizing transaction costs
- Benefiting from additional supplier support services
- Clarifying the role of procurement in all areas of spend

Strategic Sourcing Process Map

There are different variations of the strategic sourcing process. The shortest version we have seen is five phases; the longest is 14 phases. Regardless of the number of phases in the individual design, the basic components and steps in true strategic sourcing are essentially the same. It is important to note that doing it well requires a meaningful investment in personnel and skills.

We teach and mentor clients in a six-phase strategic sourcing and negotiations management (SSNM) process (see Figure 8.2 for a high level diagram). This is an advanced program that is continually enhanced based on client experience. It is supported by a considerable toolkit as any good program or process should be. In addition, it integrates strategic sourcing, negotiations management, and supplier relationship management (SRM) best practices into one seamless process.

Companies with significant experience and success in strategic sourcing often establish separate, dedicated resources or sub-teams for the tactical activities and the strategic activities. This topic came up during our discussion of organizational design in Chapter 5. This makes sense because the objectives are different, the processes employed are different, and the skill sets are often very different. The tactical and strategic personnel can be viewed as sub-teams of an overall effort that is focused on achieving significant, breakthrough results with ongoing and active supply management, all supported by utilizing efficient processes.

Negotiations Management Is Integrated

One feature of a next level strategic sourcing process is that it incorporates a robust negotiations management process directly into the strategic sourcing methodology. While this sounds obvious, the authors are aware of at least one well-known consulting firm that uses a version of strategic sourcing that omits any process for negotiations management (strategy or execution). In the words of one of its partners, "we assume our clients know how to negotiate."

The subject of negotiations management best practices, and how it integrates with the rest of the sourcing process and supplier management process, is described in Chapter 9.

Supplier Relationship Management Is Integrated

Another feature of a next level strategic sourcing process is that it incorporates supplier relationship management processes directly into the overall strategic sourcing methodology (see Phase 6 in Figure 8.2). SRM is the foundation for the next level of cost reduction beyond a successful supplier selection effort. SRM is a disciplined approach for working collaboratively with those suppliers who are critical to the success of your organization to maximize the value available within those relationships. Many negotiated agreements fail to achieve the intended benefits for both the buyer and the seller due to a failure of one or both parties to take the appropriate steps to build a collaborative relationship that unlocks value.

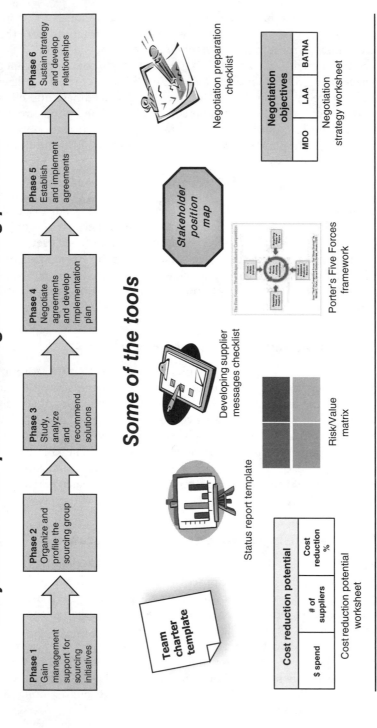

Figure 8.2   Training in strategic sourcing should include a robust process with toolkits

Source: Greybeard Advisors LLC. Copyright 2009–2010. All rights reserved.

In a worst-case situation, agreements are finalized and turned over to contract/supply managers without a detailed implementation and agreement management plan being developed prior to the agreement being finalized. On the supplier side, representatives involved in negotiations and agreement finalization often quickly shift their efforts and attention toward their next *new account potential*. In this hypothetical worst-case situation, both the buyer and the seller will likely be disappointed in the *value* achieved from their negotiated agreement.

The term *supplier partnership* is often used and in many cases misused to describe supplier relationships. True supplier partnerships require a level of information sharing, accountability for performance, and a focus on cost and value drivers for both parties that are difficult to achieve. While formal supplier partnerships are rare, there are many well-planned SRM programs, as well as supplier-driven customer relationship management programs, that have successfully moved buyers and sellers closer to maximizing the value potential of negotiated agreements. The goal should be to develop a level of collaboration and information sharing that allows the supply chain partners to function as a linked supply chain.

Well-designed SRM programs go far beyond supplier scorecards that simply measure or monitor supplier performance. Collaboration with key suppliers in identifying opportunities for both the buyer and the seller to achieve maximum value from an agreement should be the goal of SRM. Achieving this goal often involves establishing targets and measuring and monitoring the performance of both the customer and the supplier.

It is not practical for all suppliers to be enrolled in a formal SRM program. When evaluating suppliers to be included when launching a new program, it is important to focus on suppliers of critical materials, sole source suppliers, high volume suppliers, and suppliers serving multiple locations within a company. If the customer's supplier management resources are limited, it may be necessary to limit the number of suppliers included in an SRM program. In such cases, evaluation criteria (both value opportunities and risks of not managing the relationship) should be established for scoring and use in determining which suppliers should be included.

Formal SRM should always be a consideration for suppliers who compete for and ultimately win an award as a result of a major sourcing or resourcing effort. Strategic sourcing programs in many organizations include general information about their SRM programs in initial requests for information (RFI) to determine potential supplier willingness to meet the requirements of the program. Including this information in the RFI as a part of the strategic sourcing process provides valuable insight on potential suppliers' experience and willingness to participate in an ongoing SRM program. It also provides good evaluation criteria for use in supplier selection for the request for proposal

(RFP). Finally, it paves the way for enrolling new suppliers in a SRM program when implementing an agreement.

What Is NOT Strategic Sourcing

Earlier in this section, it was emphasized that an overriding objective of strategic sourcing is to select the most appropriate supply strategy. While this is vitally important, we regularly see examples of procurement professionals who confuse strategy and tactics.

There are some excellent tools and tactics available to support strategic sourcing. Tools such as reverse auctions and eRFXs are among the most well-known tools. However, these tools by themselves are not strategic sourcing; they may be enablers of a portion of a comprehensive sourcing process, but the tools themselves are not strategic sourcing.

An example of this confusion in action was a large U.S.-based company that, during the heyday of reverse auctions, ran more than 1000 reverse auctions per year. The company was proud of the fact that it forced virtually all areas of spend through a reverse auction format. A few years later, it changed its tune and was using reverse auctions more selectively as part of a strategic sourcing discipline; it realized that reverse auctions by themselves are not the right approach for every sourcing requirement. Figure 8.3 illustrates this point.

Strategic Sourcing Success Factors and Pitfalls

There are a number of critical success factors for strategic sourcing. First, strategic sourcing must be part of an overall, coordinated transformation plan as described in Part 1 of this book, particularly the leadership dimension. With that organizational support and context, strategic sourcing has a stronger chance of succeeding as an initiative and has an excellent chance of becoming

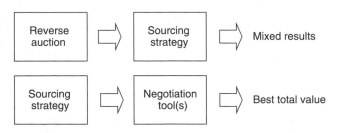

Strategy must come first and then drive tool selection to achieve best value

Figure 8.3   Sourcing strategy should determine the right tools, not vice versa

an embedded business process. Without that support and context, strategic sourcing is likely to face an uphill battle.

Strategic sourcing must also have access to cross-functional talent and resources, either through ad hoc team members borrowed from key departments and locations or, even better, through the assignment of high-potential employees to a core team role lasting two to three years. This latter idea has served companies well in terms of strengthening the sourcing process as well as providing valuable developmental experiences to employees.

A total cost of ownership (TCO) perspective is another key ingredient in successful strategic sourcing. This requires an explicit acknowledgement that *price* by itself is only one factor that needs to be considered. TCO measures all aspects of value, including price and nonprice costs, as well as other value drivers. Understanding the elements of TCO within a sourcing category is a prerequisite for determining and establishing an appropriate strategy.

Another success factor in strategic sourcing is avoiding something we call the *captive mindset*. When you self-constrain your consideration of alternatives, you have a captive mindset. A practical way to combat this condition is to form teams with personnel who understand the reasons why something has been done a certain way in the past, plus personnel who have no such historical perspective but are focused on applying the sourcing process to a *new area*. The probing questions asked by the naïve team members often create highly productive working sessions.

We cannot say enough about the importance of stakeholder involvement throughout the sourcing process. This involves identifying the key stakeholders early in the sourcing process, inviting them to play one or more roles in the sourcing effort, and regularly communicating with them as the sourcing effort proceeds. The final role of the stakeholder is often *signing off* on the negotiated results (and the associated calculation of benefits) and commissioning the implementation phase.

Beyond the role of stakeholders with specific sourcing teams, the executive officers of the company can assist by asking for periodic report-outs from teams. In particularly challenging situations, we have found it to be powerful when an executive officer assumes the role of sponsor for one or more sourcing efforts.

Another key success factor is recognizing that leverage and competitive bidding may not be the right approach to supplier selection. A collaborative approach or even an alliance may be more appropriate.

We recommend selecting sourcing team members with an eye toward who may be necessary for the implementation phase. Why is this important? The ultimate benefit from strategic sourcing comes from effective implementation. Sometimes only the commercial terms change while the supplier and materials specifications stay the same, making for an easy implementation. However, the possibility exists that all key elements change—the supplier, specifications of what is being purchased and delivered, commercial terms, and operational integration. Since this is a possibility with every sourcing effort, the authors strongly suggest selecting team members who are crucial to a successful implementation of the sourcing strategy.

Speaking with One Voice

A key component of a successful SSNM program involves training an organization to *speak with one voice*. The results of many carefully planned negotiations have been compromised as a result of uncoordinated communications with suppliers.

Simply stated, the speaking with one voice practice and expectation is for all employees within the organization to speak with one voice in all discussions or activities involving suppliers. Speaking with one voice does not necessarily mean that a single person will speak on behalf of a company. Rather, all individuals within a company will deliver consistent messages when communicating with suppliers.

While this sounds straightforward, creating a culture that understands the importance of speaking with one voice can be difficult to achieve. Suppliers have many communication channels within the companies they deal with—ranging from the executive level to engineers to the end users of their products and services. Identifying these communication channels and coordinating the messages that flow through them can be a challenge. Some critical success factors in speaking with one voice are described.

Creating awareness: All employees, including executives who communicate with suppliers in any way should be made aware of the goals and benefits of speaking with one voice. They should also understand the potential consequences of failing to do so. A key point is that any interaction with a supplier—no matter how innocent or technical it may appear to be—is in fact part of the negotiations process.

External communications planning: A detailed communication plan should be developed when initiating a sourcing effort. The plan should identify who may communicate with suppliers in any way. The list typically includes key management employees, executive sponsors, key stakeholders, team members, and in some cases end users of the products or services being sourced. The plan should include:

- What should or should not be communicated
- When information should be communicated
- Who should communicate information
- Who information should be communicated to
- How information should be communicated (i.e., letter, e-mail, phone, or in person)

Ongoing development and distribution of carefully scripted messages to be used in response to anticipated questions during each phase of the sourcing process strengthens the possibility of employees speaking with one voice. Diligence in updating a communication plan is a key success factor in all sourcing and negotiations management efforts.

Effective internal communication: Speaking with one voice strengthens a company's position in negotiations with suppliers. The absence of frequent and consistent internal communication often results in inaccurate speculation and the expression of various personal opinions that can severely damage, if not completely destroy, efforts to speak with one voice. When organizations fail to effectively communicate sourcing project status, planned next steps, and appropriate messages to be delivered in response to supplier inquiries, less than desirable things often occur. Timely and effective communication internally enhances the possibility of a company speaking with one voice.

Formal training: Formal training of individuals who interact with suppliers is critical to developing a speaking with one voice culture. Training that includes videos of role playing showing what can go wrong when individuals fail to speak with one voice, as well as examples of proper techniques to be used when corresponding with supplier representatives, can be valuable.

One of the best practices we have seen is to create a short DVD program, explaining what can happen when a company does not speak with one voice with suppliers. This is done via short scenes or vignettes, based on actual experiences. It's distributed throughout the organization with the support of top management. If you'd like to see an example of what we're talking about, go to http://www.greybeardadvisors.com/SwOVexcerpt/ to view an excerpt from one company's speaking with one voice program.

Speaking with One Voice

One of the authors recalls a challenging sourcing effort from his experience as a chief procurement officer. The supplier sales rep was arrogant, and smug when dealing with the sourcing team. The supplier rep had reason to be confident—he had contacts throughout the customer's organization: from the corporate office to plant locations, from the general manager level to the loading dock. This supplier rep was *plugged in* to the customer's organization. As a result, he knew more about the company's current activities, and near-term plans, than the sourcing team.

It took a while for the sourcing team to realize what was going on and why it was having difficulty with this supplier rep. But once it did recognize the issue, it went into action. It identified, over the course of several weeks, all of the internal contacts that the supplier rep had in his network. Then came the brilliant move: it explained to each of these fellow employees that the supplier rep was *using them* to collect information for his negotiations advantage. With that awareness created (Step 1), the sourcing team then explained the value of *speaking with one voice* (Step 2). Finally, it requested that these fellow employees abide by some simple *one voice* rules and help deliver carefully scripted messages back to the supplier. The sales rep lost his arrogance and began working constructively with the sourcing team.

Special Topics in Next Level Strategic Sourcing

This part of the chapter presents a variety of topics that are part of or related to strategic sourcing. This includes supplier recognition events, Six Sigma and strategic sourcing, the sourcing of indirect materials, the need for a strategic sourcing toolkit, cost reduction planning and tracking, and applying strategic sourcing principles to transportation and logistics.

Supplier Recognition Events

If your company has gone through the effort to strategically select suppliers, why not take the process a step further and publicly recognize the *best of the best*? Many good reasons exist in favor of supplier recognition events. Recognition events:

- Demonstrate to your supply base that you are serious about rewarding excellent performance
- Raise the bar for your entire supply base once they understand how they benefit from public recognition
- Demonstrate internally that it's not just the negotiated agreement that counts, it's how well the parties perform after the agreement that matters
- Involve your internal clients/users in assessing and actively managing the supply base
- Energize your supply base and generate a significant return on investment (ROI)
- Motivate your suppliers to compete for your recognition
- Support the development of closer buyer-seller relationships
- Create a return that far exceeds the cost of the event

This is not to say that supplier recognition events are easy or without issues. This process requires leadership, budget support, effective project management skills, and commitment from executive management. Based on experience, the recognition event usually has a long planning lead time during the first year. Furthermore, the event can subject your company to behind-the-scenes criticism if it is inconsistent with how you manage your suppliers during the year.

Your company is probably ready for a supplier recognition event if it has good data on supplier performance; agreement on the selection criteria; a belief that strategic suppliers are essential to your success; a corporate culture that recognizes employees; and a CEO who is willing to participate. Obviously, your company is probably not ready if it falls short on one or more of these conditions.

Immediately following the recognition event, your company should run a full-page color ad, naming your top suppliers, in at least one trade magazine;

communicate a press release about the top suppliers to your entire supply base; and possibly even offer to conduct a local awards ceremony at your supplier's location for the benefit of its employees. As with all activities, we need to evaluate what went well and what could be improved for the next event. Supplier recognition, when performed well, can be a valuable part of an overall transformation plan for your supply management activities.

Six Sigma and Strategic Sourcing

Are you receiving unsolicited attention from your in-house Six Sigma experts? Are they pushing to implement Six Sigma as *the process* in your supply management practices? Actually, the principles underlying Six Sigma and a robust strategic sourcing process are surprisingly similar—and once strategic sourcing is explained, it can allay the concerns of even the most strident quality fan.

A core concept behind Six Sigma is Define, Measure, Analyze, Improve, and Control (DMAIC). It was inspired by W. Edwards Deming, a founding father of the total quality movement.

Take any premier sourcing process and examine its components. It should reveal a parallel between elements of the sourcing process and the DMAIC components. A high level view appears in Figure 8.4 as an example. When you perform a deeper dive into the individual process steps, the alignment becomes even more evident.

So, any interest in supply management shown by your quality group doesn't need to be reason for concern. In fact, once they understand true strategic sourcing, quality experts can be your greatest friends in the corporate world—including volunteering to participate on teams. An in-depth discussion of Six Sigma and DMAIC as it applies to next level supply management appears in Chapter 18.

Indirect Materials and Services Opportunities

One of the striking outcomes from strategic sourcing is that the opportunities for cost reduction in indirect materials and services (nonproduct spend) are often higher than that for categories of direct spend (product spend). Often, it is possible to achieve major cost reductions in indirect spend categories if they are approached properly.

The primary reason behind the opportunities for cost reductions in indirect materials and services is because purchasing attention historically has focused on direct spend categories and has been focused there for years. Second, indirect spend management is fragmented at most companies and may even be handled by nonprocurement personnel who do not use a strategic sourcing process. Finally, the gross margin (profitability) of some indirect spend suppliers is higher than for many direct spend suppliers—allowing greater pricing flexibility in response to customer demands.

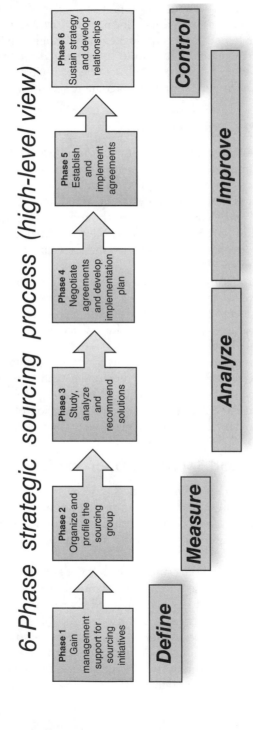

Figure 8.4 A robust strategic sourcing process is consistent with DMAIC principles

Turning the opportunities for indirect spending cost reductions into reality can be a challenge. One of the principal challenges relates to the historical *ownership* of indirect spending. Outside legal services, for example, is typically *owned* by the law department, marketing-related services is typically owned by sales and marketing, and *relocation services* is often owned by human resources.

A common pitfall that a procurement department can fall into is to aggressively go after those areas of spend and, in the process, give the impression that it is trying to undermine those areas that have been managed by other departments. As you can imagine, this can create confrontation and suspicion rather than cooperation and collaboration.

One of the best ways to handle this challenge is to recognize that while procurement processes should be involved in all areas of external spending, the role of the procurement department can vary. There are three possible roles:

1. Procurement *manages* or *owns* the category while still involving user departments in the sourcing process (example: office supplies).
2. Procurement *facilitates* the category by leading the sourcing process and sharing the decision-making responsibility with key departments/ users (example: energy procurement works with engineering and operations to collaboratively manage energy matters).
3. Procurement *supports* the category by providing sourcing process expertise to the user department. The user department provides subject matter expertise and owns the decision (example: outside legal services).

Some other challenges that cause indirect sourcing opportunities to be overlooked include:

- Accurate spend and usage data is often difficult to obtain.
- Knowledgeable and experienced resources are not available for the spend categories being targeted.
- Standards, specifications, and brand preferences vary widely from location to location within the same company.
- Indirect materials and services are perceived to be *necessities* with little opportunity for cost avoidance or cost reduction.
- Personal preferences and long-term relationships with local suppliers exist.
- For many nontraditional areas of spend, the role of procurement is not well defined.

Overcoming these challenges requires skillful data gathering and analysis, strong communication skills, product and process knowledge, market knowledge, and experienced user input. This broad range of needs can be effectively delivered by careful selection of cross-functional sourcing teams with experienced leadership. Organizations that commit to strategic sourcing teams to address indirect materials and services often achieve documented cost savings in excess of 25% from previous agreements.

Services sourcing opportunities: Service contract costs are driven primarily by wage rates and levels of service required. Many service agreements remain in place on an evergreen basis for many years without regular review. Over a period of time, service level requirements, as well as marketplace options available to satisfy the requirement, may have changed dramatically.

In addition to the building blocks to identify opportunities for indirect materials, the following should be considered for contracted services:

- Periodic analysis of skill level needs versus skill levels and corresponding wage rates being billed
- Regular review of wage rate and markup structures
- Analysis of the ratio of supervision to service provider costs versus industry standards
- Implementation of a process to carefully monitor service level needs on an ongoing basis
- Ongoing analysis of opportunities to insource or outsource as a result of changes in requirements and supply markets

The ability of individual purchasing professionals to gather and analyze the data required to carry out detailed indirect materials and services strategic sourcing efforts is frequently constrained by the time required to manage day-to-day buying requirements. Unfortunately, many indirect materials and services procurement professionals spend too much time addressing emergencies, resolving billing or payment discrepancies, or processing routine purchasing orders. These requirements can be a major roadblock to engaging in strategic activities.

Toolkits

A robust strategic sourcing process should include a healthy amount of tools, checklists, and templates for use during each phase of the strategic sourcing process. This would include frameworks for RFIs, and RFPs, as well as guidance on identifying and selecting relevant sourcing strategies, guidance for constructing an appropriate negotiation strategy and executing that strategy, guidance for constructing contracts, and guidance for ongoing supplier management. The subject of strategic sourcing toolkits is covered in Chapter 19.

Are You Making Strategic Sourcing So Complicated that No One Uses It?

A large company had invested a great deal of time and effort to create an elaborate sourcing process. There was a problem, however. No one at the company, neither the procurement professionals nor their internal clients, used this process.

Have you *audited* your own sourcing process to determine its level of adoption? Experience confirms that performing periodic process checks provides valuable, and actionable, information. Using this information can then lead to further advances in practices and improved bottom line results.

Cost Reduction Planning and Tracking

The battle for credibility of the supply management function can be won or lost in a number of areas. One of the most fundamental is the calculation, tracking, and reporting of benefits derived by using strategic sourcing and other business processes. There are some key best practices in this area:

- The calculation methodology for cost reductions, and separately for cost avoidance, needs to be established upfront, ideally with input from finance.
- For each sourcing team project, the stakeholder ultimately must agree on the proposed method of calculating benefits, as well as the estimated benefits from the new sourcing arrangement. This typically is identified in a *stakeholder signoff*.
- For each sourcing project completed, the financial office agrees with the calculation, and, ideally, they perform the calculations on behalf of the team.
- To ensure relevance to the profit and loss statement, efforts need to be made to track successes, shortfalls, market factors, and volume changes. One of the easiest ways for supply management departments to lose credibility is to report only successes. If you do that, your internal clients have no ability to track what you're reporting against their total change of costs in materials and services.
- Never add operating cost reductions to capital cost reductions and report a total cost reduction. The combined total has no relevance to the profit and loss statement.
- Ensure that budget adjustments occur so that benefits from completed projects are not diverted elsewhere.

Applying Strategic Sourcing Principles to Transportation and Logistics

Surprisingly, many companies start out with mixed feelings about applying structured sourcing processes to transportation and logistics. This is a mistake since many companies spend close to 10% of their total revenue on transportation and logistics-related activities. Anyone who believes in the value of strategic sourcing would never ignore such an important spending category. Strategic sourcing principles apply to any purchase category, not just direct materials.

Strategic sourcing proponents often encounter internal resistance that comes from fear of change, concerns about additional workload, and a lack of understanding of the underlying process. Change comes slowly in the transportation industry, and the old ways have persisted even as other areas of supply chain management have seen major shifts in business practices.

Well-run strategic sourcing projects in transportation and logistics result in significant savings and improved service. The benefits from these initiatives come in many forms, including:

- Cost reductions from reduced waste and improved pricing
- Stronger relationships based on performance and cost benefits to both parties
- An understanding of the true cost of doing business and what further improvements can be made
- Lasting tools and processes to manage spend, quality, and provider performance

How do we get these benefits? Just like with any other category, transportation and logistics sourcing projects require the right approach and knowledge to succeed.

Build consensus to ensure success: Transportation and logistics functions are often managed in stand-alone silos alongside the typical procurement and supply chain management functions. This separation often causes friction as projects span across sourcing categories and move into what was previously protected turf. For this reason, it is very important to build support at the level in the organization where the management of supply chain, procurement, and logistics comes together. With these leaders onboard, the project can proceed, and the parties involved will generally work together to reach the common goal. Many projects never get to this level of consensus, and the risk of failure is high in these situations.

Analyze the data: The first step is to gather relevant information on shipment volumes, costs, and service requirements. This data is further broken down into lane-specific information, mode of transport, commodity, business unit, and carrier name and type. Use this time to assess and streamline product flows and consolidate the network before building the sourcing event(s) and requesting proposals or quotations.

Optimize and strategize: After analyzing the data, determine an appropriate high-level strategy for each subset of transportation spend. Potential segmentation methods can include category of service, modes of transport, divisions of the business, or other stratifications (see Figure 8.5). Be sure to aggregate complementary services and transportation lanes. Note that some categories may not be appropriate for strategic sourcing.

Where appropriate, develop multimodal strategies (e.g., rail, truck, barge, intermodal) for strategic rate negotiations and to allow for flexibility in dispatch decisions. A good transportation sourcing strategy takes into account organizational structure, the geographical and modal scope of the project, project resource requirements, and related spend categories. It also features clear goals for pricing and service improvement, consolidation, and efficiency gains.

Look for related opportunities: Be sure to include vendor-paid freight and private fleet lanes in any analysis. Coordinating transportation and materials procurement strategies and contracting activities yields the best overall results. Best of breed strategic sourcing initiatives consider delivered cost and maximize opportunities to collect pricing for bundled and un-bundled services. Without this, it is difficult to assess the competitiveness of the collected pricing for materials or freight.

Category	Segments
Transportation Modes	Ocean
	Air
	Rail
	Truckload
	LTL
	Intermodal
	Drayage
	Parcel
	Special moves
	Other
Locations	Divisions and sites
	Commodities
	Geography
	Global
	NAFTA
	US
	Lane-specific
Services	3PL, 4PL, and related services
	Freight audit and payment

Figure 8.5 Potential segmentation methods for transportation and logistics
Source: Greybeard Advisors LLC. Copyright 2005–2010. All rights reserved.

Build sourcing processes that work well for everyone: Transportation and logistics providers need highly detailed operational information to price services effectively. It is important to share details about the commodities you intend to ship and store. Spend time working with experts in the organization to identify all necessary parameters. Relevant categories of information can include:

- Commodities and characteristics such as weights and densities
- Average shipment sizes
- Origins and destinations by 5-digit zip code or address
- Transport and warehouse equipment and service requirements
- Pickup and delivery site information
- Special handling requirements

Be sure to request pricing in forms that can be properly applied, audited, and invoiced. While pricing can be set in many creative ways, most transportation pricing is calculated based on a combination of the cubic volume, weight, and distance moved. Ensure that the pricing structure selected can be implemented by you, your carriers, and your freight audit and payment service.

Create lasting value: After the primary sourcing effort is completed, develop tools to drive and track compliance to preferred routing instructions. The project may be done and recommendations made, but implementation is the only way to realize actual savings. To ensure lasting results, create routing guides, build compliance management processes, and develop systems that reward good decisions. While it is tempting to discount this part, routing and compliance reporting tools are important deliverables from any transportation and logistics sourcing project.

Freight audit and payment is another piece that can add significant value (or difficulty) to the process. Outside freight audit and payment services can help collect detailed transportation data, ensure that the proper pricing is applied to shipments, and help facilitate transfers of funds to large numbers of providers. The best freight audit and payment providers can also develop detailed compliance reports, build and implement routing guides, and provide platforms to simplify tracking and tracing.

Transportation and logistics is an important area of spend. Using the right tools, skills, and providers with specialized knowledge is the best way to achieve success in this category. The benefits can be large and often go far beyond just reductions in cost.

A Next Level Idea

A major U.S.-based corporation took the idea of strategic sourcing to the next level. It developed—and coordinated—materials strategies involving incoming raw materials sourcing, transportation strategies for outgoing product shipments, and cross-modal transportation options. By leveraging not just cross-modal options within the realm of transportation, but also the materials sourcing options, it created exceptional results in both areas. Prior to that, it had done what most companies do: sourced each area independently.

Pressure to Deliver Quick Wins

What can you do to sustain the discipline and commitment to strategic sourcing if you are under extreme pressure at your company to deliver *quick wins*? It can be tempting to shorten the time horizon and turn your team's attention to projects that can generate results in the immediate future: these are the so-called quick wins. When the economy weakens, the CFO and other senior colleagues will often look to the chief procurement officer (CPO) to pull some rabbits out of the hat—quickly. The immediate temptation is to redirect your entire team's attention away from their current plans (presumably including a comprehensive list of true strategic initiatives) to focus on generating some fast results.

Something we have noticed during the recent economic downturn is a temptation to revert to adversarial relationships with suppliers. After all, what quicker way is there to save costs than to place this burden on suppliers? Unfortunately, *quick wins* return only a fraction of what can be achieved with a strong strategic sourcing process. The returns are rarely long lasting.

If you find yourself going down the quick win path, this is the reality: Speaking from extensive experience, there are some classic and powerful quick wins that any good CPO should have in mind during a tough business environment. That isn't the real challenge. The real challenge is to find ways to continue making steady progress on the strategic initiatives and, at the same time, deliver quick wins.

In our experience, the best approach is to build a hybrid, explicit plan comprised of quick wins and strategic projects. The quick wins—if chosen properly—can generate the short-term *fix* that everyone seeks. They can also help fund the strategic initiatives that offer the greatest long-term, sustainable value to your organization. Figure 8.6 illustrates this point.

- Strategic cost and working capital initiatives create significant, sustainable and long-term value. They also require an investment (time and resources) to do properly, which can be challenging in tough business environments

- Quick wins can serve two purposes: *feed the monster* with short-term results and create a self-funding mechanism to support strategic initiatives

- A typical profile would look something like this:

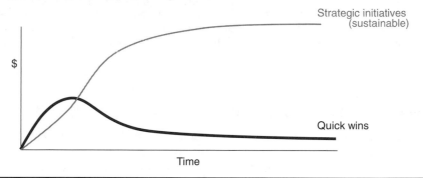

Figure 8.6   In a tough business environment, it is essential to retain focus on strategic initiatives while pursuing quick wins

Source: Greybeard Advisors LLC. Copyright 2009–2010. All rights reserved.

Next Steps in Strategic Sourcing

Let's examine five categories in the use or limited use of strategic sourcing. We'll offer suggestions for companies in each category.

Category I: Strategic Sourcing—What Is That?

Years after the birth of strategic sourcing as a business process, a majority of companies are still not aware of strategic sourcing. If your company is in this category, it is leaving significant value on the table. Also, you are trying to do the job of supply management without a full set of techniques at your disposal—a sure prescription for personal and professional frustration. There are some productive actions that you can take to get your supply organization up-to-speed quickly on what real strategic sourcing is all about. Chapter 13 of the book *Straight to the Bottom Line®* identifies a range of actions that can be taken. Also, refer back to the section *Strategic Sourcing—A Review* to identify the kinds of factors that make strategic sourcing possible. The first step is to develop awareness of the potential strategic sourcing may offer your company. This requires a leader with a vision that can be communicated across the company. Strategic sourcing also requires an organization that is comfortable with centralized or centrally led decision making.

Category II: Bells and Whistles, but Not Strategic Sourcing

In audience polls at conferences, we have confirmed that a surprising number of companies think they are using strategic sourcing, but when we probe further, it is clear they are not doing much more than adding a few bells and whistles to conventional purchasing. The confusion can arise from several different directions: a common error is a belief that doing certain activities, like reverse auctions, is the same thing as strategic sourcing. While reverse auctions, and other tools like eRFXs, can play an important role in enabling certain elements of strategic sourcing, they do not constitute strategic sourcing by themselves.

Companies in this category are also leaving value on the table. An important action here is to arrange for a candid assessment of procurement processes compared to best practices. The resulting gap analysis will provide input to two important deliverables: an opportunity assessment (the financial impact possible by addressing the gaps) and a detailed roadmap for transforming into a world-class performer.

Category III: Dumbed Down Sourcing or Quick Win Purchasing

Some companies that previously used a robust version of strategic sourcing have *dumbed down* their process into a tactical ghost of what it used to be. In some cases, this situation is due to the pressure to accomplish quick wins in a tough business environment. (Some companies seem to have a chronic preference for *quick win purchasing* regardless of the business environment.)

As with the other two categories, companies here are leaving value on the table. If your company falls into this category, an action you can take is to examine why you've strayed from the process your company had been using—and try to address the root cause. If the motivator was pressure from executive management to achieve quick wins, then develop a hybrid plan comprised of quick win projects and strategic sourcing projects.

As outlined earlier, it can be productive to build a hybrid, explicit plan comprised of quick wins and strategic sourcing projects. These wins—if selected properly—can generate the short-term *fix* or *relief* mandated by executive management. They can also help fund the strategic initiatives that offer longer term, sustainable value. No senior executive will knowingly discontinue projects that have clear, strategic value. The key is to lay out a plan with specific projects—and savings projections—for quick wins and strategic initiatives. Most CEOs and CFOs respond well to business cases that feature positive, compelling ROI.

Category IV: Stand-alone Strategic Sourcing

Companies have tried to introduce and embed strategic sourcing without the supporting pillars of a transformation roadmap—and as a result, have usually had a difficult experience. Leading-edge companies introduce strategic sourcing as one element of a comprehensive transformation roadmap. That point is well made in this quote attributed to the Institute for Supply Management: "Without real procurement transformation, only 60% of the value of procurement initiatives are retained by year two. This value drops by 10% for each subsequent year."

If your company is in this category, like the previous categories, it is not maximizing the value available from strategic sourcing. For background on the essentials of the transformation process, refer back to Part 1 of this book. Do not underestimate the importance of the transformation process.

Category V: Doing It Well but Need to Re-energize

Without question, there are companies that have done all of the things we advocate and have been staying the course for an extended period. The original excitement may be diminishing as the sourcing and transformation process has matured, and the enthusiasm associated with early successes is giving way to an almost-predictable pace of new and perhaps diminishing results. How does your organization maintain its intensity? How does it re-energize everyone? Here are a few ideas to consider from a long list of possibilities:

- Rotate category sourcing and contract management assignments among personnel at least every three years (provides opportunities for *fresh looks and new perspectives*)
- Make a visible commitment to talent management, including a minimum 40 hours of training per person per year
- Institute an internal certification for demonstrated strategic negotiations expertise (e.g., a certified negotiator program)
- Expand involvement of technical experts and end users as sourcing team members
- Develop and implement a supplier management program to drive continuous improvement and measure performance
- Implement a supplier recognition and reward program as well as a supplier suggestion program
- Implement a recognition and reward program for key stakeholders who demonstrate cost reduction innovation or contribute ideas to be explored

- Encourage ongoing development of market knowledge for high volume spends or critical materials, to be formally updated at least every two years
- Encourage, on an annual basis, the nomination of a specific number of products or services to be evaluated for potential outsourcing or insourcing based on changes in internal capabilities or external markets
- Continue to set aggressive supply base improvement targets that are reported to executive management.

Concluding Thoughts

Perhaps the most important part of strategic sourcing involves the need to communicate internally and externally the objectives of this process. Developers will say the key to real estate success is *location, location, location.* Perhaps the key to successful strategic sourcing is *communicate, communicate, communicate.*

Supply organizations should take a cue from our friends in sales, marketing, and advertising. How much is spent trying to persuade your internal customers to take the action you suggest? To be truly effective communicators, we must understand our internal customer's *buy motive* and be sensitive to company culture. Communication gets complicated in a hurry when there are different business units to support. It gets even more complicated when communicating with personnel from different functional groups located in different geographic locations. Strategic sourcing can be a great thing. Having internal participants who buy-in to the outcomes of the strategic sourcing process is even better. That means stressing the importance of effective communication.

Chapter Notes

1. Adapted and updated from Robert A. Rudzki, Douglas Smock, Michael Katzorke, and Shelley Stewart Jr., *Straight to the Bottom Line®* (Fort Lauderdale, FL: J. Ross Publishing, 2005).
2. The authors acknowledge the important contributions of Jim Baehr, Ron Casbon and Jon Gilbert to this chapter.

This book has free material available for download from the
Web Added Value™ resource center at *www.jrosspub.com*

9

Negotiation Management Best Practices

Negotiations are a way of life. We negotiate from the time we wake up in the morning to the end of the day when we retire. Negotiation comes in many forms. Some negotiations we don't think much about. In fact, it's probable that we don't see what we are doing as negotiating. These negotiations tend to be instinctive. Among families and friends, matters as simple as deciding what to have for dinner or what movie to see typically require some level of innate negotiation. There may be some preparation, such as searching the web for restaurant menus or checking the theater listings, but not much more.

For procurement professionals, negotiations are frequently tactical,[1] made or carried out with only a limited or immediate end in view. A requisition becomes an inquiry for a price. The supplier gives you a price. If you don't like the price, you go back and forth until reaching agreement. These bargaining events are, for the most part, tactical or impromptu. For basic purchases, this course of action works and can produce acceptable results.

When pursuing a comprehensive sourcing opportunity, where the stakes are high in the form of cost, process, and risk, then negotiations take on the next level of significance. Handled deliberately and thoughtfully, the negotiators can deliver improved value for their stakeholders. These types of negotiations are regarded as strategic.

There are many good books on negotiation. *Bargaining for Advantage* by G. Richard Shell provides insights on ways in which we conduct ourselves, as individuals, when negotiating.[2] In *3-D Negotiations* by David A. Lax and James K. Sebenius, we are introduced to tools that, when applied, enable negotiators to move beyond relying solely on tactics.[3] In *Getting to Yes*, Roger Fisher and William Ury offer methods for dealing with conflict resolution that can make a real difference if applied to disputes that arise during negotiation.[4] If you expect to negotiate often, you would benefit greatly by taking some time to study the differences between positional bargaining and integrative bargaining (from *Getting to Yes*).

This chapter addresses two distinct phases of negotiation. These include preparation (planning) and execution (negotiating). Along the way, we will point out some insights and best practices from experience and research.

Preparation

Preparation is the process of devising methods to achieve a desired end. (We use the terms preparation and planning interchangeably.) Out of necessity, we are often called on to make decisions with limited information. Emergencies, threats, and confrontations require that we rely on experience and instinct to arrive at swift resolutions to immediate challenges. Bargaining is a similar action. The term bargaining implies that an event is transactional in nature and is based on a position or power. Preparation isn't fundamental to the activity. The previous example of a buyer trying to agree on a price with a supplier can be looked at as bargaining. Conversely, negotiations are more likely to be strategic.

It is an old axiom that *good negotiators are made, not born*. It's also widely held that negotiation is integral to good decision making and that decisions result in outcomes and that outcomes generate impact, as illustrated in Figure 9.1.

How can a negotiator become good at making the decisions that drive outcomes and impacts? Decision making in the context of negotiations requires preparation, information, and a plan. It's reasonable to state that negotiators who are well prepared will be the negotiators that have the ability to lead and manage the negotiations process. We are expected to be well prepared before entering into negotiations that are strategic.

In order to develop a framework for preparation, it is possible to draw on the distinction that is commonly made about negotiation. Negotiation is either distributive (i.e., competitive), in character with win-lose outcomes, or it is an integrative, problem-solving process leading to win-win results.[5] What follows in this chapter is directed to integrative negotiations for the purpose of delivering strategic outcomes.

Figure 9.1 The linkage between negotiations and impacts

Management of Negotiations Starts with Preparation

Consider the following scenario. The exterior of your house needs painting. You bring in professionals to tell you what they can do and when. Painter A tells you that the job can be done in a few days—just a few quick coats and your house will look great. Painter B tells you it will take a few weeks to do the job. He explains that to do a job that looks good and lasts will take time. This involves planning the job, selecting a paint that's appropriate for the environment, scraping, sanding, repairing, and priming the surfaces. "If I don't do all of this, the job will look good for a while, but it won't last," says Painter B.

Negotiations are much the same. To be effective at negotiations and to deliver outcomes that will last (are strategic) requires preparation and the added dimension of management. As described throughout this chapter, the development of a negotiations strategy is dependent on facts and findings. This information is the product of the diligence associated with following the processes laid out in Phase 3 of the strategic sourcing and negotiation management (SSNM) process presented in Chapter 8. Phase 4 of the SSNM process details the steps for managing negotiations. Preparation, homework, and planning must precede negotiations.

Internal and External Data Gathering

The first measure of preparation is to gather requirements. Gathering business requirements seems easy enough to do, but is it? Knowing who wants what, how many, and when is important, but really knowing the business requirements is becoming more important. This is what attracts attention at senior management levels.

Identifying, developing, and acting on business requirements is essential for procurement groups that want to be accepted as a strategic resource rather than just another corporate function. The strategic sourcing process relies on the ability of procurement professionals to engage all areas of the business to understand what is happening when, how, and, most importantly why. Procurement professionals who demonstrate awareness to business requirements typically earn the confidence of senior management and are viewed as a valued resource by their colleagues.

Understanding what business requirements are: Business requirements are the needs of the stakeholders within a company. At the highest level, business requirements complement the strategies of a company. At the user level, they become more specific and must be identified to ensure that the requirements can be addressed based on timelines, resources, market conditions, and budgets. Meeting and exceeding business requirements directly affects the ability of a company to deliver on its strategies.

How to develop business requirements: For procurement professionals to be effective at developing business requirements, they must follow the processes that are embedded in strategic sourcing. By applying a disciplined, cross-functional course of action, they can verify the needs of the business. Teaming, interviewing, and listening are all essential to defining requirements.

How and when to use business requirements: Business requirements become the basis for a sourcing strategy as well as a major part of the total cost of ownership assessment. Business requirements are written into requests for proposals, typically as a *scope of work*, and must be addressed by suppliers to satisfy stakeholders. Business requirements determine the priorities in negotiations. Meeting the established requirements becomes the metrics by which effectiveness of both the supplier and the strategy is measured.

Accepting that the Other Side Has Requirements

The preceding section provides insights on the importance of business requirements. This is a good spot to call attention to the importance of being cognizant that the other (the supplier) side has requirements as well. The best way to get what you want is to help the other side get what they want.[6] As an individual or team assembles requirements for the purpose of negotiations, it's essential to keep this point in mind.

The general thinking about sellers is that all they want to do is sell something. However, the motivation of a sales professional is often more than the commission awarded when the negotiations are complete. Consider some of the following possibilities:

- It may be that the sales professional will make his quota for the end of quarter sales, or he or she may be eligible for a bonus by going beyond the quota. The same could apply to the sales management involved. They may have regional or product/service sales objectives that they must meet.
- The company, which has corporate objectives, may have targets (e.g., revenues, long-term contracts/commitments) that must be achieved. The chief financial officer will be sensitive to how a negotiated agreement affects these commitments.
- Breaking into a new market where an agreement represents the potential for establishing a presence.
- Fending off a competitor who may be gaining momentum in a market segment.
- Delivering a new product or service offering.

There are other examples of requirements that could apply. As mentioned earlier, if a sourcing team has carefully followed a strategic sourcing process, it already has a sense of what will motivate the sales professional. Conversely, most sales professionals understand the *best way to get what you want* concept. The top performers will follow their own prescribed selling processes and identify value-based alternatives that exceed the customer's defined requirements.

From the sales perspective, the purpose of negotiation is to bring it to a successful conclusion. Sales professionals are savvy enough to understand that negotiations are not a contest. The reality is that sales professionals are trained to be collaborative and solve problems. Even if they're not trained in this discipline, they often learn on the job because their customers expect them to be problem solvers. Most importantly, sales professionals understand the value of relationships.

The Difference between Wants and Needs

Before the negotiators for the sourcing side set down their requirements, they must first evaluate their stakeholders' requirements to sort out needs from wants. It's probable that the request for proposal that brought the sourcing and selling teams to the point of negotiating included both wants and needs. A need is something that you have to have, and a want is something you would like to have. Knowing the difference between the two will often affect the success of negotiations.

Knowing Your Constraints

Beyond wants, needs, and opportunities, negotiators must accept the realities of constraints such as deadlines, existing contractual obligations, resource limitations, and stakeholder concerns. Constraints create boundaries that influence behavior during negotiations. They must be understood in advance of negotiations. If identified while negotiations are in process, the result could be a loss of confidence that suboptimizes decisions and outcomes.

Establish Negotiations Objectives

An understanding of price, delivery, quality, and service requirements should be defined internally whenever a proposal is developed by a sourcing team or procurement professional. These elements are drawn from a number of sources, including spend data, performance records, quality reports, and dialogue with affected stakeholders. It is helpful to isolate each element to determine its importance; however, each represents a need that must be addressed. None of these can be neglected during negotiation (see Figure 9.2).

Surrounding each of these elements are variables that must be taken into consideration. The following are some examples:

Price—Plant A currently pays price x for a product, and Plant B pays y for the exact same product. This is because Plant B requires a quantity of parts to be inventoried on site at the supplier whereas Plant A does not.

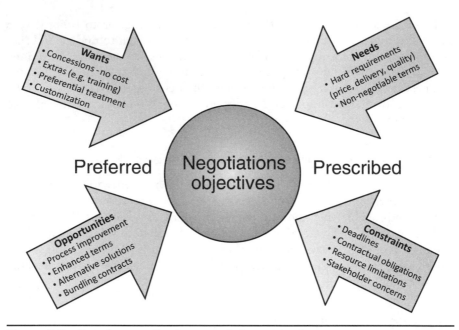

Figure 9.2   Four factors affecting negotiations objectives

Delivery—When Plant C needs parts, they need to be delivered the next day. This adds a premium to the cost of delivery. Plant D uses the exact same parts but doesn't have the same need for immediacy required by Plant C.

Quality—Plant A continually has issues related to the quality of a material. Plant B uses the same material but seldom, if ever, has problems with the quality.

Service—Plant C has a need for the supplier to provide technicians on site. None of the other sites has the same requirement.

All of these examples show that there will be a level of complexity in negotiating a corporate-wide agreement that will meet the needs of all the stakeholders. From the supplier's perspective, meeting all of these varying needs will have a price. Suppliers will refer to this as the *cost to serve.*

There are a number of techniques for determining which requirements become priorities during negotiation. The following is recommended:

- Quantify the requirement—how will the team and stakeholders measure achievement of the objective? Identify which element is the highest priority, second highest, and so forth.

- Why is this important?[7]—understand why stakeholders believe that their priorities are the right priorities. Drill down to the level of needs and then prioritize them.

- Differentiate needs from problems—is a stakeholder need actually a problem that can be addressed outside of the negotiations?
- Discover alternatives—are there other ways to meet the needs of some stakeholders without negatively influencing other stakeholder groups?
- Predict issues—if a commitment is made that benefits 80% of the stakeholders, what will be the consequences of coming up short for the other 20%?

Providing an Opportunity that is Appealing to the Supplier

When a sourcing team constructs a proposal, it should be with a clear understanding of attracting interest in the opportunity. Interest in the offer will motivate suppliers so that they are willing to put forth the effort to deliver an equally attractive response. Offering a longer-term agreement instead of a one-year contract should capture a supplier's interest. Also, opening the door to future business, opportunities for early involvement during product development, or earning a place on the supplier preferred list should also intrigue suppliers.

Some Important Acronyms

The fact base that was developed in the earlier phases of the strategic sourcing process drives the analysis and the conclusions regarding three very important concepts: most desirable outcome (MDO), least acceptable agreement (LAA), and best alternative to a negotiated agreement (BATNA). While some may look at these concepts as the means for establishing leverage, it's more productive to treat these concepts as a roadmap that will take you to a destination.

The MDO is the best (most favorable) scenario that a team feels is possible as an outcome of the negotiations. The key word here is possible. Defining the MDO is essential to a negotiations strategy. Be careful not to lead off with your MDO. It can send messages that the team isn't serious about negotiating or that the team is testing the supplier. This can lead to no agreement, or what we call *deadlock*.

The supplier will also have an MDO. If the team drives hard for its MDO, they will move the negotiations away from the overlap area that is crucial for a successful outcome. The concept of overlap is addressed later in the chapter. Seldom do suppliers enter into negotiations by advancing their MDO. They understand that relationships follow successful negotiations.

The LAA is the minimum agreement that a sourcing team and their stakeholders will accept without forgoing their must-have requirements. This can be called the reservation point/price because it represents the least favorable point—the maximum they are prepared to pay or the bottom line to a condition. The same applies for the sales team. The LAA is the minimum price it is willing to accept or the maximum on a point that it is willing to concede. At the point of LAA, an agreement is still possible.

The BATNA is the preplanned course of action in the event that an agreement cannot be reached. BATNA is a widely recognized acronym and also a misunderstood one. When asked what BATNA is, many negotiators will tell you it's their *walk away* option.

Fisher and Ury tell us that the reason we negotiate is to produce something better than the results that are obtained without negotiating. They tell us BATNAs are not always readily apparent, and they offer a simple process for determining your BATNA:

- Develop a list of actions you might conceivably take if no agreement is reached
- Improve some of the more promising ideas and convert them into practical options
- Select, tentatively, the one option that seems best[8]

Having a BATNA is a safeguard that allows the team to recognize if they are accepting a bad agreement or rejecting one that may be in their interest. By comparing the BATNA to the offer on the table, the team can assess if the deal, while not what they may have wanted going into the negotiations, is acceptable.

BATNA is about alternatives beyond *walking away*.

A young man has a car that is mechanically sound and looks good, with the exception of some normal wear and tear. Recently, he received a promotion and a boost to his income that has enabled him to consider buying a new car. The young man does his research and prepares well before shopping for a new vehicle. He takes into consideration what he believes to be all the aspects of the total cost of ownership for both his current vehicle and a new one—gas, insurance, maintenance, etc. He also takes the extra measure of preparing a BATNA. "If a new car isn't affordable, then I can look at fixing the dents and scratches on my current car, buy new tires and maybe even have it detailed," he tells himself.

When he starts shopping, he spies a car that has just about every feature that can be had. He decides this is the best car that he will ever own. Maybe it's more than he needs, but *wow*, it's his MDO. When the salesperson gives him the price, the young man balks. The price is more than he expected. After thinking for a few hours, he goes back to researching the possibilities. He identifies options in the car that he convinces himself he doesn't need and maybe even doesn't want. He heads back to the dealership with his LAA in mind.

He now has what he needs to negotiate. If he can't reach an acceptable deal, he knows that he can take some of the money that he was going to spend for the new car and use it to dress up the one he currently owns—his BATNA. He's set to negotiate and make a decision. It's not about *walking away*. It's about knowing all of his options.

Identifying Trade-Offs and Concessions

During the course of negotiations, there will be give-and-take, or what is termed *trade-offs* or *concessions*. The team should identify and document possible trade-offs or concessions in advance of the negotiations. Undoubtedly, some unexpected possibilities will come to the forefront during negotiations; however, the more the team can anticipate the trade-offs, the better.

We know some things about concessions. To make the negotiating process work, all parties must be willing to demonstrate flexibility. Failing to do so often leads to deadlocked discussions (failing to reach an agreement). Regardless of your opening position, leave room to maneuver. If you take a flexible position, make sure your counterpart is also taking a flexible position, or you will be offering most of the concessions. As the negotiation progresses, make sure the frequency and value of concessions diminishes. Smaller and smaller concessions indicate a likely resistance to further concessions. Finally, remove the audience, especially managers, during a negotiation. The larger the audience, the more difficult it becomes to offer concessions. The possibility exists that offering concessions will come across as weakness when others are present. In the final analysis, it is important to offer concessions during negotiations—but not too many.

The Need for Overlapping Positions

Believing that you will always achieve your MDO, or at least come close, is not realistic. Unfortunately, procurement professionals can be stubborn and inclined to resort to tactical power plays that, while they may be effective in the short term, may not create longer-lasting value. Recognizing that buyer and seller positions need to overlap is the difference between an accomplished negotiator and a frustrated one. Both sides have objectives, needs, and positions.

At the highest level, a sourcing team is after reducing the total cost of ownership for an agreement while improving, or at a minimum preserving, quality, delivery, and service objectives. Similarly, the sales team is after establishing a new customer relationship, or preserving an existing one, with an eye on profitability. These are not opposing points of view. When the buyer and seller positions do not overlap, there can be no agreement.

Consciously, the sourcing team takes this into account as they evaluate responses to its proposal. Before entering into negotiation, the team needs to thoroughly assess the elements that comprise the overlap of the buying offer and the selling proposal. Figure 9.3 illustrates the concept of overlap.

Writing It Down

The sourcing team needs to have the discipline to assemble the information it has gathered when preparing for the negotiations. Documenting its research

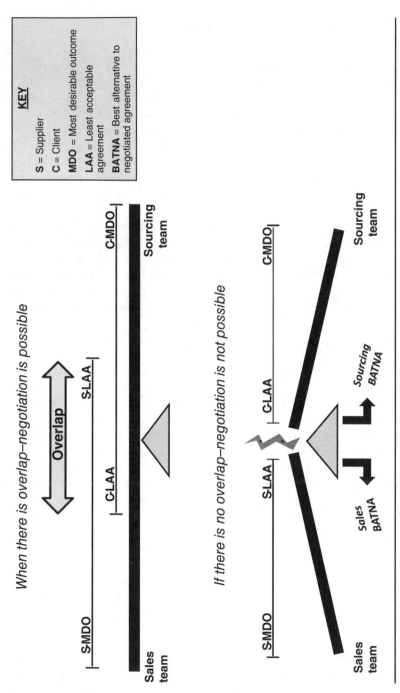

Figure 9.3 The importance of overlap

provides the team with a medium for sharing information with stakeholders and management to make sure the buying side is *speaking with one voice*. Chapter 8 discussed the importance of speaking with one voice during the strategic sourcing process. The worksheet in Figure 9.4 is an example of a tool for gathering information relevant to negotiations with a supplier.

The focal point of this worksheet is the messages section. A responsibility of any sourcing team is to develop a communication plan that will strengthen its position during the negotiations. The messages and subsequent actions should be consistent and a natural extension of the overall negotiations strategy. Some examples of the messages to consider are:

- Here's what we expect and here's what you (the seller) can expect—this establishes the overall objectives upfront
- This is an important undertaking for our company—expresses the visibility and commitment within the buyer's company
- This sourcing initiative will take place with or without you—builds credibility by taking a firm position

Why Does Preparation Often Fall Short?

We have spent considerable time discussing the importance of preparation. The hard reality, based on experience with many supply professionals, is that preparation does not occur at the same level as it does on the selling side of the negotiating table. Too many negotiators want to jump right into negotiations. There are many reasons for this—negotiations are action oriented, which some consider fun or fulfilling. Preparation just isn't as interesting. It requires patience and discipline. However, as experienced negotiators tell us, preparation is a critical prerequisite to negotiating success. The preparation process is often characterized by some serious weaknesses. These weaknesses include:

- Failing to commit sufficient time
- Failing to establish clear objectives
- Failing to formulate convincing arguments or support for positions
- Failing to consider the needs of your counterpart
- Believing that quick and clever is enough

If you feel your negotiating efforts lack in preparation, you are certainly not alone. The key is to identify your planning weaknesses and then take corrective action to overcome those weaknesses. The first step is to recognize the inseparable link between effective planning and strategic negotiating success. Failing to plan effectively can *lock in* mistakes for a long time.

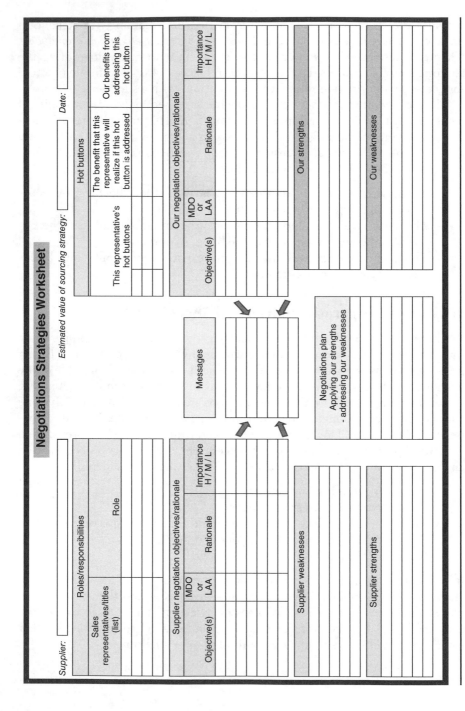

Figure 9.4 Negotiations strategy worksheet

Execution

Part of the negotiation planning process is determining the strategy for carrying out the negotiation. As Gordan Eubanks, the former CEO of Symantec, commented, "Strategy gets you on the playing field, but execution pays the bills." This quote also applies to negotiation. Planning is great, but execution brings it home.

Certified Negotiators

As discussed in Chapter 6, talent management is a differentiator of next level supply management organizations.

One of the authors, as a chief procurement officer at several large companies, decided to reinforce the importance of professional skills building in a novel manner. He appointed a team of supply management and human resources professionals to develop a certification program for negotiations expertise in the supply management function. When rolled out, the program had several levels of certification, clearly communicated expectations and criteria, and appropriate recognition and awards. This program and process went a long way in reinforcing a new paradigm of strategic negotiations management, versus the old school of tactical bargaining.

The execution phase of negotiations demands attention to some important decisions. Even something as simple as the location of a negotiating session can have a major impact. While these decisions appear to be simple, they are not. They deserve careful consideration.

Execution Decisions

Two major decisions related to execution are where to negotiate and who should negotiate. Deciding the timing and location for negotiations is a mix of art and science. There are clear psychological factors about time of day, day of the week, meeting facilities, length of the sessions, and many other facets that influence negotiations. The sourcing team should make it clear to the selling team that it will manage these conditions. The art comes in the form of making changes as negotiations proceed to limit any loss of momentum.

Another key issue during the execution phase is who will be part of the negotiation process and what role each party will play. On the sourcing side, will the team be empowered to make a *buy* decision and *reach agreement*? A lack of empowerment adds to the degree of difficulty as the negotiations turn into a *stop-and-go* process. This is sometimes an issue with international negotiations when the senior member of an organization is expected to provide approval. Any time a team reaches a decision point, it will need to ask for judgment before it can go forward. Figure 9.5 summarizes various roles that are part of the negotiating process.

Negotiators for the sourcing team should be relieved of as many day-to-day responsibilities as possible so that they can make the negotiation a priority.

Functional role	Negotiating role	Types of messages
Lead negotiator	*Driver* • Seeks alternatives • Explores options • Keeps process moving forward • Pushes for decisions	• Change is possible • Change can be good • Nothing is sacred • We have needs / expectations
Purchasing representative (process expert)	*Neutral/Driver* • Looks for common ground • Results oriented	• We value our suppliers • Relationships are important • Relationships are only as good as performance / scorecards • TCO matters
Technical representative (subject matter expert)	*Neutral/Challenger* • Wants change without cost • Pushes for alternatives • Concerned about quality	• What support will you provide? • Looking for new (technologies) • How can we stay current?
Production/operations representative (subject matter expert)	*Neutral/Good guy* • Relationships matter • Risk(s) averse • Seeks improvement	• We like you but … • We currently receive (services) • Production can't be disrupted • We're interested in new ways • Certifications are an issue
Marketing representative (subject matter expert)	*Neutral/Challenger* • Looking for competitive edge	• How do we compare? • We need to be out ahead • We're value driven
Data manager (information technology expert)	*Neutral/Good guy* • Eye to existing systems • Looking for assistance on changes	• What can you do to minimize the need for (system) changes? • What assistance is available?
Finance representative (finances/numbers expert)	*Challenger/Neutral* • Numbers matter • Results oriented	• Show us the money • How much? • How soon? • What are the risks?
Legal representative (terms and conditions expert)	*Challenger/Neutral* • T's & C's are important • Assess risk	• Will you agree to?

Figure 9.5   Various roles are part of the negotiations process

Some companies staff their negotiating teams with supply personnel that specialize in supplier negotiations. These individuals may not even become involved with the strategic sourcing process until the planning phase or even later. All members of a sourcing team that are involved in negotiations will be responsible for communicating the key themes to the supplier.

The decision about the number of suppliers to invite to a negotiation affects the execution phase. Simply stated, it makes the negotiation much more complex. Incumbents tend to be invited, provided that past performance has, at minimum, met expectations. New suppliers bring a competitive element to the process. We are aware of a major company that negotiates with up to three suppliers for a given proposal. And it has no intention of reaching an agreement with all three. This approach creates a competitive tension among suppliers and makes them *sharpen their pencils* that much more.

The selling team should be comprised of individuals who are knowledgeable of their proposal and able to address specific questions about their bid. Also, the sourcing team should confirm that the supplier representatives assigned to the selling team are fully empowered to make decisions on every element of their offer, including the ability to address the legal terms and conditions needed to sign an agreement. If not, the sourcing team should consider taking a position that they will not negotiate until these conditions are satisfied.

In the experience of the authors, cross-functional selling teams tend to be more productive than the lone salesperson interacting with cross-functional sourcing teams. The survey results described in Chapter 20 confirm that conclusion from both the sales and procurement perspectives.

As business becomes more global, it is imperative that the negotiator accepts the realities of cultural differences. The sourcing and selling teams must be sensitive to the difference in both social and business practices. Attitudes about formal communications, exchanging documents, time management, personal space, gifts, humor, and even food can vary widely. While procurement and sales professionals are more knowledgeable than ever about cultural differences, it is necessary to take these into account during the planning phase. Having a representative of each team who can skillfully address these diversities can be the difference between success and failure. A good translator during the negotiation, even if negotiations are in English, will be invaluable.

The Negotiation Session

During the negotiation, there are some important points to remember. First, it is usually a good idea to keep the atmosphere surrounding the negotiation less formal whenever possible. After all, you are not negotiating a Mideast peace agreement. A less formal atmosphere should facilitate an open dialogue between the parties.

Next, as the negotiation progresses, we recommend periodically summarizing positions and points of agreement. Stressing points of agreement reinforces that the parties are capable of coming to agreement. Some negotiators like to begin with simple issues that are easily resolved. This creates a momentum to take on more complex topics. Summarizing points of agreements also helps ensure the parties understand what they have agreed upon. At the end of the session, we highly recommend conducting an internal lessons learned session while the negotiation is still fresh in everyone's mind.

Behaviors of Effective Negotiators

An effective negotiator is a valuable asset to his or her organization. The good news is we know the kinds of behaviors that define what an effective negotiator looks like. So think about this set of behaviors as you engage in your next negotiation with a supplier. Effective negotiators:

- Are willing to compromise or revise their goals, particularly when new information successfully challenges their position. They understand the need to be flexible during the negotiation.
- View issues independently. They do not create complicated linkages between issues that lower the probability of reaching agreement.
- Establish upper and lower ranges for each major issue. Again, this supports flexibility.
- Explore almost twice as many options per issue compared with average negotiators. They are expansive rather than limited in their search for solutions.
- Do not publicly gloat or claim victory after a negotiation. This only serves to embarrass the other party and make future negotiations more difficult.
- Make almost four times the comments about the common ground between the parties compared with average negotiators.
- Give fewer reasons for the arguments they advance. Too many supporting reasons can dilute an argument.
- Make fewer counterproposals. While a willingness to make counterproposals is an important part of negotiating, making too many counterproposals can result in too many concessions.
- Understand clearly that how concessions are presented affects the expectations of the other party.
- Are comfortable with silence. Talking simply to fill an uncomfortable void is not usually in the negotiator's best interests.

Vested Outsourcing—Taking Negotiation to the Next Level

Next level supply organizations will engage in vested outsourcing agreements with suppliers.[9] With conventional outsourcing agreements, a buyer attempts to reduce costs while a supplier attempts to maximize the size of the contract. It is not hard to see how each party, regardless of what they may say, works to protect its interests. With vested outsourcing, the parties sit *on the same side of the table* rather than across from each other when developing a contract. In a vested outsourcing arrangement, the economics are structured so that the company that is outsourcing reduces its costs, improves its revenues, and/or receives increased service levels while the service provider improves its profits. Vested outsourcing agreements represent complete sharing of information within a collaborative environment. They are designed to achieve performance results that are above and beyond what two parties might normally achieve— results that can impact top and bottom line performance. It represents the next level of negotiated agreements.

Reaching a vested outsourcing agreement requires the application of five rules that, when followed, should result in a vested agreement. Rule 1 is to focus on outcomes or desired states rather than transactions. Vested outsourcing agreements *buy* desired outcomes rather than individual transactions. Rule 2 is to focus on the *what*, not the *how*. With vested outsourcing the company that outsources specifies what it wants and moves the responsibility of determining how to accomplish a scope of work to the outsource provider. Rule 3 stresses the importance of agreeing on clearly defined and measurable outcomes.

Rule 4 is to optimize pricing incentives for cost/service trade-offs. Inherent in the business model is a reward for the outsource provider to make investments in process, service, or associated product that will generate returns in excess of contract requirements. The next section of this chapter explores the idea of relationship-specific investment. And finally, rule 5 maintains that the governance structure that oversees the relationship should provide insight, not merely oversight. Insight represents the power of acute observation and deduction while oversight represents watchful care and general supervision. When pursued properly, vested outsourcing offers a creative way to realize formerly unrealized value through the negotiating process—value that can enhance revenue performance.

Looking Toward the Future

We witnessed a shift from bargaining to strategic negotiation after some major supply model changes occurred. The first change was a shift from a supply base that featured many suppliers with short-term contracts to a smaller supply base featuring longer-term contracts. Longer-term contracts are almost always negotiated because they address more issues than short-term agreements. The second shift involved the development of strategic sourcing. Effective strategic sourcing processes include negotiation as an important and integrated part of the process. As supply groups apply a strategic framework to an expanded set of purchase requirements, especially services and equipment, the amount of negotiation should increase.

While we do not expect movement away from longer-term agreements, and an emphasis on strategic sourcing will not disappear, we do see a trend that could reduce, perhaps dramatically, the need for negotiation. That trend is a reduction in process cycle times.

The pressure to reduce the time it takes to perform virtually every process within an organization demands new ways of doing business. A supply organization may no longer have the time to plan and negotiate with suppliers, particularly when sourcing opportunities are connected to new product development. It is well accepted that the time to develop new products has shortened dramatically over the last 20 years. Any sub-processes that support product development must also shorten dramatically.

As a supply organization converges on a supply base that remains relatively stable over a longer-term period (and many organizations have achieved this convergence), supplier switching becomes a less common occurrence. A buyer often knows early on which supplier will receive new business. Furthermore, if the supply organization has developed collaborative relationships with a smaller group of suppliers, open sharing of information within a win-win environment will be the norm rather than the exception.

The last piece of this puzzle here is something called target costing (some call this target pricing). With target pricing, the price that a supplier receives is calculated within a framework that considers all elements of cost within a new product. The price that a supplier receives is not the result of negotiation. In fact, with target costing, no formal negotiation takes place. We have every reason to believe the use of target costing will increase, thereby lessening the need to engage in supplier negotiation, at least for direct materials.

Concluding Thoughts

The next time you negotiate with a supplier, keep in mind that statistically, your sales counterpart has received at least four times the amount of training in negotiation than you have received. The real possibility exists that you are at a disadvantage the minute you walk into the negotiating room. Next level supply organizations understand this discrepancy as they develop their talent management plans. They know supply negotiators will be a valuable asset for the foreseeable future. While the question of what we negotiate may change, the need for skilled negotiators within supply management will not go way.

Chapter Notes

1. *Webster's Ninth New Collegiate Dictionary* (Merriam-Webster, 1987).
2. G. Richard Shell. *Bargaining for Advantage Second Edition* (New York: Penguin Books, 2006).

3. David A. Lax and James K. Sebenius. *3D Negotiations* (Boston: Harvard Business School Press, 2006).
4. Roger Fisher, William Ury, and Bruce Patton. *Getting to Yes*, 2nd ed. (New York: Penguin Books, 1991).
5. Ray Fells. "Preparation for Negotiation: Issue and Process." *Personnel Review*, February 01, 1996.
6. Ronald M. Shapiro and Mark A. Jankowski. *The Power of Nice: How to Negotiate So Everyone Wins—Especially You!*, rev. ed. (New York: John Wiley & Sons, 2001).
7. R. L. Keeney. *Value-Focused Thinking: A Path to Creative Decision Making* (Cambridge, MA: Harvard University Press, 1992).
8. Fisher, Ury, and Patton.
9. The material in this section is adapted from Kate Vitasek, Mike Ledyard, and Karl Mandrodt. *Vested Outsourcing—Five Rules that Will Transform Outsourcing* (New York: Palgrave Macmillan, 2010).
10. The authors acknowledge the important contributions of Jim Baehr to this chapter.

10

Comprehensive Energy Management

The use of energy has been part of the human existence for as long as anyone can remember. For most of its history, energy was consumed without thought for efficiency or economy. Energy was always considered in limitless supply and cheap when compared to other necessities in conducting an enterprise. The consumption of energy achieved its zenith in the 20th century with the development of vast natural gas pipeline systems, electricity transmission grids, and various modes for transporting hydrocarbon fuels on a worldwide basis.

Energy was managed in the sense that it needed to be transported, stored, generated, and transmitted. It was not managed from the perspective of reducing consumption or lowering cost. In fact, in some instances, it was considered too cheap to measure.

Energy began to be thought of with a scarcity mindset after the oil embargoes of the 1970s. Terms like efficiency, conservation, and energy independence started being associated with energy consumption. Within industrial companies, specific disciplines were established that dealt exclusively with energy consumption with the aim being to reduce its use and gain competitive advantage. Consumption of energy per unit of output became a prevalent unit of measure. There was also a great deal of effort to develop new technologies to improve energy use efficiency.

We now know that energy management offers attractive opportunities for supply managers, particularly at companies that have not developed a comprehensive strategy to procure and manage this valuable commodity. This chapter presents seven key areas that are essential for comprehensive energy management, including:

- Energy procurement
- Energy risk management

- Consumption management
- Energy project development
- Participation in the regulatory and legislative process
- Carbon footprint management
- Internal energy management organization

Deregulation Creates Opportunities and Risks

Before presenting the seven key areas of comprehensive energy management, let's first understand energy regulation and deregulation. In the early 1980s, natural gas and electricity were still regulated in the United States. Pricing was approved by the Federal Energy Regulatory Commission (FERC) and by state public service commissions. There was no procurement process for companies to follow for acquiring these commodities, as there was only a monopoly provider for each regulated franchise area. Price management for natural gas or electricity was relegated to participating in regulatory proceedings, and this was done only by very large sophisticated companies that consumed large quantities. Fuel oils and coal were not regulated and could be procured in competitive markets.

Relatively few companies, except for utilities, used fuel oils or coal as part of their commodity mix. Coal, for example, was bought by utility and steel companies and very few others. For most other enterprises, there was still little to no active energy price management.

As natural gas was deregulated during the 1980s (see Figure 10.1), it became possible to purchase it directly from producers. However, there was little established procedure as this was a totally new market. Additionally, there was no expertise within companies, so the responsibility for natural gas procurement, in most instances, was given to the technical groups that were already responsible for the consumption management. As the natural gas market evolved, some companies established new procurement functions to manage energy acquisition.

Electricity deregulation started to occur in stages about 10 years after natural gas deregulation. Because of the nature of electricity supply, where generating plants are located locally, retail deregulation occurred on a state-by-state basis. And not all states have enacted electricity deregulation. The electricity markets, as a result, are much more confused than the natural gas markets with degrees of complexity varying with geographic location.

In the deregulated market areas for electricity, it is probable that electricity cost has risen faster than in the still regulated areas. The impetus for deregulation, to instill competition in monopoly markets and drive cost down, has backfired somewhat for the end user. The new deregulated suppliers have used the confusion of increased complexity to exercise greater market power and exert higher premiums for the unbundled services. In the deregulated states, it

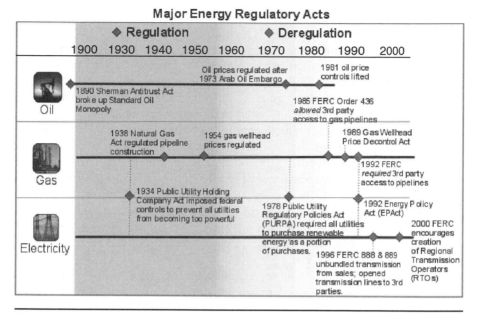

Figure 10.1   Deregulation timeline

has become a *buyers beware* environment. Most end users are not aware of this reality and have come to be dependent on suppliers for hopefully the effective price management of their electricity supplies. Only the more sophisticated users with large expenditures for electricity take the trouble to be informed and proactive in the markets to mitigate the negative aspects.

Many believe that when natural gas and electricity were deregulated, the state and federal regulatory bodies no longer had a role to play. This is far from reality. Deregulation only applies to the commodity portion of the total energy service. The natural gas pipelines and distribution systems and the electricity transmission and distribution systems are still monopoly providers and are still regulated. It is still prudent for end users to be aware of regulatory proceedings and actively involved, as it was before deregulation.

Comprehensive Energy Management

In today's energy complex, there are many influences and drivers of energy cost for an end user (energy consuming) company. It has become critical for companies to mitigate as much of these cost drivers as possible. If a company only focuses on achieving lowest purchase price and ignores other influences, it is possible and most likely probable that all the benefit achieved with aggressive purchasing and hedging methods can be eroded through the regulatory process as public service commissions grant rate increases to natural gas pipelines or electricity transmission companies. It has also been documented that as companies succeed in reducing the purchased cost of a particular energy commodity, the efficiency of consumption of that commodity usually suffers, thus potentially resulting in higher overall cost because of increased consumption. It is vital that a company aggressively manage all aspects of the energy equation so that gains achieved in one area are not reversed through negative impact in another.

Comprehensive energy management refers to participation in all of the disciplines and commodities that impact the total cost of energy. It also implies that the participation needs to be coordinated in a deliberate and cohesive manner. As an example, knowledge of market trends are critical as part of an intervention in a rate proceeding by a utility company. Additionally, development of an energy efficiency project opportunity cannot be fully achieved without knowledge of longer-term market values. In addition, as mentioned earlier, it does no good to lower the price of a commodity if that in turn reduces motivation to conserve.

A company needs to have an organization for managing energy that is cross functional as well as centrally coordinated. Only in this way can a united, aggressive effort on total energy cost be successful. Figure 10.2 shows the various functions included in a comprehensive energy management program. Later in this chapter, we will discuss how to implement such a program.

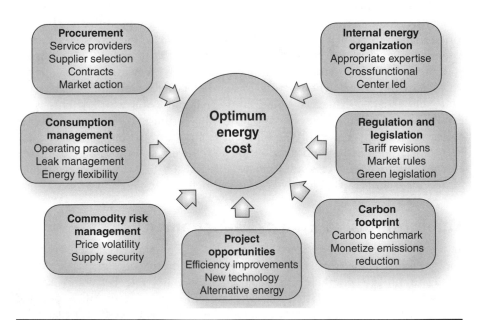

Figure 10.2   Components of comprehensive energy management
Source: Greybeard Advisors LLC. Copyright 2010–2011. All Rights Reserved.

Energy Procurement

Prior to natural gas deregulation in the mid-1980s, energy procurement practices were limited to coal and liquid fuels. Coal was and continues to be purchased through contractual arrangements from competing suppliers. But procurement experience with coal is limited to utility companies who purchase coal as a fuel for electric generation and the steel industry, where coal is a raw material in the steelmaking process. Liquid fuels such as gasoline, heating oil, diesel, and no. 6 fuel oil have been purchased broadly as commodities for a long time. As a percentage of total energy used by companies though, liquid fuels do not play a significant role, except with trucking companies.

The majority of energy consumption by companies today is in the form of natural gas and electricity. Before the natural gas commodity was deregulated in 1986, it was supplied by monopoly providers, and there was little any company could do to affect price. The same was true for electricity supply until it was deregulated in the late 1990s and early 2000s. But unlike natural gas, electricity was deregulated in a state-by-state process, and many states still remain regulated.

In the deregulated market environment, it became incumbent upon consuming companies to become knowledgeable about the workings of the markets, both natural gas and electricity, and develop procurement methods to achieve competitive supplies and manage supply risk. Today's markets for energy commodities have developed into a complex system of suppliers, service providers, transportation and transmission arrangements, and local distribution tariffs. It is a buyer beware environment and requires specialized skills to navigate within it.

Natural Gas: Prior to being deregulated into a competitive commodity market, natural gas was supplied to end users by local monopoly suppliers (utility companies), and pricing was established through regulation by public service commissions. After deregulation, it became possible for end users to negotiate their contracts with producers, but this introduced a significant level of complexity to the process that required end users to get on a steep learning curve. Not only was it necessary to negotiate a competitive contract with suppliers, but the end user now had to make arrangements for the transport and delivery of the natural gas to his location.

During the same period, natural gas pipelines were transformed into common carriers and developed a myriad of new services for those wishing to establish transportation arrangements on their systems. For larger end users, it became necessary to have contractual service with multiple pipelines and natural gas suppliers. As a result of the new complexities introduced by deregulation, new companies were formed that provided sales and marketing services to both the wholesale suppliers and the end users. Over time, these new companies filled the void created by traditional utilities and pipelines after they became only transporters.

In the current market environment for natural gas, the role of purchasing has three basic components.

1. Arrangements for the supply of the commodity. This is usually done through a request for proposal (RFP) process where the primary consideration is the ability to perform on the part of the suppliers. Contracts for natural gas supply have been standardized by the North American Energy Standards Board (NAESB). The aspects of the arrangement that are negotiable are price and volume. Since natural gas is traded on commodity exchanges, price is usually determined by indexing formulas and is hedged using derivative instruments by suppliers and sometimes by more sophisticated end users.

2. Arrangement for the transportation of the commodity. The supplier delivers to a point on an interstate pipeline, and the gas must be redelivered to the receipt point of the local distribution company (LDC). For larger end users, these arrangements can involve multiple delivery and receipt points as well as multiple pipelines. Transporting natural gas adds a layer of cost to the price of the commodity. This cost can be fixed by tariff or be variable as a basis, depending on market action. Basis is the price difference between two trading points—in this instance, the point of receipt for the commodity and the point of redelivery. While a tariff transport rate is established through regulation and contract, a basis cost can be variable based on market action or be fixed through financial hedging by suppliers and marketers as well as end users. The advantage of using basis to establish transport cost is that it can be less than the fixed tariff rate and thereby result in minimizing overall cost. However, the risk exists that basis can also be greater than the tariff rate. Choosing the best method is highly dependent on which pipeline is used for transport and on current market conditions.

3. Delivery by the LDC. The LDC, while no longer the monopoly supplier of the gas, is still the monopoly provider of the last leg of transportation. In addition, as part of the delivery service, there are usually rules that require volume management so that quantities scheduled do not deviate from quantities delivered. This has evolved into a daily function and differs between various LDCs. The cost of delivery and any associated penalties for imbalances are set by tariffs approved by the public service commissions. These costs are a third layer on top of the commodity cost. It is at this point that the all-in *burner tip* price of purchased natural gas is established (see Figure 10.3).

It is important to note that the rates for services on interstate pipelines as well as rates for delivery service by LDCs are still regulated. These services can

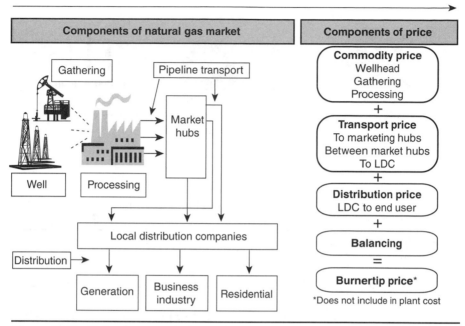

Figure 10.3 Natural gas market components

comprise from 20 to 50% of the total delivered *burner tip* price of natural gas depending on location and market conditions.

Electricity: Unlike natural gas, which was deregulated on a national level by the FERC, retail deregulation of electricity happened on a state-by-state basis. Currently, 16 states have deregulated electricity on a retail level. They are clustered in the Midwest, Mid Atlantic, New England, and Texas. Some states have programs enacted that are limited to large industrials only. Other states continue to have a regulated electricity market environment with monopoly providers.

The role of purchasing in a deregulated electricity market has evolved similarly to that in the natural gas markets. Electricity markets, though, are even more complex than natural gas markets and require significant technical expertise to navigate all the new services that have developed over the years. But unlike the natural gas market, electricity markets are limited to geographic control areas. Each control area has its own market rules for price discovery and transmission access. An end user can interact only with marketers and suppliers that control generation assets within the end user's specific control area.

In states where electricity supply remains regulated by the public service commissions, acquiring electricity has no opportunity for any competitive processes. There is only one monopoly supplier, which is the local utility company,

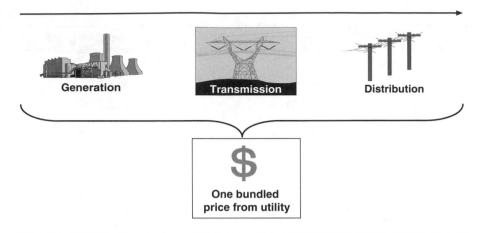

Figure 10.4   Components of regulated electricity price

and the end user has no choices when dissatisfied with the rates (see Figure 10.4). But the utility company tariffs are designed to vary rates based on types of consumers, time of use, degree of reliability required, and economic incentives for new load. Commercial and industrial companies usually have separate tariffs that are discounted from the standard residential rates. This is due in part to the fact that larger consumers take power at higher voltages and are more level loaded in their consumption.

The purchasing manager who is familiar with details of the local utility tariff and is equally familiar with his facilities consumption patterns will usually discover opportunities to reduce electricity cost. As an example, switching operations to lower cost off-peak periods or agreeing to be interruptible for a fixed period can yield significant benefits with minimal risks. Each utility is unique in its tariff treatment as is each company's consumption profile. The opportunities that may be identified will also be unique to each company's specific situation. These efforts in the regulated market are not procurement practices in the traditional sense and require the participation of operations and engineering skills to implement.

Deregulated electricity: Like natural gas, deregulated electricity service is divided into three basic components: the commodity, transmission, and distribution (see Figure 10.5).

1. *Arranging commodity supply*. The electricity commodity can be acquired through an RFP process from local marketers. Again, as with natural gas, the primary consideration for the purchasing manager is the supplier's (load serving entities) ability to perform. Price is set by indexing the marginal cost on the system or through price risk

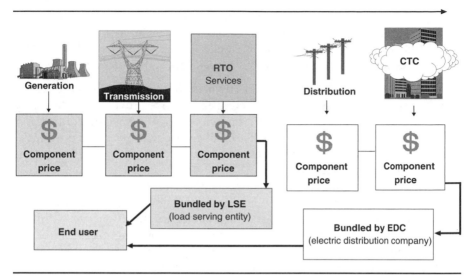

Figure 10.5   Components of deregulated electricity price

management instruments. Depending on the volume, multiple suppliers may be required to service the end user's total requirement. As with natural gas, electricity supply contracts have been standardized by NAESB. The electric distribution company (EDC) is the supplier of last resort, but they too have to purchase electricity in the deregulated market. Many purchasing managers take the path of least resistance and continue to deal with the EDC. This, invariably, is the more costly choice.

2. *Arranging for transmission.* Electricity needs to get from the point of purchase to the point of consumption. This happens instantaneously. It is therefore necessary to contract for access to the transmission grid in the control area. This may involve financial transmission rights and auction revenue rights. This is a very esoteric area of electric markets and requires specialized expertise. In most instances, the supplier or marketer makes arrangements for transmission rights and contract for delivery to the end user. However, because of the complexity, any opportunity that can be developed in the transmission access markets remain in the marketer's domain and will not accrue to the end users. Some very large end users have acquired the knowledge to be able to take advantage of specific opportunities through use of expert consultants and intimacy with market rules in their specific control area.

3. *Distribution for consumption.* Like natural gas, the LDC is the last leg for delivery of electricity. The EDC charges a tariff rate for the service that is approved by the public service commission. Again, there

must be volume management for electricity, like for natural gas, so that scheduled quantities and actual quantities are in balance. This can be an hourly activity, usually handled by sophisticated software. This has also become the province of marketers and service providers.

As with natural gas, one of the purchasing manager's primary roles is to establish effective relationships with marketers and service providers. Additionally, he or she must continue to acquire knowledge of the specific control area market rules and market dynamics. This will ensure that market opportunities will be recognized and taken advantage of rather than passively allowing the suppliers to reap those benefits.

Purchasing deregulated energy: Because of the complexity introduced into the function of acquiring energy, many larger consumers developed their own internal expertise and associated staff to manage the function. Over time, as complexity increased, many companies began outsourcing much of the activity to service companies that specialized in the area as a line of business. In today's energy markets, most companies use the services of marketers and service providers to perform most of the requirements in getting energy delivered to their facilities. This can include price setting and risk management. These outsourcing companies will charge fees based on the level of service required. The purchasing manager needs to be mindful of companies that claim they charge no fees to the client. These companies extract their revenues from the upstream suppliers they deal with, and consequently, their fees become imbedded in the price of the commodity paid by their clients.

One of the dangers of using services providers and marketers for energy supply is that the purchasing manager usually will have little knowledge about the workings of the markets and, as a result, will have poor judgment as to whether or not his company is receiving optimum service. In addition, he or she will have little appreciation of the cost reduction opportunities unless they are made aware by the service provider. Over time, the purchasing manager, as well as the company, may become dependent on the service provider and make no effort to actively manage their energy supply costs.

Having said all that, the reality of the current market is that the use of service providers has become a necessity. As a matter of fact, the primary function of the purchasing manager charged with energy procurement is establishing and maintaining effective arrangements with marketers and service providers. By being selective as to which functions are outsourced and using multiple service providers, the purchasing manager can establish a situation where he or she can ensure that their company will receive best available service.

The total cost of ownership (TCO) for a particular commodity will therefore not only include the commodity and transport or transmission costs to the meter or burner tip as described but will also include additional fees imposed by service providers, brokers, hedging gains or losses, and in-plant maintenance costs. These additional costs must also be managed aggressively as part of a comprehensive energy management program.

The effective way to achieve optimum results is by enlisting independent advisors whose loyalty is to the client. The independent advisor has in-depth market knowledge and can advise on service providers, market dynamics, and project opportunities. The independent advisor is not conflicted in his loyalties as a marketer/service provider might be. Will a marketer also acting as a service provider advise a client about new technologies or practices that would reduce consumption?

Other energy commodities: In addition to natural gas and electricity, most companies require other commodities related to energy to operate and produce their products. These include:

- Hydrocarbon liquids—fuel oil, heating oil, and gasoline
- Coal
- Propane
- Industrial gases—oxygen, nitrogen, hydrogen

These commodities were never regulated like natural gas and electricity. They continue to be purchased by purchasing professionals and are in competitive markets. The strategic sourcing process will result in the best outcome. As with natural gas and electricity, hydrocarbon liquids are exchange traded commodities, and price variation will be in a very narrow band. In purchasing liquid hydrocarbons, it is important to be aware of market trends of the individual commodities and as they relate to each other, including natural gas and propane. Often, natural gas commodity prices are impacted by the price action of crude oil as well as the price action of the other traded fuels. This happens because, in many instances, some of these hydrocarbon liquids are substitutable for each other and therefore act as price ceilings or price drivers. The purchasing manager needs to maintain significant market knowledge on this issue as well as promote interchangeability of fuels within the company to achieve optimum pricing leverage and lowest TCO.

Coal, considered an energy commodity as well as a raw material, is usually purchased through longer-term forward contracts within specific pricing formulas. Coal is not leveraged by natural gas or oil and has historically been the least cost energy source.

In reality, very few companies purchase coal. Those that do purchase coal are utility companies that use it as a fuel for electricity generation and steel companies that use it to make coke for the iron making process.

Most companies do not consider industrial gas as energy commodities because they are not an energy source per se. But we include them in our discussion of energy procurement because their prices are driven by the underlying raw material used to generate them. Fully 70% of the cost of producing oxygen is the producer's price for electricity, and nitrogen is a byproduct of oxygen generation. Hydrogen is generated by reforming natural gas.

The purchasing manager needs to be fully aware of the total operating costs of industrial gas producers in the same manner he or she has to keep current on electricity and natural markets. Although industrial gas contracts are usually longer term in nature, there are tracker mechanisms installed in the contracts that reflect changing energy market conditions. In effect, when a company is negotiating an oxygen contract, they are really making a long-term electricity supply arrangement. The purchasing manager must reflect his or her understanding of energy market trends in contractual arrangements made for industrial gases.

Risk Management

As mentioned earlier, energy commodities display significant price and supply volatility; one doesn't have to look further than today's news headlines to find the reasons why. As a result, various strategies are employed in an effort to achieve control of the uncertainty. Individual circumstances and motives as well as whether the market area is regulated or deregulated determine which are employed (albeit with no guaranteed results).

The simplest option is to merely buy supply from a reputable utility or marketer and let the supplier handle all *upstream of meter* issues. This is generally the choice of small volume consumers, although this may change as contemporary *smart metering* efforts and *choice* programs are deployed. Another option can be aggregating supply requirements with other companies of similar circumstances in the form of a purchasing consortium. Besides trying to create larger volume for better price leverage, these consortiums and *pools* can also be used to mitigate balancing penalty exposure.

Larger players can use additional options. The simplest is to buy one's physical future requirements on any trading day. The physical commodity is now owned, is available for delivery, and its cost is known. For storable energies like natural gas and crude oil by-products, user accessible storage facilities can also lead to strategies involving buying low, storing, and then withdrawing during times of higher pricing. A further refinement of fuel flexibility can involve arbitrage opportunities.

An additional opportunity is to temporarily curtail consumption and release associated unused energy for sale to the market. As an example, when price differentials are favorable, stored oil can be switched for delivered natural gas and vice versa, or stored oil might be used to internally generate electricity that displaces purchased merchant electricity for financial compensation. These opportunities normally arise during periods of strained supply and/or deliverability. Evaluation of the TCO is necessary to determine economic benefit.

Not everyone has access to the storage facilities (Figure 10.6) required to take advantage of the aforementioned. Furthermore, the capital (or credit worthiness) necessary to contract physical ownership is generally significant and may even be unavailable. As an alternative or in addition to the above, hedging activity can employ financial derivatives. A simple version might involve the right to purchase physical ownership of a commodity at a certain future date. The pricing and sale of this futures contract, as well as other types, is traded on a futures trading platform such as the New York Mercantile Exchange.

Needless to say, extensive market knowledge is required in the effort to determine favorable market conditions to hedge future prices. This effort is subject to either success or failure relative to the *strike* price that is chosen. Existing hedge positions can be unwound (sold) ahead of expiration if deemed prudent to do so, but some companies may frown upon such activity as speculative. Special accounting rules must also be followed. Developing a written hedging policy is mandatory when contemplating the use of financial hedging. (More about the subject of risk management and hedging can be found in Chapter 19 of *Straight to the Bottom Line*.)

No matter what strategy is employed to mitigate risks in energy, caution should be used. Each requires observance of appropriate accounting rules, knowledge of market trends, and dealing with trustworthy and credit worthy supply and service providers. For the energy end user, hedging should not be

Figure 10.6   Oil storage

viewed as a profit generating activity but rather as an effort to try to meet desired business plan budget estimates for either part or all of the energy requirements for future periods. If better than budget cost is achieved, there is reason to smile, but it can also go the opposite way. Again, developing a written hedging policy is mandatory when contemplating the employment of hedging.

Consumption Management

The traditional goal of consumption management is simple: decrease energy cost by improving energy efficiency. At the basic level toward achieving this goal is the creation and use of energy efficient procedures and operating practices. This includes maintaining infrastructure, equipment, and controls in a condition that assures on-spec performance. Examples include the tuning of controls (i.e., fuel to air ratio), efficient insulation, leak prevention (steam, water, air and other utilities), and special practices that minimize energy consumption during start-up, shutdown, or delay and idle. All of these assure the best physical performance of process equipment, and the key to their sustainability and consistency is continuous process monitoring for out-of-spec operation followed by correction (see Figure 10.7).

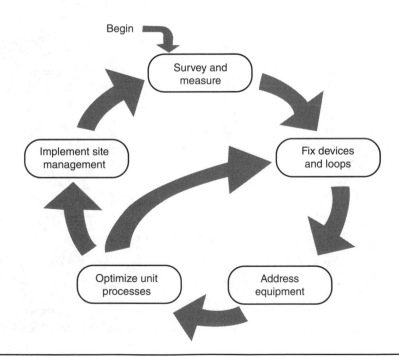

Figure 10.7   Efficiency improvement

A step up from the fundamental on-spec operation is efforts that improve existing performance. This normally involves the substitution of original process equipment or the process itself with a more efficient alternate. Examples include the better matching of equipment size to process requirements (i.e., replacing oversized or inefficient motors and pumps), replacing a wasteful throttling process with a variable output prime driver (i.e., replacing a constant speed fan employing modulating louvers with a variable speed motor and non-modulating louvers), lowering the prime operating system pressure or temperature, substituting convection type heating with radiant heat, switching to more efficient lighting sources (LED and CFL instead of incandescent light, T8 fluorescent light bulbs for T12). Examples are quite extensive as well as varied in complexity. The primary goal is substituting a more efficient process for the original one.

There is one area of consumption management that doesn't try to reduce energy but instead makes a decision to use it or not for a special financial reward. This *interruptibilty* of consumption is rewarded by utility companies or other suppliers as part of prearranged interruptible contracts. For natural gas, interruptibilty is rewarded through contracts whose transport rate is generally less than that of a non-interruptible transport contract (firm) or at least carries no long term *take or pay* commitment. For electricity, the end user typically curtails its operation to reduce load and receives an upfront reward for volunteering ahead of time to do so. There are many other aspects to this topic. A new *smartmeter* initiative by many utility companies across the nation is extending this concept to the small consumer (including homeowners).

Beyond the traditional efficiency focus of consumption management, a decade of daily energy headlines has brought a new consideration and dimension to contemporary consumption management. Today, it also contributes to solving environmentally related concerns as well as associated public image and responsibility. Today's energy consumption management is so globally compelling that governments worldwide have major programs to help achieve better performance. The U.S. government has stepped up its effort and commitment dramatically. It now offers help not only to the typical consumer but to commercial and industrial companies as well. Today's global consumption management mission goes beyond efficiency interest to include the development and use of alternate energy forms that help to conserve the world's fossil reserves themselves. All of this helps to reduce global warming and pollution. If you haven't joined in the effort, it's time to do so. It's all part of a comprehensive energy management effort.

Energy Project Development

The motives of energy project development include cost reduction, retaining competitive edge, and positively impacting a company's carbon footprint. The opportunities are usually derived from technological and practice changes. Project opportunity areas typically fall within the following categories:

- Recovering waste heat (Figure 10.8)
- Replacement of pumps and motors
- Improving lighting technology
- HVAC improvement
- Installing back-up generation or co-generation
- Hosting alternative energy projects by developers

Historically, many project returns derived from efficiency improvement alone typically have not had sufficient short-term return or urgency to motivate investment, especially when compared to other competing project categories within a company. The contemporary situation is changing though, due in part to the higher costs for energy, but just as importantly, with the need for compliance with more stringent environmental regulations and concerns. Besides ongoing examples that include the Reasonably Available Control Technology Rule and the Clean Air Act, new, more stringent and broader environmental regulations are evolving, and energy's inherent tie with contemporary

Figure 10.8   Heat recovery unit

environmental issues brings increased weight to the energy project justification equation. A recent example is the 2010 United States requirement of the metering and reporting of fuel use associated with greenhouse gas (GHG) emissions for large consumers of energy (typically utilities and large commercial and industrial companies).

The introduction of government incentives and voluntary participation programs are additional sources of project funding and motivation. Other federal legislation is on the horizon. Also, many states have already enacted renewable portfolio standards (RPS) for electric generation, in effect, requiring a certain percentage of total electric generation to be from renewable sources. The RPS requirements are a key driver in the development of projects like wind and solar generation.

The internal funding of projects has always been challenging. As an alternate, one can engage in outside financing. In this arrangement, an investment group provides the funding for either part or all of the project's capital requirements and then shares in the project's benefit. For the end user, aside from the financial stability of the financing company, the most important aspect of the relationship is the establishment of a valid benchmark of performance to which the new performance will be judged. This requires accurate past data and clear expectations.

Many renewable energy sources (i.e., solar, biodiesel, wind, etc.) enjoy favorable funding and tax and depreciation treatment from both federal and state sources. Examples include wind farm development (Figure 10.9), which, without favorable treatment, would have been much more difficult to get underway and sustain. For solar development, New Jersey is a lead U.S. state, while Germany by national choice has been a world leader in support of solar-based electricity generation. Biodiesel and flex fuel development has also been supported through favorable tax treatments.

The government's DOE and EPA partnering programs have given industry new resources for evaluating and teaching energy efficiency at the process level (fans, pumps, motors, lighting, and steam systems). They offer extensive *assessment* programs, as well as standardized yet in-depth programs for end-user application. This renewed interest in energy prudence has rekindled the all but idled end-user efficiency programs of the mid-1970s and 80s. New technical advancements in equipment such as lighting, motors, fans, and process control equipment are all sources of project opportunity.

Enhanced versions of computer-based sophisticated supervisory control and monitoring help to improve operational efficiency. They lessen individual operator error while helping to tie together previous stand-alone improvements to help reduce energy consumption and predict maintenance requirements and reduce downtime. While providing centralized reporting and monitoring, they also provide the reporting capability for federal requirements.

Figure 10.9   Wind turbines

When energy supply deregulation was enacted, the unbundling of energy supply in participating states introduced new opportunities for cost reduction. On the operations side, depending on the electrical end-user's load size and generation capability, various opportunities can be employed to create revenues. One example might be the installation of in-house electricity generation capability (Figure 10.10). This could be used to participate in the interruptible tariffs of utilities. The capital involved is offset by yearly lump-sum rewards for the utility's right to interrupt load to the participant, as well as more favorable electricity costs.

A noncapital way of taking advantage of electricity pricing differential between peak and non-peak hours is the scheduling of production during off-peak demand times. In addition, on-peak interrupted production can be made up during off-peak hours. For natural gas, an alternate fuel like fuel oil or propane may be used as a substitute for natural gas volume sold into the market during periods of high pricing differential. The capital for the storage facilities is offset by lower interruptible transport costs and arbitrage revenue.

Figure 10.10   Generator

In the end, for a company to derive maximum benefit from energy project opportunities, the participation of all of the components of the equation, from the regulation to the provider to the consumer, is necessary.

Participation in the Regulatory and Legislative Process

Before deregulation, natural gas and electricity providers were, in effect, monopolies. Because of the significant investment in infrastructure required, it was not practical to have more than one system of pipes or wires competing for the same customers. To ensure that customers would be treated fairly, regulatory bodies in the form of public utility commissions were formed in each state to control rates for services from the monopoly suppliers.

As a result of this structure, there was little opportunity for an end user to influence the price of energy service for his operations. During the rate making process, it was possible to intervene independently or as a group to offer testimony and try to influence commission decisions on cost allocations for the utility company. In this way, industrial companies were able, because of their unique circumstances, to establish rate structures more favorable than other customer classes. But this did not alleviate the problem of geographic price disparity and lack of competitiveness among utility companies. Customers with facilities in higher priced territories were at a disadvantage against competitors in lower priced territories. This situation was a prime driver in the path to deregulation.

When deregulation occurred in natural gas and electricity markets, it was only the commodity portion of the service that was deregulated. The pipeline transport or wire transmission still remained regulated. The public service commission in each state still determines the rates that the utilities, now LDCs for natural gas and EDCs for electricity, can charge for the final leg of delivery of the commodity. There still remains a disparity among LDCs for this service, and it can be a significant portion of the total delivered cost to the end user.

Additionally, the interstate pipelines that transport natural gas and the high voltage long distance transmission lines that move electricity continue to be regulated by FERC.

So, it remains vitally important for the end user of energy to participate in the regulatory process and maintain a detailed understanding of rates and tariffs that pertain to his facilities. The gains made in the effort to lower the purchased cost of the commodity can be and usually are eroded by increases in the regulated transport services. Participation in rate proceedings through the intervention process will continue to be a vital cost management process. Also, in those states where electricity has not been deregulated, the issue is even more critical since it is the only way to mitigate cost increases in electricity services.

Just as participating in the regulatory process is important to mitigate cost increases, participation in the legislative process on the state or federal level can be equally important. In the current global warming sensitive environment, there is much proposed legislation at the federal level and the state level to push energy consumption toward *cleaner* fuel sources. It is almost a certainty that any legislation that is enacted will increase costs for any company. Being involved in the legislative process through lobbying groups or even individually, when appropriate, may not eliminate the negative implications, but it will certainly mitigate the outcome, so it is as favorable as possible to the end-use companies.

Carbon Footprint Management

Carbon footprint can be defined as the total set of GHG emissions caused by an organization, event, or product. It is often expressed in terms of the amount of carbon dioxide equivalent of all categories of GHGs emitted. It benchmarks how *green* something is. Since carbon dioxide equivalents are to a large extent the byproduct of most common fossil fuel burning activities, it's tied to *everyday* energy use by default. Figure 10.11 depicts the global sources of carbon dioxide.

Ever since the United States acknowledged climate change in the mid-2000s, much work has gone into adopting (and adapting to) programs and rules that support its control and reduction. Key U.S. senators continue to work for a congressional consensus for legislative action. Stringent automotive (CAFÉ) emissions reduction along with *cap and trade* of CO_2 equivalents are the prime components, although the latter remains very contentious. In the meantime, the government has asked industry members to participate in a voluntary 25% *energy intensity* reduction over ten years.

To help reduce climate change, individual states are requiring utilities to generate a certain portion of their electricity from renewable energy sources (solar, wind, waves, geothermal, other). In some states, entities that purchase this electricity can receive renewable energy credits in an effort to become

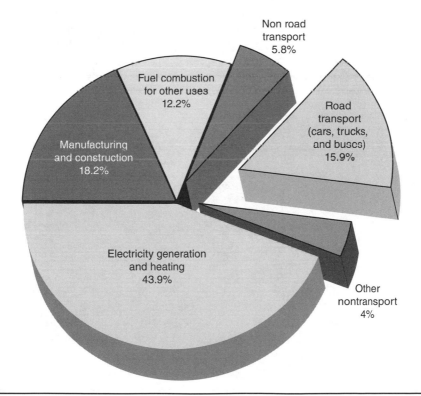

Figure 10.11   GHG sources

carbon neutral and green. Along the same line, since natural gas produces about half the emissions that coal burning does (50% of electricity generation is coal based), the industry is substituting natural gas fired gas turbines for coal and fuel oil based power stations. Efforts to convert automotive vehicles to natural gas are also underway. Natural gas has become the preferred green fuel.

To recognize energy awareness and its advancement by progressive participants, the United States has many programs that identify, certify, and credit energy prowess. Examples include the Leadership in Energy & Environmental Design for fostering green energy efficiency in office building design and ISO 50000 that certifies and credits ongoing excellence in green manufacturing efficiency advancement. A *GHG protocol* is now available for identifying and accounting all of the different GHG emissions that an entity causes as it produces a product. The method defines three *scopes* or phases of emissions generation. Figure 10.12 is a simple illustration.

This inventory process is still voluntary, but at some point, it will likely become mandatory. Recently enacted, large consumers are now required to measure and annually report their fuel use that contributes to their GHG emissions. These kinds of programs fit well into the strategic sourcing philosophy in that they provide a way of identifying and associating oneself with *best in class*—and hence assumed best in cost—supply partnering. Enhanced public image can also be a benefit. All of these programs can aid in the justification of energy projects. They are old intangibles that have new tangible value in today's energy focused world.

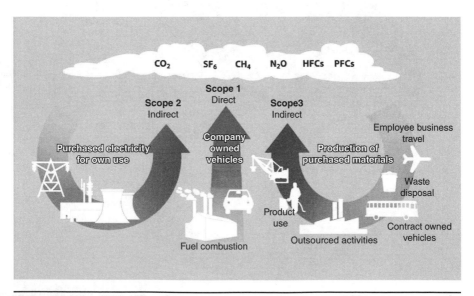

Figure 10.12   GHG emissions protocol

The uncertainty of what final form proposed legislation and proposed regulation will eventually be enacted into law is a major contributor to a company's indecision and inaction. In the end, the best course of action is good sense and an awareness of what is being considered and what its potential effect on the company may be. A proactive approach will serve best.

Internal Energy Management Organization

As has been discussed throughout this chapter, there are many aspects to a comprehensive energy management program. It is vital for a company, especially when energy cost is a significant expenditure, to be proactively involved in all the aspects discussed. Many companies have ignored, or are unaware of, the opportunities available to manage cost in the energy arena. Some are intimidated by the complexity or are content to relegate energy management to a service supplier they are forced to deal with because they have no internal knowledge or capability.

There is no one size fits all comprehensive energy management organization that will be effective for all companies. Each company is different and organizing a comprehensive energy management effort will depend on each company's individuality. Factors such as size, overall energy spend, number of locations, corporate culture, central or decentralized management style, diversity of product lines, whether industrial or commercial, will all weigh in the final design of an effective organization. However, regardless of a company's individual factors, there are aspects to a successful comprehensive energy management organization that are absolutely necessary.

Senior executive stakeholder: Experience has shown that comprehensive energy management must be a *top down* effort. A senior executive must take ownership of energy management and ensure a high level of awareness throughout the organization. The senior executive is the stakeholder.

Energy manager: There must be someone in the role of energy manager or energy director. The person's responsibilities will be devoted full time to energy. He or she will be charged to coordinate all of the aspects of the comprehensive energy management effort and will derive authority from the senior executive. The energy manager usually resides in the procurement function but works closely with all the other disciplines that are involved in the process to provide leadership and direction. In many instances, the energy manager will determine if external expertise is required and will manage the selection process. In companies where the energy spend is very large, the comprehensive energy management effort can be a staffed group with appropriate expertise that manages the company's energy spend. The energy manager will also be charged within maintaining a central energy market knowledge resource that supports the various participants within the company.

Local energy coordinator: When there is more than one operating location, there must be a person responsible for being the local energy coordinator. This may even be a full-time position. The role of the energy coordinator is to focus on those aspects of comprehensive energy management that are unique to the operating locations, such as consumption management.

Mechanisms for sharing knowledge: There must be a mechanism established to exchange information among divisions and locations about energy successes and failures. This will prevent sub-optimization and drive the organization to next level in the energy management arena. For example, successes in one location with innovative lighting programs can usually be repeated at other locations. Sharing failures among locations will prevent them from being repeated.

Additionally, a periodic gathering of energy-focused personnel, led by the energy manager, will ensure a common goal within the organization and dispense leading edge market knowledge as well as identify project opportunity.

For companies where energy spending is less significant or for companies with a single location, the stakeholder, energy manager, and energy coordinator will most likely be combined into a single responsibility. Much of the required expertise necessary to manage the various aspects of comprehensive energy management can be outsourced.

When dealing with service providers, it is critical for the company's energy manager to maintain appropriate market knowledge and not relegate his or her responsibility to the service provider. This happens all too often in the current realities, and as a result, the company loses its capability to manage its energy affairs with internal staff.

Concluding Thoughts

Effective energy management demands aggressive participation in the energy arena with attention to all the issues that can impact the total cost of energy. Next level supply organizations know that energy management offers substantial opportunities to manage a cost category that is often taken for granted or largely ignored. After all, when we turn on the light switch, the lights go on. What more could we ask? Just as transportation deregulation in the early 1980s opened a world of possibilities for managing transport costs, energy deregulation, as well as advances in technology, offers this generation of supply managers a similar world of possibilities. But these opportunities are only open to those organizations that develop the expertise to manage this very complex commodity.

Chapter Note

1. The authors acknowledge the important contributions of Peter Franolic and Ted Eichenlaub to this chapter.

11

Enhanced Sourcing with Idealized Design

This chapter is about a process called idealized design that has a track record of generating real and lasting impact, both on the bottom line and on innovation in how procurement work is performed. It creates fruitful collaboration among procurement professionals, their clients, and suppliers. Despite its academic-sounding name, idealized design provides a practical approach for bringing to life the key concepts in this book so that supply management transformation is successfully executed. The process is so versatile that it can be applied to any aspect of supply management.

We'll try to make this chapter interesting by walking you through a variety of cases showing how the process is applied and the bottom-line impact it makes. The examples provided are from experience applying idealized design to procurement at pharmaceutical giant GlaxoSmithKline (GSK). A transformation began in 1999 when the vice president of global procurement systems, processes, and operations decided that idealized design would become the centerpiece of how his systems and processes group engaged its user base and planned the department's activities. This initiated a ten-year journey applying idealized design, first in procurement and then throughout the company. By the end of this chapter, you should see that idealized design can be used in any aspect of supply management to help reduce cost, generate revenue, improve return on invested capital (ROIC), accelerate the sourcing process, and mitigate risk.

Idealized Design Overview

The key feature of idealized design session is that participants pretend that a process, system, or product that they are designing was destroyed the previous night. They are designing what they ideally want today if they could have whatever they wanted. Doing this allows people to *think outside the box*, unleashing creativity and generating momentum, buy-in, and consensus that support implementation of innovations and breakthroughs. In essence, participants start at the end—where they want to be—and work back from there. This removes perceived obstacles and generates consensus and commitment on *how to get there*.

During an idealized design session, the participants perform two main activities, which Figure 11.1 summarizes. They start by making a list of ideal *specifications* or characteristics of something they would like to create. Then, they begin creating a *design* that will bring about the chosen specifications.

A specification is a statement of a desired property or characteristic of a function, a process, or input. For example, if a person pushes a button for the wrong floor in an elevator, having the ability to cancel it is a specification of desired functionality. A design is a structure and a process that will bring about one or more desired specifications. Continuing with the example, a design to bring about the desired specification of canceling wrong floors on an elevator might be to develop *cancel* buttons that would be placed by each floor button.

When the initial idealized design session is finished, a small core team takes the outputs and iteratively turns them into a practical design to move forward. The design that is ultimately implemented must be financially viable, so the team pursues those ideas with an acceptable return. The cases we present later will illustrate the bottom-line impact.

Idealized design is different from prevailing procurement practices for defining requirements and streamlining processes. Many supply chain organizations engage in lean improvement efforts, but where are the breakthroughs that take them to the next level of performance? The way many lean tools are applied nearly guarantees reproducing or tweaking the status quo. Teams spend time analyzing the current state, identifying root causes of problems,

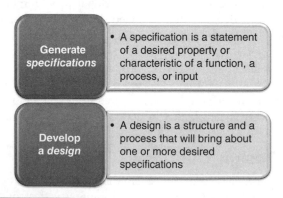

Figure 11.1   Participants perform two major activities

Specifications	Design
• Specific statements should begin with *There ought to be* or *I would like* • *Don't wants* should be converted to *Ought to be* • Record specifications in real time • Remind participants to stay in *design-from-scratch* mode • Facilitators should prompt further discussion by saying *Tell me more about that* or *Say more about that*	• Participants to create or draw structure and processes to bring about specification • Start design with what is most important • Group should make design choices by consensus • Document as much as possible so that all design ideas are captured • Design phase is most difficult ... some teams will struggle

Figure 11.2   More *how to* for specs and design

and then developing solutions to problems. But if you fix problems in the current system, don't you only get back to where you were? The problem is that little or no time is spent focusing on what is ultimately wanted without regard for what's in place today. That's a major reason we don't see many breakthroughs, and why idealized design can be helpful. It's the difference between *continuous improvement* and *discontinuous improvement*. Idealized design allows for unconstrained thinking and for stakeholders to go into depth designing and discovering what they really want. Figure 11.2 provides more insight into idealized design process.

Planning And Setting Up Idealized Design Sessions

This section provides detailed guidance to sourcing managers about how to arrange and lead idealized design sessions. The process of planning and setting up idealized design sessions includes the following key elements, which Figure 11.3 also summarizes.

Setting the Idealized Design Session Scope: In planning one or more idealized design sessions, the sourcing team will need to define what will be the session scope. This is a brief statement—one or two sentences—on what the participants will be asked to design. Getting the correct scope is important but can be tricky and requires some thought. This is where multiple sessions can be helpful. The initial session(s) could be broader, and subsequent sessions could focus in more detail on specific aspects that stakeholders have identified as important.

Facilities: A single idealized design session will require a room for 12-15 participants (i.e., users) and as many of the *providers* (i.e., those who provide a service or product) as can attend. The providers are there to listen. The room should include flip charts, a big screen, and an LCD projector for use when

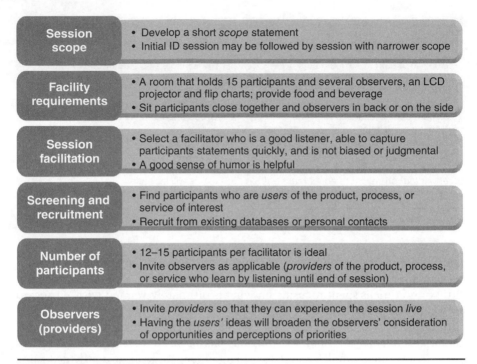

Session scope	• Develop a short *scope* statement • Initial ID session may be followed by session with narrower scope
Facility requirements	• A room that holds 15 participants and several observers, an LCD projector and flip charts; provide food and beverage • Sit participants close together and observers in back or on the side
Session facilitation	• Select a facilitator who is a good listener, able to capture participants statements quickly, and is not biased or judgmental • A good sense of humor is helpful
Screening and recruitment	• Find participants who are *users* of the product, process, or service of interest • Recruit from existing databases or personal contacts
Number of participants	• 12–15 participants per facilitator is ideal • Invite observers as applicable (*providers* of the product, process, or service who learn by listening until end of session)
Observers (providers)	• Invite *providers* so that they can experience the session *live* • Having the *users'* ideas will broaden the observers' consideration of opportunities and perceptions of priorities

Figure 11.3 Organizing an idealized design session

introducing the process and displaying the specifications as they are captured. The participants will use the flip charts during the design phase to record diagrams and/or text.

Idealized Design Session Facilitation: The sourcing team identifies a facilitator for the idealized design session(s). The activities the facilitator will perform are discussed in more detail later in this chapter.

Screening and Recruiting: A key step is identifying the session participants. The most important criterion is that the participants should include those who actually use a process, service, or product of interest (e.g., employees who use manufacturing equipment; employees who use legal services; employees who travel frequently; employees who requisition). The next step is to identify how participants will be recruited. They could be identified from databases of users or, less formally, recruited from personal contacts of people in the organization itself.

Number of Participants: The sourcing project team should recruit 12-15 participants per facilitator. Idealized design sessions are designed as group sessions rather than one-on-one sessions because people can contribute their individual ideas, build on each other's ideas, and are stimulated to think of things they would not likely have come up with on their own.

Another advantage of having 12-15 participants per facilitator is that they can work together on specifications, then split into two or three breakout groups of five people to work separately on their designs during the design phase. The use of three groups creates more opportunities for design ideas to emerge. When there is more than one breakout group, it is beneficial to have the groups present their designs to each other at the end of the session. It is possible to engage dozens of participants at one time by using multiple facilitators. In such cases, the lead facilitator could introduce the process to the entire group and, when starting specifications, have the other facilitators support the breakout groups.

Observers: Invite as many *providers* as possible to the session, so they can experience it *live*. A broader involvement of observers lessens the need for those who did attend to go back and *sell* the results to others. As many sourcing team members as possible, as well as others who support the service or process, should attend. It will also be helpful for one or more high level sponsor and individual/group who supports the project team to attend, so they can be exposed to the ideas.

Providers should sit on the perimeter of the room and take notes, having been advised prior to the session that they are there only to listen, at least until the session nears its end. Experience has shown that observers in the room do not distract participants because the participants become so focused around designing their ideal design that they forget about their surroundings. Observers can also listen remotely when it's not feasible to bring everyone together.

Leading an Idealized Design Session

At the beginning of the idealized design session, a facilitator tells participants they will be taking part in a process called customer idealized design, in which they become all-powerful designers of their ideal process, service, system, etc. At this point, the facilitator briefly reviews the scope of what they will be designing. Next, the participants briefly introduce themselves with providers acknowledged but not individually identified. This is followed by an introduction to the idealized design process, which typically ranges from 15-30 minutes. This introduction includes guidelines for the idealized design session (discussed later in this chapter). It should also include a story about an application of idealized design. Doing so makes things clearer for the participants and gives them a sense of what they will be doing for the remainder of the session. A story also helps people understand what the specifications phase is about and how the design is derived from the specifications.

Guidelines for Facilitating the Session

During the introduction to the idealized design session, the facilitator creates the right environment by instructing the participants to follow a set of inter-related guidelines:

- *The current process/system was destroyed last night.* This assumption is critically important because referring to the existing system holds participants back from thinking about what they really want. Their minds tend to get caught up in the constraints of the current situation, and they do not allow themselves to think beyond that, which is the most common constraint to breakthroughs.
- *Focus on what you would like to have if you could have whatever you wanted: think of it as your ideal; stay in design-from-scratch mode.* The idea is to get the participants to not hold back.
- *Don't focus on what is not wanted.* Focusing on negative aspects saps positive energy and takes time away from focusing on ideals.
- *Don't worry about whether resources are available to implement your wishes/ideals or whether it's even possible to implement the wishes.* Imparting this message is critical because worry or skepticism about whether the design will ever be implemented frequently limits imaginations. Furthermore, breakthrough thinking often increases available resources because decision makers will see additional areas that are attractive and worthy of investment.
- *If you disagree with someone else's specification, simply state an alternative specification.* The facilitator must not allow participants to criticize each other's specifications since this often destroys the constructive and creative mood. He should tell them that evaluation and prioritization (i.e., critical analysis) come after the session.
- *Providers must agree to remain in listen-only mode.* Providers must remain listeners until the end, when they may ask questions. Following this guideline prevents providers from asking questions that divert the users from talking about what they want.

On occasion, providers want to make sure their concerns are addressed in a session, or they want to hear the participants' reactions to topics they feel are important. It is best to delay the introduction of providers' topics until later in the session or even until the end so the creative flow of the users' own ideas is not disrupted. In some cases, the facilitator can get a list of topics from the providers at or near the end of the specifications phase and ask the participants to give their thoughts (and possibly specifications) on the providers' topics that haven't been covered. It is also possible to build in time for questions near the end of the session where the providers can talk with the participants about topics of interest. Figure 11.4 summarizes the facilitator guidelines.

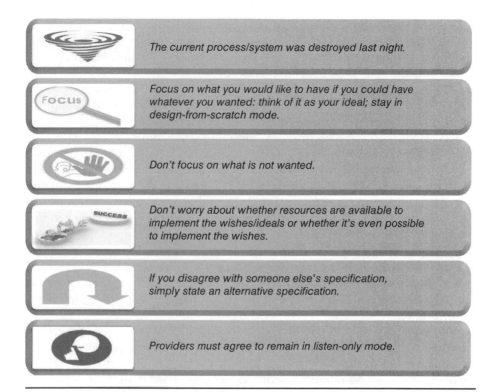

The current process/system was destroyed last night.

Focus on what you would like to have if you could have whatever you wanted: think of it as your ideal; stay in design-from-scratch mode.

Don't focus on what is not wanted.

Don't worry about whether resources are available to implement the wishes/ideals or whether it's even possible to implement the wishes.

If you disagree with someone else's specification, simply state an alternative specification.

Providers must agree to remain in listen-only mode.

Figure 11.4   Six facilitator guidelines

Specifications Phase

The facilitator should start the specifications phase of the session by asking the participants to give their bullet statements about what they would like in their ideal. He should:

- Instruct participants that their specification statements should begin with phrases such as "There ought to be . . ." or "I would like . . ." If participants start talking about what they don't want, they should be asked to convert that into a specification of what *ought to be*.
- Record all specifications so everybody can see them being written in real-time. This not only captures everything but also shows participants that their input is being taken seriously. The facilitator should ask participants to speak up whenever something has not been captured accurately.
- Remind participants that it is important that they stay in design-from-scratch mode. If participants refer to the existing process or complain about current problems, the facilitator must remind them that the process was destroyed last night and that there are no problems to complain about.

There's one aspect of facilitating that appears subtle but is important. Often, people state specifications that are worth following up in order to learn more about what they want or why they want it. Probing further will get at the underlying emotional and rational basis for the specification. The facilitator should probe by simply saying, "Tell me more about that" or "Say more about that." These phrases keep the discussion open-ended and encourage people to expand on their specifications.

Knowing when to probe further is something that comes with practice, but there are a couple of situations where it is clearly needed. One is when it's apparent that to implement what the person is saying, more detail or explanation is needed. If the facilitator does not follow up, the sourcing team will never know what the user had in mind. The other situation is when someone uses words that are emotion laden. Further probing can shed light on product or service features and/or emotional benefits that may be important. This also shows that the facilitator is interested in what the person has to say, making it safer for other participants to offer what they may personally feel are outrageous ideas but in reality could be major breakthroughs. In some cases, the facilitator can reveal deep insights about a particular statement by following up multiple times to the participant's responses to her probing.

The facilitator should be careful not to judge ideas—either negatively or positively—because this discourages the participants from offering them or can guide them in the direction they think the facilitator wants them to go. Instead, he or she should simply write ideas down. There will be plenty of opportunity after the session to evaluate specifications. The facilitator needs to *go* wherever the participants' design takes him.

Design Phase

In the design phase, the participants create (or draw on) structures and processes that would bring about the specifications. Design is essentially about showing possible ways that selected specifications could be brought about.

There are a few things the facilitator can do to get the design process moving efficiently. A way to begin is to ask the participants to think about the specifications and start with what is most important to them. It is not necessary to go back through the specifications to see what was discussed; experience shows that this just takes up time that could be spent working on the design. The participants should be instructed to start with what they collectively feel was most important. To determine this, a group will sometimes have a brief dialogue, create a short list of candidate items they might work on, and then choose one or more for which they will create a design. It is better for the group to make its choices by consensus than by voting since voting implies winners and losers.

Designing is a creative process, meaning no one ever knows for sure what will emerge or exactly how the groups will work. The design phase is the hardest part of the process, and it is not unusual for some groups to flounder, at least for a while. Reassuringly, there will be many good ideas in the specifications—and accordingly, no shortage of possibilities to develop.

Having 12-15 participants allows the group to form two or three breakout teams during the design phase. It is helpful for the facilitator to step aside and allow the participants to self-lead the breakout sessions. Having participants facilitate the design phase also helps solidify ownership of their designs, which helps promote full participation and leadership. The facilitator should tell the teams that they should try to document as much as possible so that all ideas are preserved.

During an initial half-day idealized design session, the participants will spend one to two hours working on their design. When more than one half day is available, it can be productive to have participants go into greater detail. The facilitator should instruct the participants as to how long they should work on their designs, taking into account when the session is scheduled to end. In cases where the breakout teams will be reporting their designs back to the entire group, about ten minutes per group should be factored in. In cases where the *providers* want to ask the users questions at the end, approximately 15 minutes total should be factored in. Reporting back with questions and answers takes time away from designing, so this trade-off should be taken into account.

The Post-Initial Idealized Design Session

The next step following the initial idealized design session(s) is to establish a relatively small design *core team* (often three to five people) that will lead the process of iteratively taking the idealized design further. The core team often includes some or all of the sourcing project team members if the team has already been formed. The time commitment required of each of the team members varies widely depending on the scope, complexity, priority, and timeline of the sourcing initiative.

The core team will draw on ad hoc input as well as the periodic participation of an extended team, while continually reconnecting with users in the process of iteratively enhancing the design. The core team continues the design process by *mocking up* design possibilities and working with users and other providers to refine and enhance the design over the following weeks or months. The more complex the process and the more diverse the stakeholders, the longer the process will take. The iterative design process typically goes through ten or more iterations of additions, refinements, enhancements, and deletions before the design is sufficiently fleshed out.

The mockup process involves not only continual development by the design team members and others in the sourcing project team, but also periodic input from users, senior management, functional heads, and other key stakeholders. The sourcing project team should get the input of not only those directly affected by the design, but also of those who are likely to influence the new process launch. This allows relevant personnel to shape the new process or product, which in turn helps generate buy-in.

Additional noteworthy benefits of an iterative design process include:

- It allows the team to make mistakes and corrections before the product, service, or system is physically designed.
- It helps reveal potentially flawed assumptions about the needed solution(s), helps identify details about what is needed, and points to how the solution would work in practice.
- It shows the sourcing team it is making progress, which gives them satisfaction and momentum. This further promotes buy-in within the team itself and gives members confidence that the product or service will be aligned with stakeholder needs.
- Often, many of the specifications are converted into requirements and/ or questions for requests for information and requests for proposals. Designs can also be attached so suppliers are more likely to understand the users' detailed needs.

Case Examples of Using Idealized Design

The following cases show the many ways that idealized design can be used to take organizations to the next level. As you will see, this process is robust, which means it can be applied across many kinds of settings and situations.

Using Idealized Design to Develop a Risk Mitigation System

GSK was sole sourcing a key raw material from a Japanese supplier who produced that material in only one plant. In 2008, that supplier's plant exploded and burned to the ground. In another case, GSK sourced a raw material for one of its blood thinning products. In 2008, Chinese supplies of this key material became contaminated, and hundreds of people around the world died from allergic reactions. While other companies were forced to issue product recalls, GSK was unaffected. Despite these disasters, GSK didn't lose a single dollar in sales and experienced no disruptions to its supply chain.

How did GSK avoid disaster? To answer this question we need to go back to 2007. At that time, the direct materials procurement team maintained a spreadsheet-based, manual, and fragmented risk-mitigation process. Raw materials were often looked at separately, and there was not a holistic bill-of-materials view of each product's supply chain. No one had a quick, company-wide way to see sources of supply, stocks of raw material across the company, which sites handled each raw material, and how materials were processed and moved through the supply network.

This process began to change when GSK's chief procurement officer charged a team with creating a system that would protect the company's top 25 product revenue streams by putting in place supply risk mitigation action plans for key materials. The key word here is *action*. GSK created a system that enabled them to take action not only after a disruption but, critically, take action beforehand to minimize or eliminate the impact from certain risks.

Here's how the supply risk project proceeded. A team was formed and charged with building a risk mitigation action plan (RMAP) system. The team engaged more than 100 stakeholders (including manufacturing personnel, buyers, sourcing managers, finance, suppliers, and IT) in an idealized re-design of the risk mitigation process. This team reviewed the bills of materials for each of the top 25 products and mapped the supply chain for each material—how these materials were transported, where they were stored around the world, and where they were processed.

A key goal for each material was to identify high, medium, or low supply risk along two scales: probability of occurrence and severity of impact. The idealized design process resulted in the creation of a system that required category managers to enter information for each raw material. The system then calculates a risk factor. The category managers then use this system to complete RMAPs for important risks.

Some action plans call for doing things before a potential incident can occur. For example, in the case of the sole-source Japanese supplier whose plant exploded, the category manager had protected the company by setting aside a six-month safety stock of the raw material that was specifically marked for mitigating risk. In the case of the tainted Chinese supply, the company wasn't using Chinese supply because the RMAP had indicated the risk was too high. When the Chinese crisis hit, the category manager was able to quickly view key information in the system, including which products the raw material was being used in, the level of material in stock, and the suppliers currently being used. He was then able to move stock around the network so none of the plants would run short, particularly since other companies would be entering the supply market in search of non-tainted supplies.

The RMAP system also has sections that help the category manager review other types of risks, including:

- Quality risks
- Supplier legal and financial/commercial risks
- Regulatory risks
- Supplier performance issues
- Environmental, health, and safety risks

The bottom line is that the idealized design process helped GSK protect its revenues, profits, reputation, and safety of its products.

Using Idealized Design to Shorten Product Development

This case is about the use of idealized design to help generate business/user requirements for procured goods. In this case, GSK got away from the norm of reproducing existing requirements for lab test equipment. The company accomplished this by engaging scientists in designing new lab equipment that reduced the cycle time for developing new medicines.

When pharmaceutical companies develop new medicines, they need to test drug dosage forms to determine how they dissolve and release their medication into the body. One laboratory machine simulates the human digestive system. It contains six clear glass *vessels* that look a bit like lab beakers and are the size of the stomach. These vessels are kept at body temperature via a water bath. The equipment contains paddles inside the vessels that turn the contents slowly in order to simulate the churning of the stomach. Scientists can check to see the rate at which various tablet *candidates* release the medicine.

The challenge to the procurement category manager and lab manager was to generate breakthrough user requirements that a supplier could utilize to create new equipment that would help scientists work more efficiently and effectively. To meet the challenge, the research and development procurement manager involved users—nearly 60 scientists—in designing their ideal machine for accomplishing this task.

Here are some of the design features the scientists generated:

- The vessels would be wrapped in a transparent heating film that keeps them at body temperature instead of the conventional heated water bath. (This change eliminates hazardous waste water, as well as the 20 minutes it takes to heat the water to body temperature.)
- Instead of the current six vessels, it would be designed as a tower that holds 12, 18, or 24 vessels within the same footprint on the laboratory bench-top.
- For easy servicing, the tower could be opened like a side-by-side refrigerator.
- Enable the 24 vessels to run independently so that if one or more of the experiments in the 24 vessels fails, the others will continue uninterrupted.
- Enable the user to receive a text, phone call, and/or e-mail if any experiments fail.
- Enable the user to monitor and operate the system remotely from anywhere in the world.
- Here's what one of the senior scientists said about the idealized design process:

My team was struggling to identify a good process to define business requirements for some new lab equipment. Within six weeks after we learned about idealized design, we had completed several sessions at five sites, generating hundreds of creative and original ideas from nearly 60 users. With just some minor additional categorizing and prioritizing, the result was a document that will be used by a selected vendor as the design basis for the new equipment. The biggest benefits from idealized design were to place some needed structure around the requirements gathering process and to engage and provide a sense of ownership to a broad population of users.

The bottom line is the new equipment design, created through the idealized design process, accelerates drug development, enables scientists to obtain higher-quality test results in less than half the time, and frees them to work on other projects during much of that run-time. Getting new drugs to the market sooner has resulted in more time in which a medicine can be sold under patent, which often means an incremental $1,000,000 or more in sales per day. With this lab equipment costing around $100,000, the higher throughput and utilization contribute to a higher ROIC. Directly enhancing a higher ROIC is something all next level supply organizations strive to achieve.

Using Idealized Design to Improve Corporate Travel Services

The director of corporate services procurement at GSK, Janan Johnson, applied idealized design to travel procurement. Her objective was to engage employees to generate ideas on how the travel experience could be improved and what suppliers and *internal providers* could do to improve the process.

Johnson invited multiple suppliers to participate—GSK's airline partners, corporate card supplier, hotel partners, and car rental agencies. These companies attended several idealized design sessions where they were observers while internal customers—employees who use their travel services—designed their ideal system. Subsequently, the suppliers worked with the procurement team to execute initiatives to make key aspects of the design a reality.

Reflecting on the idealized design process, Johnson identified four things she liked about the application of the process to travel:

First, it validated that what my team was already doing and planning was right and gave me additional insight and detail from users about how we should execute our ideas and make them more usable. Second, I can count on the process to be the source of the next innovative idea. Third, involving the supply base helped build a better partnership between my team and the suppliers. It gave them better transparency on what my internal customers (i.e., users) want—rather than my speaking for the customer and the suppliers not being sure that I truly understand what my users want. In other words, not having a procurement middleman helps create better buy-in to the ideas from the suppliers. And fourth, another interesting result came from working so intimately with suppliers who participated in the idealized design workshops. The process really built our confidence in these suppliers and strengthened relationships profoundly—to the point where we have changed how we approach contracts. For example, we've never signed a five-year contract before, but we just did with American Express when we renewed our corporate card program.

Johnson also added that a number of specific improvements resulted from the process:

One thing that was clear was that employees want a lot of transactional/back-end processes related to travel—expense reports, for example—to take place automatically, with the forms prepopulated with card charge data. This validated the expansion of a system we had in place in one country to additional countries. Employees also said they ideally want to have one integrated process, so they can handle all of their travel needs, such as air, hotel, and chauffeur cars, together rather than calling separate groups or using multiple systems. Consequently, we are now piloting a system that allows booking and tracking all of these together.

During the sessions, it became clear that participants were not aware of all the services currently available to them. A communication plan was created as a result. Johnson elaborated: "We found that there were a number of travel-related services, such as visa expediting, that already were being provided but which people were still asking for. This was easy to address—we initiated a series of communications about the available services and made them more prominent in the travel website. This is a good example of a low-cost, quick-win solution that comes out of listening to the users." A major part of the idealized design process is about better listening.

Using Idealized Design to Reduce Purchasing Cycle Time

This case illustrates how an internal team used idealized design with a supplier to generate new revenues while shortening the cycle time it takes to perform part of the procurement process.

First, some background is in order. When the U.S. Food and Drug Administration approves a medicine, it often requires changes to the prescribing information that accompanies the medicine in the box. This necessitates making changes to the leaflet that comes with the medicine, approving the changes, getting printing film set up, transporting materials, printing the inserts, and placing them into the packaging.

A packaging engineer at GSK and the stakeholder group he assembled, including the supplier, had a goal of reducing the time it takes to get the leaflets printed. The project team quickly used several lean sigma tools to map out and measure the existing process and analyze inefficiencies. They made note of the time that each step was taking and noticed that the biggest time waster was transportation of print films from the existing supplier location to the manufacturing site.

The team eventually set aside its work on the existing process and used idealized design. During the initial idealized design session, the team generated many ideas, including specifying that "there would ideally be zero transportation time." The out-of-state supplier they were using for printing had recently acquired a company located much closer to the manufacturing site, and the supplier representative in attendance suggested that they could use that company in the printing process. At the manufacturing site, the team figured out how to reduce even more time from the process.

Commenting on the idealized design process, the team leader said, "My team used idealized design to generate one extra day of sales under patent without increasing cost. We shortened by 65% (from 17 hours to six) the time required to print prescribing information leaflets at launch. This improvement translates to an additional $4 million in sales for each product that has $1 billion in sales at the end of patent life."

Using Idealized Design to Reduce Product Life-cycle Costs

The president of GSK's consumer health care business tasked a team with reducing costs by £125 million annually. In response to this daunting challenge, the team initiated various savings projects. One project, for example, reduced costs by £3 million by creating multi-language packaging for a dental product.

After realizing similar savings on several other projects, the team concluded it had reached a savings plateau. The team also concluded it would need creative approaches to reach the next level of savings. That's when it turned to idealized design. The team began by brainstorming the ideal process for saving money, evaluated the best ideas objectively, and turned the best ideas into implementable designs. The team concluded, for example, that the richest savings opportunities were at the beginning of the product life cycle rather than later in the cycle. In response, the team designed a process to become engaged early on with new product development groups. Some of the things they focused on included developing global standards for packaging, active ingredients, flavors, and components; getting product teams to utilize existing materials and specifications wherever possible; and product formulation harmonization.

To support the use of standards, the team designed a system so that various country teams could easily access standard materials and specifications, as well as access standard artwork and marketing materials. Significant savings were achieved simply by not paying multiple times across the world for similar artwork and marketing materials. The team also crafted a preferred supplier list, so employees could easily locate the preferred rates already negotiated.

Other initiatives were put forth that are too numerous to discuss here. In case you are wondering, the team easily surpassed the president's £125-million savings goal.

Concluding Thoughts

A central theme of this book is about the need to achieve the next level of supply management excellence. This chapter showed clearly how idealized design can be used to achieve breakthrough performance results. While many approaches encourage creative thinking (kaizen workshops, value analysis, value stream mapping, to name a few), few offer a way to design an ideal system featuring intense integration with suppliers, internal stakeholders, and even external customers. Most approaches stress the incremental improvement of existing products, process, and services. And most approaches are applied narrowly rather than broadly. If next level supply management excellence is your ideal, then an idealized design process is one approach your organization wants to practice regularly.

Chapter Note

1. The authors acknowledge the important contributions of Jason Magidson and Gregg Brandyberry to this chapter.

12

Lean and Supplier Development

It is always easier to save money in a deflationary period or one of stagflation. Challenges begin to arise during periods of inflation, market share losses, and shifts in exchange rates. How do successful companies challenge themselves and their supply base to generate a continual flow of savings when those savings are hard to come by?

Successful companies understand the value of creating strong relationships with their supply base. Partners go the extra mile for each other, and the relationship bound by common interests creates financial benefits for both parties. One way of fostering a successful supplier relationship is through a supplier development program that embraces the concepts of lean deployment, and when we refer to lean, we don't simply mean a program that focuses on finding and fixing quality problems or short-term kaizen events at suppliers.

Lean thinking is a journey down a number of roads. Most of us are familiar with the Toyota production system, kaizen, kanban, value analysis/value engineering, and other quality and value enhancement concepts. However, one area that is not usually considered is using supplier development to promote lean across the supply chain.

This chapter first presents some essential knowledge about supplier development, a process that is still on the *to do* list of most supply organizations. Next, we provide an overview of lean, including the need to make lean deployment a major part of supplier development. The third section identifies some of the arguments and challenges typically faced when pursuing processes such as lean and supplier development. The chapter concludes with a case example of applying lean within a supplier development project, something that next level supply organizations should routinely do.

Developing Supplier Performance Capabilities

Something that most buying organizations, particularly in North America, have not pursued rigorously is the development of supplier capabilities. Supplier development is a broad concept that represents any activity or effort on the part of the buying company to improve the performance of suppliers.[1] Development efforts fall into a variety of categories:

- Working with current suppliers to resolve a problem
- Working with current suppliers to continuously improve performance capabilities
- Developing a new supplier to bring it up to speed
- Working with suppliers to create a performance capability where none previously existed
- Working with a supplier to introduce a new technology that is critical to the success of a product

One expert explains supplier development this way: "Supplier development requires that both firms commit financial capital and resources to the work; share timely and sensitive information; and create effective means of measuring performance and progress. Executives and employees at the buying firm must be convinced that investing company resources in a supplier is worthwhile. Executives at the supplier's firm must be convinced that their best interest lies in accepting direction and assistance from their customer. The convincing may not be congenial at first, but eventually it should evolve into collaboration based upon mutual goals."[2]

It should come as no surprise that early in the history of supplier development, particularly in the United States, most development efforts focused on working with suppliers to resolve existing problems. Actually, this probably has not changed much over the years. We expect next level supply organizations to view supplier development as a strategic activity that focuses on improved performance and creating new supplier capabilities and technologies. Other initiatives, such as a world-class supplier evaluation and selection process, will hopefully minimize the need for reactive responses to problems at a later date.

The logic behind the need for supplier development is straightforward. Without question, most supply organizations have reduced the size of their supply base to a more manageable level. A reduction of up to 90% in the number of suppliers maintained compared with ten or 15 years ago is not unusual. Once this reduction occurs, the amount of supplier switching that takes place usually decreases as a supply organization converges on a set of suppliers it views as critical to longer-term success. In addition, many of the remaining suppliers receive a longer-term purchase agreement, further limiting supplier switching. But, guess what? The need for continuous supply chain improvement is never ending. With fewer remaining suppliers, improvement will occur primarily through the improvement of existing supplier capabilities rather than from large-scale supplier switching. This improvement will often involve supplier development initiatives.

Any company that is experienced with supplier development projects knows these projects must be pursued selectively. First, some suppliers are world class and will not benefit appreciably from development efforts. They know what they must do to improve on their own. Second, no amount of supplier development efforts will transform some suppliers into world-class performers. Investing in a supplier development project with these suppliers will not yield the kinds of benefits that generate a desired return. These suppliers eventually become candidates for elimination. Third, too many business-to-business relationships are still adversarial, prohibiting the use of an approach that requires high levels of trust and cooperation. Finally, some suppliers do not want any development support. Forcing your vision of supplier development may only harm a relationship. It is important to target carefully those suppliers and performance areas that will provide the greatest return.

Next Level Supplier Development Practices

Companies that pursue supplier development activities should be aware of the practices that characterize next level supply organizations. We have identified these practices after working with leading companies across an array of industries. Next level supply organizations will:

Treat development initiatives as investments rather than expenses: It is important for supply leaders to convey the notion that supplier development projects represent an investment rather than expense. Companies that view supplier development as an expense are often quick to reduce these expenses when business declines. As organizations allocate scarce resources to their development efforts, it becomes critical to manage these resources carefully.

Calculate the financial return from supplier development projects: Applying financial metrics such as pay back, net present value, and internal rate of return will become more common once the development projects are treated as investments. It is important to speak the language of finance here. When your supply organization begins thinking like a CFO by highlighting the financial benefits that can be achieved, not only will your company support this effort, but suppliers will recognize the value as well.

Manage supplier development opportunities as projects: The use of project management tools will help instill a sense of discipline to supplier development initiatives.

Establish a central system for controlling and monitoring development efforts: Too often supplier development efforts happen in a decentralized or uncoordinated manner. When this is the case, the ability to report the extent of performance benefits from development projects often becomes difficult. A central system for reporting and updating supplier development activities will provide wider visibility across a company.

Establish baseline performance and track and report the impact of changes: This is critical for establishing a link between cause (the supplier development effort) and effect (the resulting performance improvements). Failing to identify the baseline performance level before the development activity increases the risk that performance results will be confounded by other extraneous variables.

Develop a standard approach for supplier development projects: Supplier development, like many supply management approaches, benefits from taking a process view. The following is one possible way to approach supplier development:[3]

Step 1: Identify improvement opportunities

Step 2: Target specific suppliers that should benefit from development activities

Step 3: Meet with the supplier's executive leadership to obtain buy-in, agree on the development opportunity, and develop project plans and clear measures of success

Step 4: Identify the type of supplier development support to provide

Step 5: Make resources available to support the project

Step 6: Perform the development project

Step 7: Measure and report the return from supplier development

Systematically identify development opportunities: A process for identifying the best development opportunities will help ensure supplier development occurs systematically rather than on an ad hoc or reactive basis. One leading company maintains a continuous listing of development projects, four of which are worked on simultaneously. After completing a project, it is replaced with another. A committee of senior supply leaders is responsible for evaluating development ideas and maintaining the potential project list. This committee also has the authority to sponsor project teams and allocating resources.

Identify core and as-needed supplier development support personnel: Access to personnel within and outside of supply management who have the necessary skill sets to support a development project is critical to success. Having the time to commit to development projects is also a critical success factor.

Allocate budget to support travel, living, and other expenses incurred during development projects: A complaint we sometimes hear concerns the reluctance, rightfully so, of functional groups to bear the travel and living expenses of their personnel when supporting development projects. A dedicated budget to support specific supplier development projects supports two purposes. It eliminates any complaint that expenses are being incurred by nonsupply groups. Perhaps more importantly, it provides an easy way to track financially the cost side of supplier development projects.

Share savings from development activities with suppliers: Never underestimate the link between supplier participation in development projects and rewards. Some supply organizations evaluate a supplier's performance improvement and include that as part of their scorecard rating. Others share any direct savings from the development project, either as payments to the supplier, adjustments to the selling price that reflect the supplier's share, or as credits toward cost reduction commitments. Direct payments require working closely with accounting since it can be difficult to write a check for an improvement rather than an invoice.

Conduct lessons learned sessions at the end of each development project: At the end of a development project, the participants should identify what went right, what did not work as well as planned, and how to improve the development process. In short, what was learned here? These lessons are then shared with others across the organization.

The Merging of Supplier Development and Lean

While there are many ways to practice supplier development, research from the late 1990s, a period when supplier development entered the supply management conversation, revealed that the most common types of supplier development support, at least in the United States, included enhancing working relationships with suppliers, requiring supplier capability improvements, and increasing supplier performance goals.[4] These are hardly hands-on or direct types of supplier development activities. Other examples of development support include allowing suppliers to attend a buyer's training program, placing engineers or other support personnel at suppliers, and providing equipment and technology. Conducting kaizen workshops to improve supplier operations, conducting Six Sigma quality improvement projects, and providing capital also qualify as development approaches.

Increasingly, we expect to see the transfer of lean thinking and lean capabilities to external suppliers through supplier development activities. Far too many firms still view lean from strictly an internal perspective, a narrow view that does not align well with today's competitive realities. Lean must also extend up and down a supply chain. This does not mean that combining lean and supplier development will be easy. Similar to the combining of chocolate and peanut butter, however, the time has come to make lean initiatives a major part of supplier development.

Remember that development requires a mutual commitment and effort between parties. It is important to focus on shared business plans and value streams for each product that your company and a supplier have in common. Keep in mind that cost, quality problems, and inflexibility are usually the direct result of shared processes. Furthermore, recognize that both the supplier and the customer must change because they share processes. Be sure to acknowledge that both the supplier and the customer must make an adequate return from any development projects.

Understanding Lean

Up to this point, we have talked about but not really elaborated on the concept of lean. While we all have heard the term, it is subject to different interpretations.[5] Our intention is not to provide an in-depth presentation of lean, something that hundreds of books do already. Our intention is to provide an overview since the concept is a central part of this chapter. Figure 12.1 presents, at a high level, various elements that are part of a lean deployment.

The reality is that while most managers have a basic understanding of lean, few organizations have truly achieved lean, partly because it is a never-ending pursuit. Furthermore, most lean adopters focus narrowly on their internal

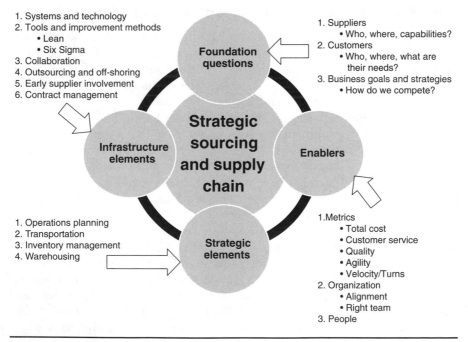

Figure 12.1   Elements of lean deployment

operations, ignoring the idea that lean is an end-to-end concept where everyone along a supply chain has a role to play. Far too many benefits from lean are left on the table.

A logical place to begin involves the definition of lean. Like total quality management, we view lean as a business philosophy rather than a set of tools and techniques. At a broad level, lean involves the relentless elimination of waste across an extended supply chain. This applies to any organization and any industry, whether it is profit or nonprofit, industrial or nonindustrial, service or manufacturing. The range of activities that fall under the lean umbrella is broad. We can make a convincing argument that any activity that eliminates waste across a supply chain is a legitimate part of lean.

Elimination of waste: Central to lean, and what must clearly be a focus during supplier development, is the elimination of waste. Waste is any activity that adds no value from the customer's perspective or an activity for which the customer would not willingly pay as part of a product or service. The presence of waste, and there is always waste at some point along a supply chain, can lead to too much time to perform an activity or process, too much inventory spread across the supply chain, and costs that are too high compared with what they should be.

It is important to realize that supply chains are populated with three kinds of activities—value-adding activities, nonvalue-adding activities, and wasteful activities. A value-added activity is one that transforms material or information into what a customer requests and is willing to buy. The focus here is to constantly improve and exploit these activities. A nonvalue-added activity is one that often has to be performed to move or deliver material or information closer to the customer but with no physical *value-add* taking place. All supply chains require some level of nonvalue-adding activities to operate. Supply chain designers should minimize or improve nonvalue-added activities wherever possible. It's hard to imagine a supply chain that does not have some nonvalue-adding activities. A third set of activities are those that are pure waste, or what the Japanese call muda. These activities create additional costs and are immediate candidates for elimination. Figure 12.2 presents the traditional categories of waste as well as various other types of waste that are more specific to supply management.

Confusion sometimes exists regarding the differences between nonvalue-adding activities and waste. In fact, the two terms are often used interchangeably. One way to think about this is to realize that all wasteful activities are nonvalue-adding. However, the reverse is not true. Nonvalue-adding activities are not necessarily wasteful. In fact, customers are often willing to pay for these activities, at least up to some point.

Consider the movement of a product or material within a supplier's facility. No change occurs to a product's physical characteristics during the movement, yet material handling is required to move a product closer to the place where

Traditional wastes—manufacturing and services	Additional wastes
1. Overproduction–produce more than required 2. Idle time–time to repair or set up equipment 3. Delivery–travel time and steps between stations or suppliers 4. Work processes–set-up time or P.O. processing 5. Inventory–raw, WIP, finished goods 6. Operator movement–nonvalue add 7. Rejected parts	1. Early supplier involvement (ESI)–No formal process to control upfront supply selection, design, and final product total cost. 2. Contract management process–No standard template, no central repository; are multiple sites paying different prices for the same product? 3. Low-cost country–global sourcing–LCC can be the home market: Have you leaned out both your and suppliers processes? Is your company creating costs for your suppliers? 4. Organization design–Does the current organization suboptimize ESI, transportation, and planning? 5. Metrics–Do you have the right metrics in place to create and drive sustainable cost reductions? Or, are you driving the wrong behavior?

Figure 12.2   Elimination of waste

value will be added. Another example involves machine setups or change-overs. During changeovers, no physical value or enhancement takes place, yet they must occur or nothing is produced. The challenge here is to identify that portion of the setup that can be improved or even eliminated.

Lean Objectives

Regardless of your perspective on lean, there will be some important objectives or outcomes that underlie this philosophy. Before identifying a robust set of objectives that help define lean, let's be clear about two important terms—objectives and goals. There are some key differences between these two concepts, although they are often used interchangeably. The short version is that objectives are aspirations that are often broad and open-ended. Objectives point us in a direction. Goals tend to be more specific and represent accomplishments. Once a goal is achieved, it should be superseded by new goals. A key point is that effective goals align directly with objectives. Objectives, which provide direction, drive the development of goals.

Why is this important to our discussion? Failing to achieve key objectives usually leads to waste. Falling short of an objective of providing world-class quality to customers, for example, obviously means that quality problems are present that create costly waste. Next, once we understand our key organizational objectives, we start to understand where we need to establish goals, allocate resources, and develop the action plans (i.e., tactics) for achieving the goals that align with our objectives.

In the broad area of lean, there are some clear objectives (i.e., aspirations) that provide direction to our development efforts with suppliers. (These objectives also provide guidance when pursuing internal lean opportunities.) Organizations that do a good job satisfying the following seven objectives will have done a good job with lean. Areas where these objectives fall short offer clear opportunities for supply chain improvement. Some of these opportunities might even be structured as supplier development initiatives. So, what are these lean objectives or outcomes?

Understand customers and their requirements: The critical starting point for lean thinking is value, which is defined by the ultimate customer. And this is only meaningful when expressed in terms of a specific product, good, or service that meets the customer's needs at a specific price and a specific time.[6] Total quality and lean are similar here—they both recognize the importance of the customer.

Keep material and information flowing: Flow means keeping the right material continuously moving toward a downstream entity that requires that material. There are a variety of flows across a supply chain, including payment flows, information flows, ownerships flows, vehicle and equipment flows, people flows, and reverse logistics flows. Interruption to the flow of any of these areas can be wasteful, and every organization has flows of some kind. From a supply chain perspective, it makes sense to organize activities so that work flows uninterrupted and at a rate that matches the demand pull from the customer. Constant stopping and starting adds little value that customers appreciate. Are there bottlenecks in your supply chain that limit flow?

Pull, don't push: It is amazing how two simple words, pull versus push, can have such an impact on how supply chains operate. What is the difference between the two? Pull systems relay information or a signal from a downstream entity to an upstream entity about what material, part, or service is required; the desired quantity; and where and when it is needed. In a pull system, action is taken in direct response to a downstream request rather than in anticipation of a need or request that may never occur. In a push environment, action is taken by an upstream entity in anticipation of a request and delivered to a downstream entity, whether that entity actually wants something or not.

The reality is that few firms operate in a purely pull environment. Across the supply chain, there are usually boundaries that separate push processes from pull processes. A company may have pull systems within their internal operations, for example, but suppliers still build to their own forecasts and internally derived economic models. Internal production is based on a pull system, but material replenishment with suppliers still occurs on a push basis. An obvious supplier development opportunity is to help suppliers make the transition from a push to a pull environment.

Make it as perfect as possible: The notion that poor supply chain quality creates waste is not even in question. Quality experts have long argued that any deviation from a desired target carries with it an associated loss. In a lean supply chain, there simply is little to fall back upon when quality errors occur, making the pursuit of perfection a critical lean objective.

Never underestimate the interrelationship between lean and total quality management. Lean organizations commit themselves to the pursuit of perfection. Supply organizations that expect to make lean a major part of their supplier management efforts are urged to become well versed in the philosophy and techniques of total quality management and Six Sigma. It is safe to conclude that a large percentage of supplier development initiatives will have quality implications.

Optimize the supply chain: Optimization as an objective is usually not included within lean discussions, an omission that is a serious mistake. To optimize is to make something as perfect, effective, or functional as possible. While many observers will equate optimization with reduction, less of something does not have to be the case.

There is no shortage of areas that can be optimized within a supply chain, both internally and with external suppliers. A sample of potential optimization opportunities include:

- Number of suppliers
- Design of products and physical processes
- Flow of material through a facility
- Number, size, and location of distribution, retail, and dealer outlets
- Number of component parts and stock keeping units
- Number, size, and location of production facilities
- Order delivery network
- Any major process, such as new product development, supplier selection, demand estimation, and customer order fulfillment

Each of these areas should be made as perfect, effective, and functional as possible. Do your suppliers need help optimizing any of these areas?

Establish the standard: Standardization means to conform to something that is established as a model or ideal example (i.e., the standard). Too many firms fail to standardize their common parts, processes, practices, documents, contracts, measurements, policies, and procedures across their business units when opportunities for standardization exist. A failure to standardize usually leads to wasteful duplication of effort that fails to promote best practices. Helping a supplier to identify and then converge on an accepted standard for an internal process or component is a logical supplier development task.

Make life simpler: Simplification seeks to diminish the scope or complexity of something without diminishing its effectiveness. Two areas that often benefit from simplification include process design and product design. A process is a set of interrelated tasks designed to achieve a specific outcome. Virtually any work that is meaningful has an organizational process underlying it. They do not relate only to physical processes.

When simplifying processes, nonvalue-adding and wasteful activities are targeted for improvement or elimination. Process improvement teams will search for creative new ways to perform necessary tasks, which should logically lead to shorter cycle times and cost reductions. It is also safe to conclude that working with suppliers to simplify products and processes will lead to an abundance of development opportunities.

Why be concerned with simplifying product designs? A simplified product nearly always requires fewer components, resulting in fewer suppliers, fewer material releases, less transportation, less inventory, and lower inventory management costs. Eliminating unnecessary components also reduces a product's cost, which reduces the value of the inventory required to support customer demand and service requirements. It can also be shown mathematically that fewer components support higher product reliability, thereby reducing the cost of poor quality. This particular objective is covered extensively in Chapter 13 on complexity.

The point of this discussion is to point out that lean deployment must achieve some specific objectives, as described. Failing to achieve these objectives with external supply chain members presents supplier development opportunities. Even if these objectives are being achieved at a satisfactory level, the need for continuous improvement is never ending.

The Challenges

Making lean thinking a cornerstone of supplier development can represent a radical change. As with any change process, we expect to hear an abundance of arguments why something will not work. The following is an anecdotal sampling of the reasons we hear why lean supplier development simply won't work:

- Larger companies complain that rigid silo structures make it difficult, if not impossible, to promote flow between functional areas or processes. Smaller firms say they do not have the resources to work on improvement efforts like the larger companies.
- Process industries are convinced that lean principles work fine with discrete products. Companies that make discrete products know it is impossible to apply lean methods with all the individual parts, processes, and complexity they must deal with.

- Some companies know for a fact that this concept will never be accepted. Other plants tried something similar once, and everyone in production disliked it so much that there is no reason to even consider trying again.
- A high percentage of doubters are convinced that lean is much easier in Japan because "they have a different culture and work ethic."
- We simply do not have the time, money, or resources to commit to supplier development.
- If we are successful at lean, I risk losing my job.
- Our suppliers do not trust us enough to let us in the door. They think the only reason we want to help is to reduce the price we pay.
- Our own performance is questionable. Who are we to think we can help anyone else?
- We have way too many suppliers to identify the best supplier development opportunities.

We are sure you have heard your own set of reasons why change of any kind will not work in your unique setting. Organizationally, the challenge of combining lean and supplier development is not trivial:

- A shift in practices and many times a cultural change within your own company and at suppliers with the concepts of lean and supplier development will not be easy.
- The willingness of suppliers to open the door to a supplier development team to work both operational improvements with open book costing can be problematic.
- Selling the return on invested capital value of lean and supplier development will always be a challenge when some participants view supplier development as an expense.
- It is important that a supply organization *walks the talk* internally with supplier development before it can successfully pursue supplier development with suppliers.

While none of these violate the laws of physics, they can present some serious hurdles to lean supplier development. As with any resistance to change, a business case must be made that shows, in no uncertain terms, the payback from any initiative. Other hurdles will require more time and energy to overcome.

Putting It All Together—a Case Study

This case presents the experiences of a supply leader who was tasked with addressing a serious delivery problem at a major supplier.[7] "Soon after I started an assignment with a new employer, the CEO brought to my attention the constant delivery problems we were having with one of our largest suppliers. I immediately contacted the strategic sourcing manager who had responsibility for this supplier, requesting background details on our operations, as well as details about the supplier. I came to learn that the supplier had the capability of shutting down two of our biggest plants and that the delivery challenges we were experiencing had been on-going for almost six months."

After an initial review, the supply manager proposed a multi-step action plan to address this situation. These steps included:

- Meeting with internal stakeholders to understand the drivers behind the late deliveries
- Scheduling a separate call with the transportation provider to learn about the buying company's material planning, scheduling, and supply chain planning linkages with the carrier as well as learning about the supplier's processes after they receive an order from the buying company
- Meeting with the supplier to learn about their material planning, scheduling, manufacturing, and transportation processes

The story continues. "Soon after, we were on a plane to our supplier. Our approach into the airport took us directly over their manufacturing plant (over 500,000 sq. feet). I looked down to the ground and then asked one of my managers, 'What do you see outside the plant?' He replied, 'Trailers!' I suggested that before we start our meeting, we take a tour of the outside of the facility." During the tour through the yard, the visitors counted 32 trailers in the yard with only eight dock doors to process them. It became clear that the flow of inbound material was being impeded. The initial visit to the supplier set the stage for developing the team, tools, and processes for achieving four key objectives:

1. Identifying the areas of opportunity that need to be addressed
2. Creating the team that would resolve any problems
3. Identifying and implementing problem resolution actions
4. Calculating detailed savings opportunities

During supplier development, most companies look at the first three items and not the fourth. If the fourth is evaluated, it is on a high level rather than in-depth to understand the sustainable cost savings. Most companies negotiate a one-time tactical savings associated with the *pain threshold* of having to do the suppliers work. This is noncollaborative and leads to strained relationships.

Using a Lean Six Sigma methodology (Chapter 18 reviews the Six Sigma methodology), the supply organization identified a development project to assist the supplier with improving material planning, scheduling, and leaning out its operations. A development team was established with personnel from the buying company, supplier, transportation provider, and several major tier-two suppliers. The team included members from finance, strategic sourcing, operations, transportation, sales, and engineering. A project scope was outlined to address two prime products that the supplier shipped to the buying company.

Using value stream mapping, the team detailed the current material planning (starting with the customer order process), scheduling, transportation, and delivery processes. This included identifying personnel requirements, the cost of current processes, and the cost of future state processes. The team identified not only root causes of problems that were affecting material flow but also ways to overcome them. Within two weeks, the team developed a revised project plan.

The changes produced a host of impressive benefits. Benefits included reduced inventory at tier-one and tier-two suppliers as well as to the buying company. The members of the supply chain realized reduced working capital requirements of $250,000. A reduction in premium freight charges was also realized. This allowed the supplier to lower its unit price since the supplier factored its poor planning abilities into its original bid. The supplier understood it did not have good material planning and scheduling processes, so it included these costs as part of its cost base.

Tier-two suppliers also added some costs into their price, knowing their shipments would sit in the tier-one supplier's yard after delivery. A better flow of inbound material at the tier-one supplier resulted in improved relationships with its suppliers. Better material flow eventually netted the tier-one supplier an automatic 4% cost reduction from its suppliers, the amount the tier-two suppliers had added into their price. Total unit cost savings of $650,000 and a reduction in premium freight costs of $56,000 per year were now realized. And this doesn't factor in the benefit to the buying company of receiving deliveries that are consistently on time.

Perhaps the biggest win for the buying company was that the supplier understood the supplier development team was working to achieve mutual success. The supplier realized additional savings of nearly $300,000 per year as its improved processes were applied to other customers. Shared equipment and processes improved absorption rates for the supplier, enabling the supplier to reduce its unit costs on two primary product lines.

Supplier Development and a Redesigned Lean Supply Chain

This case features the development of a redesigned supply chain between an OEM of transportation equipment and two suppliers.[8] Perhaps the best way to appreciate the redesigned supply chain is to look at the before and after pictures of a logistics system that involves two suppliers located in the Midwest. The OEM's production facility that these suppliers support is located hundreds of miles away in Georgia.

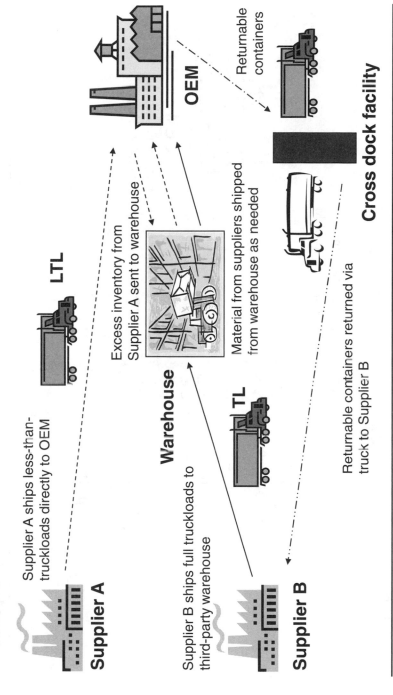

Figure 12.3 A traditional supply chain

Source: Robert J. Trent. *End-to-End Lean Management*. Ft. Lauderdale, FL: J. Ross Publishing, 2008.

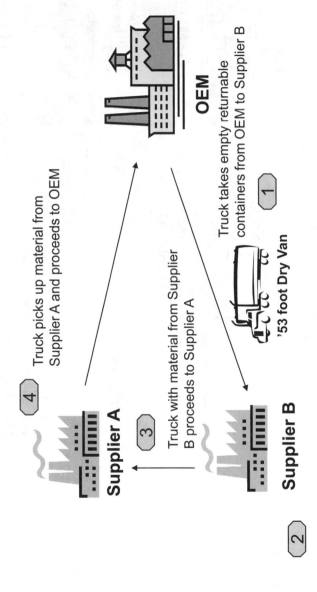

After

Truck picks up material from Supplier A and proceeds to OEM

4

Supplier A

3

Truck with material from Supplier B proceeds to Supplier A

Truck takes empty returnable containers from OEM to Supplier B

1

OEM

'53 foot Dry Van

Supplier B

Truck drops off containers and picks up material from Supplier A

2

Figure 12.4   A redesigned supply chain

Source: Robert J. Trent. *End-to-End Lean Management*. Ft. Lauderdale, FL: J. Ross Publishing, 2008.

Supplier A provides the OEM with fans, producing a total of four different part numbers. As shown in Figure 12.3, before the redesign this supplier shipped its parts via less-than-truckloads (LTL) carriers to the production facility two times a week. While not shown here, LTL shipments go through their own series of steps as material moves between a supplier and the customer. Any unneeded inventory at the OEM's production facility was transferred to a third-party warehouse to join the other excess inventory. The warehouse maintained, on average, 32 days worth of inventory from this supplier.

Supplier B provides hoods and side panels, comprising a total of nine part numbers. Before the redesign project this supplier shipped full truckloads of material directly to a third-party warehouse three times a week. On average the warehouse maintained 20 days worth of inventory from this supplier. This third-party would transfer material from the warehouse to the OEM's production facility on an as-needed basis. Empty returnable containers would then be sent from the production facility to a separate cross-dock facility. These containers sat in this facility until enough were accumulated to justify a truckload trip back to the supplier. The complexity and wastefulness of this system should be obvious. The demand schedules between the OEM and the two suppliers were clearly not in sync.

The redesigned system, which Figure 12.4 illustrates, is a closed-loop transportation system, something that is a central part of many lean systems. The OEM's supply management group worked with the two suppliers to ensure they could support this new system. The supply group also selected a contract carrier to handle pick up and deliveries according to a regular schedule. The two suppliers ship only the quantities that are required directly to the OEM's assembly line five times a week. The third-party warehouse and cross-dock facility are no longer part of the supply chain.

The original system, which featured multiple transfers of inventory between facilities, holding inventory for extended periods, and extensive transportation resulted in total logistics cost of nearly $700,000 annually. The redesigned system, which eliminated multiple handling and storage of inventory, resulted in annual total logistics costs of just under $300,000 annually. There are certainly better ways to use $400,000 than committing this capital to unnecessary transportation, inventory carrying, and other wasteful activities.

Concluding Thoughts

An objective today should not be about being a lean company but rather being part of a lean supply chain. Ignoring the importance of lean across the entire supply chain shows an unhealthy adherence to a narrow and outdated vision of lean. A broader view means we must also address lean supply, which means that lean will become a key part of your supplier development efforts. Next level supply organizations will transfer what they know internally about lean to their suppliers through their supplier development efforts.

Chapter Notes

1. Robert J. Trent. *Strategic Supply Management: Creating the Next Source of Competitive Advantage* (Ft. Lauderdale, FL: J. Ross Publishing, 2007), 187.
2. David Burt, Donald Dobler, and Stephen Starling. *World-Class Supply Management: The Key to Supply Chain Management* (New York: McGraw-Hill, 2002), 514.
3. Trent, 189.
4. Robert M. Monczka and Robert J. Trent. "Purchasing and Supply Management: Key Trends and Changes throughout the 1990s." *International Journal of Purchasing and Materials Management* 34, no. 4 (Fall 1998): 2–11.
5. Some of the ideas in the following sections are adapted from Robert J. Trent, *End-to-End Lean Management: A Guide to Complete Supply Chain Improvement* (Ft. Lauderdale, FL: J. Ross Publishing, 2008).
6. James Womack and Daniel Jones. *Lean Thinking: Banish Waste and Create Wealth in Your Corporation* (Simon and Schuster, 2003), 16.
7. The authors want to thank Mark Berlin for his generous support when developing this case and chapter.
8. This case is adapted from Robert J. Trent, *End-to-End Lean Management: A Guide to Complete Supply Chain Improvement* (Ft. Lauderdale, FL: J. Ross Publishing, 2008). The author would like to thank Brian Fugate for sharing this example.

13

The Value of Reducing Complexity

A number of years ago, a fire destroyed the Japanese supplier that provided a critical brake P-valve to Toyota.[1] While the source of the fire was a mystery, what followed was not. Perhaps first and foremost, Toyota's obsession with lean caused the company to shut down all Japanese assembly operations within hours because of no backup supply or supplier. Next, the response from other suppliers to help Toyota was nothing less than astounding. Seeing a direct linkage between Toyota's and their destiny, suppliers, even those that did not normally produce brake parts, did whatever was possible to build tooling and parts, all without contracts, lawyers, or negotiations. Finally, Toyota's engineers came to realize that over time, they had designed 200 P-valve variations, many of which had complex tapered orifices that required highly customized jigs and drills. This made the recovery from the fire that much more challenging. A Toyota executive said the fire provided the company with an opportunity to trim its parts variations.

In another example that is not quite as dramatic as a fire, one of the authors of this book purchased a home theater system. It quickly became obvious that no mere mortal could install this system. After two professionals completed the arduous tasks of mounting to the wall the heavy 55-inch TV and wiring a variety of boxes to the system (the DVR box alone has eight separate cables that mysteriously disappear into the wall), a technician handed the owner three separate remote controls for operating the system. Combined, the three controls have over 160 buttons with instruction manuals that total several hundred pages. The owners have concluded that if they ever sell their house, the home entertainment system is a permanent fixture that will stay with the home.

Welcome to the world of complexity. It is a world where companies and consumers wake up one day, look around, and wonder how they ever got to the point where life became . . . so complex. This chapter explores various topics related to supply chain complexity, including an attempt at defining the term, explaining why it is a problem, identifying why it happens, and presenting some next level strategies for removing complexity. The chapter concludes with an example of how a leading company has launched a serious attack on complexity.

Defining Complexity

In 1964, U.S. Supreme Court Justice Potter Stewart expressed his opinion on what is obscene in a free society and what constitutes an expression of art. When commenting about the difference between pornography and art, he famously said, "I know it when I see it." Complexity is much the same way. While there are no hard and fast rules telling us if something is too complex, we usually know it when we see it.

In one sense, complexity is an easy word to define since it simply refers to something that is complex.[2] Another way to look at complexity, then, is to examine its root word—the adjective complex. (Complex is also a noun, as in the apartment complex.) To be complex means to be composed of two or more parts, which in business relates to just about everything. A complex system is defined as one in which many independent agents interact with each other in multiple, sometimes infinite, ways.[3] The issue here is not whether something is complex or not but rather at what point does something cross a threshold and become excessively complex.

A second and perhaps more appropriate perspective views something as complex if it is hard to separate, analyze, or solve. More revealing are the synonyms that describe the word complex. These include complicated, intricate, involved, and knotty. While there are academics who have provided cumbersome definitions to this concept, in reality, the word complexity is not that complex. Perhaps we should stay with our original position that we know complexity when we see it.

Let's provide a nonbusiness example where you can decide if the following appears too complex. At a private, eastern U.S. university, any sort of change to an academic business course or program must pass through a sequential series of steps before ultimate approval:

- Members of the department who put forth a proposal must review and approve it.
- The proposal is reviewed by a dean's committee comprised of department chairs.

- A college policy committee made up of business faculty reviews the proposal.
- Members from the entire business college vote to accept the proposal.
- A subcommittee of the university educational policy committee reviews the proposal.
- The full committee of the university educational policy committee reviews the sub-committee's recommendation.
- The full faculty of the university vote whether to accept the proposal.

The cycle time for this process can be up to a year before final changes are put in place. How may processes does your company have in place that seem like nothing more than a series of hurdles? And we wonder why tuition is so high.

Types of Complexity

McKinsey researchers have studied the topic of complexity probably as much as anybody. They have concluded that two broad categories of complexity exist. The first category, institutional complexity, stems from strategic choices, the external context (such as regulations), and from major choices about organizational and operating systems.[4] Some refer to this as macro complexity.

Some researchers have argued that organizations that learn how to manage and exploit institutional complexity can generate additional sources of profit and competitive advantage. When managed well, complexity can also increase corporate resilience by enhancing the ability to adapt to change. Serving more customers, selling in more countries, and introducing new products all contribute to institutional complexity. They also have the potential to create new value when managed properly. Some types of complexity are not necessarily bad.

The second category is individual complexity. Some also refer to this as internal or micro complexity. It includes the way employees experience and deal with complexity. In other words, individual complexity deals with how hard it is for employees to get their jobs done. Employee role ambiguities, conflict, administrative burdens, duplicate roles, and ill-defined processes all contribute to individual complexity.

Not surprisingly, researchers have concluded that most companies focus exclusively on institutional complexity. Some argue that a better response for attacking complexity is to identify and reduce individual complexity by making detailed organizational and operating-model choices, including clarifying roles, refining key processes, and developing appropriate skills and capabilities among the employees who face complexity.[5] In fact, McKinsey research determined that companies reporting the lowest levels of individual complexity had the highest returns on capital employed and returns on invested capital.[6] Organizations as a whole learn to adapt to institutional complexity. Complexity at the individual level is not so easy to overcome.

The McKinsey research further elaborates on four more specific types of complexity.[7] These include:

1. *Designed complexity*—this results from choices about where the business operates, what it sells, how it sells, to whom its sells, and so forth.
2. *Inherent complexity*—this is intrinsic to the business and can only be removed by exiting a portion of the business.
3. *Imposed complexity*—this includes laws, industry regulations, and interventions by external organizations.
4. *Unnecessary complexity*—this results from a misalignment between the needs of an organization and the processes in place to support it. This is probably the easiest complexity to address.

Figure 13.1 offers one way to evaluate whether something is too complex at the individual level. This figure supports a point made earlier—there are no hard and fast rules for identifying complexity. Oftentimes complexity is a relative comparison of one situation against another.

Complexity is like cholesterol. Our bodies have good and bad cholesterol, and even the bad cholesterol is tolerable until it reaches a certain level. Complexity is much the same way.

Why Complexity Is (Generally) Bad

Even after conceding that some types of complexity are a natural part of business, it is safe to conclude that other types of complexity should not be a

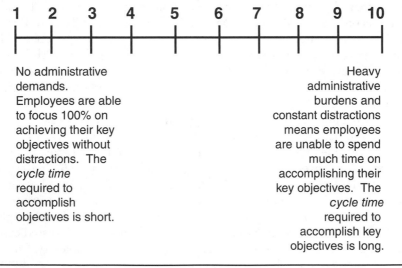

Figure 13.1 Assessing internal organizational complexity

natural outcome. This is true when even good complexity reaches a point (call this the tipping point) that impedes our ability to achieve our objectives. Excessive complexity wastes valuable human and organizational resources, drives up direct and indirect costs, frustrates those who have to deal with it, and often stifles creativity. Whatever our beliefs about complexity, the one perspective we should all share is that at some point complexity increases costs, often with no corresponding financial returns. Higher costs elevate the risk that a company will no longer be profitable or competitive.

Part of the reason why complexity is difficult to grasp is few people really understand the concept. Furthermore, accounting systems rarely capture complexity's true cost. Similar to trying to capture the true costs of poor quality or transactions, complexity costs are usually not measured, are scattered across many different accounts and spread across different organizations within a supply chain, or are buried within overhead accounts. Complexity also carries huge opportunity costs. As we deal with the effects of complexity, we are not as able to focus our attention toward more productive pursuits. Unfortunately, economists have not yet developed a way to calculate a society's complexity tax. Trying to argue that cost accounting systems provide much help in the battle against complexity would be a hard position to defend. Not surprisingly, we have yet to see any key indicators that capture the complexity construct.

Let's drill down and show the many effects of a specific kind of complexity. Without question, most U.S. companies have historically suffered from having too many suppliers, and it's clear that many still maintain too many. Procter and Gamble, for example, recently announced its desire to eliminate 20,000 suppliers from its worldwide supply base. The company also announced plans to reduce the number of distribution centers it maintains from 400 to 200.[8] While maintaining multiple suppliers for every purchase requirement was often seen as a way to create competition and guarantee access to supply, we now realize that a supply base that is too large in terms of numbers creates many adverse consequences. Unfortunately, these consequences are rarely identified or quantified. Turning the case of too many suppliers around, think about the beneficial effects of a pared-down supply base:

- Fewer contracts or purchase orders to negotiate and write
- Fewer material releases and receipts
- Less effort expended to process and handle material receipts
- Easier material traceability
- Better communication and relationships that support the pursuit of value-adding activities
- More attention given to supplier selection, thereby improving the effectiveness of that process
- Fewer accounts payable transactions
- Fewer requests for quotations (RFQs) or proposals to manage

- Improved supply base quality and delivery as lower performers are removed from the base
- Lower unit costs due to better leveraging of purchase volumes
- Fewer supplier performance reports or scorecards to generate
- Fewer supplier performance review meetings

Looking at another scenario, what are the effects of overdesigning or excessively customizing a product, another common area of complexity? Overdesigning a product can adversely affect quality (this will be shown mathematically in a later section), create supply chain complexity due to more suppliers and components, increase production time while decreasing overall throughput capacity, and increase product costs. As with a too-large supply base, an overdesigned product, including excessive customization, brings with it an impressive list of less than desirable outcomes.

Besides the impact that complexity has on costs, and these costs are not trivial, there are other reasons why excessive complexity is not something you should welcome into your life.

Complexity Is the Antithesis of Lean

A key objective of lean is simplicity, a term that is in obvious contrast to complexity. The relentless elimination of waste forces companies to address those activities that add minimal, if any, value within a value stream. Companies that are serious about lean should also be serious about attacking complexity since lean and complexity do not go well together.

Let's look at one aspect of lean and see how it reduces complexity. Larger manufacturers have increasingly relied on closed-loop transportation systems to support their just-in-time initiatives.[9] These systems feature regular pick up from suppliers, usually with private or contract transportation carriers, with the trip back bringing returns and containers. While few companies have benefited from closed-loop systems (they are usually managed by large companies), their appeal is obvious to most supply chain managers.

A supply chain mapping exercise at one leading company revealed that supplier deliveries featuring less-than-truckload shipments build in an unusually large number of steps between the supplier's dock and eventual use by the industrial buyer. A traditional inbound supply chain can require 27 steps or activities simply to move one item from the end of a supplier's production process to the start of the buyer's production process. This assumes the buyer stores the material upon receipt for eventual use. The redesigned supply chain, featuring a just-in-time, closed-loop network, requires only six steps or activities.

We can probably conclude that 21 of the 27 steps in the traditional supply chain created complexity. Imagine the waste that takes place for products with hundreds of first-tier suppliers and potentially thousands of sub-tier suppliers, all operating within a traditional production and logistics network. Do not believe that complexity and lean will ever get along well.

Complexity Works against Speed and Flexibility

Without question, the way that companies compete today is different from just a few years ago. Characteristics such as speed and operational flexibility are becoming as important as quality and cost. It should be intuitive that excessive complexity creates barriers to speed and flexibility.

It is not hard to find examples where speed and flexibility have become major parts of what separates one company from another. Consider the case of Polaris, a maker of four-wheel utility vehicles and snowmobiles.[10] After the downturn of 2008, the company slashed inventory levels at its dealers. When demand began to rebound, the company found itself with too little inventory in its distribution channel, causing missed sales opportunities. This resulted in the company examining closely its ordering and inventory management practices. Its long-standing practice of having dealers place large orders twice a year did not provide the flexibility to better respond to shifts in customer demand. Demand planners know that the longer they look into the future, the more variable their demand estimates become. Now the company allows dealers to order smaller quantities of products every two weeks to better match supply with customer demand. Polaris has also slashed its product development time by 50%, allowing it to get to the market more quickly with products that customers want.

Other companies, including Boeing and the locomotive unit of General Electric (GE), know that faster customer order fulfillment times win orders. After GE slashed the order time for its locomotives from 90 to 45 days, it saw its sales increase. Railroads appreciated the faster delivery of a revenue producing asset. Boeing now builds two popular models, the 737 and the 777, on assembly lines that require a fraction of the time to make a plane that lines using traditional assembly methods need. Companies do not achieve gains in speed and flexibility when excessive complexity is the norm.

Complexity Affects Quality

The effect of complexity on product quality provides perhaps the strongest argument we have for simplifying product designs. The reason the argument against complexity during product design is strong is because we can show numerically the effect it has on parts per million defects (ppm). This ppm metric has become the standard that nearly all Six Sigma organizations use to report component and product quality levels.

Let's show how we can calculate the affect of complexity on quality levels. Assume a design team creates a product with seven components, each with an average reliability of 99%. The overall reliability of this product is $.99^7$, or 93% reliability. This corresponds to a 70,000 ppm defect level (7% defects per one million opportunities). Next, a design simplification project eliminates the need for two of the components, making the overall reliability $.99^5$, or 95%. This now corresponds to a 50,000 ppm defect level, nearly a 30% reduction from the original ppm level. Further assume that another improvement project increased the average reliability of each component to .995. The overall reliability now becomes $.995^5$, or 97.5%. This further reduces the ppm defect level to 25,000 ppm. Of course, these levels are nowhere near Six Sigma performance levels. These numbers were used to show how complexity in product designs mathematically leads to higher predicted defect levels. More components create more opportunities for error.

How Supply Chains Become Complex

As many companies realize, complexity is not something that is in short supply. This is ironic because no company has a stated objective of becoming more complex from a negative perspective. For a variety of reasons, however, complexity is often the state where we find ourselves. Mergers and acquisitions (M&As) often lead to duplicate systems, parts, employee skills, and suppliers, all of which add to complexity. Adding features to differentiate a product in the marketplace will naturally lead to more product complexity, making complexity a normal part of the supply chain trade-off process. In addition, deciding to sell products in 120 countries will lead to channels of distribution that are anything but simple.

We call this tendency to become more complex over time *complexity creep*. While complexity within an organization can grow quickly, it usually evolves at a pace that ensures it does not draw any unusual attention. In our experience, the battle against complexity is nearly always a reactive one. At some point, the realization becomes clear that steps have to be taken to regain control. Enough is enough.

Much of the complexity we see across supply chains is the result of organizational strategies. Many observers refer to this as self-inflicted or self-imposed complexity. The following, while certainly not an exhaustive list, will provide some insight into why complexity often becomes an organizational norm rather than exception.

Engineers Gone Wild

One of the most visible sources of complexity involves products that are overdesigned. Overdesign means they have too many components, more features than what the customer wants or can even use, or are overly complex to produce. While the purpose of this section is not to attack engineers, if product designs often lead to complexity, it becomes logical to look at the source of the design. As the opening to this chapter illustrated, no one intends to wake up and find hundreds of variations of even the most basic components. Spreading design responsibility across different centers, failing to check whether a previous component is available for reuse, or inheriting components and designs after a merger can all make the complex-o-meter go up. And let's not forget the tendency of engineers to want to create the next Mona Lisa during the design process.

Marketers Gone Wild

Staying with the previous theme of going wild, product proliferation has clearly resulted in *designed complexity*, a type of complexity mentioned earlier in the chapter. With product proliferation, a company has made a conscious decision to extend its brand offerings to attract more customers. While product extensions can create market excitement and advantage, they also create complexity. At some point too much really becomes too much. How many varieties of Cheerios are on store shelves today? How many varieties of Tide detergent do supermarkets carry? One supermarket manager commented that in an earlier era, his store carried 5000 stock-keeping units (SKUs). A typical supermarket may now carry as many as 30,000 SKUs. While not all of this increase is due to product proliferation (the growth in store brands and buying products around the world have also increased SKUs), a good part of the increase can be traced to brand extensions.

Product proliferation and mass customization are closely related. Mass customization recognizes that markets are not homogenous and that product life cycles are shortening, on average. While the ability to mass customize is a strength that can win new business, it is a complex model to master. Figure 13.2 contrasts a traditional business model from a mass customization model. A traditional business model is based on predictability and stability while a mass customization model is dynamic and subject to rapid change. It also results in many product varieties and configurations.

Faster Product Development

Although it may seem counter-intuitive, complexity is also a consequence of faster product development cycle times. While shorter cycle times, on average, are a good thing, an interesting consequence of improved product development processes is the introduction of more new products. Companies find that when they streamline their development process, they are able to introduce more products with few, if any, additional resources. More new products mean more complexity. Ideally, more products will also mean more sales and growth that offset any increases in complexity. A bit of an irony is at work

Traditional business model	Mass customization model
• Emphasis on efficiency, stability, and control • Stable demand with large homogeneous markets • Long product development cycle times • Limited product variety and configurations • Long product life cycles	• Rapid product development • Produce low-cost, high quality, and low-volume customized goods and services • Extensive product variety and configuration • Variety and customization through flexibility and quick responsiveness • Fragmented demand and heterogeneous niches • Shorter product life cycles

←───→

| **Predictable and stable environment** | **Dynamic and complex environment** |

Figure 13.2   Traditional vs. mass customization business models

here. As the complexity around product development declines, the complexity related to product proliferation often increases.

An interesting analogy here involves production cycle times. Companies find that when they increase their product throughput within a facility (i.e., reduce the time it takes to produce a product), the capacity of that facility increases. Faster throughput means more units can be produced without more human and physical assets. The facility has become more efficient. New product development throughput operates much the same way. Faster development times mean the development of more new products using a consistent amount of resources.

Lack of Process Thinkers and Ill-Defined Processes

A process is a set of interrelated tasks or activities designed to achieve a specific objective or outcome. Developing innovative new products or selecting world-class suppliers are examples of desired process outcomes. Process thinkers, a breed that is far too rare, seek to understand holistically how the pieces come together. Most individuals understand their part of a process but do not grasp how that fits into a bigger picture.

Most organizations suffer from a shortage of process thinkers because most individuals are trained to think functionally. Unfortunately, most organizational processes cross functional boundaries. They simply do not know any better. Complexity arises when individuals try to optimize their work within a process that they do not understand or cannot conceptualize. Even those individuals who understand processes sometimes fall into the trap that engineers fall into. In other words, they over-engineer rather than simplify a process.

Another scenario that creates complexity is the presence of poorly designed processes. Just because a process is in place does not mean it is a good process, and just as products can be overly complex, so can processes. Processes may also be poorly understood. As mentioned earlier, a major cause of poor processes is decentralized structures that fail to build in best practices or coordinate the development of consistent processes. A lack of central coordination means that each operating unit is ultimately responsible for developing, and usually sub-optimizing, a range of processes. Duplication of effort also results when the operating authority for process development is dispersed throughout an organization.

Strategic Choices

We cannot ignore the fact that some organizations choose to be inherently complex. They make strategic choices about introducing new product lines, buying other companies, or expanding into new geographic regions. No one would dispute that Federal Express is a more complex organization today compared to when it served only the U.S. market. Growth brings complexity, and that's the way it will always be. Good companies learn how to manage the complexity that results from strategic choices.

Continuous Reorganizations and New Programs

Continuously reorganizing the corporate governance structure is often seen as a way to show visible progress. Unfortunately, reorganizations also cause chaos, confusion, and complexity (and probably some other words that begin with *c*). The following quote, whose authorship is disputed but is believed to be several thousand years old, summarizes the effect of reorganizations:

> "We trained hard but it seemed that every time we were beginning to form up into teams, we would be reorganized. I was to learn later in life that we tend to meet any new situation by reorganizing, and a wonderful method it can be for creating the illusion of progress while producing confusion, inefficiency and demoralization."

The same is true about new programs. It seems like every challenge can be overcome with a program that has a clever acronym. Actually, the acronyms are often the most creative part of these programs. Programs to improve quality, reduce costs, improve customer satisfaction, improve supplier relationships, or improve employee morale are constantly being added, revised, and sometimes deleted. A constant churning of programs breeds not only complexity, it also breeds cynicism. It is not a sign of endearment when employees refer to a new program as the flavor of the month.

Bureaucracy

Bureaucracies are systems of administration characterized by officialism, red tape, and a proliferation of rules, procedures, and positions.[11] It would be hard to argue that bureaucracy does not lead to complexity. Bureaucracies are notorious for stifling innovation, lengthening decision making times, and erecting barriers to change. While we often think that bureaucracy relates to government, corporate structure and governance, particularly at larger corporations, can often rival some of the worst bureaucracies.

Government bureaucracy, rules, regulations, and laws that are in the thousands of pages show complexity at its finest, or worst depending on your perspective. Any supply organization that does business with the U.S. government is familiar with, for example, a large body of work called Federal Acquisition Regulations. An anecdotal account showing a tangible cost of complexity can be found when comparing two companies that compete in the same industry with roughly the same level of sales and purchases. One company sells strictly to the private sector while the other sells exclusively to the Department of Defense. What is revealing is that the company that sells to the private sector has 20 buyers working for it while the company that sells to the government has 40 buyers. While other factors could confound this comparison, an executive at the defense contractor is adamant that the difference is due primarily to dealing with complex rules and regulations.

Mergers and Acquisitions

Probably the quickest way to create complexity, not to mention anxiety and role confusion, is through M&As. The process nearly always features a complex set of legal and financial issues. After the ink is dry on an agreement, it becomes evident how much duplication, overlap, and even conflict exists between the newly formed entities, a complexity that does not go away simply because the legal part of the process is completed. When brought together, different organizations bring different cultures, systems, policies, procedures, suppliers, customers, part number schemes, etc. We think you see the connection to complexity here.

Complexity Creates Job Security

It should come as no surprise that some individuals, and even organizations, have a vested interest in keeping complexity alive and well. Some will fight vigorously anything that seeks to make life simpler. Lawyers and accountants, for example, have a keen interest in keeping some things overly complex. What if the tax and legal codes were simplified so everyone understood them? Would we even need the services of lawyers and accountants?

We all know someone who works hard to protect the status quo by resisting even the most logical changes. These individuals earn their living formulating or enforcing the many rules, policies, laws, and regulations that an organization must follow. Or perhaps they earn their living managing supply chains that probably should not be as complex as they have become. They owe their job to complexity. You may even know a union representative or two whose very reason for being on earth is to point out which paragraph you just violated within a 250-page labor agreement. And don't forget the OSHA representative who plays a solid game of I Gotcha by faithfully pursuing every one of the thousands of edicts that government regulators produce annually. We have complexity because some people want complexity. Their living depends on it.

Complacency

At some point corporations, particularly larger, well-known ones, suffer from two sins that bring forth a swift and painful decline. The first sin is complacency, which reflects a high level of self-satisfaction, often with an unawareness of actual dangers or deficiencies.[12] Complacent organizations are not concerned with complexity because they like the ways thing are right now. They have no idea of the costs, dangers, or deficiencies associated with being overly complex, nor do they probably care, at least in the short run. A lack of urgency leads these organizations to ignore the subject until it is far too late.

The second great sin is arrogance, which reflects an often unfounded attitude of superiority. One does not have to look further than any well-known company that has fallen from grace to find arrogance at the root of their downfall. General Motors, and more recently Toyota, come quickly to mind. While not linked to complexity as directly as complacency, arrogance does fit nicely within the theme of corporate sinning.

Let's Go Global

Statistics that reveal a steady growth in international purchasing over the last 25 years are hard to refute. While most international decisions likely reflect sound courses of action, something that is often overlooked is the impact these decisions have on supply chain complexity. Take a close look at Figure 13.3, which lists the logistical issues that arise when buying on a worldwide basis. These issues are not as prevalent when sourcing domestically. Unfortunately, few companies account for the costs of logistical complexity or the total cost of international sourcing decisions. In addition, few have any idea about how many people work in supply chain management to manage this complexity.

- Longer pipelines in distance and time
- Increased risk (damage, theft, etc.)
- Different shipping terms (Inco terms versus U.C.C. terms)
- Increased use of agents and other third parties
- Extensive documentation requirements

- Delivery variability
- Reduced ability to plan due to longer cycle times
- Increase in supply chain touch points and handlers
- Multiple modes of transportation required
- More challenging to identify the true cost of ownership

Figure 13.3   Logistical complexity from international purchasing

Other areas of complexity arising from international purchasing include working across different cultures, language and communication barriers, different legal systems, time differences, challenges obtaining reliable information, possible counter-trade requirements, a total landed cost that never equals the unit cost of what is being purchased, and increased risk management requirements, including currency risk management.

A U.S. medical devices company provides a perfect illustration of how international purchasing and production creates supply chain complexity. This company markets a product that requires 20 components sourced from ten countries. After consolidating these components in the United States, final product assembly takes place in a Caribbean country with product sterilization taking place back in the United States. The production time from start to finish was close to 80 days, which did not include supplier lead times. Even after a supply chain redesign project reduced the production cycle time by nearly half, it still includes 12 days of nonvalue-adding travel from the United States to the Caribbean and back. There is no question that international purchasing creates supply chain complexity.

Anyone reading this chapter will likely have his or her own views about how complexity happens. Table 13.1 lists probable causes of complexity as identified by supply leaders at a well-known chemical company. Understanding the causes of complexity is half the battle against complexity.

Approaches for Driving Out Complexity

Next level supply excellence requires a relentless attack on complexity. Most published sources address this topic by putting forth general rather than specific actions for battling complexity. These actions often include streamlining the organizational design, creating clear processes, and eliminating employee role ambiguity. While these recommendations are well and good, it might help to include more specific courses of action, particularly actions that relate directly to the supply chain.

Table 13.1 Root causes of complexity—a preliminary list of possibilities

• Imbalance between control/management and leadership
• Many layers of management combined with matrix decision making
• Too many simultaneous changes underway
• Conflicting objectives, initiatives, and roles
• Many different data reporting and data collecting approaches
• A tendency to *over engineer* everything
• Shifting objectives and priorities (short-term focus today, long-term focus next month)
• Trying to solve performance issues through structure and reorganizations
• Building jobs around people instead of around the process or function
• A heavy reliance on administrative processes rather than achieving key objectives (stressing activity over accomplishment)
• Subjecting strategic activities to the same metrics as tactical activities
• Staffing project teams with external consultants or internal staff who lack practical experience and expertise
• Too much focus on *who gets credit* instead of who can benefit
• Lack of accountability

The purpose of this section is not to present detailed descriptions of the activities that reduce complexity. These descriptions can be found easily in other books. Rather, the objective here is to raise awareness about the variety of specific complexity-reducing actions that are available. Of course, the complexity battle is already lost if executive leaders do not make the war on complexity a strategic objective.

Simplify Product Designs

The logic behind simplifying product designs was presented earlier in the chapter. For many companies, simplifying product design offers one of the fastest ways to eliminate complexity. Besides the reduced cost and complexity benefits from simplified designs, the bottom line is that customers appreciate the virtue of simplicity. Although it has been an electronic eternity since Apple introduced the iPhone, and others have entered the market with phones that do some things better than Apple, the iPhone is still a hot-selling item because it has retained its *cool* factor. Besides being cool, some analysts attribute part of the product's success to the simplicity of its use.[13]

Product design is the time to think about simplification. Industry leaders understand the power of the development process to satisfy some important aspirations or objectives. The term X represents different aspirations that development teams consider even before beginning design work. Design for X aspirations can involve design for quality, reliability, serviceability, sustainability, end-of-life recycling, target price, assembly, cycle time, and simplicity of design and use. This is a powerful concept because it ensures that important objectives are considered early on during product development.

Standardize and Reuse Components

Few supply managers would dispute the notion that custom designed components nearly always cost more than standardized components. Related to the notion of standardized components are reuse components. Reuse components are already available from previous designs.

In addition to the cost issues, over-customization often limits a customer's ability to respond to demand changes. Customized components are usually provided by a single or few suppliers that may be unable to respond when market conditions change abruptly. They are also more expensive than standard or readily available components. Using Apple again as an example, the company experienced financial problems during the 1990s when demand for several of its products increased dramatically. Suppliers of custom designed components, which Apple relied on heavily, were slow to respond to demand increases. Furthermore, over-customization meant that Apple was unable to achieve the kinds of rapid cost reductions that competitors achieved. Young people today only see the hip and cool Apple. They do not realize how close this company came to extinction on several occasions due to its reliance on custom designed product architecture.

As with product simplification, one way to address the complexity that comes with over-customization is to make standardization and reuse a key objective during product design. One leading company assigns a reuse engineer to each product development team. This individual's responsibility is to ensure design engineers are not over-customizing designs when previously designed or standard items are available.

A word of caution is required here. Excessive use of standard and reused components creates a risk that customers will not be able to differentiate a new product from a previous product or one product line from another. One study found that the tipping point of negative impact from design reuse percentage on innovativeness for new offerings is 43%, beyond which novelty suffers.[14] An automotive design engineer once noted during a research interview with one of the authors that if a customer feels it, touches it, sees it, or smells it, then it better look new and improved. He went on to say it better not look like what they have already designed or like our other new models.

Pursue Center-led Supply Management

Something that center-led leadership provides is the ability to coordinate company-wide supply and supply chain initiatives. This coordination will go a long way toward reducing the institutional complexity that comes with managing global supply networks. Decentralized authority structures lack the ability to look beyond a local or business unit level. No matter how hard we try to argue otherwise, this will remain the case. Decentralization does not bring with it the authority to engage in the kinds of coordination that will remove complexity. Please refer back to Chapter 5 for an in-depth discussion concerning the need for center-led supply leadership.

Rely on Organizational Design Features to Help Reduce Complexity

Chapter 5 discussed the important role that organizational design plays when pursuing the next level of supply management. Design features can also help with the battle against organizational complexity. Research findings are clear, for example, that early supplier and procurement involvement on product design teams helps avoid costly and complex rework as products move through the design process. A co-location design model simplifies patterns of communication as supply personnel work in close proximity to their internal customers. And cross-functional commodity teams bring different perspectives together to make important supply decisions, often enhancing the decision-making process. Never underestimate the important relationship between an effective design and an effective supply organization. Also, never underestimate the power of an effective design to streamline channels of communication, reduce complexity, and enhance communication accuracy.

Become More Rational

Rationalization is a continuous process of determining the right mix and number of something to maintain. It is a powerful concept that has wide application across every part of a supply chain. It is also a concept that offers one of the most powerful ways to battle supply chain complexity. While rationalization should be of ongoing interest, it is usually of most interest when we finally realize we have too many of something. At some point, we reach a point where the marginal cost of one more of something outweighs the marginal contribution of that next *something*. Areas where companies should continuously evaluate the right mix and number to maintain include their:

- Supply base
- Component SKUs
- Product lines and product features
- Customer base
- Purchase contracts
- Retail outlets
- Production sites
- Engineering centers

An observation that is subject to debate is that many consumer products companies have gone overboard in their quest to offer product variety. As mentioned earlier, the inevitable result is a proliferation of brands and brand extensions. The question becomes what to do about this proliferation.

There are some ways to attack product proliferation.[15] First, do not ask consumers if they want more variety. The answer to that question will inevitably be yes. Second, classify goods into a classification scheme for analysis. One company found it was able to easily categorize its products into core, seasonal, promotional, export, and new products. Third, create cross-functional product-pruning teams. These teams are responsible for reaching collective agreement about what products truly add value to the portfolio and those that do not. Fourth, limit product choice. Retailers often apply this approach by removing those products from stores that do not pull their weight in terms of sales and turnover. Finally, implement mass customization. If product variety, which can lead to proliferation, is a worthwhile pursuit then set up a production capability that is designed to accommodate variety.

Empower Employees

To empower means to give an individual or team official authority or legal power. What most managers fail to recognize is that a failure to empower a team or individual to perform basic tasks or make decisions (up to a point) creates organizational and individual complexity. A newly hired MBA at a global manufacturer was surprised to find, for example, that he could not organize a meeting without a manager's signature. Unauthorized meetings of nonmanagers violated company policy.[16] In reality, competent adults who are treated like untrustworthy children will not stay around too long.

Figure 13.4 details four kinds of authority that relate to work teams, which will remain a common part of organizational designs for the foreseeable future. The first dimension, scheduling authority, allows a group or team to schedule meetings without external approval. Selection authority allows a group to select new members as required or solicit external support. Internal process authority allows teams to manage their activities, such as budget allocation and goal setting, without management approval. Finally, external authority allows a group or team to bind or commit an organization through team decisions. It should come as no surprise that granting specific kinds of authority to work teams should lead to positive performance outcomes, including reduced complexity.

Standardize and Redesign Processes

A primary responsibility of a centrally led supply organization is to look across an organization and identify those processes that create real value. Furthermore, a center-led group must lead the effort to design processes that build in best practices and eliminate duplication of effort. It is hard to justify having every

Scheduling authority	Selection authority
Represents the ability to schedule meetings without others approving the decision	Represents the ability to select leader(s) and/or new team members as required to complete assigned tasks

Internal authority	External authority
Represents the ability of a team to control internal activities, such as allocating budget and material resources, determining goals, making timing decisions regarding the completion of activities, and requesting nonteam members to support assignments as needed	Represents the ability of a team to make decisions that bind or commit an organization, similar to Legal Agency rights. This is conceptually the highest level of authority because it allows a team to operate independently of external managers

Figure 13.4   Dimensions of organizational team authority

work center develop essentially the same set of processes. The complexity that results from sub-optimal processes and duplicate effort is not a source of pride.

Unfortunately, some interpret standardization to mean that every location or group must conform to a defined process with no deviation or flexibility allowed. A standard process should provide a best-practice framework that allows modifications where necessary, particularly when working across different geographic locations.

Process development or redesign efforts should have the removal of waste and complexity as a primary objective. Process modeling using standard ANSI symbols and value stream mapping are two recommended approaches when standardizing and redesigning work processes.

Create Low-dollar Purchase Systems

Many supply organizations still spend too much time chasing relatively insignificant items. These low-dollar and usually low-volume items create complexity that detracts from the time that could be spent on more important activities. Next level supply organizations will exit, perhaps completely, the transaction business by providing internal customers with the systems to seamlessly manage low-dollar items. Each of the following approaches has the potential to reduce the time and complexity associated with obtaining low-dollar items:

- Procurement cards issued to internal users
- Blanket purchase orders that allow internal users to issue material releases directly to suppliers

- Local purchase order books that allow internal users to issue orders below a certain dollar limit
- Electronic funds transfers to suppliers
- Online supplier catalogues and ordering capability
- Electronic purchase orders issued to suppliers
- On-site suppliers to manage and replenish inventory
- Electronic requisitions issued to procurement
- Use of full-line maintenance, repair, and operating distributors
- Electronic data interchange to manage transactions

Next level supply organizations will reduce complexity by getting out of the low-dollar acquisition business.

Use Information Technology

Every day we use technology to make our lives less complex. We take for granted that we can bank online, use ATM machines to get some quick cash, renew library books, buy airline tickets, renew prescriptions over the Internet, or search for information using powerful search engines. However, have we seriously thought how less complex our lives have become as the uses of information technology grow daily?

Using information technology to support our supply chain needs also grows daily. Whether stated or not, most IT applications are designed to remove, simplify, and streamline transactions. They also make the transfer of data from one system to another seamless while making information more transparent. Given that IT is a complexity killer, next level supply organizations will continue to be relentless in their search for IT applications that simplify supply chain applications. Information technology supports something that we call *complexity transfer*. The system takes the complexity away from the users.

Survey Suppliers, Employees, and Customers

Do you want to know where complexity exists? Ask suppliers, customers, and employees directly where they are experiencing complexity. With easy-to-use online survey technology, the barrier to using surveys is low. Ask suppliers, for example, if your company is doing anything that makes their life unnecessarily complex. It is possible that your material planners change release quantities right up to the delivery due date. Or perhaps your company has a cumbersome accounts payable process. If suppliers, customers, and employees take the time to provide feedback, then the requestor must take the time to respond to that information. Supplier, customer, and employee suggestion programs can also be used to request ideas about how to remove supply chain complexity.

Streamline Contract Reviews

If your legal department is a source of frustration, then welcome to a club that has way too many members. This frustration is due to a contract review process that can often take months rather than days. It can be the result of working with a group that thinks in terms of legal and punitive contingencies rather than collaborative possibilities.

For whatever reason, the review process for contracts is often far too complex. At a leading logistics company, supply managers were dismayed to see the longer-term agreements they negotiated with suppliers take up to nine months to work their way through the legal review process. They were more dismayed to see nine months of contract benefits forgone as original contract terms remained in place. In another example, a chemical company spent nine months reviewing a warehouse lease consolidation contract, thereby delaying the start of $80,000 in annual cost reduction savings. The savings from that single contract would have paid a buyer's salary. The reality is the legal review process should not be that complex.

Streamlining the review process can happen in a number of ways. One way is to create contracts that are not overly complex. Trust us when we say that most suppliers do not appreciate 50 page contractual agreements. While he was at IBM, the late Gene Richter reduced contracts from 40 pages on average to six pages. He understood precisely the need to reduce contract complexity.

Another streamlining method involves the use of preapproved contract language. Contract development relies extensively on *cut and paste* as agreements are negotiated. Legal involvement occurs only when preapproved language is modified. Instead of reviewing an entire contract, lawyers review and initial only the changes. The legal department could also assign a representative specifically to the supply organization, presumably resulting in better response times. Finally, metrics can be compiled to track legal review times. The point here is that a variety of methods exist to take complexity out of the review process.

What we presented here does not represent an exhaustive listing of ways to battle complexity. For example, organizations that are serious about waging war on complexity will develop a set of measures that reflect progress in this arena. Next level supply leaders know they have to take the lead in the battle against complexity. Far too often, however, complexity seems to be winning the battle.

Beating Complexity—How Leaders Do It

The following case example describes how a leading company has taken the battle against complexity to a higher level. It shows what can happen when reducing complexity becomes part of the supply leadership model.

Whirlpool's Approach to Beating Complexity[17]

Whirlpool is a premier manufacturer and marketer of home appliances. Not long ago, Whirlpool was a $3 billion company that focused its design, manufacturing, and selling operations largely within North America. Today, with $17 billion in annual revenue, thousands of employees, and dozens of manufacturing and technology centers worldwide, the company boasts an impressive global portfolio of brands that includes Whirlpool, Maytag, Amana, KitchenAid, and Jenn-Air.

With so many acquisitions and brands, plus the normal tendency for engineers to design new components each time a product is introduced, it should not come as a surprise that complexity has crept into the Whirlpool supply chain. An exciting initiative at Whirlpool involved a global attack on component proliferation and waste. Engineering and sourcing leaders have evaluated the components within every one of the company's 52 commodity categories. Whirlpool formed what it calls component architecture management (CAM) teams to accomplish this evaluation.

This initiative involves component rationalization. Recall that rationalization refers to trying to find the right mix and number of something to maintain. Here rationalization involves a search for the right mix and number of components to support worldwide production requirements. Entering the rationalization process, Whirlpool had, for example, 150 different water valves for dishwashers. Whirlpool's goal was to reduce this to 40 or 50 valves.

At its onset, the component rationalization process had several expected outcomes. First, the primary outcome was to remove complexity and redundancy from product and component designs. A second outcome involved creating a cultural change that requires personnel to justify why Whirlpool needs another variation of a part rather than trying to justify why there are so many. And finally, the company used the rationalization process as an opportunity to refresh its global commodity strategies.

CAM teams included representatives from procurement, engineering, technology, and global consumer design. Suppliers were also part of the process, particularly when providing data attributes about components. This process brings sourcing, engineering, and suppliers together in an environment that one senior leader describes as being intensely collaborative. Each CAM team had 16 weeks to finalize its component review.

The review process started with a determination of how many variations of a component were needed. A formal sign-off process was established that placed each CAM project in the engineering project system. The formal tracking that goes along with being a recognized engineering project lends credibility to the rationalization process. Tracking also provided visibility about each commodity's rationalization progress.

At the onset, the expected financial improvements from this process were $1 billion annually in direct material savings. This figure does not include the benefits from reduced supply chain complexity, any accounting for cost avoidances, improvements to product quality, or reductions in product development cycle times from having component designs available for reuse. While these types of benefits should be meaningful, they are also difficult to quantify.

Whirlpool's efforts align nicely with a goal of removing supply chain complexity. In fact, senior managers are confident this process represents a next level engineering and supply practice. Any company that has not coordinated the activities of its design centers or has grown through mergers and acquisition should expect to find too much of too many things. As Whirlpool has discovered, the time had arrived to declare war on complexity.

Concluding Thoughts

An objective of this chapter was to create awareness that supply chain complexity is a real issue that does not go away by itself. It is often an inevitable outcome of business decisions. Furthermore, we must realize that not all complexity is created equally. The battle against complexity should be a selective one. We need to broaden our thinking about the kinds of activities that can reduce supply chain complexity. We also need to think about the consequences of activities that at first glance appear to provide savings but in reality make life more complex. A relentless search for lower labor costs around the world comes quickly to mind.

The pressure to reduce costs is relentless and severe. Since complexity often increases cost with no commensurate benefit, the next generation of cost management strategies should place the battle against complexity at the forefront.

Chapter Notes

1. Valerie Reitman. "Toyota Motor Shows Its Mettle After Fire Destroys Parts Plant." *The Wall Street Journal*, May 8, 1997, A1.
2. These definitions come from www.merriam-webster.com.
3. Wendy Mason. *Complexity Theory*. www.referenceforbusiness.com/management/Bun-Comp/Complexity-Theory.html.
4. Suzanne Haywood, Jessica Spungin, and David Turnbull. "Cracking the Complexity Code." *The McKinsey Quarterly*, May 2007, 86, citing Trond

Riiber Knudsen, Cedric Noret, and Evan S. Van Metre, "The Power of a Commercial Operating System." *The McKinsey Quarterly*, Web (August 2006).

5. Heywood, Spungin, and Turnbull, 86.
6. Julian Birkinshaw and Suzanne Heywood. "Putting Organizational Complexity in its Place." *The McKinsey Quarterly*, May 2010, 2.
7. Birkinshaw and Heywood, 6.
8. Paul Teague. "P&G is King of Collaboration." *Purchasing* 137, no. 9 (September 11, 2008), 46.
9. Robert J. Trent. "Managing Inventory Investment Effectively." *Supply Chain Management Review*, March–April, 2002.
10. Joann S. Lubin. "After Slashing Inventory, Polaris Now Struggles to Meet Demand." *The Wall Street Journal*, May 24, 2010, B1.
11. Adapted from www.merriam-webster.com.
12. Adapted from www.merriam-webster.com.
13. Associated Press. "Despite Competition, Apple Still Cool." *The Express-Times*, May 19, 2010, B1.
14. John E. Ettlie and Matthew Kubarek. "Design Reuse in Manufacturing and Services." *The Journal of Product Innovation Management* 25, no. 5 (September 2008), 457.
15. Barry Berman. "Products, Product, Everywhere." *The Wall Street Journal*, August 23, 2010, R6.
16. Liz Ryan. "5 Ways to Ensure Mediocrity in Your Organization." Retrieved May 17, 2010, www.finance.yahoo.com/career-work/article.
17. This is adapted from a case written by Robert J. Trent and appearing in *Managing Global Supply and Risk: Best Practices, Concepts, and Strategies* (Ft. Lauderdale, FL: J. Ross Publishing, 2010).

14

Risk Assessment, Prevention, and Mitigation

Nothing about the Boeing 787 Dreamliner is evolutionary. From its advanced composite materials, radically new engines, swept aerodynamic wings, and an interior cabin that will make flying enjoyable again, the Dreamliner is an aerospace game changer. Even the way it was designed was revolutionary, as Boeing assigned extensive design and build responsibilities to a small cadre of suppliers. Unfortunately, the dream has not quite worked out the way it was envisioned on paper, exposing the company to costly delays, lost customer goodwill, and financial risk. While Boeing is reluctant to reveal how much the delays will eventually cost, analysts estimate the company faces billions of dollars in payments to compensate airlines and reimburse suppliers.[1]

A large part of the Dreamliner's problems resulted from supply lapses. Some suppliers that were good at what they did previously were not necessarily good at system design and integration, forcing Boeing to step in and take control, and sometimes even ownership, of supply chain members. Parts shortages and poor workmanship also forced the company to send hundreds of its employees to work at supplier facilities. Boeing experienced firsthand the risks that are present when pushing the boundaries of technical and commercial innovation.

This chapter approaches the important topic of risk from a variety of perspectives. We provide an overview of risk, including its definition, differentiating between prevention and mitigation and presenting the major categories of risk. Next, four major trends affecting supply chain risk are discussed. The chapter then addresses a set of next level activities for preventing supply chain risk. The chapter concludes with examples of what leading companies are doing to manage their risk exposure.

Supply Chain Risk—the New Normal

Risk management will continue to be a hot supply chain topic for reasons that are explained shortly. In fact, we could even say that an era of heightened risk represents a condition called the new normal. Do we expect supply chain distances to suddenly become shorter or will the constant pursuit of lower purchase prices no longer take us to new and untested sourcing locations? Will we ever see the Homeland Security threat level at U.S. airports go below high? The new normal means that supply chain risk will be of interest for the foreseeable future.

Something that all supply leaders should understand is the relationship between their actions and possible unintended consequences, something that often elevates risk. A reliance on Chinese suppliers, for example, sometimes leads to operational risk in terms of quality problems and long ordering lead times. The unintended consequences of longer lead times are delivery uncertainty and a reduced ability to plan. An emphasis on longer-term contracting, another popular sourcing action, often results in higher supplier switching costs and the shutting out of new ideas from suppliers who feel they do not have a chance to receive a contract from a buyer. An unintended consequence of some well-intentioned supply initiatives is higher risk.

So, what is risk? For our purposes, risk refers to the probability of experiencing a less than desirable event that affects one or more of the parties within a supply chain. A standard perspective of risk is that it involves the possibility of loss or injury. When risk events occur, they have the potential to negatively influence the achievement of business objectives.

The Supply Chain Leadership Council, established in 2006, has worked to create a common definition of supply chain risk management (SCRM). The council defines SCRM as the practice of managing the risk of any factor or event that can materially disrupt a supply chain whether within a single company or spread across multiple companies. The ultimate purpose of SCRM is to enable cost avoidance, customer service, and market position.[2]

Two other concepts related to risk are vulnerability and resilience. Risk vulnerability represents the combination of the likelihood of a disruption combined with its potential severity. Resilience refers to the ability to bounce back from disruptions of any type. Obviously, resilience will differ according to the risk occurrence and the steps taken to help with a recovery. A company with redundant data systems located physically apart will have a higher resiliency to systems failures than a company that lacks this redundancy.

If we think hard enough about it, the reality is there is risk in everything we do, whether it is crossing the street or providing personal information online. Did you know that within the next 50 years, there is a chance the earth may be hit and possibly destroyed by an asteroid? If that depresses you, then you might not want to look up in the sky when you go outside. Or you can be comforted by the fact that the probability of this occurring is nearly infinitesimal. This is a key point about risk and risk assessment. It is not enough to identify potential risks but rather to understand their nature and the probability that a specific risk might occur. This is why many organizations undertake scenario planning by examining potential outcomes and assigning probabilities to these potential outcomes.

A common misperception is that risk is something bad and should be avoided. Anyone who commits their life to not taking chances, and these chances always carry an associated risk of failure, will not get far. An important consideration when evaluating risk is the trade-off between risk aversion and the willingness to accept a risk, or what we will call a risk appetite. Entrepreneurs, for example, have a high-risk appetite and a low-risk aversion. Those who are completely risk averse would never invest in the stock market.

Risk Mitigation vs. Risk Prevention

One way to view risk is to divide the steps taken to manage risk into two broad categories—mitigation and prevention. Risk mitigation is the process of proactively managing risks with a focus on minimizing their potential impact. To mitigate is to cause something to become less harsh, hostile, or less severe. The important point here is that mitigation often, but not always, takes place after a risk becomes a reality. While buying commercial property insurance is often seen as a way to mitigate the risk of a fire, for example, changes that have to be made to qualify for the insurance (such as improved electrical wiring) might help prevent future negative occurrences.

Instead of simply thinking of risk in terms of mitigation, leading supply organizations think of what can be done to prevent certain occurrences from happening in the first place, particularly operational risk. Our perspective views prevention as a means to keep something that is negative from happening. For example, diplomats might undertake negotiations to prevent war from breaking out between countries. And if we eat our broccoli every day, we might prevent certain types of cancers.

Let's illustrate the concepts of mitigation and prevention with an everyday example. Each time we travel in a car, we are exposed to risk. These risks include the possibility of an accident, getting lost during our travels, becoming delayed because of traffic, or breaking down due to mechanical problems. Clearly, there are actions that can prevent these risks from occurring. To prevent a breakdown we can have our car regularly serviced (there is a reason it is called preventive maintenance), make sure the tires are not worn, and purchase gasoline from reputable outlets. To prevent getting lost, we can determine our route ahead of time and keep a map or GPS in the car. To avoid traffic jams, we can check our state department of transportation website to identify scheduled roadwork and listen to radio updates or traffic reports. Also, driving carefully and sober is always a good idea.

What if our car does break down? At this point, the focus shifts from risk prevention to risk mitigation (i.e., make the situation less severe). Now we will be glad we have a cell phone, emergency roadside flares or warning signs, and an up-to-date AAA card. A good spare tire may also come in handy. If we get into an accident, a secure seat belt, air bags, a five-star safety rating on your vehicle, and fully paid automobile insurance should help mitigate that event.

The same logic between prevention and mitigation applies to supply chains. Steps can be taken that will help prevent certain types of risks from becoming reality while other steps help mitigate a risk situation after it occurs. A later section identifies various activities that can help prevent supply chain risk. Many organizations simply refer to any steps taken within the risk arena as part of their risk management process.

Risk Categories

Not all supply chain risks are created equally. It makes sense to segment risk into different categories and then develop approaches that are suitable for each category. For some risks, such as earthquakes and hurricanes, the best some companies can hope to do is manage the risk after an occurrence, although taking into consideration major earthquake fault lines before building a new facility might help manage that particular risk. Reinforced structures can also mitigate damage if an earthquake occurs. For other risks, such as poor supplier performance, steps can be taken to anticipate and even prevent these risks from occurring. While no industry standard topology of risks exists, many supply organizations categorize their risks into four major groups. An important point to remember is that risks can be interdependent. For example, a strategic decision to locate a new facility in China can affect operational supply chain risks.

Hazard risk: Pertains to random disruptions, some of which are acts of nature. This category also includes accidents and fires. Other disruptions could be malicious, including crime, terrorism, and product tampering.

Financial risk: Relates to internal and external financial difficulties. A later section will address the monitoring of supplier financial health, including some of the tools available for monitoring supplier health. We also include supply prices that are unnecessarily too high as part of this category.

Operational risk: Arises out of daily operations, including supply chain risks. Poor supplier quality, late deliveries due to port delays, and poor forecasts are examples of operational risks.

Strategic risk: Relates to strategic decisions made by executive management. Buying another company, for example, presents potential strategic risk.

Trends Affecting Supply Chain Risk

Surveys reveal that supply managers perceive their risk exposure to be greater than just a few years ago. In a recent report on risk, nearly 75% of risk managers say their company's supply chain risk levels are higher than in 2005. Over 70% of study respondents say the financial impact of supply chain disruptions has also increased.[3]

Beyond the risks associated with an imploding economy, other, less obvious trends continue to occur that have the potential to expose supply organizations to greater risk. Four trends in particular include a steady growth in international purchasing, an increased reliance on higher level outsourcing, supply market volatility, and stock keeping units (SKUs) proliferation and mass customization.[4]

Let's Go Global!

Since 1980, the total value of goods exported from the United States has increased over 475% (from $224 billion to a peak of $1.3 trillion). The value of services exported from the United States for this same period increased 1000% (from $47.5 billion in 1980 to a peak of $534 billion in 2008).[5] The figures for 2009 and beyond declined due to a general decline in economic activity. Whether we like it or not, the globalization of business activity is a continuing trend that brings not only increased complexity, but also increased risk.

While globalization can contribute to increased profitability, it also creates a new set of risks. It is nearly a given that lead-times and logistics costs will increase. Longer lead-times also mean that inventory must increase to ensure product availability. As supply organizations buy internationally, delivery variability, possible loss of quality control, currency fluctuations, and longer lead times that make planning less certain all become concerns. While globalization offers tremendous opportunity for reward, particularly lower prices, it also creates opportunity for risk. Increased globalization has increased the need for global risk management.

Higher Level Outsourcing

Another trend involves outsourcing those parts of the supply chain where a company offers nothing distinctive while investing in those areas that represent core competencies or capabilities. Businesses should be systematically examining their processes to determine what will remain internally and what will be outsourced. A result of this examination has been a well-established trend toward outsourcing to suppliers that presumably can add new value. Outsourcing has resulted in an increasing number of OEM's that are proficient at designing and assembling final products but no longer as proficient at making the parts that go into those products.

Outsourcing has some definite risk implications, as the Dreamliner example at the start of this chapter points out. First, the practice creates an increased dependence on third parties that are often located throughout the world. This dependency brings with it any risks involved with relinquishing control. Are these suppliers qualified to take on extensive design work that was previously performed by the buyer? Furthermore, outsourcing often leads to a transfer of supply chain power and decision rights from one party to another. In addition, companies that outsource to third parties become reliant on them to effectively manage supply chain risk for component suppliers, something the buying company previously managed. Finally, companies that outsource usually lose capabilities that will never be recovered. It is a fallacy to believe the use of third parties or agents automatically leads to lower costs, higher performance, or reduced risk.

It Is a Volatile World

If you think supply markets seem more volatile compared with days past, you are probably right. Consider the following headlines from the last five years—prices for molybdenum are at historic highs; spot gold predicted to double in coming months; zircon rises as demand exceeds supply; crude oil hits new trading high; copper leaps to record high; and titanium dioxide is about to rise. Buyers then witnessed some rapid price declines due to the economic meltdown of 2008. Recently a handful of cocoa traders took possession of nearly all the cocoa beans in certified warehouses in Europe in an attempt to squeeze the market and force prices above their already historic highs.[6] Unfortunately, these rapid price gyrations, sometimes created by market manipulations, create volatility, a condition that elevates supply chain risk and makes planning more difficult.

Proliferate and Customize Is the Name of the Game

Chapter 13 addressed product proliferation and customization in terms of its affect on supply chain complexity. It is clear that the number and types of products offered by most producers are increasing. Furthermore, customers are asking for products that are less standardized and more tailored to their unique requirements. In many market segments, success will belong to those that are able to mass customize their product or service offering. Mass customization involves producing products in small batches tailored to individual customers at an economical rate.

It is reasonable to conclude that customers will continue to demand more mass customized products and services. It is difficult to take something away from customers once they experience its benefit. One of the implications for distribution is that although overall demand may remain relatively stable, the number of SKUs will increase, resulting in a fragmented array of product offerings. Forecasts of product mix, the demand at different distribution points and locations, and required volumes will become increasingly difficult to predict and manage. This difficulty is a breeding ground for risk.

Companies will also be expected to provide value-added services, such as kitting, to meet the demand for specialized products. Kitting involves packaging a variety of items together to create a new item, such as a subassembly. Furthermore, the use of postponement as a means of supporting mass customization, while still keeping inventory at acceptable levels, will become increasingly important. With postponement, the final process steps that differentiate a product are delayed until a customer provides insight into the product's final configuration.

Business practices such as mass customization, kitting, and postponement all require a flexible and responsive supply chain. Coordinating SKUs in global distribution centers, as well as the handling, packaging, and transportation issues that arise from offering specialized SKUs, is a global challenge. A failure to create the capabilities to accommodate increased product proliferation and customization can leave a producer in a risky position.

As we lament over the prospect that supply chain risk is increasing, we should not forget that much of this risk is self-induced. Most of the trends just discussed represent conscious decisions arising from the strategic planning process. Chapter 13 featured a story about a fire at Toyota's single supplier for a critical brake component—the supplier's facility burning down is a type of risk (hazard risk) where Toyota had no direct control. However, the fact that Toyota relied on a single supplier with no backup plan and designed hundreds of variations of the same component created risks that were self-induced.

A Risk Management Framework

Various typologies exist that seek to guide users through a risk management integrated framework. Figure 14.1 presents one such approach adapted from the Council of Sponsoring Organizations of the Treadway Commission (COSO).[7] This group defines enterprise risk management as:

> Enterprise risk management is a process, effected by an entity's board of directors, management, and other personnel, applied in strategy setting and across the enterprise, designed to identify potential events that may affect the entity, and manage risk to be within its risk appetite, to provide reasonable assurance regarding the achievement of entity objectives.

1. Internal environment	Encompasses the tone of an organization, and sets the basis for how risk is viewed and addressed, including the risk management philosophy and risk appetite, integrity and ethical values, and the environment in which people operate.
2. Objective setting	ERM requires that management has in place a process to set objectives and that the chosen objectives support and align with the entity's mission and are consistent with its risk appetite.
3. Event identification	Identify internal and external events affecting the achievement of an entity's objectives, distinguishing between risks and opportunities. Opportunities are channeled back to management's strategy or objective-setting processes.
4. Risk assessment	Risks are analyzed, considering likelihood and impact, as a basis for determining how they should be managed.
5. Risk response	Management selects risk responses (avoiding, accepting, reducing, or sharing risk) and develops a set of actions to align risks with the entity's risk tolerances and risk appetite.
6. Control activities	Management implements and establishes policies and procedures to help ensure the risk responses are effectively carried out.
7. Information & communication	Identify, capture, and communicate relevant information in a form and timeframe that enable people to carry out their responsibilities.
8. Monitoring	ERM is monitored through ongoing management activities, separate evaluations, or both and modifications made as necessary.

Entity level   Divisional level   Business unit level   Subsidary level

Figure 14.1   Enterprise risk management framework
Source: Adapted from Council of Sponsoring Organizations

The definition reflects certain fundamental concepts that underlie its risk management framework. Enterprise risk management is:

- A process, ongoing and flowing through an entity
- Effected by people at every level of an organization
- Applied in a strategy setting
- Applied across the enterprise, at every level and unit, and includes taking an entity-level, portfolio view of risk
- Designed to identify potential events that, if they occur, will affect the entity and to manage risk within its risk appetite

- Provides reasonable assurance to an entity's management and board of directors
- Geared to achievement of objectives in one or more separate but overlapping categories

The COSO risk management framework has eight levels encompassing four levels of risk management planning, which Figure 14.1 describes. Risk management planning can occur at the entity, division, business unit, and subsidiary level. This framework is geared toward achieving an entity's objectives across four categories. These categories are strategic (high level goals, aligned with and supporting a corporate mission), operations (effective and efficient use of its resources), reporting (reliability of reporting), and compliance (with applicable laws and regulations).

The purpose of this framework is to present risk management within the context of a comprehensive process. Risk management is not something to be performed haphazardly or on an ad hoc basis, although research still reveals that far too many organizations approach risk management in this manner.

Why Manage Risk When You Can Prevent Risk?

Oftentimes we simply use the broader term risk management when talking about the actions taken to address supply chain risk. It is a nice *catch all* term. In line with the precepts of quality management, this section takes a slightly different approach by focusing on a powerful set of approaches that have the potential to prevent unwanted consequences from happening in the first place. While clearly not a comprehensive set of preventive actions (a comprehensive set would fill volumes), you should get the idea that some things do not have to happen and that proactive and reactive behavior are different ways to approach risk.

Monitoring and Predicting Supplier Financial Health

The continuous monitoring of supplier health is without question the area that has received the most attention within the risk management arena. We have no reason to believe this will change within the foreseeable future. This is due largely to the increased awareness of financial risk brought about by the economic meltdown that started in 2008. It is also due to an abundance of available third-party data.

In an ideal world, suppliers would readily inform customers about financial difficulties. Unfortunately, suppliers are often fearful of divulging this type of information for fear of losing a customer's business, further accelerating their decline. Next level supply organizations will have strong analytic and financial capabilities to analyze a variety of internally derived and externally provided data.

Financial statement analysis: Balance sheets, incomes statements, and cash flow statements provide a wealth of insight when analyzed by a financially trained individual. Next level supply organizations will maintain a strong financial competency, possible through a finance expert collocated with supply personnel.

A wide range of ratios that use data from financial statements are available. While different sources may disagree on the final categorization, financial ratios typically fall into one of four broad groups:

- Liquidity ratios indicate a supplier's capability in meeting its short-term financial obligations.
- Leverage ratios reveal a supplier's capability in paying its longer-term debt obligations.
- Activity ratios reveal how efficiently a supplier manages its assets, including its working capital.
- Profitability ratios show the return the supplier is earning.

For several reasons, the quantitative assessment of financial data using financial ratios is not enough when evaluating supplier health. First, data access and reliability can be a concern, especially when dealing with international suppliers in emerging markets. Second, ratio analysis is simply a tool that should be part of a broader approach for monitoring supplier health. Third, care must be taken when comparing companies from different industries. The interpretation of financial ratios is not always consistent from industry to industry. Finally, financial statements, which are the primary source for ratio analysis, provide insight only for a point in time (the balance sheet) or a relatively short period of time (the income statement). Multiple time periods should be used to identify possible trends.

Watching for signs of supplier distress: Beyond the analysis of income, balance sheet, and cash flow data and ratios, buyers should be aware of some qualitative warning signs that might reveal supplier distress. Various signs that a supplier may be experiencing financial difficulties include:[8]

- A large portion of a supplier's sales go to customers in depressed industries.
- A supplier cannot meet agreed upon lead times because of late purchase order placements for its materials.
- A supplier is shipping early due to a lack of business.
- The supplier announces plant closings.
- The supplier has reduced its investments in research and development, IT, equipment, or resources.
- The supplier is reducing staff and workers.
- Unusual turnover occurs at the executive level.
- Quality is deteriorating.

- Additional discounts are offered for early payment or payments are required in advance.
- The supplier is restating financial reports and projections.
- The supplier's product is labor intensive, requiring large payrolls.
- The supplier has absorbed upfront research and development and tooling costs on new products that are delayed getting to the marketplace.

Third-party tools: A variety of third-party tools are commercially available when monitoring supplier financial health. Some of these tools even provide scores that relate to benchmarks of financial health.[9] Four sources of supplier financial information that we will highlight include (1) Altman Z-reports, (2) Dunn & Bradstreet (D&B) ratings, (3) FactSet Research Systems, and (4) Rapid Ratings. While we do not endorse any particular risk management product, we do endorse the need to have access to timely and relevant third-party data. You can decide which, if any, of the offerings satisfy your risk management needs.

Altman Z-reports: Perhaps the most widely known tool for assessing supplier financial health is the Z-score. Developed by Dr. Edward Altman of New York University, the Z-score combines a series of weighted ratios for public and private firms to predict financial health. It is nearly 90% accurate in predicting bankruptcy one year in advance and 75% accurate in predicting bankruptcy two years in advance.

The Z-score methodology has several things going for it that makes its use attractive for supply organizations. The first is its simplicity. Only four ratios are needed to calculate the Z-score for private firms and five ratios for public firms. The second positive attribute is it provides a single score that provides tremendous insight into a supplier's financial condition. Supply organizations use the Z-score during the preliminary evaluation of suppliers, as well as during ongoing operations. Altman Z-reports are available on many financial websites. Figure 14.2 presents the Z-score framework.

D&B reports[10]: Over the years, D&B has developed a suite of products and reports that support supply managers by monitoring, predicting, and reporting supplier risk. One of D&B's primary offering is its Supplier Risk Manager product. This is a suite of offerings that the company maintains will help supply organizations certify suppliers as approved and bring new ones on-board through an online portal that aggregates, validates, and enhances supplier data to determine potential risk. It provides ongoing alerts and profiles that provide operational, financial, and supplier performance data. The tool also analyzes risk and identifies trends with suppliers through scorecards, graphs, and charts that combine your data with D&B data. All of this is done to provide insight that helps mitigate risk.

A second major D&B offering is the Supplier Qualifier Report. This report evaluates suppliers and potential suppliers according to risk, financial

Private company:

$$Z\text{-Score} = 6.56 \times \frac{\text{working capital}}{\text{total assets}} + 3.36 \times \frac{\text{retained earnings}}{\text{total assets}} + 6.72 \times \frac{\text{EBIT}}{\text{total assets}} + 1.05 \times \frac{\text{net worth}}{\text{total liability}}$$

Where:

Z-Score <1.1 — Red zone—Supplier is financially at risk

Z-Score between 1.1 and 2.6 — Yellow zone—Some area of financial concern

Z-Score > 2.6 — Green zone—Supplier is financially sound

Public company:

$$Z\text{-Score} = 1.2 \times \frac{\text{working capital}}{\text{total assets}} + 1.4 \times \frac{\text{retained earnings}}{\text{total assets}} + 3.3 \times \frac{\text{EBIT}}{\text{total assets}} + 0.6 \times \frac{\text{net worth}}{\text{total liability}} + 1.0 \times \frac{\text{net sales}}{\text{total assets}}$$

Where:

Z-Score <1.8 — Red zone—Supplier is financially at risk

Z-Score between 1.8 and 3.0 — Yellow zone—Some area of financial concern

Z-Score > 3.0 — Green zone—Supplier is financially sound

Figure 14.2 Z-score formulas

stability, and business performance. This report is especially helpful during the pre-qualification stage of supplier evaluation. Included in this report is information about a supplier's business overview, history and operations, payment information, risk assessment, financial information, and any public filings.

FactSet Research Systems[11]: This resource is used widely by the financial community. It provides a wealth of data by creating internal databases supplemented by content from hundreds of third-party data providers. Users can integrate streaming real-time market data, prices, financials, earnings estimates, research reports, and news in a presentation platform the user can customize. The user can select an extensive set of financial and non-financial criteria to identify, select, and sort public and private companies. The output can further be customized by selecting the analytics and data that match your specific needs.

Rapid Ratings[12]: Rapid Ratings is an independent ratings, research, and analytics firm that rates the financial health of companies for investment and risk management purposes. Its quantitative ratings system produces something called Financial Health Ratings (FHRs). FHRs are predictive and comprehensive measures of the true financial health of a company. FHRs identify a company's ability to remain competitive in the future against a global industry peer group. According to the company, FHRs are based on adaptive models that combine financial ratio analyses with nonlinear modeling techniques. From the FHR methodology, the company offers a variety of value-added products. One such product that should be of interest to supply managers is Estimated Probabilities of Default (EPD). The EPD is based on an analysis of historical defaults. It is a risk management tool for analyzing the prospective default risk of a company.

The Risk Management War Room

Imagine walking into a room where risk management information is collected, categorized, analyzed, prominently displayed, and widely disseminated to the right people at the right time. Imagine having a dedicated staff with responsibility for monitoring supplier health, collecting and analyzing third-party data, spotting disruptive weather patterns, tracking material movement around the globe, following political and business news and trends, responding to specific risk-related information requests from internal customers, and sending early risk warnings to those who would benefit from that information. This staff would also help local units develop their risk management capabilities. The war room should also allow users to flag supplier names for notices when noteworthy information becomes available. Welcome to the risk management war room, a room that is a dream of many organizations.

Several trends make the risk management war room something to consider when thinking about preventing supply chain risk. First, we are seeing a general movement toward greater centralization and centrally led leadership within supply and supply chain management. Chapter 5 provided data that showed this movement for a host of strategic supply management activities. It is time for risk management to join the list of activities that would benefit from strong central leadership. Second, widely dispersed supply chains and economic uncertainty are combining to make risk more rather than less critical as a supply chain topic. Greater risk requires aggressive ways to battle this beast.

The predominant model of risk management that we see today is what we call the *pockets of excellence* model. Within a typical organization, groups develop risk management capabilities simply because they need to develop risk management capabilities. Some of these groups are even quite good at managing various kinds of risk, particularly operational risk. At other times, the *pockets* are not quite so capable. Unfortunately, the pockets model does nothing toward creating a coordinated *center of excellence* that supports an entire organization. This model usually results in risk management techniques that are dispersed, incomplete, sub-optimized in their sophistication, uncoordinated across a company, and often duplicated in their development. Other than that, the pockets model works just fine. It is time to set up a risk management war room that is supported at the highest organizational levels.

World-class Supplier Evaluation and Selection Process

Supplier evaluation and selection is one of the most important responsibilities of any supply organization. While most supply managers recognize the truth of this statement, supplier evaluation is often an afterthought performed by buyers who pursue the lowest possible price rather than the lowest total cost. A strategic emphasis on core capabilities and competencies, which often results in the outsourcing of major requirements, now makes supplier evaluation a critical organizational process. A realization that some upfront work can prevent some problems later has not gone unnoticed by leading supply organizations.

The primary objective of the evaluation process should be the selection of suppliers with a solid track record of performing at world-class levels. When this occurs, many of the issues that create risk mysteriously disappear. For the most important goods and services, a buying organization should approach supplier evaluation much the same way it would approach due diligence in an acquisition. Cross-functional teams should routinely be used to evaluate a supplier's financial condition; capacity; logistical networks; cost structure; supply management practices; technology innovation; and design, engineering, and process capabilities. While the cost of making supplier visits can be high, the value of preventing future problems can far outweigh these costs. Supplier evaluation and selection is a process that next level organizations will get right.

A methodical approach for selecting suppliers: A world-class selection process incorporates many supply management topics, including strategy segmentation and development, risk prevention, measurement, longer-term contracting, and negotiation. While not all selection decisions are equally important, the more important ones should follow a logical flow from recognizing a need to reaching an agreement with selected suppliers. A capable selection process should create output (i.e., selected suppliers) that meets or exceeds performance expectations. The following presents a generic framework for progressing through the supplier evaluation and selection process:

- Recognize a supplier selection need exists
- Identify supply requirements
- Determine the appropriate supply strategy
- Identify potential suppliers
- Reduce suppliers in selection pool
- Conduct a formal supplier evaluation
- Select supplier and reach contractual agreement

Chapter 8 provides an in-depth treatment of a comprehensive process (strategic sourcing) incorporating these and other factors.

Next level supply organizations will require the development of risk management plans that are part of supply strategies and selection decisions. In fact, this is a best practice as it relates to supplier evaluation and selection. The truth is that supplier selection represents the beginning of what could be a long commercial relationship. Over time, the focus must shift from evaluating and selecting suppliers to managing supply risk and developing supplier capabilities. Next level supply organizations recognize that supplier evaluation is not only one of their most important organizational processes, it represents perhaps the preeminent way to prevent risks from beginning realities.

Taking time out of the selection decision: Most supply chain experts will agree that nothing good happens as planning horizons and cycle times become longer. In fact, longer planning horizons are a primary cause of increased supply chain risk. Next level organizations know that competitive advantage can result by shortening the planning and execution times of just about everything we need to do, including supplier evaluation and selection.

Many supplier evaluation and selection decisions support new product development. Since development times for new products and services are declining rapidly, it nearly goes without saying that any supporting cycle times must also decline. Major supplier selection decisions often have to occur in weeks, sometimes even days. Supplier selection is a process that must not only be performed well but also performed quickly.

Supply organizations have a wide array of options to shorten the cycle time for supplier selection. A sample of approaches include a preferred supplier list; preapproved contract language; templates for internal customers to forward their requirements electronically; supply management participation on new product development teams; and the use of third-party data to pre-qualify suppliers. Knowing that longer cycle times often create risk, progressive supply organizations will diligently pursue approaches that shorten each step of the selection process.

Total Cost of Ownership Modeling

Managing a supply chain from a total cost of ownership (TCO) perspective is perhaps one of the best ways to prevent the risk of making poor decisions or paying too much for goods or services. Total cost includes the expected and unexpected elements that increase the unit cost of a good, service, or piece of equipment. Total cost systems or models, and there are a variety of them, attempt to capture these cost elements. The development of reliable total cost models is without question a best practice that, unfortunately, far too many companies have yet to perform well. Because their incorrect use can create rather than alleviate risk, at least a cursory understanding of TCO modeling is recommended.

TCO models: TCO models belong to a family of measurement systems called cost-based systems. A primary objective of these systems is to replace subjective measurement or assessment with data that are more objective. Two other types of measurement systems include categorical systems and weighted-point systems. Categorical systems involve subjective check-off ratings for various items. Categorical measurement is the lowest level of measurement in terms of sophistication. Weighted-point systems, which are widely used in supplier performance scorecards, use scales with defined values. This approach weighs and quantifies scores across different performance categories. Neither categorical nor weighted-point systems usually consider total cost directly. As with any measurement system, cost-based systems offer advantages and disadvantages. What limits their use is the fact that they can be extremely challenging to develop and use. If these systems were easy to develop, then everyone would have them.

Across a supply chain we generally see total cost models applied within three major areas. A total landed cost model is ideally suited for use when evaluating suppliers prior to making purchase decisions. This is what makes their use ideal for risk prevention. Landed cost is the sum of all costs associated with obtaining a product, including acquisition planning; unit price; inbound cost of freight, duty, and taxes; inspection; and material handling for storage and retrieval.[13] Each of these cost categories will contain numerous sub-categories. As it applies to total landed cost models, cost elements are often divided into categories that reflect a logical progression of material through the supply chain, within country of manufacture, in transit to country of sale, and within the country of sale. Total landed cost models are recommended when making international purchasing decisions.

Various models attempt to capture the true cost of doing business with a supplier on a continuous basis. Perhaps the best known of these models is the supplier performance index (SPI). Just as total landed cost models consider total cost during the evaluation phase of supplier selection, SPI measures costs incurred during a supplier's ongoing performance. The SPI is a cost model that presents its output in the form of an index or ratio. It assumes that any quality or other infraction committed by a supplier during the course of business increases the total cost (and hence the total cost performance ratio) of doing business with that supplier. SPI calculations are helpful when tracking supplier improvement over time, quantifying the severity of performance problems, deciding which suppliers should exit the supply base, and when establishing minimally acceptable levels of supplier performance.

Life-cycle cost models may be what comes most readily to mind when thinking about total costs analysis. This type of model is most often used when evaluating capital decisions that cover an extended time period, usually for equipment and facilities. Life-cycle models are similar to net present value models used in finance. The flow through of a life cycle is essentially one of buying, shipping, installing, using, maintaining, and disposing. Most life-cycle cost models are used (or should be used) to evaluate capital decisions rather than the purchase of everyday components and services. Other cost models are more applicable for repetitively purchased goods or services.

Why total cost models are usually wrong: A popular misconception is that total cost models provide better information than not having total cost models. The reality is that total cost models, like forecasting models, nearly always have some degree of unreliability, and this unreliability can create risk if it is excessive or managed improperly. The question becomes how much unreliability is embedded in the model.

Why are these models usually wrong, at least to some degree? The data that populate a total cost model can be segmented into four categories that represent a hierarchy from most to least reliable, as illustrated in Figure 14.3. These categories also conveniently start with the letter A.

Regardless of the cost model used, the need to understand the data populating the model cannot be understated. Supply managers may make decisions based on data that fall largely at the bottom of the reliability scale. Like forecasting models, total cost models usually arrive at some number to report in the way of total cost. But are you confident in that figure? What is the confidence interval around that number? Used correctly, TCO models can help reduce operational and financial risk. Used incorrectly, these models can elevate rather than alleviate risk.

Financial Risk Management through Hedging

One of the most widely talked about risk management approaches is financial hedging. And one of the most widely misunderstood topics in risk management

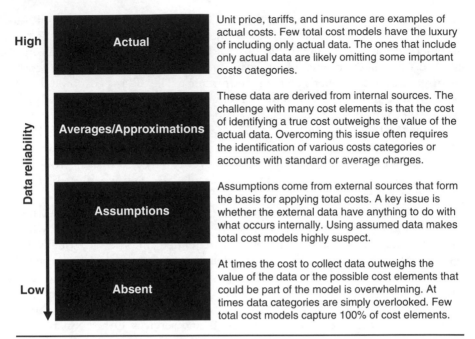

High	**Actual**	Unit price, tariffs, and insurance are examples of actual costs. Few total cost models have the luxury of including only actual data. The ones that include only actual data are likely omitting some important costs categories.
	Averages/Approximations	These data are derived from internal sources. The challenge with many cost elements is that the cost of identifying a true cost outweighs the value of the actual data. Overcoming this issue often requires the identification of various costs categories or accounts with standard or average charges.
	Assumptions	Assumptions come from external sources that form the basis for applying total costs. A key issue is whether the external data have anything to do with what occurs internally. Using assumed data makes total cost models highly suspect.
Low	**Absent**	At times the cost to collect data outweighs the value of the data or the possible cost elements that could be part of the model is overwhelming. At times data categories are simply overlooked. Few total cost models capture 100% of cost elements.

Figure 14.3 Levels of total cost data

is hedging. Hedging involves the simultaneous purchase and sale of material (i.e., commodity) or currency contracts in two markets. The purpose of hedging is to lock in a position for a future point in time. In simplified terms, a gain on one contract will be offset by a loss on the other. The objective of hedging is risk aversion rather than a monetary gain. Speculating is the process of playing commodity and currency markets for a financial gain.

Hedging contracts involve either futures exchange or forward exchange contracts. Futures contracts are traded on commodity exchanges and are open to any party with a need to hedge or a desire to speculate. Speculators, which are essential for creating markets where hedging can occur, usually practice their trade on commodity exchanges. Forward contracts, the second type of hedging contracts, are issued by major banks, primarily to other banks, brokers, and multinational companies.

Hedging can result in lost opportunities. Assume a supply organization hedges copper at $3.00 per pound six months into the future, and at the six-month point copper is now valued at $2.50 per pound. The buyer is still responsible for copper at $3.00 per pound even though it now sells for $2.50 per pound. Conversely, copper could increase to $3.50 per pound, resulting in a cost-avoidance for the owner of the hedging contracts. Hedging locks in a forward position, which is important for planning and budgeting.

Because of its complexity, hedging is rarely the responsibility of supply organizations, nor should it be. This does not mean that hedging is not an important tool for managing supply and currency risk. Supply organizations that want to engage in hedging of any kind are encouraged to work closely with their treasury or finance groups. Next level supply groups will have internal financial expertise or have finance representatives collocated within their organization. Hedging is a complex risk management approach that should increase in use. This will force closer collaboration between supply management and finance.

Mapping Supply Chain Risks

A popular way to approach risk management is through mapping. Figure 14.4 presents the ever popular 2 × 2 matrix that looks at risk from two perspectives—the impact of a risk occurring and the likelihood of a risk occurring. It is operationally impossible to develop approaches for managing every kind of

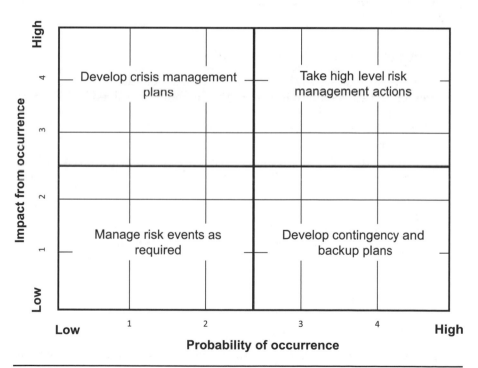

Figure 14.4   Mapping supply chain risks

Source: Robert Trent and Lew Roberts. *Managing Global Supply and Risks*. Ft. Lauderdale, FL: J. Ross Publishing, 2009.

conceivable risk that might occur across a supply chain. The 2011 Japanese tsunami demonstrates this point. This makes having a technique for segmenting and prioritizing risk occurrences nearly a necessity.

This technique is best used with an assembled group of supply chain professionals. First, the group works together to identify the range of risks that might occur across the four categories presented earlier (hazard, financial, operational, and strategic). Some companies may choose to focus on certain kinds of risks when using this approach, such as operational risks. Next, the group maps the various risks within the matrix. While this can be done by group discussion and consensus, a more efficient way is to ask each member to rate each risk along a 0 to 5 scale for likelihood and impact. Electronic surveys and group voting tools make this a relatively efficient process. This will reveal quickly if consensus exists and, hopefully, allow placement of the risks along the two continuums. A final step involves identifying ways to prevent or mitigate each key risk.

It's hard to imagine having a single risk map for an entire company. Different geographies and diverse business units will likely have their own set of risks they face.

Building in Supply Chain Flexibility

Flexibility represents a ready capability to adapt to new, different, or changing requirements. It can be present in areas that are not only valued by customers but that also help an organization respond quickly and in many cases prevent different kinds of risk from becoming a reality. For example, the ability to reroute a shipment in transit can help avoid delays at a port with striking workers. While flexibility helps mitigate risk, it can also help prevent risk occurrences from becoming amplified in their effect. Possible areas of supply chain flexibility include:

- Routing and logistical
- Production process
- Lead-time
- Scheduling
- Product configuration and variety
- Physical expansion and capacity
- Design change
- Supply and order quantity

Supply chain flexibility enhances a firm's ability to respond to change and unforeseen circumstances. The quest for flexibility is not as simple as it sounds, especially when it involves working with suppliers with different agendas (some types of flexibility can be accomplished internally). Consider the apparel industry. Retailers and apparel companies are increasingly pursuing a business model based on flexibility. They want suppliers to move production quickly to new locations to keep prices as low as possible and provide short lead times for follow-up orders when styles catch on. They also want suppliers to ship smaller orders more frequently, again with shorter lead times. Unfortunately, the suppliers that produce clothes are reluctant to add capacity, want firm order commitments many months in advance, and want to pass through material and labor costs to preserve their profit margins. Retailers and apparel companies want flexibility while suppliers want stability. This highlights the importance of cooperative suppliers whose supply chain vision aligns with your vision.

Shortages of electronics components as global demand increased highlight the value of flexibility.[14] Polaris, a maker of ATVs and snowmobiles, has had to reduce the number of vehicles with power steering it produces due to chip shortages. In response, the company switched production to products, such as electric vehicles, that do not have power steering. This is an example of production process flexibility. In an example that shows the value of design change flexibility, HTC Corporation experienced shortages of active-matrix organic light-emitting diodes that it uses in many of its products. HTC switched to a comparable technology from Sony called Super LCD that it now uses in several of its product lines. Flexibility can be a beautiful thing when addressing risk. It provides options that mitigate risk.

Predictive Risk Metrics

Most companies rely on supplier scorecards as a means to report supplier performance. Unfortunately, unless the scorecard helps spot trends that could be detrimental, most scorecards suffer from some serious shortcomings. They are not effective at preventing risk, usually measure each supplier the same way (cost, quality, and delivery), lack timeliness, are backward looking, and are populated with measures that are often subjective. In addition, they are usually completed by buyers who have a vested interest in how well a supplier is performing.

Next level supply organizations will use something called predictive risk metrics to anticipate risk situations with suppliers before they occur. Once potential risks are identified, corrective action can be taken using Six Sigma tools and techniques. A company-wide tool being developed at a high-tech company relies on a common set of 20 core risk indicators, a secure data platform, specified performance targets, and algorithms to provide early detection of process risk. Both the buying company and supplier input data for the core risk indicators on an ongoing basis. Included in this tool is the means to assess sub-tier supplier performance. This approach to risk prevention is leading edge and has received endorsement from the company's highest executives. Predictive risk metric systems are designed to overcome the shortcomings associated with supplier scorecards.

Digging Deeper: Multi-tier Supply Chain Analysis

It is not uncommon for less than 100 tier-one suppliers to receive over 80% of total purchase dollars. Furthermore, many of the suppliers in this relatively small subset perform extensive design and systems integration work (refer back to the Boeing example at the beginning of the chapter). A consequence from relying on large systems suppliers is a shift of supply chain responsibilities and a possible loss of control away from the focal firm and to the tier-one supplier. Suppliers that were previously located at the tier-one level are now pushed to the tier-two level or even lower as large systems suppliers are slotted into the first tier. Are you confident these large, tier-one suppliers are capable of managing component and sub-system suppliers?

Supply organizations need to be aware that the source of supply chain risk is often several tiers below where they reside. Next level supply organizations will need to be creative regarding how to dig deeper into the supply chain to manage risk at the sub-tier level. Four ways that offer opportunities to prevent risk beyond the first tier include mapping the supply chain, placing capacity buffers along the supply chain, specifying or approving the suppliers that tier-one suppliers use, and evaluating the supply base management capabilities of tier-one suppliers.

Map the supply chain: Supply chain mapping involves taking a part or system and breaking it down to identify sub-tier suppliers. Let's be clear about a stark reality here. While your large, tier-one suppliers may be a strong link in your supply chain, most supply chains have a set of minor suppliers that are vulnerable to market and financial uncertainties. These are the links that supply chain mapping attempts to uncover. While these maps require resources to develop, the insight they provide can easily outweigh their costs. Ignorance is not always bliss.

Operationally place capacity buffers along the supply chain: An analysis of sub-tiers along your supply chain should reveal the pinch points where operational problems are likely to occur. While the lean purists are clutching their chests and gasping for air right now, it may make sense from a risk prevention perspective to request the placement of additional inventory along the weakest points of your supply chain (at least until other steps are taken to address any issues).

Specify or approve the suppliers that tier-one suppliers use: Some high technology companies have gone as far as identifying the component and sub-system suppliers their tier-one suppliers must use, particularly for their contract manufacturers. At other times, they reserve the right to approve selected suppliers. This level of engagement is not as prevalent as we move away from the high technology sector, which likely will change as supply organizations push further upstream with their risk management efforts. At a minimum, you will want to be aware of the suppliers that your suppliers are using. After all, it is your supply chain.

Evaluate supply management capabilities of tier-one suppliers: Rarely do we see in-depth assessments of a supplier's supply management capabilities during the selection process. This should be weighted as much as a supplier's technical capability. If this is done correctly, your supply group will have confidence that its suppliers' suppliers are being managed well. If your tier-one suppliers make effective supply base management a major selection criteria for their tier-one suppliers (your tier-two suppliers), you should gain confidence that your tier-three suppliers are being managed well.

Best Practice Company Approaches to Risk Management

A growing number of companies are taking steps to ensure that supply chain risk does not affect the continuity of their operations. For many supply organizations, managing supply chain risk means taking an active role in monitoring the health of their suppliers. These companies often rely on third parties to provide data, sometimes combining this with company-provided information, to arrive at supplier risk profiles. The following summarizes the efforts of two companies that are recognized for their ability to manage supplier risk.

Boston Scientific

Boston Scientific, a maker of medical devices, relies extensively on suppliers to support its innovation and growth strategies.[15] The company's biggest risk concern involves suppliers that do the majority of their business with non-medical industries and do not consider companies like Boston Scientific when making longer-term strategic plans. The company defines supplier risk management as "a proactive and systematic process for cost, effectively identifying and reducing the frequency and severity of unwanted events in the inbound supply chain that have an adverse effect on the business."

The company became interested in how it could get better intelligence by using certain criteria and data that would allow Boston Scientific to predict potential risk issues with suppliers. The company's risk management strategy has four goals:

1. Use a variety of information and data to become aware of high-risk suppliers.
2. Identify and understand the drivers that increase supplier risk.
3. Proactively manage and reduce supply chain risk by determining risk mitigation responses, develop business continuity plans, develop contingency plans, and prioritize mitigations.
4. Measure risk mitigation and impact.

The company first identified all suppliers that have more than $10 million worth of revenue with Boston Scientific. Next, supply leaders developed a set of questions for different categories. The responses to these questions enabled the company to categorize suppliers according to a risk probability index (RPI). This index provides a measure of the company's risk exposure for each supplier. Boston Scientific relied on a number of sources, including third-party data, to gather the answers to their questions.

The company uses the RPI to identify potential problem suppliers, which supports early intervention to address issues before they become major problems. In one case, early quality issues that were identified at a supplier resulted in the development of short-term, mid-term, and long-term mitigation plans. The short-term plan addressed the supplier's issues directly, the mid-term plan began to search for a second source in the event the improvement plan did not work, and the long-term plan specified an exit strategy, if needed.

United Technologies Corporation

United Technologies Corporation (UTC), a global powerhouse that includes Carrier, Pratt & Whitney; Hamilton Sundstrand; Otis; and Sikorsky (among others) knows that supplier bankruptcies present serious risk to business continuity. The company relies on an online tool that provides early warning if a supplier is becoming financially distressed.[16] An alert is provided once a supplier starts replicating a pattern that is consistent with other companies that have entered bankruptcy. UTC monitors 25,000 suppliers on a regular basis with this tool.

The tool that UTC uses is called SBManager, developed by Open Ratings. It is a pattern-recognition model that looks at past bankruptcies of suppliers and the events that preceded the bankruptcies. SBManager relies on third-party data about financial, legal, and government compliance and combines it with a customer's information on the supplier's quality and reliability. It then profiles, evaluates, monitors, and alerts managers of potential problems within the supply base. The tool reportedly has a 92% success rate predicting bankruptcies six months before they occur.

Concluding Thoughts

Experienced supply managers understand something important—supply chain success demands an understanding of supply chain risk. This understanding demands the development of appropriate risk prevention and mitigation strategies. Unfortunately, risk planning can come across as busy work, particularly when we realize that the objective of a good part of risk planning is to never have to use these plans. One thing we know for certain, however, is that global supply chains and global supply chain risks are highly correlated. More than one company has realized that failing to take these risks into consideration can have catastrophic consequences. Next level supply organizations will elevate SCRM to a strategic level.

Chapter Notes

1. Doug Cameron and Peter Sanders. "Boeing Hedges on 787 Delivery." *The Wall Street Journal*, July 16, 2010, B2.
2. Andrew K. Reese. "The Paradox of Supply Chain Risk." *Supply and Demand Chain Executive* (February/March 2010): 37.
3. Donovan Favre and John McCreery. "Coming to Grips with Supplier Risk." *Supply Chain Management Review* 12, no. 6 (September 2008):26, citing statistics from Marsh and *Risk & Insurance* magazine.
4. We have intentionally avoided including climate change as a contributor to greater supply chain risk due to the volatile and inconclusive nature of this topic. We will let readers draw their own conclusions regarding this topic.
5. From www.census.gov.
6. Caroline Henshaw and Holly Henschen. "Cocoa Play in Europe Raises Alarm." *The Wall Street Journal*, July 17–18, 2010, B12.
7. This section is adapted from "Enterprise Risk Management—Integrated Framework" *Executive Summary*, September 2004. http://www.coso.org/documents/COSO_ERM_ExecutiveSummary.pdf.
8. AMR Research as cited in *Industry Week*. April 2009, 38; Paul Teague. "Watch for the Warning Lights," *Purchasing*, January 2010, 54.
9. Teague, 57.
10. www.dnb.com.
11. investor.factset.com.
12. www.rapidratings.com.
13. K. Cowman. "Material Costs." *Materials Management and Distribution* 49, no. 7 (September 2004): 73.
14. Dana Mattiloi. "From Snowmobiles to Cellphones, a Scramble for Parts." *The Wall Street Journal*, August 6, 2010, B1.
15. This is adapted from William Atkinson, "Boston Scientific Develops Supplier Risk Management Program." *Purchasing*, February 12, 2009, P. x.
16. Adapted from James Carbone, "Suppliers Join in the Design Huddle." *Purchasing Magazine Online*, September 7, 2006, www.Purchasing.com.

15

Central Role in Working Capital Management

Without question, next level supply organizations will have a healthy obsession with working capital management. While accountants will formally define working capital as the difference between current assets and current liabilities, we will present a different and more workable perspective from an operating perspective. We view working capital as the money a firm invests to run its supply chain and operations while managing its cash flow cycle. In equation form, working capital equals:

$$(\text{Raw materials} + \text{work-in-process} + \text{finished goods}) + \text{accounts receivable} - \text{accounts payable}$$

Certain working capital improvements can and should be spearheaded by procurement and supply management professionals. Other working capital improvements deserve participation by supply chain professionals. In the process, you can add real value to your company and demonstrate that supply management is able to drive strategic value across both price and nonprice dimensions.

To frame this subject, let's examine working capital management from the perspective of a chief financial officer. Figure 15.1 shows the main components of working capital management, namely:

- The cash tied up in inventory (days of inventory outstanding [DIO])
- The cash tied up in accounts receivable, while waiting for payments by your customers (days of sales outstanding [DSO])
- The cash contributed by supplier payment terms (days of payables outstanding [DPO])

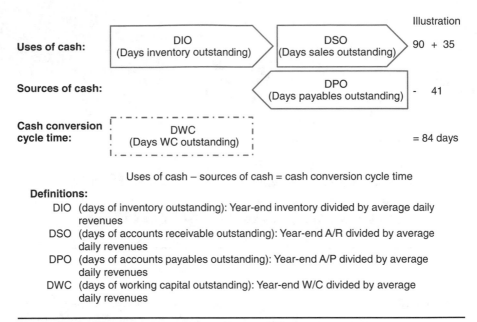

Uses of cash – sources of cash = cash conversion cycle time

Definitions:

   DIO (days of inventory outstanding): Year-end inventory divided by average daily revenues

   DSO (days of accounts receivable outstanding): Year-end A/R divided by average daily revenues

   DPO (days of accounts payables outstanding): Year-end A/P divided by average daily revenues

   DWC (days of working capital outstanding): Year-end W/C divided by average daily revenues

Figure 15.1   The components of working capital management

- The net result of the first three components is the net cash conversion cycle time, which is the number of days it takes to convert production and sales into cash (days of working capital [DWC])

In the example noted on the right side of Figure 15.1, the company has a 90-day inventory investment and additionally waits on average 35 days for customers to pay invoices. The 125 days is partially offset by the 41 days contributed by payables, resulting in a net DWC of 84 days.

In next level supply management, the supply management department plays an important role in each of the three drivers of working capital performance: inventory, revenue collection, and payables. Given the size of the opportunity relating to payment terms, we'll address that area first.

Payment Terms with Suppliers

One of the greatest areas of opportunity is changing payment terms. This is an often-overlooked area in companies due to any number of reasons:

1. No one has specific responsibility for proactively managing payment terms.
2. People assume that the accounts payable department manages payment terms (they don't in most companies; their role is to efficiently process invoices according to the established terms).

3. It is assumed that the *sales terms* are established by the supplier and are nonnegotiable, when in fact payment terms are one of many negotiable dimensions of the commercial relationship.
4. Supply management departments are uniquely positioned—as the function whose job it is to manage suppliers—to take the lead on this important subject.
5. A smart payment terms initiative begins with profiling your annual spend according to payment terms categories. Such a profile might look similar to Table 15.1.

The data in this table suggests a *sweet spot* of sizeable spend in the Net 25 to 35 range. We say sweet spot, because experience has shown that—if approached properly—suppliers will often respond positively to an overture to shift from Net 30 terms to a combination of discount and net terms, for example, 1% 15, Net 45 days. (There are other conclusions about the rest of the chart, but let's focus on this particular sweet spot for this chapter.)

Too often, the simple objective in payment terms initiatives is to try to extend pre-existing net terms to longer net terms; e.g. taking Net 30 to 45 or to 60. This may be due to a variety of factors, including single-minded focus on increasing DPO—as a way to improve DWC.

It is better, and more valuable, to obtain the option of paying either discount or net, at your company's discretion. Ask any finance person and they

Table 15.1 Payment terms analysis

$ Invoices past 12 months	Payment terms
$8,200,000	Due upon receipt
$200,000	Net 5 days
$7,500,000	Net 10 days
$11,000,000	Net 15 days
$15,000,000	Net 17 days
$1,000,000	Net 20 days
$18,000,000	Net 25 days
$355,000,000	Net 30 days
$4,500,000	Net 35 days
$1,200,000	Net 45 days
$55,000,000	1% 10 net 30
$4,500,000	1½% 10 net 30
$3,250,000	2% 10 net 30
$1,000,000	1% 30 net 45

Source: Greybeard Advisors LLC. Copyright 2008–2011. All rights reserved.

will tell you that having an option (on nearly any topic) is valuable. Then, based on company finances and liquidity objectives, you have the flexibility to pay earlier and earn the discount (which flows directly to your bottom line) or pay longer and hold onto your cash.

As part of your working capital initiative, you should be able to explain internally the value of changing payment terms. Figure 15.2 offers some insight on this subject, on a program-level basis.

The other thing that leading companies do is they create a detailed table of all possible payment terms and their *values* as a quick reference for their procurement professionals to use when comparing one set of terms to another in supplier discussions. One such table is available through the WAV download for this book, accessible by going to the publisher's website, www.jrosspub.com.

There are some classic errors regarding how some companies have approached the subject of payment terms. All of the following examples are based on real situations in the business world:

- The *dictator customer* ignores previously agreed-upon terms, and dictates new terms (as opposed to *selling* the proposed change). This often results in damage to the company's reputation and damage to the supplier's attitude to help the customer in other, critical areas (such as innovation). Such behavior is indicative of a company who does not fully appreciate the strategic opportunities—and ramifications—of supplier management.
- The *narrow focus* procurement department fails to look at the entire relationship with a supplier. This can cause negative impact by not realizing that some suppliers may also be large customers.
- The *incorrect scorecard* causes purchasing to focus only on extending net payment terms. That can result in lost opportunity by not providing the option to discount, which, as noted earlier, can be of great value.

Example:

- For each $100 million of annual purchases, moving from net 30 days to Net 45, 1% -15 offers your company the **option** of:
    - (a) improving earnings by about $ 1.0 million/year (minus the interest earnings on the cash used to pay early), ***or***
    - (b) the ability to grow accounts payable and cash balances by about $ 4.0 million by paying in 45 days instead of 30 days.

Figure 15.2 The value of changing payments terms
Source: Greybeard Advisors LLC. Copyright 2005–2011. All rights reserved.

Avoid This Classic Mistake

One area of opportunity is payment terms. It is also an area ripe for disaster, if approached improperly.

When we work with companies to design and execute a procurement transformation plan, one aspect typically involves analyzing current payment terms and making recommendations for changes (and how to approach suppliers).

One classic error companies can make is to take an arrogant approach, literally *dictating* that their supply base accept a new, aggressive payment term.

An example of taking that approach appears to be AB InBEV, the large global brewer. News stories both in the United States and in Europe report that AB InBev has changed payment terms from 30 days to as much as 120 days (in one fell swoop). To say that this has generated controversy and ill will is an understatement.

In general, an effort to successfully improve payment terms—without damaging other important elements of your suppliers' support—involves considerable homework and analysis, careful planning and messaging, and a willingness to treat each supplier as a valued part of your supply chain. After all, the next level of supply management excellence will involve energizing your supply base to work preferentially for your company's success. If your suppliers feel *damaged* through a thoughtless approach to extending payment terms, you may have won a battle but lost the war.

Inventory Management: a Supply Management Opportunity

Inventory management is another area where supply management can add value; in this case, it's not so much a leadership role as it is a collaborative role with its internal clients within operations, although supply management activities directly affect the value of inventory. Inventory value also directly affects working capital requirements.

There are three principal ideas worth pursuing here:

1. Inventory consignments
2. *Leaning out* the production process in conjunction with suppliers and your operations people
3. Financial hedging as a way to reduce reliance on physical inventory

The idea behind inventory consignments is straightforward. Rather than assume that raw materials, or parts, inventory needs to be owned by and *on the books of* the customer, explore with your suppliers their willingness to maintain an inventory consignment either on your property or nearby. The way this typically works is a supplier holds the inventory for a specified number of days (e.g., 30 days or 90 days) at which point the inventory—if it has not already been drawn down—is invoiced and transferred to the customer. If the inventory item is used earlier than the specified transfer date, it is billed at that time.

In our experience at medium and large companies, a proactive approach to inventory consignments can generate millions of dollars of working capital benefits. However, the key is to open the conversation with suppliers on this subject. A natural window of opportunity to do so occurs during the request for proposal (RFP) stage of the strategic sourcing process. We generally recommend that for subjects that have a meaningful inventory component, you should build into your RFP an invitation for the suppliers to propose inventory consignment type programs and terms.

A final word on inventory consignments: be sure to involve your accounting department as you proceed down the consignment path. There are some important bookkeeping issues that each company may treat differently.

Leaning out the production process to accomplish a variety of lean objectives, including optimizing inventories, is another great way for supply management to work with its suppliers and internal stakeholders to add value. (Since this subject is covered in some detail in another of the author's books, *End-to-End Lean Management: A Guide to Complete Supply Chain Improvement*, we won't review it here.)

Hedging (financial risk management) is typically thought of in the context of managing price volatility. Hedging can also play a role in working capital and liquidity management by eliminating or reducing the need for physical inventory hedging.

The Three V Perspective of Inventory Management

In our view, most companies take a far too limited view regarding how to manage inventory. How managers view inventory and how to manage it will differ depending on where they reside in the supply chain or corporate structure. While finance views inventory in terms of dollars, which is reported on the balance sheet, supply chain planners usually view inventory in terms of units. What is the right view if we expect to effectively manage inventory investment? Assuming multiple perspectives about inventory is actually a worthwhile way to approach this topic.

Companies that are serious about managing inventory must visualize how their practices and approaches will impact the three Vs of inventory management—the volume, velocity, and value of inventory. Volume relates to the amount of inventory that a firm owns at any given time. Key volume measures will relate to total units on hand, including safety stock levels. Velocity refers to how quickly raw material and work-in-process inventory can be transformed into finished goods that are accepted and paid for by the customer. Faster velocity requires a lower commitment of working capital and improves cash flow. Key velocity measures include material throughput rates, inventory turns, and order-to-cash cycle times. Finally, value pertains to the unit cost of the inventory. Key measures include standard costs and the total value of inventory, including raw materials, components, sub-assemblies, and finished goods.

The activities that are pursued to affect the three Vs will be a function of the resources available to implement an approach along with how inventory is currently managed. The point here is that organizations must pursue activities and approaches that positively affect the volume, value, and velocity of inventory through and across the supply chain. If they do that, they will see a direct affect on their working capital requirements.

Accounts Receivable as an Area of Awareness for Supply Management

Earlier, we noted that one classic error in managing payment terms is the *narrow focus* procurement department that fails to look at the entire relationship with a supplier. This can cause negative impact by not realizing that some suppliers may be large customers. Angering large customers who also happen to be suppliers is generally not a good idea; it can result in at least two consequences: slower payment of invoices and shrinking or discontinuing the business relationship.

In Table 15.2 we show scenarios based on the size of the customer/supplier relationship and the nature of the payment performance. For example, in the top right corner of the 2 × 2 matrix, we have the situation where the customer/supplier buys more from us than we buy from them, and they currently

Table 15.2 What can happen when a supplier is also a customer

	Customer currently pays our invoices faster than we pay their invoices	Customer currently pays our invoices slower than we pay their invoices
Customer buys more from us than we buy from them	This is a favorable situation to be in. Hope the customer does not realize the imbalance, given its buying power in the relationship. Be careful about seeking to extend or change your payments to them—lest you wake the sleeping giant.	This is the most unfavorable situation to be in—significant adverse WC situation (they buy more from us than we buy from them, compounded by their slower payment performance). Evaluate carefully the basis for changing your payments to them.
Customer buys less from us than we buy from them	From a working capital perspective, this is a favorable situation to be in.	This is an unfavorable situation to be in—with perhaps an opportunity to rebalance.

Source: Greybeard Advisors LLC. Copyright 2008–2011. All rights reserved.

pay our invoices slower than we pay their invoices. As a result, there is an adverse working capital situation with this business partner. However, given the size of their customer relationship with you, the situation needs to be carefully researched before action is taken on how you will pay them going forward. In addition, in situations involving suppliers that are also customers, it is wise to involve your in-house legal counsel to ensure that no inappropriate actions are taken.

Asset Recovery as an Additional Working Capital Recovery

The concept of asset recovery is well described in the original *Straight to the Bottom Line®*. A quick recap of the concept appears in Figure 15.3. The point we want to make here is that asset recovery can be viewed as a source of working capital, even though it did not appear in our operational definition of working capital presented at the beginning of the chapter. Performed well, it helps to monetize the value of idle or surplus plant and equipment. It is certainly not one of the sexier topics in modern supply management; however, executed well, it can be a recurring generator of value for your organization.

Successful asset recovery programs are built around these principles:

- An accurate, up-to-date database showing all idle or surplus plant and equipment (with reasonably detailed descriptions, history, and, ideally, digital photos of the asset from various views)
- Access to that database for all internal users
- A responsible person at each major location/department, who is designated the asset recovery *point person* for that location, and who also functions as part of the internal network for asset recovery management
- A professional who is responsible for overseeing the program, the database, and the network of internal contacts
- Connection between the asset recovery process and the process for ordering *new* plant and equipment
- Internal policies (management and accounting) which facilitate the fair value transfer of idle equipment among internal locations
- Access to market expertise for used equipment or idle real estate (often accomplished via a master agreement that was the result of a strategic sourcing effort to select an appropriate third party service provider)
- Use of the master agreement service provider to determine fair value for internal transfers, and to monetize the asset in a best-in-class manner where no internal transfers are appropriate

Figure 15.3 Asset recovery—another opportunity to add value in working capital

For sizable companies, a well-constructed and well-executed asset recovery program can consistently generate millions of dollars of value per year.

Concluding Thoughts

Working capital management is a next level supply management topic. Unfortunately, and for various reasons, it has taken us quite a while to reach this point. First, the role of inventory within a company is somewhat deceptive from a financial perspective. Accountants place inventory squarely under the heading of *current assets* on the balance sheet, placing it next to cash and marketable securities. Over time, this has created a false sense of security as we equate inventory with goodness. After all, assets, especially current assets, are good while liabilities are bad. In reality, life is not that black and white.

Another reason it has taken a while to focus on working capital management is due to the obvious disconnect between supply chain personnel and the financial people. In most companies, neither group really understands what the other is doing. These groups also do not understand the role they play in working capital management. The time has come to view working capital management as a way to bring together very different organizational groups to achieve a common corporate objective—the management and improvement of working capital.

This book has free material available for download from the
Web Added Value™ resource center at *www.jrosspub.com*

16

Early Involvement in Capital Project Procurement

A look toward the future suggests that supply personnel will be involved with just about every category of purchase expenditure. While managing direct materials has been the historic responsibility of procurement, why not also manage those troublesome indirect items? While we are at it, let's have procurement personnel apply their commercial expertise to the many services required to operate a business. But why stop there? Why not apply that procurement magic to capital expenditures? After all, capital projects require suppliers and financial resources. They practically beg for procurement involvement.

This chapter explores procurement involvement within capital expenditure projects. As the term is used throughout this chapter, involvement refers to an earlier rather than later point in the capital expenditure process. Research shows that on average the benefits of involvement are greatest when that involvement comes earlier in a project, such as during the concept or feasibility planning stages, rather than later.

We begin the chapter with an overview of procurement involvement in general, including where we typically see early involvement initiatives. Next, a more detailed coverage of procurement involvement with capital expenditures occur, followed by the need to understand life-cycle and financial cost modeling techniques. The chapter concludes with a presentation of how leading supply organizations use procurement involvement with capital expenditures to become next level supply organizations.

Understanding Early Involvement

Let's step back and talk about early procurement involvement in general. Early involvement is the process of relying on procurement personnel and resources, either physically or virtually, to provide support during functional and strategic planning, demand and supply planning, continuous improvement projects, capital project planning and when developing new products and technologies. Involvement can take place formally, such as by membership on a project team, or informally through a consultative role. The reasons behind early involvement of supply personnel, whether in demand and supply planning, product development, or capital projects, are not difficult to understand:

- The need for continuous improvement demands new ways of conducting business.
- Competent supply professionals provide a wide range of expertise and value within a process, including insight into materials, suppliers, and labor markets.
- The need to compress project development times demands different ways of doing business, and research shows that early involvement can take time out of a process.
- A continuing focus on the outsourcing of non-core capabilities and competencies results in a stronger reliance on suppliers, an area where supply professionals must step up and demonstrate leadership.
- Design changes become exponentially more complex and costly as product and project designs move through development stages, which encourages bringing competent players to the table early so that better decisions will emerge.
- Early involvement supports various quality management principles, particularly quality at the source and the prevention of defects.
- Early procurement involvement is the catalyst for early supplier involvement.

Let's take a look at these reasons more closely. Perhaps foremost, at a broad level the need for continuous improvement demands new ways of doing business. Existing ways of doing business just won't satisfy the demands of a global marketplace. Since most firms have yet to tap into the possibilities that early involvement offers, especially during capital expenditure projects, this model offers intriguing possibilities. Turning this concept into a reality will be the challenge.

Another reason to consider early involvement is because competent supply professionals can provide a wide array of expertise and value. This value comes in the form of identifying potential suppliers, providing cost and other performance data (particularly from the request for proposal process), negotiating complex contracts, analyzing supplier proposals and supply market data, and bringing new perspectives that may challenge the status quo.

Third, the need to compress project development times demands different ways of doing business, making the involvement of procurement personnel an appealing option. In fact, in the product development space, the need to get to market quickly may be the primary driver behind early involvement. We see similar pressures affecting the capital expenditure side of the business, which a later case will illustrate. Ramping up new capacity quickly, for example, may be essential for meeting corporate growth expectations.

Another early involvement driver is a continuing focus on the outsourcing of non-core capabilities and competencies. Early involvement will be a necessity when so much of an OEM's content and design originates with external suppliers. Someone must be the conduit to external suppliers that are an integral part of project success. Furthermore, early involvement here does not involve only procurement and supply personnel. It also involves suppliers. This is especially true for capital expenditures since most companies do not design and build their own buildings or transportation, production, or material-handling equipment.

Next, a realization exists that design changes become exponentially more complex and costly as product and project designs move through development stages. This is true whether we are talking about product development

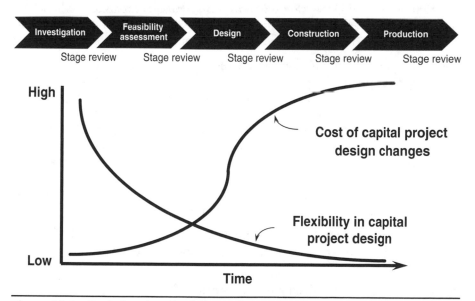

Figure 16.1 Capital project flexibility and change costs

Source: Stage gates from http://www.pd-trak.com/phasegatetemplates.htm.

or capital planning projects. Figure 16.1 illustrates the inverse relationship between the flexibility to change a design, whether it is a product, equipment, or facility design, and the cost of design changes. While design costs are a relatively minor part of total costs, decisions made early in the process lock in a disproportionate amount of final costs. It is well accepted that the flexibility to make changes decreases rapidly as development progresses. Within project management we call this progression *stage gates*, which this figure also shows. Early involvement seeks to include qualified participants so that better decisions will emerge that are not changed at a later date. Research reveals that the primary benefit of using cross-functional teams, for example, is to bring greater knowledge and skill together at one time.

Early involvement supports various quality management principles, particularly quality at the source and the prevention of defects. In the words of the quality proponents, "do it right the first time." Preventing costly pushbacks of development decisions should be an important objective for any design group. For firms that are looking for their next major source of improvement, early involvement is likely an untapped opportunity area.

Finally, early procurement involvement is the catalyst for supplier involvement. We have been aware for some time of the benefits that early supplier involvement can provide. Research reveals that most organizations appreciate the potential benefits of closer inter-organizational relationships. Research also reveals that relying on supplier input when the task warrants involvement results in a more effective task outcome, on average, compared to when suppliers are not involved. Specifically, research reveals that a host of benefits are realized when an organization involves suppliers early. These include:

- Greater satisfaction concerning the quality of information exchange with suppliers
- Higher reliance on suppliers as a resource to support project goals
- Fewer problems coordinating work activity with suppliers
- Greater effort put forth on project assignments
- Greater supplier contribution and suggestions about how to achieve cost reductions, including material, design, development, and manufacturing costs
- Greater supplier contribution and suggestions about how to improve quality, delivery, process technology, and cycle times

The reasons for early procurement involvement are compelling. The barriers to early involvement are usually self-inflicted and can be overcome.

Where Do We See Early Involvement?

A phrase that readers may have heard as it relates to procurement is *a seat at every table*. Unfortunately, as it relates to a traditional purchasing group, that seat usually means a seat at the lunch table. This phrase now refers to being involved early in the commercial and even the technical activities of nearly every functional group to support their supply related requirements.

The scope of procurement's early involvement must expand once supply groups evolve from a transactional-based purchasing model to a strategic supply model. While a seat at every table sounds good on paper, turning this into a reality is a bit more challenging. It requires human resources that are available to support other groups as well as personnel who have a solid knowledge of the needs of these groups. Let's be clear about an important point here. Procurement is an organizational support function, and as a support function, it has, by definition, internal customers. It just so happens that the domain of those internal customers has expanded over time.

Examples where supply professionals become involved early in the activities of internal customers are easy to come by. Consider the following:

- The marketing strategy development team at a major consumer products company now includes a supply professional. This individual negotiates trade show and promotional contracts on behalf of marketing. She also helped marketing reduce the number of printing suppliers it uses from 600 to 5.
- At a major automotive OEM, a supply professional is assigned to work within human resources. The supply representative leads the effort in creating health care service contracts with local hospitals that feature favorable pricing.
- At a leading electronics company, supply personnel work closely with engineering at the start of any product development project. One of the responsibilities of procurement is to prequalify suppliers in anticipation of future needs, an activity that has helped reduce product development cycle time.
- The supply group at a major chemical company was responsible for leading an initiative that radically changed the way the company designed and retrofitted production facilities.

We think you get the idea that today's supply professionals are much like a Visa card—they should be everywhere you want to be.

Procurement Involvement with Capital Expenditures

A review of procurement involvement in various purchase categories reveals that involvement with capital expenditures represents a logical progression. Most would agree that the primary focus of supply professionals over time has been with direct materials. Responsibility for services, indirect spending, and capital equipment were often left to those groups that required those goods and services. These items simply were not on the radar screen of most procurement organizations. At a major logistics company, for example, the procurement group until recently was directly responsible for only 16% of total company expenditures. The remainder of the expenditures was spread across various operations, logistics, engineering, and marketing groups.

Historically, if early procurement involvement outside of direct materials occurred within companies, it was primarily during new product development. Most of the research and writing regarding early involvement to date has focused on procurement and supplier involvement in product development. Since procurement involvement with capital expenditures is an evolving process, we expect that research will someday catch up with industry practice.

Interestingly, one study that concluded a lack of early procurement involvement was detrimental to overall project performance involved the U.S. federal government. An analysis that evaluated procurement involvement in major acquisitions, including capital projects, found involvement is sorely lacking at the Pension Benefit Guaranty Corporation (PBGC). The PBGC insures pensions for more than 44 million workers covered by employer-sponsored defined benefits plans.[1] The general accounting office (GAO) found that procurement had no input into major purchase decisions involving capital projects and contracting. The GAO concluded that procurement was responsible for implementing the policy decisions made by executive management teams but had no voice in making those decisions. It further stated that procurement involvement on strategy boards would improve strategic planning by:

1. Identifying and managing the relationships among the parties involved in the acquisition process
2. Analyzing aggregate agency needs to devise strategic acquisition plans
3. Taking into consideration the effects of external factors on the timing and execution of major contracts

In summation, the GAO concluded that procurement's lack of involvement in strategic decisions makes its unable to identify, analyze, prioritize, and coordinate agency-wide acquisition needs.

It is clear we believe that the domain of early involvement is expanding. That expansion is taking us to involvement with capital expenditures. Procurement involvement with capital expenditures should increase primarily for two reasons. First, the magnitude of the spending in this category is high. Second, it is largely an untapped opportunity area.

A primary reason why procurement should be involved early in capital expenditure projects is due to the magnitude of the spending in this category. The U.S. government defines capital expenditures as the total investment in new and used structures and equipment for a particular period. New structures and equipment include expenditures for new buildings and other structures, structures that have been previously owned but neither used nor occupied, new machinery and equipment, and other new depreciable assets. Used structures and equipment include the expenditures for buildings and other structures that have been previously owned and occupied, secondhand machinery and equipment, and other used depreciable assets. The government also includes new structures and equipment acquired through capital lease arrangements.[2] Capital expenditure items are usually subject to depreciation over multiple years. Over the last three years for which data are available, around 37% of total capital expenditures are for structures and 63% are for equipment.

Historically, the largest share of capital investment comes from the manufacturing sector. Not far behind manufacturing is the finance and insurance industry. These two industry segments comprise around a quarter of all capital investment for all industries in the United States. While the amount that many companies commit to capital expenditures has dropped dramatically due to the economic downturn that started in 2008, total expenditures at the macroeconomic level in the United States are still over a trillion dollars a year. This rivals total logistics

Table 16.1 Capital investment expenditures

Company	Sales	Capital assets	Capital expenditures	Expenditures/ Sales
Intel	$37.6B	$17.5B	$5.2B	13.8%
Alcoa	$26.9B	$17.7B	$3.41B	12.7%
Southwest Airlines	$11.0B	$11.0B	$.92B	8.4%
Caterpillar	$51.3B	$12.5B	$4.01B	7.8%
Target	$63.4B	$24.1B	$4.37B	6.9%
DuPont	$32.8B	$11.2B	$1.98B	5.7%
UPS	$51.5B	$18.3B	$2.64B	5.1%
Eli Lilly	$20.4B	$8.6B	$.95B	4.7%
Nucor	$23.7B	$4.10B	$1.02B	4.3%
Dow Chemical	$57.5B	$14.3B	$2.28B	4.0%
Procter & Gamble	$83.5B	$20.6B	$3.05B	3.7%
American Airlines	$23.8B	$15.7B	$.876B	3.7%
Apple	$32.5B	$2.50B	$1.09B	3.4%
Kraft Foods	$42.2B	$9.9B	$1.37B	3.2%
Wal-Mart	$404.4B	$95.7B	$11.5B	2.9%
Boeing	$60.9B	$8.8B	$1.67B	2.7%
Hewlett-Packard	$118.4B	$10.8B	$2.99B	2.5%
United Technologies	$58.7B	$6.3B	$1.22B	2.1%
Bank of America	$124.1B	$13.2B	$2.1B	1.7%

*Represents 2008 data rather than more recent data due to the distorted figures from the economic downturn.
Source: finance.yahoo.com.

costs in the United States, which includes inventory carrying costs (but not the cost of inventory), transportation costs, and the administrative costs of logistics. It is easy to see the potential economic value of managing capital expenditures well.

Table 16.1 identifies the sales, capital expenditures, and plant and equipment assets (capital assets) of some well-known firms. The table also shows the percent of total sales that capital expenditures represent. Sales data are obtained from the income statement, capital assets are from the balance sheet, and capital expenditure figures are from the cash flow statement. All data in this table are from 2008 rather than more recently available data. This was done purposely because after the economic crisis that started in 2008, capital expenditure figures, as well as revenue and income figures, declined dramatically for some companies, sometimes by 50% or more compared with earlier figures. This distorts what we are trying to achieve from this analysis, which is to present what the world looks like in a more steady state as it pertains to capital investment levels. Hopefully, current data are an anomaly rather than a new normal state. When times become difficult, one of the first things corporate executives slash is capital expenditures. Reduced travel expenses, training, hiring, and supplier development activities are also early victims of economic downturns.

A review of Table 16.1 shows that industries, and companies within those industries, differ widely in their capital investment requirements. Airlines, for example, commit a large portion of their capital expenditures to aircraft. A single Boeing 777, for example, can cost $250 million. Contrast that to the relatively meager capital expenditure requirements of Apple and, to a lesser degree, HP. These companies rely extensively on an outsourcing model that utilizes the assets of other companies. Some companies are simply more capital intensive than others. Intel, for example, now spends $2-3 billion just to build and equip a single semiconductor facility.

A central focus of next level organizations involves the need to exceed some key financial metrics. Without question, one of these metrics is the return on invested capital (ROIC). Recall from an earlier chapter that capital expenditure investment comprises a major part of ROIC. This metric is important because when a firm's ROIC is lower that its cost of capital, the firm is slowly liquidating itself. For this reason, any methods for improving ROIC, including early procurement involvement with capital expenditures, should be of interest.

In reality, when all goes well, procurement's early involvement with capital projects appears in the shadows, making it difficult to identify cost savings or avoidances from doing things the right way. When something goes wrong on a project, the absence of early involvement is one of many factors that might be responsible. Root cause analysis usually focuses on the technical aspects of failures rather than the lack or quality of early procurement involvement.

While some purchases will never be the direct responsibility of procurement (spot-market oil purchases at oil companies, for example, are usually not procurement's responsibility), the trend today is for supply professionals to apply their skill wherever corporate funds are being committed. The bottom line is that capital expenditures represent serious cash outlays, both at the macroeconomic level and at the firm level. Because the items that comprise capital expenditures usually bring with them a stream of expenses that extend for years, the effective management of this purchase category is important. At a leading global company that we work with, procurement will continue to expand its involvement by attempting to get a better view of all upcoming project concepts. While this can be challenging, especially in large companies, supply leaders will want to know what is occurring in the concept stage of capital projects so they can evaluate involvement opportunities at the earliest possible date.

Many companies have specific policies that prohibit nonprocurement personnel from making commitments with company funds. With that said, variability often exists regarding the level and timing of procurement involvement as well as the level of expertise and sophistication of local procurement personnel. On smaller projects and in parts of a company where there are no dedicated capital procurement personnel, project managers usually drive the bid process and negotiations, and procurement carries out the contract. Strategic, complex projects should have dedicated capital procurement professionals assigned to the project team. On larger projects where there is a need for dedicated personnel, procurement personnel can even be collocated with the project design team.

Evidence of Tangible Support

This section is based on the experience of a major chemical company. There are different kinds of support provided by procurement during capital projects. The first type of support involves working with engineering to develop the project scope and estimate project costs. The second type of support involves identifying long lead items that may need to be pre-funded and ordered before total project scope is approved or funded. A third support involves developing sourcing plans for materials and contract plans for construction labor. Finally, the fourth type of support is the development of comprehensive bid packages with a determination of what to include in materials and contract plans.

Involvement leads to some tangible outputs provided by procurement:

- An execution strategy plan identifies whether the project will be carried out in house or outsourced.
- A material control plan identifies materials that must be expedited due to their criticality to the project schedule.
- A material sourcing plan identifies equipment fabricators and manufacturers that have the capabilities and capacity to supply the critical equipment. Also, the material plan considers low-cost country sources.

The material sourcing plan can also consider leverage opportunities with other projects.

• A contract plan is a comprehensive construction plan that addresses issues such as contract types, bidders, and construction planning efforts. The contract plan is integrally linked to the engineering plan, project schedule, and the availability of detailed information for bidding.

Adding Value through Early Involvement in Capital Projects

At many companies, procurement has been involved early with capital projects for many years with success differing on a project-by-project basis. Historically, involvement was not always consistent or viewed as valuable by project managers. This is due partially to the project manager's experience with procurement as a lower-level functional group that was not suited for strategic thinking or did not understand the technicalities of capital projects. In fact, as with many organizations, the procurement organization was not the most widely respected or sought after group. In the eyes of the project manager, would involving procurement justify the costs of their service?

While specific value should accrue from involving procurement early in capital projects, supply leaders often find it challenging to separate the unique value derived from early involvement within complex capital projects. It is difficult to identify or partition specific causes that lead to a desired effect within dynamic environments. However, what is known for certain is that when a project has some level of failure, whether due to a lack of early procurement involvement, poor engineering, inadequate construction, or poor planning, the costs can be significant.

Early procurement involvement is sometimes not considered when project managers try to go it alone by getting suppliers to assist for free by developing preliminary designs. While at first glance this seems like a good thing, this often locks in that supplier's design, thereby eliminating a competitive selection process. Procurement creates value by avoiding a practice that serves to increase project costs by eliminating competition.

A number of issues can affect the success of capital projects—and this is exactly what early procurement involvement seeks to prevent. Perhaps first and foremost, the largest project issue involves *pushing the button*, and the process does not work. A second issue involves being late with project completion, and a third issue is being over budget. Being too far under budget can also come into play. One major company found that to compensate for these issues, project managers develop cost estimates that are too high, buy locally as much as possible to eliminate potential shipping issues, and spend freely to consume most of an inflated budget. Procurement's early involvement forces project leaders to look for the best total value, including low-cost country sourcing.

Early procurement involvement in itself does not guarantee success unless the supply organization adds value to the process. Project managers may or may not value procurement involvement based upon past experience. In general, procurement personnel add value by understanding the needs of the project, which requires a more technical procurement perspective than normal procurement; understanding the market for the goods and services needed to support a project; and allowing project personnel to focus on the technical aspects of capital projects while procurement covers the commercial aspects. Value is also added by assisting in developing realistic material sourcing plans and contract plans and by negotiating agreements for the project team and business unit that address topics such as capital costs, total cost of ownership (TCO), and post-project support.

Additionally, early procurement involvement supports a coordinated (and leveraged) view across projects and businesses. Project personnel often see only their individual projects and at times may want to use a supplier that a company is struggling with on another project. Procurement can leverage or bundle information and demand across projects, determine shop and contractor loads across projects, and provide a broader, more strategic view compared with project teams acting in relative isolation. The ability to see the big picture helps preclude situations where a company finds itself competing against itself when dealing with suppliers.

The bottom line is that engineers are conservative by nature and are not likely to endorse perceived risks (such as unknown or untested suppliers) unless they are convinced the risks are acceptable, including a contingency plan to address those risks. Therefore, procurement personnel must understand the engineer's perspective and be ready to address those concerns proactively by demonstrating the value of early involvement.

The Alcoa case at the end of this chapter provides greater insight into the specific benefits that companies can realize when procurement is an early participant with capital expenditure projects.

Life-cycle Costing for Capital Projects

A major part of capital project planning involves the use of life-cycle cost models, which are a subset of total cost models. In fact, procurement is often responsible for obtaining a good part of the data that populate these models. This makes a working knowledge of life-cycle models essential for any supply professional who becomes involved early with capital expenditure projects. Chapter 14 reviewed TCO models as a means for managing supply risk. Here our attention will be on the application of life-cycle models when evaluating capital projects.

Life-cycle cost models are often what comes most readily to mind when thinking about total costs analysis. This type of model is most often used when evaluating capital decisions that cover an extended time period, which is common for equipment and facilities. Buyers at a global energy company, for example, cannot propose the purchase of any pumps or compressors unless they attach life-cycle cost models that show a sourcing option will result in the lowest total cost. The competition to provide the next generation of refueling tankers for the U.S. Air Force highlights the challenges associated with calculating life-cycle costs for complex projects.

Life-cycle models are similar to net present value (NPV) models used in finance, which a later section builds upon, in the sense that they usually deal with multi-year periods. When we start talking about present values, we are entering a more complex type of analysis. Most life-cycle cost models are used (or should be used) to evaluate capital decisions rather than the purchase of everyday components and services. As Chapter 14 revealed, other cost models are better suited for repetitively purchased goods or services.

Several important points are relevant to life-cycle models. First, life-cycle costs apply whether equipment is sourced domestically or internationally. The international model will have additional cost categories (and complexity) that are not part of the domestic model. This includes items like exchange rate issues, possible hedging costs, and duties or tariffs. Second, as it becomes available, actual data should replace the projections made during model development. It is essential to validate the model while providing insights regarding how to improve the cost-modeling process. It is a good idea to replace cost estimates with actual data within any type of total cost model.

Developers of life-cycle cost models often allocate their cost elements across four broad categories that reflect their usage over time:[3]

- Unit price is the unit price including any purchase terms taken.
- Acquisition costs includes all costs associated with buying, ordering, and delivery to the customer.
- Usage costs includes all the costs to operate equipment and facilities, including installation, energy consumption, maintenance, reliability, spare parts, and yield and efficiency during production.
- End-of-life costs are all costs incurred when removing equipment from service or exiting a physical structure less any proceeds received for resale, scrap, or salvage.

The flow through of a life-cycle model is essentially one of buying, shipping, installing, using, maintaining, and disposing.

Life-cycle Cost Model Example

Figures 16.2, 16.3, and 16.4 illustrate a life-cycle model for a company that is evaluating the purchase of 1000 computers. These figures show the kinds of data that a life-cycle model could require. The request for proposal process

	Supplier A	Supplier B
Unit price		
Quoted price	$1,200	$1,310
Software license A	$275	$200
Software license B	$152	$160
Software license C	$85	$80
Acquisition costs		
Shipping cost	$58	$79
Supplier negotiation and contracting costs	$15,200 (total, not per computer)	$17,500 (total, not per computer)
Usage costs		
Installation	$210	$185
Equipment support (increase 3% per year)	$25 per month	$29 per month
Network support (increase 3% per year)	$35 per month	$45 per month
Electricity usage (increase 4% per year)	$9 per month	$7 per month
Repair costs	$65 per year	$45 per year
Lost productivity due to estimated downtime	15 hours per year per PC @ $45 per hour	11 hours per year per PC @ $45 per hour
End of life		
Salvage value	$75	$92

All figures are per computer unless otherwise noted—1,000 total computers

Figure 16.2   Life-cycle cost data

is often a primary way to capture a good part of the data required for a life-cycle cost analysis. Notice that in these tables, all figures represent current and expected future costs except for the projected salvage value that appears in the last year. Because the salvage value is a revenue stream and not a cost, it appears in parenthesis. Something that is missing in this model is any attempt to bring future cost and salvage value streams back to today's value. In other words, the NPV of the two alternatives is missing. The next section shows how to extend the life-cycle analysis using a more complex financial perspective.

Every cost model has challenges regarding their use. For life-cycle models, it is difficult to underestimate the importance of identifying the proper set of cost elements to include and then developing reliable costs figures that extend into the future. Unfortunately, total cost models share a dubious similarity to forecasting models. Both are nearly always inaccurate to some degree, which is common with models that look into the future. Just as forecast accuracy should be regularly measured, so too should life-cycle model accuracy since some important decisions are made using these models as a guide.

	Year 0	Year 1	Year 2	Year 3
Unit price				
Quoted price	$1,200,000			
Software license A	$275,000			
Software license B	$152,000			
Software license C	$85,000			
Acquisition costs				
Shipping cost	$58,000			
Supplier negotiation and contracting costs	$15,200			
Usage costs				
Installation	$210,000			
Equipment support		$25,000	$25,750	$26,523
Network support		$35,000	$36,050	$37,132
Electricity usage		$9,000	$9,360	$9,734
Repair costs		$65,000	$65,000	$65,000
Lost productivity due to estimated downtime		$675,000	$675,000	$675,000
End of life				
Salvage value				($75,000)
Total costs	**$1,995,200**	**$809,000**	**$811,160**	**$738,389**

Figure 16.3   Life-cycle total cost data for Supplier A

Evaluation Techniques for Capital Expenditure Projects

It is possible that capital expenditure projects will have finance personnel assigned to support complex analytic requirements. It is also possible these resources will not be available. In either case, it is in the best interests of procurement personnel to understand the relevant financial terminology and approaches that support the analysis of capital projects. Remember an important point here. For procurement to be an active contributor during capital projects, it must have the respect of the groups it supports. That means bringing a wide range of knowledge and project understanding to a project. Increasingly, that includes technical and financial knowledge.

Next level supply organizations understand the need to merge supply management, supply chain management, and finance. In fact, the term *supply chain finance* is becoming increasingly commonplace when describing the application of financial tools and techniques within the supply chain space. Supply

	Year 0	Year 1	Year 2	Year 3
Unit price				
Quoted price	$1,131,000			
Software license A	$200,000			
Software license B	$160,000			
Software license C	$80,000			
Acquisition costs				
Shipping cost	$79,000			
Supplier negotiation and contracting costs	$17,500			
Usage costs				
Installation	$185,000			
Equipment support		$29,000	$29,870	$30,766
Network support		$45,000	$46,350	$47,741
Electricity usage		$7,000	$7,280	$7,572
Repair costs		$45,000	$45,000	$45,000
Lost productivity due to estimated downtime		$495,000	$495,000	$495,000
End of life				
Salvage value				($92,000)
Total Costs	**$1,852,500**	**$621,000**	**$623,500**	**$534,079**

Figure 16.4   Life-cycle total cost data for Supplier B

organizations must attain a certain level of financial competency since capital projects are usually evaluated on their financial merits. A study conducted by Aberdeen concluded that less than one-third of companies consistently consider financial topics such as cash flow and working capital elements as part of their procurement goals.[4] Poor financial awareness will make procurement a less respected part of the capital expenditure process. It is hard to talk about capital expenditure projects without acknowledging their financial implications.

While the following three techniques are used widely during the analysis of capital expenditures for plant and equipment, by no means are these the only areas where they are applied. Other applications include the financial evaluation of new products, business acquisitions, and information technology decisions. These techniques can even be used, for example, when evaluating the financial return of supplier development initiatives. Next level supply organizations will routinely treat supplier development activities as a potential investment opportunity rather than as an expense.

Payback Period

The payback method, often used when evaluating equipment purchases, looks at an initial capital expenditure and then compares that to the estimated annual net savings per year to arrive at a payback period. The savings are usually calculated over the life of the equipment. The payback period can then be compared to a target payback to see if the project meets some predetermined threshold. This method is popular because it is relatively simple (it does not require a calculation of the NPV of future savings or cost streams), and for companies that are in a tight cash position, it is often interesting to know how soon they will recover their invested funds.[5] It is also good for less complex projects with relatively short planning horizons.

Let's provide an example of a simple financial payback. Assume a company decides to put forth a cash outlay of $700,000 to purchase returnable containers. Project planners have identified all the relevant savings, backed out any new costs from the returnable containers, such as the cost to return empty containers, and estimate the project will save $400,000 annually over a five-year expected project life. The payback is simply $700,000/$400,000, or 1.75 years, assuming the savings occur in a constant manner.

Figure 16.5 presents two projects where the benefit streams are not uniform each year. In Project A, the Year 0 cash outlay is $400,000 with a Year 1 cash inflow of $300,000. That leaves $100,000 of the initial outlay still to be covered, which occurs in the first half of the cash inflow for Year 2. So, the payback period for Project A is 1.5 years. For Project B, the Year 1 cash inflow covers $100,000 of the $400,000 cash outlay in Year 0. Year 2 cash inflow covers $200,000 of the remaining $300,000 cash outlay, leaving $100,000 of the original cash outlay to be covered in Year 3. Since the Year 3 cash inflow is

A	Projects	B
$(400)	Cost (outflow year 0)	$(400)
300	Cash inflow year 1	100
200	Cash inflow year 2	200
100	Cash inflow year 3	300
	Accumulated cash inflow	
$300	Year 1	$100
500	Year 2	300
600	Year 3	600
1.50 Years	Payback period	2.33 Years

Figure 16.5 Payback period illustration

expected to be \$300,000, it will only take $1/3$ of the year to cover the remaining \$100,000 of the cash outlay. So, the payback for Project B is 2.33 years.

Net Present Value

A company may require a more complex financial assessment of its capital projects, such as the calculation of the NPV of a project or competing alternatives. It is defined as the present value of future cash flows or benefits discounted at an appropriate cost of capital or hurdle rate, less the cost of the investment. Whenever the reader sees the word *net* in a financial indicator, he or she can assume something has been subtracted to arrive at a final result. More complex financial evaluations, such as NPV, require a multistep process, which the following summarizes:[6]

- *Estimate the initial cash outlay*. This includes the initial project costs, such as the cost of equipment or new building.
- *Determine annual incremental operating cash flows*. This requires quantifying the net savings that result from the project. One way to do this is to prepare an estimated income statement and cash flow with and without the project. The difference represents the incremental impact of the capital project. Actual data should replace estimated data as the project progresses.
- *Project the terminal cash flow or expected salvage value*. Add the salvage value of equipment or a facility to the final project year's operating cash flow. Equipment figures usually represent the scrap or residual value at the end of the equipment's usable life.
- *Determine the present value of the future cash flows*. This represents the value in today's dollars of the benefit stream over each year of the project. Future flows are discounted by some percentage, such as a hurdle rate, provided by the finance department. Taking future flows down to a present value level requires the following equation:

$$PV = FV/(1 + r)^N$$

where:

PV = present value
FV = future value
r = return or hurdle rate
N = number of years

Please note that present value tables are available that will provide the discount factor for a given period and interest rate. Consult a finance textbook for this table.

Determine the NPV of the project. It is the sum of the present values of the inflows (benefits received each year) less the outflows (investment cost) in a given project. A positive number means the current value of the discounted future benefits exceeds the project hurdle rate. If more than one proposal is under evaluation, the one with the higher NPV is expected to provide a better return.

Probably the best way to illustrate NPV is through an example. Let's say your company is evaluating two competing proposals for new production equipment. Table 16.2 summarizes the initial investment and projected net savings streams for the two alternatives. This example discounts the future inflows to Year 0 using a 12% interest or hurdle rate. This table shows how the NPV method allows project planners to arrive at an *apples to apples* compari-

Table 16.2 Capital project options

Project A		Project B
($600)	Cash outflow year 0	($645)
$200	Cash inflow year 1	$250
$300	Cash inflow year 2	$330
$300	Cash inflow year 3	$330
$225	Cash inflow year 4	$250

Interest rate return requirement: 12%
*All figures are in thousands.

PROJECT A CALCULATIONS

Present value for year 1 inflow: PV = $200/(1 + .12)^1 = $178.57
Present value for year 2 inflow: PV = $300/(1 + .12)^2 = $239.16
Present value for year 3 inflow: PV = $300/(1 + .12)^3 = $213.54
Present value for year 4 inflow: PV = $225/(1 + .12)^4 = $142.99

Present value of inflows: $774.26
Less year 0 outlay: $600
Project A net present value: $174.26

PROJECT B CALCULATIONS:

Present value for year 1 inflow: PV = $250/(1 + .12)^1 = $223.21
Present value for year 2 inflow: PV = $330/(1 + .12)^2 = $263.07
Present value for year 3 inflow: PV = $330/(1 + .12)^3 = $234.89
Present value for year 4 inflow: PV = $250/(1 + .12)^4 = $158.88

Present value of inflows: $880.1
Less year 0 outlay: $645
Project B net present value: $235.10

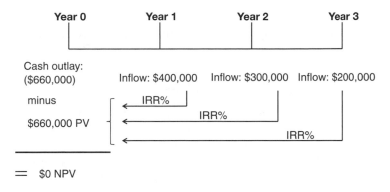

The internal rate of return that results in a present value stream of
$660,000 and an NPV of $0 is **19.7%**

Figure 16.6   Understanding internal rate of return

son between project alternatives. Because Project B has the higher NPV, it is
considered the better choice from a financial perspective.

Internal Rate of Return

Internal rate of return (IRR) is the interest rate that equates the total present
value of future cash inflows to the Year 0 investment expenditure. The IRR is
what we often think of when we refer to the term return on investment for
a specific project. Figure 16.6 illustrates a capital project with an investment
cash outlay of $660,000. In the previous section, the rate we use for the NPV
calculation would be provided by the finance department in the form of a
target or hurdle rate. With IRR, no such rate is provided. The point of the IRR
exercise is to identify the return rate where the present value of future inflows
equals the initial investment outlay in Year 0. Solving for the IRR figure can
be accomplished by trial and error or through the use of financial calcula-
tors, which is beyond the scope of this discussion. For this example, the IRR
that discounts the future cash inflows to the level of the initial investment is
19.7%. This number can be used for comparison purposes when evaluating
multiple project options or as a benchmark figure. As it pertains to IRR, higher
values are better than lower values.

Each benefit and cost from a capital project should be quantified or mod-
eled before making a financial assessment. This will involve, at a minimum, the
participation of finance, purchasing, operations, and engineering. These groups
will each bring some relevant information to help arrive at the net savings
realized from a capital expenditure project. While our discussion seems like

it should be in a finance book, let's not lose sight of the fact that procurement involvement with capital projects will require a growing level of financial awareness.

Early Involvement by Design at Alcoa

Alcoa, one of the preeminent aluminum companies in the world, is a company that appreciates the importance of well-planned and executed capital projects.[7] Operating in dozens of countries in a variety of businesses, Alcoa is a capital-intensive entity that requires, among other things, mines, equipment, smelters, and aluminum refineries. At any given time, Alcoa is executing multiple capital projects across its global businesses. These projects will range in cost from hundreds of thousands of dollars to over $10 billion.

Alcoa divides capital expenditures into sustaining projects and growth projects. A sustaining project is a capital project that is undertaken to sustain or improve current operations. Safety and environmental projects are included in this category. Growth capital projects often feature the greatest early involvement opportunities since they are usually the most expensive, complex, and visible. These projects involve capacity increases and often include the construction of new facilities. Across the company, Alcoa has many growth projects in its pipeline at different points in the process, ranging from concept/feasibility study to execution, although the number varies with timing and economics.

The scope of some of the capital projects at Alcoa requires the company to work with third-party engineering and construction firms such as Bechtel, Fluor, and Hatch. These companies are called engineering purchasing construction management (EPCM) firms and are considered partners by Alcoa. When working with EPCM's, Alcoa typically leaves the responsibility for developing the detailed requests for proposals (RFPs), issuing the RFPs and the subsequent analysis of the bids, and the final contract development to the EPCM firm. However, all of this work is performed with the involvement of capital procurement personnel and commercial managers from Alcoa. Given the scale of the projects where EPCM firms become involved, developing RFPs and contracts is no simple undertaking. Alcoa often works with the EPCM to specify the equipment and technology to use and will influence what suppliers will be used in EPCM managed projects, especially where the opportunity for synergies with existing Alcoa spending exists. On projects where either the business chooses not to use an EPCM or the project does not justify the cost of an EPCM, then Alcoa's own capital procurement group takes on the role of project procurement.

The early involvement of a dedicated capital procurement group on capital projects has become a mature process at Alcoa. In some cases procurement had to convince internal customers to request its support, which was sometimes resisted because of the view that procurement only drove supplier selection based on lowest price. It was necessary to show that procurement could deliver a value proposition that focused on the total value to the project based on all total cost factors, including schedule compliance, delivery, output, maintenance costs, and warranties, in addition to price. Over time, Alcoa's capital procurement group has demonstrated that the greatest value is delivered when procurement is involved during all phases of the project from pre-project planning through execution, commissioning, and operations. Procurement is no longer at the point where it must prove the value of its involvement. Now business units actively solicit procurement support.

Early Involvement Enablers—People and Structure

Beginning in January 2005, Alcoa procurement underwent a major transformation that resulted in the creation of a center-led global procurement organization (see Chapter 5 on organizational design). As part of this transformation, the supply group recruited additional talent (see Chapter 6 on talent management) and provided training for its existing staff. In the capital projects arena, procurement recruited engineers and other technical personnel along with career procurement professionals into capital procurement roles in the newly designed organization.

Human resources and organizational design are the two primary enablers supporting early procurement involvement with capital projects. Recall from Chapter 5 that organizational design refers to the process of assessing and selecting the structure and formal system of communication, division of labor, coordination, control, authority, and responsibility required to achieve organizational goals.[8]

Alcoa has a chief procurement officer (CPO) who oversees a center-led, global procurement organization. Supply leaders believe strongly that the current organizational structure is a primary enabler for many leading supply practices, including early involvement with capital projects. Procurement involvement with capital expenditures is not an accident at Alcoa—it happens by design. The executive responsible for capital procurement, the director of capital commodity management, reports directly to a vice president who reports to the CPO in charge of global procurement. The director of capital commodity management is also on the lead team of the executive in charge of all growth projects for Alcoa, which assures him a seat at the table.

Alcoa uses a matrix organizational design, which is not unusual with a center-led structure. While all supply personnel report into global procurement, many supply personnel are located in the businesses they support and have a dotted-line reporting relationship into that business. Alcoa's organizational design ensures that procurement's involvement at the corporate and business unit level is not an issue.

Three businesses make up Alcoa—Alcoa Global Primary Products (bauxite mining and refining and aluminum smelting); Alcoa Global Rolled Products (rolled fabricated products); and Alcoa Engineered Product Solutions (aerospace fasteners, power and propulsion, wheels, automotive, building, and construction). Procurement supports each business group and has full-time personnel who focus exclusively on capital projects for each of these global business units. There is a separate part of the global capital procurement group that is dedicated to large growth projects for the smelting and refining business. It is not unusual to transfer procurement personnel around the world to support primary growth projects. This is where some of the largest capital projects and dollars reside.

The Benefits of Early Procurement Involvement with Capital Expenditure Projects

Supply leaders are confident when they discuss the benefits and outcomes from early procurement involvement with capital projects. They have seen firsthand the benefit that early involvement makes from project concept to completion.

Early involvement at the project concept stage helps with the development of clear specifications and scopes of work that require minimal changes later. It is procurement's job to then clearly communicate these items to the suppliers through a formal bid process. Procurement manages the communication flow between the suppliers and the projects to ensure that all ethical standards are followed and that no room is left for a supplier to feel that the playing field was not level. The value of speaking to suppliers with one voice across the company is widely regarded as beneficial. Early involvement allows a clear set of project rules to be established that facilitates a fair process.

Project costs, including initial estimates and final costs, will be more accurate when procurement is involved early. Procurement personnel use a varied set of sourcing tools and approaches when evaluating capital projects, including leveraging common requirements across projects, developing TCO models, *should cost* models based on data from market indices on materials and labor, and historical project data. Procurement requires that suppliers provide detailed cost breakdowns when they submit proposals. These cost breakdowns cover materials, labor, and service rates. Clean-sheet cost training is part of the skills training supply personnel receive at Alcoa since the 2005 transformation.

Another benefit of early procurement involvement is that procurement evaluates a wider choice of suppliers for selection, which leads to a competitive selection process and lower costs. Specific suppliers are not designed into a project proposal.

It is still possible to provide some value if procurement involvement is later in the project planning process. Generally speaking, however, cost accuracy goes down as there is less time to fine tune specifications and less time for a supplier to provide a level of detail that allows better pricing accuracy. Additionally, the possibility of bringing in new or alternative suppliers is limited. Ultimately, this will result in an increase in project contingency costs.

Early involvement gives procurement an opportunity to provide valuable information about materials and labor availability. An assessment of labor availability in Iceland to support a growth project, for example, revealed a shortage of labor to support project construction. As a result, procurement, along with project managers, developed a plan in which suppliers built and preassembled modular construction for delivery to Iceland.

Procurement provides data that allows an evaluation of the impact of items such as schedule and terms and conditions on the total cost of a project and can balance that perspective against Alcoa's overall business needs.

Early involvement also allows procurement to investigate the potential to leverage common spending across multiple projects. Because procurement has visibility to the total capital project portfolio as well as the maintenance spending of the company, projects with some commonality can be bought together, and advantages can be shared from leveraging the total commercial position. The ability to leverage spending can reduce equipment and material costs, provide improved terms and conditions for the company, and give access to new supplier opportunities across the company. Leveraging has resulted in double-digit savings, improved schedules, and improved terms and conditions in the areas of liability, warranty, and damages.

Early involvement with projects also allows the capital procurement team to involve the indirect procurement team in providing input into the strategies for spare parts, maintenance, and ongoing service needs. This can provide benefits across the company outside of the capital spend.

All of these benefits simply are not possible if procurement is involved later rather than earlier.

Early Involvement and Global Procurement Support—Its Impact on Suppliers

A center-led procurement approach means procurement has visibility into all Alcoa capital projects worldwide. This offers the opportunity to provide additional business to suppliers who provide good support.

Suppliers have experienced tangible changes due to Alcoa's approach to capital expenditure projects. Suppliers know they have to sharpen their pencils when responding to capital project proposals. Early involvement has introduced competitive pressure as the supply organization evaluates the most qualified suppliers using advanced cost analytic approaches. Suppliers are required to provide greater cost detail in their proposals compared with earlier times. In return, they know that business is awarded fairly based on the TCO. The days of designing in specific suppliers for a project are over.

A center-led approach also results in company-wide consistency and standardization. Suppliers understand the proposal process, payment process, and the negotiation and contracting process. This is often not the case when an organization features a dozen business units developing their own supply processes, procedures, and practices. As mentioned, Alcoa now speaks with a single voice to the supply market rather than speaking with many voices across different businesses and geographic regions.

Alcoa procurement has demonstrated how applying good talent, advanced sourcing tools, and early involvement can benefit capital projects. The capital procurement group is now invited at the earliest stages of projects to work with the businesses on their capital needs. The project professionals at Alcoa would not have it any other way.

Concluding Thoughts

The reality is that procurement should be involved directly with any purchase category that involves significant dollars and where benefits are possible through involvement. Unfortunately, for a variety of often good reasons, procurement involvement has been severely lacking in the capital project arena. Many supply organizations, particularly at smaller companies, lack the resources and the expertise to become involved early with capital expenditure projects. These organizations often struggle just to manage their direct material purchases, which will remain as their primary focus. As it relates to the capital expenditure side, we often do not expect much beyond ensuring that contracts are properly loaded into the contract management system (or perhaps placed in the proper file cabinet).

Capital expenditures cover a wide range of areas that demand some level of specialized knowledge and expertise. Supply personnel who manage direct materials are expected to have a strong knowledge of the items they support. Why would a strong working knowledge be any less important when trying to support capital projects? Next level supply organizations will recognize the benefits of developing capital project expertise that is respected and asked for across the entire organization. If anyone asks why procurement personnel should be involved early with capital expenditure projects, a proper response might be, "Why would they not?"

Chapter Notes

1. "Some Steps Have Been Taken to Improve Contracting, but a More Strategic Approach is Needed." *The America's Intelligence Wire*, Access My Library, 2008. Accessed August 31, 2010, http://www.accessmylibrary.com/coms2/summary_0286-35233889_ITM.
2. www.census.gov.
3. Robert M. Monczka, Robert J. Trent, and Robert B. Handfield. *Purchasing and Supply Chain Management* (Mason, OH: Thomson-Southwestern, 2005), 364-365.
4. "Pushing Procurement Savings to the Bottom Line, Increasing Corporate Competitiveness Both Dominating the CFO Agenda, Says Aberdeen-Group." *Business Wire*, Access My Library, 2005. Accessed August 31, 2010, http://www.accessmylibrary.com/article-1G1-137408915/pushing-procurement-savings-bottom.html.
5. Samuel C. Weaver and Fred Weston. *Strategic Financial Management: Application of Corporate Finance* (Mason, OH: Thompson Southwestern, 2007), 337.
6. Weaver and Weston, 382.
7. The authors would like to thank Christie Breves and Chris Taylor from Alcoa for their generous support during the development of this section.
8. Gary Hamel and C. K. Pralahad. *Competing for the Future* (Cambridge, MA: Harvard Business School Press, 1994), as referenced in D. Hellriegel, J. W. Slocum, and R.W. Woodman. *Organizational Behavior* (Cincinnati, OH: South-Western College Publishing, 2001), 474.

Part Three

Additional Key Topics in Next Level Supply Management

17

Building a Supply Chain Organization from the Ground Up (Case Study)

Commercial Metals Company started with a clean slate in creating a shared supply chain group, but in less than a year it already saw tens of millions of dollars of cost savings.

by Andrew K. Reese, Editor, Supply &
Demand Chain Executive (reprinted with permission)

If you had the chance to build your company's supply chain function from the ground up, what would that organization look like? And more importantly, how would you go about designing the function, where would you find your staff, and how would you roll the organization out to the rest of the company?

All these questions faced Commercial Metals Company (CMC) in 2008 when the Irving, Texas-based global metals firm opted to begin moving to a centralized supply chain organization model. The ambitious goal: create a shared supply chain group that could drive savings per year per supply chain employee at a rate double or triple the industry average—in just the first year of the initiative.

Starting from Scratch

CMC manufactures, recycles, and markets steel, other metals, and related products. The company, which reported 2009 fiscal year revenues of approximately $6.8 billion, has operations in Poland, Croatia, Australia, Germany, and

Mexico in addition to its U.S. operations. It also has several trading offices, including in China and Singapore. A vertically integrated steel company, CMC has grown through acquisitions, bringing scrap yards, mills, fabrication shops, and other facilities together under its various divisions.

With diverse operations spread across recycling, mills, and fabrication and distribution groups, it made sense to set up shared services organizations to handle functions like accounts payable, human resources, payroll, safety and environmental engineering, and supply chain. The move to create shared services coincided with a rollout of an enterprise resource planning (ERP) system from SAP, with IBM acting as system integrator on the deployment.

The plan for implementing the ERP system envisioned significant supply chain benefits, says Andrew J. Houser, vice president of supply chain management at CMC. As a result, as CMC was putting together the business case for the SAP solution, it also put out a request for proposal (RFP) for consulting services to help the company ensure that it realized the best return on investment on the SAP implementation by looking at how the company should structure its supply chain organization. "We were starting from scratch in figuring out how to run our supply chain, looking at what tools to use, what processes to use, what people were going to be in the organization," says Houser. "We had a completely blank sheet of paper to start with as we designed the supply chain."

Based on the RFP, CMC brought in consulting firm Greybeard Advisors founded by Robert A. Rudzki, a former Fortune 500 chief procurement officer. Houser says that CMC went with Greybeard from among a total of eight consulting firms that the company looked at because the firm did not offer an *off-the-shelf* approach. "They genuinely got to know the business and the operation, including the culture and the people, before they put together their proposed solution," he says, adding, "At CMC, we have a very rich, defined company culture, and new initiatives are only going to be successful if you get people to participate." The consulting firm's approach also focused on communicating with senior management as well as with supply chain staff, and on transferring knowledge and skills to the client's organization to build in-house capabilities quickly.

Ambitious Goals

Greybeard's charge was to help CMC craft a roadmap for how the company should put in place its supply chain organization and business processes, and then to assist in the rollout by providing training and experienced team coaches during the first few waves of sourcing projects. Rudzki, who led strategic transformation initiatives as a supply chain executive before moving to the consulting side, says that Greybeard's approach to creating a *transformation roadmap* begins with an objective assessment of the *as is* state of the company's supply management and procurement performance against *best-in-class* organizations not only within the company's own industry, but across all sectors. That evaluation serves as the basis for a gap analysis to identify and quantify opportunities, and to assess which specific initiatives to pursue first, second and so on, in a way that builds results over time. "This is part art and part science," Rudzki says. "Done poorly, it can be the reason for *evaporating results*. Done well, the roadmap will create sustainable results and momentum and build organizational capabilities that drive superior performance."

The supply chain organization that CMC established includes: a group focused on procurement of direct and indirect materials; the logistics group, which manages the company's substantial fleet of its own trailers, trucks, railcars, barges, and leased ocean vessels, moving all CMC's products between different facilities and ultimately out to customers; the supply chain optimization group, which focuses on the sales, inventory, and operations planning process; and a supply chain capabilities group, which manages all the tools that supply chain uses, including SAP, business intelligence reporting, spend management, supplier scorecards, supplier diversity, supply risk analysis, eRFX, e-auction, e-commerce, EDI and global master data, including all of the vendor information that is loaded into SAP.

The supply chain organization launched in September 2008, just as Houser came on board with CMC. Previously, Houser worked at EDS (before the HP acquisition), where he was focused solely on the supply chain side at a time when EDS was going through a similar transformation to centralize supply chain operations. Before that, Houser was with SBC Communications (prior to the AT&T acquisition), where he did sales, operations, network management, and some procurement.

At CMC, Houser says that the roadmap for the supply chain organization provided for building a very lean group. "Our intent, when we started this, was that we didn't want to build a massive overhead or a bureaucratic organization," he says. In addition, the company elected to build the team primarily using current CMC employees drawn from the businesses. "Our logic was that while a lot of the people we were bringing in might not have a formal education in procurement or supply chain, they knew the business," Houser explains. "We felt that by teaching them the process, they would be able to use their business knowledge to drive good results."

And the results that the company was looking to drive were not trivial. Based in part on benchmark data that Greybeard had put together, CMC figured that average to high-performing supply chain organizations were achieving an average of approximately $360,000 in savings per year per supply chain employee. CMC's goal for the first year of its supply chain transformation was to drive double or triple that performance.

Building the Team

As Houser built the supply chain team, he looked for internal candidates with strong financial acumen, good communication skills, and strong knowledge of the industry and CMC's operations. "We've got a smorgasbord," he says. "Every single division gave us people for this team. We have people on the team who used to work at the mill, who used to work in recycling. And in a variety of functions, whether they ran the melt shop, whether they were in sales, whether they ran the shredder at the scrap yard. So we have a great cross-section of people with that core skills set, and with some unique business experience that really helps us understand what our internal consumer needs."

Coming from an operations background, Houser says the biggest pet peeve that people on the operations side have with supply chain is that they feel supply chain doesn't understand their needs, their business. "In a lot of cases, I think that's true. Where I've seen procurement organizations fail, it's where they have not involved their stakeholders enough or where they have not understood the business. So they go out and do deals with suppliers that don't meet the needs of the stakeholders or the business. If the business doesn't buy from that contract or changes the way that they do business, then the benefit never becomes real."

Bringing operations and sales people from the business into supply chain lends the organization credibility, Houser continues, because the people in the business see that it's their peers in supply chain, not outsiders. That means that when a supply chain person comes to the business and talks to them about changing to a certain supplier or doing a process in a certain way, it has credibility, because the people in the business know that the supply chain person has lived in their world. In the end, CMC wound up bringing in just a couple external candidates into the supply chain organization in cases where they needed particular subject matter expertise, primarily around IT sourcing.

Achieving Results

The company's original plan had been to have the supply chain organization formed in September, but they really didn't have everyone hired and in place until January 2009. That left even less time to meet the organization's ambitious goals for CMC's 2009 fiscal year, which ended August 31. And yet by the time the company reported its '09 fiscal year end results, CMC's senior management was crediting the supply chain organization with a total of $76 million in savings, including $36.2 million through the procurement group, $32.1 million achieved by the optimization group, and $7.7 million by the logistics group. Those results added up to $1.2 million in savings per supply chain staffer, or greater than three times the industry average that the company used as a baseline to rate its supply chain performance. Supply chain also helped reduce the company's inventory by 444,220 tons, worth more than half-a-billion dollars. All these results led CMC's chief financial officer, Bill Larson, to single out supply chain's contribution during the company's fourth quarter earnings call, noting, "Our supply chain management group aggressively attacked costs and achieved tens of millions of dollars of cost savings this year." Adds Houser, with a degree of understatement, "We've been very pleased with the rapid progress."

In all, supply chain initiated more than 275 different sourcing *plays* during the past year and had completed 134 by the end of the company's fiscal year. Houser points to *good progress* attacking IT categories such as wireless, fixed line network, printing, PCs, and professional services. Other broad categories they've attacked include maintenance, repair and operations (everything from safety equipment, footwear and fasteners to ropes and slings and paint); mills (including such items as electrodes, ladle brick, alloys and lime); equipment (for example, forklifts, tractors, trailers, tires and fuel); and administrative (travel and entertainment expenses and office supplies). The sourcing efforts not only produced hard-dollar savings but also helped CMC consolidate its supply base significantly, so that 80% or higher of the spend in each category now goes to five or fewer suppliers.

Supply chain also identified certain items that they were able to work with the business to manufacture themselves rather than buying from an outside supplier. Not only has this produced cost savings, but in some cases the company is getting longer life cycle out of the products because they were able to customize the items more specifically to their needs. Says Houser: "Transforming your supply chain is not just about going out and getting a better price. It's about diving in and understanding how your business consumes the product and how you can change that consumer behavior to get uplift that's above and beyond the price change."

Success Factors

Houser credits the results, in part, to the strong backing the initiative has received from senior management. "We've had overwhelming support, starting with the board of directors on down to each of the executive VPs over the various divisions. They have realized the potential benefits to their divisions, and they're doing everything they can to help us," he says, noting that the businesses have provided staff to work on the sourcing teams. In all, more than 400 people from the divisions have participated in sourcing exercises with supply chain.

Communication also has been a significant success factor, Houser adds. He went out on the road for the first 90 days of the project, visiting most of the company's U.S. locations, meeting all the staff from top to bottom, from the vice president in charge to the individual buyers, getting to know them personally. And that was done before they started running sourcing plays, so that they knew what supply chain was doing, what its intent and goals were. The supply chain organization also hosted a number of training sessions at various locations across the U.S., including for every member of the executive team, so that they understood supply chain's plans.

As the initiative unfolded, the supply chain capabilities group, with six employees, was in charge of all supply chain communications out to the businesses. They looked at how best they could communicate progress, benefits, current projects, and expectation in a way other than blasting out PowerPoint slide decks and e-mails. As a result, they did road shows at various locations, put together a supply chain magazine and monthly updates, created policy documents and executive presentations for the board, and also collected feedback from the businesses.

Houser says that he leveraged his own background in marketing to help craft an *integrated marketing campaign* to take supply chain's message out to the businesses. "I think that some of the traditional ways that supply chain has communicated have lost their effectiveness. When you throw a PowerPoint up on the screen, with most people, their brain switches off. Advertising guys are always trying to figure out how they can get their message through and get the consumer either to get educated or take action. And those are two things that we have been doing: we have been educating and we have been persuading toward action."

Finally, Houser also believes that a key success factor for any initiative of this scope is ensuring that supply chain treats its internal customers with as high a regard as external customers, if not higher. "They are the ones consuming your products," he says. "They are the ones that have to embrace the change. And if you don't look for ways to get them involved and to gain their expertise and input into the process, you're not going to be as effective."

Greybeard Advisors' Approach to Transformation

Assessment and Transformation Roadmap (Phase I)

Activities

- Current state assessments compared to best practices
- Opportunity assessments on how much cost reduction is possible and how to achieve it
- Detailed transformation roadmap development
- Business case development and presentation

Outcomes

- Comprehensive analysis of current state vs. best practices

- Opportunities identified and prioritized
- Detailed transformation roadmap finalized
- Senior management buy-in, and additional resources budgeted

Implementation & Execution Support (Phase II)

Activities

- Training in Strategic Sourcing & Negotiations Management
- Sourcing advisors (category experts) to guide teams and accelerate client results and knowledge transfer
- Ongoing transformation guidance and support

Outcomes

- Significant and credible savings results achieved by the client
- Knowledge transfer
- Capabilities enhancement

Source: Greybeard Advisors, www.GreybeardAdvisors.com.

18

Lean Six Sigma in Supply Management

Nearly everyone in business has heard of Lean Six Sigma (LSS) by now. For the last three decades, enterprises across the globe have been taking up this management strategy to guide continuous improvement efforts in their organizations, efforts aimed at pinpointing customer needs, reducing waste, and eliminating defects. It is a methodology, a set of tools, and a cultural mentality for reviewing and improving all aspects of an organization's work. Without the discipline that a LSS approach provides, learning and adapting doesn't always happen as rapidly and effectively as today's fluid technological and competitive markets require.

Sometimes, LSS efforts are eagerly applied on the manufacturing floor and result in large gains in customer satisfaction and substantial cost savings but seldom does it reach the supply management arm of the value chain. But it is an ideal approach for a strategic sourcing group. Even if your group has already launched a LSS project or two, there is likely to be potential still for using it to take your supply management organization to the next level.

How can a supply management organization put the LSS methodology and tools to work to provide better value and service to the customer? We see four areas where it can be particularly worthwhile:

1. Strategic sourcing process. LSS tools can help form or refine your sourcing strategy process, including processes for selecting suppliers and negotiating contracts. (Note: the 6-phase strategic sourcing process and toolkits described in Chapter 8 are consistent with LSS principles.)
2. Process improvement. The LSS approach will help identify opportunities for improving transactional purchasing processes and launching

improvement projects, and LSS tools will come in handy when analyzing the performance of these processes. For example, its methods can help decrease invoicing errors or reduce the variation in the delivery times of new equipment. Another example would include a launch of a LSS project to reduce the time it takes to negotiate contracts through the elimination of waste or improve the effectiveness of the request for proposal (RFP) process.

3. Stakeholder requirements analysis. Use LSS tools to gain a better understanding of stakeholder requirements so that solutions squarely hit the mark.

4. Monitor and measure performance results. The LSS approach emphasizes the imperative of ongoing monitoring. It can help you monitor supplier relationships. It can help you develop a culture that is metric-driven so that facts rather than vague feelings propel your continuous improvement efforts in the right direction at the right level of intensity.

Before we explore how LSS can be used in these four areas of supply management, we will turn first to an overview of the origins, philosophy, and methodology.

Lean Six Sigma Overview

The tools and methods of Lean and Six Sigma are built on a half century of operational improvement approaches. They were originally developed at two different companies. Lean came from Toyota, and Six Sigma was developed at Motorola. These two programs started as internal initiatives but later were diffused widely to many organizations throughout the world. The primary focus of Lean is to remove waste in a system; the main focus of Six Sigma is to improve processes and reduce variation. Today, the tools and methods of Lean and Six Sigma are usually combined to get the benefits of each discipline.

Process Excellence

LSS is nearly always considered within a larger framework that is aimed at providing more value to the customer. There are many names and variations for such a framework,[1] but we will generically label it a process excellence framework. Figure 18.1 shows a simplified subset of a more robust framework.

LSS can be the driving force that provides the methods, tools, and culture that can bind all of these activities together. It has specific connecting points that tie process inputs and outputs together to create the synergistic model that focuses efforts on providing more value to the customer. Let's discuss each component of the framework.

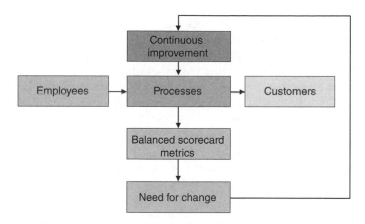

Figure 18.1   Process excellence framework

Customers: Customers are the reason that organizations exist. Ultimately, of course, excellent supply management benefits the end customer by reducing cost and improving quality. In a sourcing organization, positioned as it is at the front end of the supply chain, internal customers are also key. Strategic sourcing groups can waste no effort understanding their internal customers' true wants and needs. Instead of asking internal customers for their requirements, ask them what results or goals they are trying to accomplish. One of Henry Ford's famous quotes reveals the true meaning of understanding what customers really want, not just what they say they want. He said, "If I had asked the customer what they wanted, they would have said a faster horse." You must do all that you can to dig deep into the meaning of what the customers are telling you so that you can provide what is most valuable to them.

Processes: All work is a process. In other words, the creation of value is best understood as a series of steps that result in a finished product or service. By looking at work this way, organizations recognize that it is by scrutinizing each step and the way that steps flow together that they can deliver better quality and reduce costs. Yet it is the people performing these steps who must have the mindset of evaluating and improving the success of the processes they carry out.

One of the prominent founders of process quality was Phillip Crosby. He once said, "Those who think of quality as strictly manufacturing oriented have not thought it out. All of my writings are based on people working, not on an industry. All work is a process, and all processes can be designed, measured, and improved."[2]

If your supply management group develops a process-oriented culture, then you can take your ideas and actions to the next level. You can improve the work that you do by removing unnecessary steps, wasted time, and errors.

Balanced scorecard: Most companies today aggregate critical metrics using some version of a balanced scorecard (BSC) or dashboard to track how their processes are performing. A BSC should drive work efforts since it measures (ideally) how well you are meeting customer requirements, both internal and external. LSS efforts will provide strategic value when they take their cue from the BSC. A BSC is a great tool to ensure all efforts are aligned to the organization's highest priorities.

Employees: Employees must have the training, infrastructure, and authority to get work done. Sixty years ago, Peter Drucker said, "Any institution has to be organized so as to bring the talent and capabilities within the organization, to encourage men to take initiative, give them a chance to show what they can do, and a scope within which to grow."[3]

Teruyuki Minoura, Toyota's managing director of global purchasing, emphasized the leading role that people play in monozukuri (making things). He said, "There can be no successful monozukuri (making things) without hitozukuri (making people)."[4] Companies that invest in hiring, developing, and nurturing people are finding that this is the most important activity in supporting the long-term viability of an organization.

Lean Six Sigma Defined

What is LSS? We like a two-pronged definition:

1. A set of methods and tools that focus on improving processes, reducing variation, and eliminating waste
2. A management philosophy and culture that puts focus on the customer and on doing things right the first time

The first part of the definition is all about improving the processes of an organization. The second part is about your organization's culture changing so that everyone understands the idea of providing value to the customer. Jack Welch claimed that the biggest benefit General Electric obtained from LSS was enterprise-wide management training that unified all leaders with the same mindset and methods:

> "Overall, Six Sigma is changing the fundamental culture of the company and the way we develop people—especially our *high potentials*. We've always had great functional training programs over the years, particularly in finance. But the diversity of the company has made it difficult to have a universal training program. Six Sigma gives us just the tool we need for generic management training since it applies as much in customer service centers as it does in a manufacturing environment."[5]

So how will LSS help your supply management organization meet its goals?

- Enhances tools and processes that help everyone understand who the customer is, want they want, and how to meet those needs
- Emphasizes doing things right the first time
- Develops a mindset of continually improving all processes, both big and small
- Provides training that helps each person understand how to continuously improve
- Develops the shared practice of using data to make decisions
- Institutes a culture that drives the delivery of innovative, high-quality products and processes

Lean Six Sigma Methodology, Tools, and Complementary Skills

One of the most powerful benefits of LSS is the structure that it provides to help create new processes or improve those that already exist. It can be used to solve large, complex problems or it can be used to make small, incremental changes to a specific work activity. The same process and tool set are at work in either case.

There are two primary process methodologies in the LSS canon: DMAIC and DMADV. DMAIC is an acronym for define, measure, analyze, improve, and control. DMADV stands for define, measure, analyze, design, and verify. DMAIC is specifically used for improving an existing process; DMADV is used to create a new product or service. Table 18.1 compares the activities that are part of the DMAIC and DMADV processes.

As powerful as the DMAIC process is, it is useful to flesh out a more detailed step-by-step DMAIC flow. In Figure 18.2, note the five DMAIC activities across the top, with five substeps below each activity. This five-by-five roadmap (called the C5 method) is part of a LSS training program given to thousands of people around the world, and many have found that the additional guidance helps them make their way through a LSS project with more confidence.

Six Sigma Tool Set

The LSS tool set includes a vast number of data gathering, analysis, and problem solving methods. You have certainly encountered many of them before: project chartering, value-stream mapping, fishbone diagrams, design of experiments, and control charts, to name just a few. Some are simple and intuitive; others involve complex statistical techniques. Gathered together and put to work at the right stage of the DMAIC or DMADV process, these tools are

Table 18.1 DMAIC vs. DMADV

	DMAIC		DMADV
Define	Identify the problem and/or opportunity, get the stakeholders to agree on the goals of the project, and organize the project team.	Define	Same as Define in DMAIC but the focus is on opportunities.
Measure	Understand and document the problem and process, collect baseline measurements that validate the magnitude of the issue, and gather supporting data if needed. You also seek to understand customer requirements.	Measure	Understand what customers need, how they want to use the service or product, and what is critical to them.
Analyze	Review the existing processes and data to find root causes that are creating the problem. Determine potential solutions.	Analyze	Create, refine, and select high-level solutions that could meet the customers' requirements.
Improve	Select, pilot, and implement the solution.	Design	Design the final solution. Create prototypes and/or pilot the solution.
Control	Validate that goals were met, create a process to measure ongoing performance, and turn the solution over to the internal owner.	Verify	Ensure the solution goals were met. Stress test the solution, make sure the manufacturing or implementation process for the solution is repeatable and stable, and turn over to production for implementation.

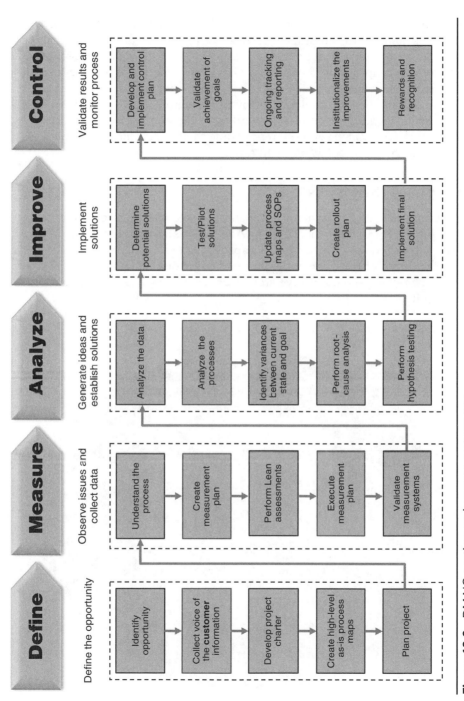

Figure 18.2   DMAIC continuous improvement process

Source: Crimson Corporation 2009.

handy for laying out dilemmas visually, collecting data in a useful format, crunching numbers to determine statistical correlations, structuring an analysis exercise, or communicating a reality. There is a tool of the right sophistication and scope to help anyone make better decisions, whether a team is a small work group making a simple enhancement to their workflow, a cadre of engineers running statistical simulations about new equipment configurations, or a cross-functional group of employees working on an interdisciplinary improvement effort. LSS training and reference guides help users learn these methods and choose the right tool at the right time.

Complementary Skills

LSS efforts are enhanced when participants are prepared with complementary skills. Figure 18.3 wraps the LSS DMAIC process around other knowledge areas that are required for successful improvement efforts.

In the center of the circle is the ultimate target of a LSS initiative: the customer. Everything should revolve around understanding and meeting customers' requirements.

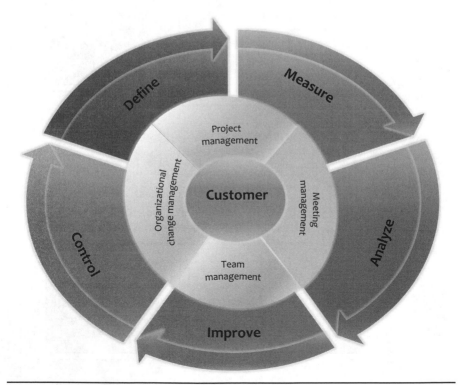

Figure 18.3   DMAIC wheel

The four knowledge areas shown in the second ring secure an excellent outcome for a LSS project or program. They are:

Project management: Bringing project management discipline to an improvement effort ensures that there is a schedule, budget, and a communication plan for the project.

Team development: Since nearly all LSS projects involve many people, it is important to understand how teams work together and to be skillful in managing these dynamics.

Organizational change management: Most projects will involve changes to processes, which will in turn have an effect on people. Since employees in an organization are the most important asset, the project should prepare people for the changes to their work routines.

Meeting management: Making certain that your meetings use the team's time well will keep the energy high and the project on track.

The outer ring of the DMAIC wheel shows how the five steps are cyclical—the last step, *control*, leading directly to *defining* the next opportunity to make a process even better. This is the *continuous* aspect of continuous improvement.

Why Use the DMAIC Process?

Organizations that are devoted to continuous improvement value managers who are not too quick to pose solutions to problems. Of course, one purpose of a manager is to ensure that the output of the group meets preset goals. However, it is a mistake to assume that she is supposed to know everything about the work, to expect that she should be the first to know how to fix problems. It is a mistake in some cases to rush to solve problems without adequately defining the problem, analyzing the current system, and testing new solutions. It is regrettable when managers are reluctant to say, "I don't know why my results aren't being achieved." It does an organization no good to program managers to respond with a solution or make a decision immediately when a process problem is presented. It is amazing how many solutions implemented under such conditions are not well thought out and sometimes do more harm than good.

Excellent managers are driven not only to know what the results of the group or process are but how the team got to those results. As James A. Belasco in *Teaching the Elephant to Dance* points out, "Management is about *how*. Management is about process. Become obsessed with *what* and you forget *how*. When you don't know *how*, you can't consistently produce the *what*."[6]

So what does this have to do with LSS? If a leader follows the DMAIC process when a problem is presented, the likelihood of finding the right solution increases dramatically. Possible solutions to a problem are not even discussed until the problem is defined, measured, and analyzed. Only then should a discussion of possible solutions be taken up at any length. Following the LSS approach puts the emphasis on the DMAIC process to obtain the best results, instead of emotional, gut level reactions.

Consider the case of a distribution company that identified a major problem in its delivery reliability process. Metrics showed 83% delivery reliability—which meant that 17 out of every 100 customers did not receive what they ordered on the first delivery. The organization tried repeatedly to improve but did not see any better results.

Why couldn't they do any better? After many failed improvement attempts, they had given up on finding the root cause of the problem and instead had created work-around processes that allowed them to meet their customers' requirements. They solved issues far downstream from their origins, thus creating extra work and building a bulky, inefficient, variance-riddled process over time. Using the LSS DMAIC process with external help, the company finally identified the root causes of its delivery reliability problems. With corrective action, it was able to improve delivery reliability to 89% in only three months, providing enormous savings and benefits internally and to customers. The success of this first LSS project led the way to many other improvements using its methodology and tools.

Lean Six Sigma in Strategic Sourcing

Now that we have a bit more background on LSS, let's turn back to a supply management organization to see how LSS can support its work. Remember that all work is a process, whether a team consciously keeps this foremost in their minds or just fumbles through without really thinking about the work step by step. The goal of any organization should be to understand their core work flows and ensure that the results of these processes meet the stated goals.

At the beginning of the chapter, we mentioned four aspects of a supply management function where it can have immediate applicability:

1. *Strategic sourcing process*: LSS tools can help you with forming or refining your overall strategic sourcing process. LSS practices can guide you when honing sub processes, such as the RFP flow or your negotiation strategy, to map and enhance them in particular.
2. *Process improvement*: Applying LSS methods can enable making incremental improvements to your day-to-day transactional purchasing work—work such as invoicing and order receipt.
3. *Stakeholder requirements analysis*: LSS practices can guide you when assembling stakeholder requirements and enrich your analysis to assure you are accurately addressing stakeholder needs.
4. *Monitor and measure performance results*: Implementing LSS methods in support of strategic sourcing will move your organization to

measure results and to act based on these measurements, creating a culture that is metric driven.

Strategic Sourcing Process

If your company has a strategic sourcing process already in place, LSS can be used for ongoing refinement. Even a well-defined process needs to be shared and understood by all areas of the organization. LSS can help.

Combined with a tried and true strategic sourcing process, the DMAIC/C5 process can be used to construct a robust strategic sourcing program for your organization. This is especially appropriate if LSS is already familiar to your organization or if launching a new sourcing process coincides with the introduction of LSS.

Figure 8.4 in Chapter 8 illustrated at a high level the consistency between a robust 6-phase strategic sourcing process and DMAIC principles. Figure 18.4 provides more detail on how the 25-step DMAIC/C5 method can be blended into a strategic sourcing process.

The key strategic sourcing activities under each of the DMAIC steps are summarized. The example here describes the process for selecting a new supplier as part of a need for a new service in an organization.

Define: In the define step, two key activities are creating the project charter and drafting the high level process maps. The project charter ensures the opportunity and goals of the request are clearly articulated and agreed upon. The high level process maps bring about a better understanding of the current work process. The maps will show which departments the process touches so that you can get all the stakeholders included in the project from the beginning.

Measure: The key activity of this step is to collect the detailed requirements of the solution so that a request for information (RFI) and an RFP can be prepared. Once this is done, the RFI/RFP is issued with the expectations established for assessing responses.

Analyze: The RFP is analyzed to see how well it meets the original requirements. The goal is to ensure that everyone completed the request and that all answers were completed correctly. If needed, any clarifications will be made during this step.

Improve: Here the solutions offered by suppliers are narrowed down, and candidates are selected. Their solutions can, when appropriate, be validated through a pilot or test process. If all goes well, the supplier is selected, and then the final contracts are negotiated and completed.

Control: This is a critical, though often neglected, step in the process. Activities here include validating that the solution met its original requirements and turning the solution over to the internal owner. Another crucial set of activities completed here is to clearly define service level agreements (SLAs) and setup business review meetings with the suppliers to assess the relationship

DMAIC	C5 steps	Inputs	Sourcing activities	Outputs
Define	Identify the opportunity	• Request	• Determine the reason for doing a project. Examples include: • Negotiate existing contract – standard annual renewal • Customer requests a new product or service • Manage problem with a vendor or service provided by the vendor • Review/Determine areas to improve or reduce costs	• Opportunity Identified
	Voice of the customer	• Current metrics • Current contract • Spend analysis	• Discuss opportunity with internal owner • Review any current information on the vendor • Review information on SLA's • Review vendor scorecards • Review Spend Analysis data • Is this a strategic relationship	• Any information on current or potential suppliers
	Charter	• Charter template • Opportunity • Goals	• Create the opportunity, goal, and scope statement • Get agreement on the goals	• Project charter
	Process map	• Current scorecard metrics • Process maps	• Understand how this process fits in with other related processes • Understand what parts of the company this process touches • Determine who is involved in this process	• High-level process map
	Plan project	• Charter • Resource list • List of risks • Team charter template	• Put team together • Create timeline • Create communications plan • Create team charter • Create risk management plan • Create org change management plan	• Team charter • Schedule • PM plans
Measure	Understand process	• Project charter • Vendor scorecards • Benchmark data • Supplier information • Industry information • Porter's 5 forces model	• Collect information on SLA's and other metrics • Review vendor scorecards • Review spend analysis data • Understand the detailed requirements for the solution • Porter's 5 forces review • Determine sourcing approach/strategy	• Detailed requirements • Sourcing strategy
	Create measurement plan	• Templates • Questions • List of possible vendors	• Create RFI/RFP • Create list of potential vendors • Create process to select the solution/vendor • Establish weighting criteria for responses	• RFI/RFP • List of potential vendors • Solution selection process

Figure 18.4　DMAIC specifics

	Lean assessment	• Vendor/supplier process	• Review RFP process to ensure it is efficient • Identify which bidding process is the most efficient • Review current vendor/supplier process specific to the vendor to ensure it is efficient	
	Execute measurement plan	• RFI/RFP • List of vendors to send to	• Send out RFI/RFP • Answer questions • Conduct any supplier meetings • Receive completed RFI/RFP	• Complete RFI/RFP's
	Measurement systems analysis	• Process to select the solution/vendor	• Validate RFI/RFP sending/receiving process was accurate • Ensure policies were followed • Ensure the process was fair	• Validated RFI/RFP's
Analyze	Analyze the data	• RFI/RFP • Analysis matrix	• Analyze the RFI/RFP responses	• Vendor response matrix
	Analyze the process	• RFI/RFP	• Validate everyone followed the right process to respond to the RFI/RFP	• Validated RFI/RFP process
	Identify variances	• RFI/RFP	• Determine if there are any significant differences between the responses that could have been caused by incorrect questions or processes • Determine gaps in responses • Validate that solutions are comparable	• Gap analysis
	Root cause	• Gaps • RFI/RFP	• Determine why there are differences or why the vendor did not supply the correct information	• List of differences
	Hypothesis testing	• RFI/RFP • Supplier information	• Determine possible ways to correct any process or question/issues • Resend RFI/RFP if needed • Get clarification on RFI/RFP	• Plan on how to reissue RFI/RFP • Validated RFI/RFP
Improve	Determine potential solutions	• Vendor selection matrix (Weighting/prioritizing) • RFI/RFP • Project charter • Contract template • Existing contract • Negotiation objectives template • Negotiation worksheet (MDO/LAA/BATNA)	• Vendor negotiations • Select vendor/Solution • Verify vendor background	• Selected vendor • Draft contract

Figure 18.4   *(Continued)*

		Potential solution		Validated solution
Test/Pilot			• Test solution to ensure vendor can provide solution • Validate SLA's • Validate process capabilities	• Validated solution
	Update process maps/docs	• Contract/proposal • Training plans	• Update any initial testing documents • Update any proposals • Conduct any initial training	• Updated proposal • Initial training
	Create rollout plan	• Solution	• Create plan to launch solution • Create transition plan from old vendor to new	• Transition plan • Rollout plan
	Implement final solution	• Draft contract	• Create final contracts • Sign final contracts • Implement solution with selected vendor	• Final contract
Control	Develop control plan	• Process maps • Project charter	• Create vendor management plan • Determine internal owner • Create processes to manage vendor • Create processes to manage upgrades/changes • Create process to manage ongoing training • Create vendor escalation process • Test escalation plan • Develop risk management plan	• Vendor management plans • Tested plans
	Validate achievement of goals	• Project charter • Detailed requirements	• Validate solution met original goals	• Validated goals
	Ongoing tracking	• SLA's • Business review calendar	• Track performance • Set vendor business review schedules and expectations	• Business reviews scheduled • Ongoing performance metrics
	Institutionalize improve	• Sourcing engagement survey template	• Turn over solution to internal customer • Updated lessons' learned • Sourcing engagement survey	• Customer has ownership • Sourcing evaluation score
	Rewards and rec.	• Supplier information • Project team member list	• Celebrate with customer and vendor	• Satisfied customer and vendor

Figure 18.4 (Continued)

and status of goals. It is critical to start the relationship with the new supplier correctly, and this is the step that really defines how the relationship will work. Scorecards are integral to this control phase.

Process Improvement

Another supply management activity where LSS can provide an advantage is the general cycle of improving existing processes. We can't reiterate Phillip Crosby's words too often: "All work is a process, and all processes can be designed, measured, and improved." For a company or department to become better, it must be clear about its current level of process performance. If you don't measure how you are performing today, you risk not knowing how your customers think you are doing. You won't know where your attempts at improvement can have the most strategic impact, and if you don't know that, you may spend time and energy fixing something that is not important to the customer.

Process improvement comes in different sizes. Larger projects generally take several months or longer to complete, engage larger cross-functional teams, and tackle more complex problems. Smaller projects generally focus on improving departmental issues in a short period of time. LSS practitioners sometimes call smaller projects kaizen events. They are part of the everyday culture of a LSS company.

Organizations that are devoted to process improvement are generally good at engaging with stakeholders to determine which issues to focus on. One method of determining what to target is to put an employee suggestion program in place. Toyota, for example, relies heavily on suggestions from employees. In 2001, the Georgetown, Kentucky plant collected over 80,000 suggestions from the employees and implemented 98% of them.[7]

LSS is an ideal choice for providing a uniform system and set of tools that can be used throughout a supply management organization for continuous improvement. The 25-step DMAIC/C5 methodology in Figure 18.4 provides a detailed framework to help pursue any improvement effort. Implemented with gusto, LSS will transform the culture to one that is dedicated to involving employees and providing value to the customer. Because supply management touches most parts of any business, and if LSS is new to your organization, there is no reason that your group shouldn't take on a leadership role in introducing the discipline of analyze and improving processes.

Stakeholder Requirements Analysis

The third area of supply management where LSS can provide immediate support is the commitment to identifying who the sourcing stakeholders are and what they want. A stakeholder is anyone who has a vested interest in the outcome of the sourcing work that you do. This could include external and internal customers, suppliers, governments, competitors, and employees. The LSS canon is replete with tools to help a company understand the critical requirements necessary to satisfy all stakeholders. Most new products fail because their creators don't do a good job of learning what the customer is really asking for. Recent studies indicate that 24% of new products fail due to inadequate market analysis—failing to comprehend what the customer really values.[8] This is a problem for procurement as well: we don't always devote the attention we could to recognizing the expectations—voiced and unvoiced—of our internal customers.

So how do we get better at correctly anticipating customer needs? In his book *What Customers Want*, Anthony W. Ulwick says that we should direct our attention to the *job* the customer is trying to accomplish.[9] Pay attention to the results of what they are trying to accomplish instead of their stated requirements. For example, if the customer says their requirement is a faster horse, you will likely give them a faster horse. But if you ask what they are trying to accomplish, and they say to get to work faster, then you will find a solution that will get them to work faster. In Henry Ford's case, you will create a car. Here is another example from Anthony Ulwick of missing the mark understanding what the customer really wanted. Kawasaki asked customers to suggest improvements to its Jet Ski stand-up recreational watercraft. They requested side padding for more comfortable standing—never dreaming of a seated craft. Competitors developed seated models, trumping Kawasaki.[10]

LSS can also help an organization become more explicit about the key roles and responsibilities between the supply management organization and the groups it serves. Bringing these relationships to light and discussing them is critical to ensuring there is a strong, working, trusting partnership between strategic procurement and other stakeholders. By following the DMAIC process and using the right LSS tools, you will be able to identify, include, and manage your stakeholders. Examples of tools that might come in handy are force field analysis, Kano analysis, stakeholder analysis, quality function deployment, and value stream maps. Responsibility charts will help clarify everyone's roles and identify a single process owner. Of course, tools are only as good as the people using them, but if there is a customer-focused culture first, then the tools can be used to understand and influence stakeholders.

Failure to make stakeholder relationships explicit can lead to disaster. Several years ago, a colleague was asked to help with a project to manage an issue with a supplier that was not providing service at the level that the company expected. He began by asking for basic information, including a list of all the stakeholders, performance metrics, SLAs, and most importantly, who owned the process. Project team members responded to each of these questions with, "We don't know, but we do know the supplier is not performing its job!" The obvious reaction was to discharge the current supplier and select a new one. The relationship was so strained, and the team was so committed to this solution before the project was even underway, that switching was the inevitable course of action. Our colleague helped the company create a sourcing plan, select a new supplier, and put metrics in place to ensure ongoing success. The one thing that did not happen was the company was unable to identify internally a relationship and process owner.

In the end, the project took over a year and a half to execute. Shortly after its completion, our colleague checked to see how the relationship with the new supplier was progressing. Unfortunately, the answer was as expected, "Not very well." The team had never agreed on who had process ownership responsibilities, so no one was managing the relationship. Procurement was in crisis mode again and finally realized that they could never count on success without a process owner to manage supplier performance.

The lesson here is that changing suppliers is no solution if stakeholder responsibilities are not made firm. The larger picture is that solutions put into practice without adequate identification of the root problem have little chance of success and result in wasted time and effort. A LSS approach would have prevented these problems.

The supply management organization should also ensure it is a trusted partner with the other internal departments and business units. Teams must focus on the customer rather than the task. Assign team members to work, understand, and be a partner with your internal customers and external suppliers.

Monitor and Measure Performance Results

The control phase of the DMAIC process is for measuring the results of a project and the ongoing contract and/or process. LSS creates a metric-driven culture that understands the importance of measurements and data accuracy. The organizational competence with measures rises dramatically by having a metric mindset.

Why is this so important? How many times have you had someone say that a process is performing well, but your data indicates that the customer is not at all satisfied? It is possible that the wrong measures are being collected and reported—measures that have little to do with customer satisfaction. Suppose you track, for example, how often a supplier meets the requirement for on-time deliveries. You sample one hundred shipments and see that the average time is exactly what was agreed to with the supplier, but this average does not reveal to you that 50 deliveries were several days early and 50 deliveries were several days late. Most organizations tend to measure averages when they evaluate process (or contract) performance. Averages, unfortunately, do not take into consideration a factor that is a priority to the customer: variation. Customers do not like variation. They expect their product or service to be consistent over time, and if it is not, they can become unhappy quickly. When Jack

Welch at GE first implemented Six Sigma, it took him three years to realize they were only measuring averages and needed to be measuring variation.[11]

Unfortunately, most people are not accustomed to looking at numbers statistically. Misunderstandings about what a metric truly reveals can lead to wrong decisions based on faulty interpretation of data. A LSS approach that includes training and mentoring about developing the right metrics will lessen this kind of mistake.

Concluding Thoughts

We've studied the history, philosophy, and methodology of LSS. We've also showed how this robust approach can be used in a strategic procurement organization. To conclude, here is a summary of how it can take supply management to the next level:

- Use LSS to enable a culture that is focused on the customer.
- At its roots, LSS employs data to identify, improve, and sustain processes. Using statistical methods to measure supply management processes—any processes—and to feed data to a score card or dashboard will give everyone a more accurate picture of the health of supply management, if not of the overall organization.
- The LSS DMAIC process and the more detailed C5 method can be brought together with strategic sourcing processes to give an organization a standard, consistent routine that can be followed to improve supply management flows.

LSS can be used to create future business leaders. After taking an LSS training class, a supply manager said "I will never look at data and processes the same way. I will manage my department differently. I only wish I had had this training earlier in my career!" While anecdotal, this type of revelation is the reason that companies are turning to LSS as a management-training program and not just a manufacturing quality program.

By endorsing LSS, your supply organization can ensure it is focusing on the customer, providing valuable business solutions, and being a complete partner to other areas of the business.

Chapter Notes

1. Some specific models include the Baldrige Performance Excellence Program and the European Foundation for Quality Management Excellence Model. They have many of the same components in common.
2. http://www.mhhe.com/business/opsci/bstat/crosby.mhtml.
3. Peter Drucker. *Concept of the Corporation* (Piscataway, NJ: Transaction Publishers, 1993).

4. Toyota. *The Toyota Production System.* http://www.toyotageorgetown.com/tps.asp.
5. Jack Welch. *Jack Straight from the Gut* (New York: Warner Books, 2001).
6. James A. Belasco. *Teaching the Elephant to Dance* (New York: Penguin Books, 2000).
7. Jeffrey K. Liker. *The Toyota Way: 14 Management Principles from the World's Greatest Manufacturer* (New York: McGraw-Hill, 2004).
8. Robert G. Cooper. *Winning at New Products: Accelerating the Process from Idea to Launch* (Cambridge, MA: Perseus Books, 2001).
9. Anthony W. Ulwick. *What Customers Want* (New York: McGraw-Hill, 2005), 23.
10. Anthony W. Ulwick. "Turn Customer Input into Innovation." *Harvard Business Review*, Jan 2002.
11. Welch.
12. The authors acknowledge the important contributions of Mark Donovan and Doug von Feldt to this chapter.

19

Toolkit for Strategic Sourcing Success

While most procurement professionals tend to think that they know how to run a sourcing initiative (yes, every time a sourcing training session is conducted, the participants will tell you they know), conducting a first rate project takes discipline. For a sourcing team to effectively develop and deliver a sourcing strategy, it helps to have and use a toolkit. We can define a toolkit in several ways. A toolkit can be defined as a set of tools, especially for a specific type of work, kept in a special box or bag. A more appropriate definition views a toolkit as a collection of information, resources, and advice for a specific subject area or activity.[1]

Tools and references, such as those built into products like Ariba, Emptoris, Oracle, and others, are integral to e-sourcing systems. If your company doesn't have such systems, then supply management professionals can rely on basic desktop software to assess opportunities, charter a sourcing initiative, and accomplish many other tasks essential to the strategic sourcing process. This same software can provide you with valuable reference information to guide you during your project.

Consider, if you will, a home renovation project. If you are handy in any way, you will pick up your toolkit and head off for the room where the work is to be done. While you may not need to use all the tools in your kit, there are some that are fundamental to the project—possibly, a ruler, screwdriver, hammer, or drill. There may be some aspects of the project where, because of limited experience, you'll need reference information—like following the directions for hanging drapery rods. You may have hung drapery rods before, but the directions will certainly make the task easier.

The Sourcing Toolkit

This chapter presents the sourcing toolkit according to the six phases of the strategic sourcing process. What follows is a description of templates, guidelines, and references that should be part of a good toolkit. The following defines these three terms:

1. Templates are primary tools. They represent established rules for ensuring uniformity and structure. Templates are mandatory documents used to ensure control by following a standardized way to do something. In most cases, if you change a template, it affects other templates, requiring that you pay attention to the interaction of processes.
2. Guidelines are documents intended to make a process more efficient according to a set way of doing something. They are practices or suggestions that when used provide organization to deliver outcomes. By definition, a guideline isn't mandatory. Guidelines are an important part of governance. They help to make certain that things are being done in an orderly manner.
3. References are papers, books, published materials, or internal works that can be utilized for support of what is being done. References provide information that can produce needed answers on a topic or practice.

Descriptions and illustrations of just some of the key tools in the sourcing toolkit are shown in Figure 19.1.

Phase 1: Gain Management Support for Sourcing Initiatives

The Role of Procurement (Reference)

The *Role of Procurement* is a reference document that enables management and procurement to determine the role that procurement or a sourcing team will take for a given project. As discussed in Chapter 8, will procurement support, facilitate or own the project? In your toolkit, there should be a reference document that provides insights for making this decision.

Phase 2: Organize and Profile the Sourcing Group

Select the Procurement Category (Guideline)

Within a commodity or category, there can be several types of spend. For example, a company may refer to its spend for copying, printing, and scanning as reprographics. In printing alone, there can be printing from desktop devices, data center printing for reports, and outside printing for sales presentations. Procurement may want to look at all of the reprographics, but the spend

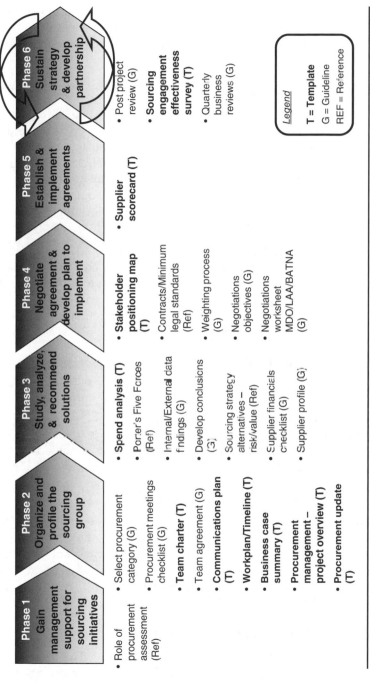

Figure 19.1 Templates, guidelines, and references for major steps of each phase

should be prioritized to ensure the best use of resources. Putting all the information into a single spreadsheet will show where there is potential for spend reductions. Sophisticated spend analysis tools are built into systems from BravoSolution, Ketera, and Zycus, to name a few.

Procurement Meetings Checklist (Guideline)

Once management determines where there are opportunities for cost reduction, it will commission sourcing projects. For the projects that are assigned to a sourcing team, the first step is to bring the team together. Since team training is not nearly as prevalent as it once was, it helps to have a meetings checklist in your toolkit to make certain that you address everything from an agenda to deciding when the next meeting will be scheduled.

Team Charter (Template Required)

If there is any one tool that every sourcing team should use, this is it. The best teams start their assignment by drafting a team charter. The Six Sigma version is a good one to use. When modified, it covers most of the basics of a sourcing initiative. Team charters are dynamic documents and should be updated throughout the sourcing process. The following template (Figure 19.2) matches DMAIC with sourcing Phases 2 through 6.

Team Agreement (Guideline)

Supporting the team charter with a team agreement is a good practice. While a team agreement isn't necessary, it helps to resolve conflicts that can arise when deeper in the sourcing process. Agreements are best when put in place at the start of the project. Signing the agreement tends to increase the sense of commitment for the team members. Team agreements should be carefully constructed and, unlike the team charter, shouldn't change during the project.

Communications Plan (Template Required)

Stakeholders, management, and suppliers want to know what you're doing—therefore, establishing a communication plan is a necessity. A sourcing team is obligated to know who it must communicate with (key stakeholders, etc.), what the team must communicate (the message), how it must communicate (the approach), why it's communicating (the purpose), when (dates and deadlines), and who from the team is responsible to ensure the communications take place.

Workplan/Timeline (Template Required)

Not all of the *whens* will be driven by communications. The team is required to declare what it will deliver and by what date. If the team isn't time bound,

Team charter

Project title:				
Business case:				
Problem/Opportunity statement:				
Goal statement:				
Project scope:				
Executive sponsor: Steering committee: Procurement sponsor: Project manager: Team members:			Stakeholders:	
Preliminary plan	Target date	Actual date	Estimated cost savings:	
Start date:				
Phase 2 / DEFINE				
Phase 3 / MEASURE				
Phase 4 / ANALYZE			Notes:	
Phase 5 / IMPROVE				
Phase 6 / CONTROL				
Completion date:				

Figure 19.2   Suggested team charter format

it can languish in analysis, meet for the sake of meeting, or just be uncertain as to who should be doing what and the deadlines. A workplan/timeline keeps a team on task.

Timelines can be developed with project related software, spreadsheets, or simply with a document listing dates and actions. A disciplined team will keep track of its accomplishments by identifying when the task was completed, even if it happened later than planned.

Business Case Summary (Template Required)

The business case is pivotal to determining whether or not a sourcing team should go forward with its project or stop. The business case provides reasoning for the project. It is initially prepared for senior management to enable making an informed decision on providing the resources required for the project. The business case is also used as the justification for stakeholder support and commitment to the outcomes.

The sourcing team should request the assistance of finance in determining and preparing the monetary benefits of the business case. If the company has a quality or continuous improvement function, then the team should request assistance from this functional group on identifying nonmonetary benefits. An effective business case addresses the following:

- Project description
- Deliverables
- Background, including initial observations
- Expected financial benefits
- Nonfinancial benefits
- Issues
- Key dependencies
- Risks
- Major milestones
- Additional information

The business case is a dynamic document and subject to change as the sourcing project evolves.

Each company's culture is unique. However, we have generally found that it is best if a business group, such as finance or quality/continuous improvement, keeps track of each proposed sourcing initiative as a neutral third party and reports the results.

Procurement Management—Project Overview (Template Required)

There are two reasons for the project overview. The first is to convince the head of procurement/purchasing of the validity of the business case for the sourcing initiative. Once onboard, the head of procurement becomes the principal advocate for the project. The second reason is the project overview is the communication vehicle for presenting the business case to senior management—to secure their support and the allocation of the necessary resources for the specific sourcing initiative. While the business case in itself is a good document for justifying the initiative, you need more. A sourcing team needs the opportunity to interact with senior management to ensure a clear understanding of the background, intent, and expected outcomes of the initiative. Note that the development and presentation of business cases for specific proposed sourcing initiatives is facilitated by first doing the overall assessment and roadmap process described in Chapters 1 and 3. That first step establishes credibility and overall support for the entire transformation program.

Procurement Update (Template Required)

Either procurement management or, better still, an oversight/steering committee comprised of management representation from the business groups (stakeholders), finance, and procurement should be updated on a regular basis on the progress of each sourcing team (Figures 19.3a and 19.3b). The team report should cover the following:

- Project title and category covered
- The sourcing objective
- Identification of the team, team leader, team members, and sponsor
- Spend history (at minimum the most recent full year)
- Estimated savings (both financial and nonfinancial benefits)
- Time to benefit (when the savings will start)
- Key milestones (both accomplished and pending)
- Issues, concerns, and risks

Phase 3: Study, Analyze, and Recommend Solutions

Spend Analysis (Template Required)

While preliminary spend data is required to identify and assess the sourcing opportunity, at this point in the process the team needs to develop spend information that is detailed and as specific as possible. Without exact information, the team will not know the full extent of the opportunity. The information becomes the prime reference point for any RFx that is issued.

Finance groups have different ways of breaking down spend information. This tool is identified as a template, making its use mandatory; however, the company and team should decide how it wants to collect, analyze, and present this information.

Figure 19.3a   Project management—project overview Part 1

Communications plan   Next steps   Timeline/Milestones

Figure 19.3b   Project management—project overview Part 2

Porter's Five Forces (Reference)

This is a reference document that no toolkit should be without. Too often, procurement professionals either don't know this information or neglect to consider the framework when preparing their sourcing strategy. This theory was developed by Michael Porter, a Harvard business school professor and researcher.[2] The theory, which is widely recognized and accepted, advocates that an organization know and understand the forces that influence the competitive marketplace. As sourcing strategies typically cover a three to five year timeframe, the team should consider these factors when assessing both the current and future state of the marketplace. An internet search will provide a team with considerable information on Porter's theory.

Internal/External Data Findings (Guideline)

The term *big picture* tends to be overused, but a sourcing team must understand all the influences on where it is and where it wants to be. The team needs to pull together a panoramic view of both the internal and external factors that will weigh on the strategy. Findings (Figure 19.4) lead into conclusions, which are then applied to the formulation of the appropriate strategy.

Develop Conclusions (Guideline)

With findings in hand, a sourcing team is now in position to develop conclusions and make decisions on how best to proceed with the initiative. Conclusions should take into account the following:

- Internal conditions
- Total cost of ownership, including transaction, usage, price, and any other total costs factors
- Supplier/marketplace conditions
- Best practices

Sourcing Strategy Alternatives: Risk/Value (Guideline)

To come up with a range of possible strategic alternatives that are applicable to the product or service, a team should use a set of risk/value criteria. A

Findings related to the use of the product/service	Findings related to the supply of the product/service

Our company
- Segregate data by company division and by supplier:
  - Volumes
  - Expenditures
  - Quality levels
  - Specifications
  - Issues/problems

Other users
- Combine intelligence on how others are *using* the product/service (benchmark data)
  - XYZ Co. outsource
  - ABC Corp. utilizes internal resources

Industry aggregate
- Total market size
- Number of suppliers
- Products offered
- Trend data
- Issues reported
- Other industry news
  - Mergers/announcements
  - Regulatory impacts

Individual supplier information
- Products/services offered:
  - Completeness of product line
  - New offerings
- Supplier capacity & risk of disruption
- Supplier cost structure and market share
- Supplier financials
  - Sales and profits
  - 5-year history

Figure 19.4   Internal/External data findings example

risk-to-value matrix must be based on facts derived through the research of the team.

Alternatives can be depicted graphically, making it easier to recognize where a recommendation fits as the team considers value against risk. There are numerous risk/value (2 × 2) matrices that can be applied to aid in recognizing the sourcing approaches that will deliver the best outcomes with least amount of difficulty. It is a simple exercise that can produce meaningful results. Some of the recommended matrices include (with value defined as spend as a % of sales):

- Segmentation of the procurement category; based on type of product or service
  - Bottleneck (high risk/moderate value quadrant)
  - Routine (low risk/low value quadrant)
  - Critical (moderate risk/high value quadrant)
  - Leverage (high risk/high value quadrant)
- Strategic alternatives are different ways that the product or service can be sourced using the same criteria applied to segmentation

- Appropriate supplier relationship
  - Preferred supplier (high risk/moderate value quadrant)
  - Approved supplier (low risk/low value quadrant)
  - Broad-based competition (moderate risk/high value quadrant)
  - Strategic alliance (high risk/high value quadrant)

Supplier Financials Checklist (Guideline)

Sourcing teams should work internally with finance to collect information on the following indicators to assess the viability of either a potential or existing supplier:

- Liquidity ratios lend insight into company's ability to meet short-term financial obligations.
- Financial leverage ratios provide information about a company's use of long-term debt.
- Profitability ratios are used to assess the ability of the business to generate earnings as compared to expenses over a specified time period.
- Certain sections of an annual report on Form 10-K include forward-looking statements that are based on management's expectations, estimates, projections and assumptions.
- Coverage ratio measures a company's ability to pay off its incurred debt. This indicates the approximate time that would be needed to pay off all debt, ignoring the factors of interest, taxes, depreciation, and amortization.

Supplier Profile (Guideline)

To better understand the qualifications of each potential supplier, the sourcing team should consider the following:

- General company information
- Geographic coverage
- Core capabilities for products and services
- Clients/references
- Ability to implement and administer the sourcing/supply strategy

Phase 4: Negotiate Agreement and Develop Implementation Plan

Stakeholder Positioning Map (Template Required)

Sourcing teams have an obligation to take into account the concerns that stakeholders might have about how they will be affected by a sourcing strategy. If the team followed through on the communication plan called for earlier, stakeholder support should be known and understood. An effective stakeholder positioning map should identify the following:

- Stakeholder or stakeholder (business or functional) group
- Issues/concerns
- A statement of the stakeholder's position (i.e., will not participate; will participate if changes are made, etc.)
- Actions required by the team to address concerns
- Actions/support required of procurement management (or oversight/ steering committee)
- Completion date
- Outcome(s)

Contracts/Minimum Legal Standards (Reference)

Most companies have standard contracts that they use when entering into an agreement with a supplier. They also have minimum legal standards for those instances when the suppliers' paperwork is used for establishing the agreement. A good example of using the supplier's document is a software license. Companies do not typically invest the time or effort in constructing their own software license unless software is core to their business.

The team should engage with the company's legal department as early as possible in the sourcing process. Minimum legal standards should be unambiguously set forth in any requests (RFxs) issued to suppliers. These should also be addressed again in advance of any negotiations.

Weighting Process (Guideline)

Decision factors should be identified in advance of issuing any requests to suppliers. It's awkward and inefficient to try to decide which criteria are important, and the degree of their importance, after supplier responses are received.

The team should either look for or establish a weighting process to use during the evaluation and ranking of supplier responses. These criteria will become the basis for measuring a supplier's performance for the duration of the strategy.

Negotiations Objectives (Guideline)

Negotiations objectives are a clear set of key parameters and relevant goals supported by rationale that define the ideal outcome. Negotiating effectiveness is likely to be enhanced if a sourcing team sets aggressive goals and clearly defined bargaining parameters. Price, specification, delivery, service, and quality are the most notable targets, but the team should challenge itself to identify other atypical targets that can bring meaningful results for all sides.

Negotiations Worksheet with MDO, LAA, and BATNA (Guideline)

Most procurement professionals will declare that they are good negotiators. While this may be true, negotiating as a team offers major advantages but also requires a different approach. Volumes have been written on how to negotiate; however, as a minimum, it's recommended that a team take the time to ascertain the following for each negotiations parameter:

- MDO—most desirable outcome—the best of all possible outcomes for the team.
- LAA—least acceptable agreement—the minimum that a team will agree to accept.
- BATNA—best alternative to a negotiated agreement—per Roger Fisher et. al., *Getting to Yes*,[3] the team needs to identify alternatives if an agreement cannot be reached. This may include turning to the supplier that provided the second best response or regrouping to identify other strategies.

This needs to be more than a discussion topic. Negotiations objectives and the MDO, LAA, and BATNA should be put into writing, then reviewed and accepted by all the team members. It doesn't matter how the team formats the information—spreadsheet, template, or a simple Word document. It just matters that it happens.

Phase 5: Establish and Implement Agreements

Supplier Scorecard (Template Required)

There are as many reasons for using a supplier scorecard as there are measurements for assessing a supplier's performance. Scorecards provide a consistent means—a mechanism—by which the team communicates to the supplier what key indicators are important. At defined points in time, the team gathers data on how well the supplier is performing to these indicators. Every company has different measurement criteria. The team should work with its quality/continuous improvement group, its management, and project stakeholders to adopt or construct a relevant scorecard. The scorecard evaluates the performance of both the sourcing strategy and the supplier.

Phase 6: Sustain Strategy and Develop Partnership

Post Project Review (Guideline)

Even if a sourcing team is attentive to detail, it can look back at the project and find aspects of the process that could have been handled differently or better. As the initiative moves into the implementation phase, the team should make the time to assess the project and identify improvements. The team should consider asking key stakeholders to participate.

It's important for the team to document the *what went well* and *what could have been done better* so the learning can be shared with future sourcing teams. It's also important to understand that the review is not intended to disparage the performance of individuals but to take a holistic approach to evaluating the total body of work for continuous improvement purposes.

Sourcing Engagement Effectiveness Survey (Template Required)

An effective sourcing process relies heavily on collaboration—within the team, with management, and especially with stakeholders. The post project review helps the team look inward to find improvements. The engagement effectiveness survey reaches outward to the businesses to ask for input. An added benefit is that the survey can disclose if actions taken to address stakeholder concerns (stakeholder positioning map) resolved the issues that were identified. The survey should cover the following:

- Results—did the team fulfill its charter and meet its objectives?
- Communications—how well did the team communicate throughout the project?
- Collaboration—were stakeholders engaged and did they become involved? Communications should go beyond *communicating to* and demonstrate *communicating with*.
- Financial compliance—were financial requirements (e.g., payment terms) fulfilled?
- Legal compliance—were legal requisites met?
- Supplier performance—even though the strategy is in the early stages of implementation, is the supplier doing what was assured under the agreement?

Quarterly Business Reviews (Guideline)

Despite the fact that quarterly business reviews are a good practice, the reality is that sourcing teams often see their assignment as complete once the agreement is signed, even before implementation is complete. To ensure that all parties are performing to both the expectations and the agreement, the team should reconvene with stakeholders and suppliers on a regularly scheduled basis.

Achieving the Next Level

Why are information technology groups viewed as delivering *projects*, but procurement is viewed as *buying stuff*? For decades, IT organizations have successfully applied project management techniques to meeting business goals. Successful IT projects don't just happen. They are carefully planned and carefully managed. For this reason, IT management has established credibility with senior management that procurement management has yet to parallel. IT managers prepare business cases, supported by project plans, to secure management's commitment to resources.

The toolkit works for any size company because it goes beyond buying and supports a strategic sourcing process. There are excellent e-Sourcing systems available, but if a procurement group cannot justify the investment in information technology, it can, at least, adopt a sourcing process. The tools in this toolkit represent:

- Taking a strategic versus tactical approach
- Company-wide (enterprise) thinking
- A willingness to be cross functional—engaging stakeholders
- Making decisions based on facts rather than intuition
- A deliberate method of negotiating
- A sense of continuous improvement

For procurement personnel who want to be viewed as professionals, it's time to pick up your toolkit and start working. A word of caution is in order here. Toolkits support a strong strategic sourcing process. They are not meant to serve in lieu of a strong sourcing process.

Concluding Thoughts

Buying is typically an independent act—a one-to-one event. Sourcing is typically collaborative and best supported by a defined process. There are ten tool examples in the toolkit that are identified as *required*. Each of these tools has a different degree of importance, but they all fit together to make sure that a process is followed and that a thoughtful strategy is designed and implemented. Throughout the process, the team should be able to present any of its templates or guidelines as a means for communicating with senior management and stakeholders. Even if a sourcing team is not used, a procurement professional is obligated to approach a large purchase (defined by a dollar amount or a multi-year term of agreement) with a project orientation. There is no excuse for neglecting these responsibilities.

Most procurement professionals will look at these tools and declare, "I do that—just without all the paperwork. It takes too long." As Saint Bernard of Clairvaux (1091-1153) stated, "Hell is full of good intentions or desires." Sourcing is seldom effective if handled as a random act. When it is done in an unstructured manner, there is often hell to pay.

Chapter Notes

1. *Encarta® World English Dictionary*, North American ed. Microsoft Corporation (Bloomsbury Publishing Plc, 2009).
2. M. E. Porter. "How Competitive Forces Shape Strategy." *Harvard Business Review*, March/April 1979.
3. Roger Fisher, William Ury, and Bruce Patton. *Getting to Yes*, 2nd ed. (New York: Penguin Books, 1991).
4. The authors acknowledge the important contributions of Jim Baehr to this chapter.

20

When the Worlds of Sales and Procurement Collide

Introduction and Executive Summary

It's been three decades since Arch McGill, then vice president of business marketing for AT&T, pushed to ensure that his sales force was certified in the process of system selling. It's also been three decades since Dr. Peter Kraljic developed a model that was a process for sourcing strategically. Despite three decades of experience, a history of *strategic* successes at select companies, and an abundance of technologies designed to support both disciplines, for the most part, sales and procurement continue to dwell on tactics.

Both sales and procurement recognize the value of being strategic in the practice of their respective professions; however, given the opportunity to *peek around the curtain*, the interest that seems to be at the forefront is to learn more about the *secret ways* of both professions. No matter how many times sales or procurement professionals are told that there are no *silver bullets*, they tend not to accept the answer.

The survey that is the basis for this chapter collected current perceptions for the purpose of developing understandings of how sales and procurement view each other. It evaluates their perceptions across dimensions ranging from *knowledge* to *performance* to assess the current state. By comparing perceptions, the survey confirms that for the most part, despite the best intentions to be strategic, it's business as usual just as it was nearly three decades ago. To say it another way, despite declaration of becoming strategic, both procurement and sales are—in general—conducting business as usual.

In the responses, there is evidence of respect for the other side; working cross functionally; sales/procurement collaboration; and acknowledgment that there's value in looking beyond the tactical. Unfortunately, there's also evidence that the focus is on price rather than cost (or value); there's too little interest in engaging the other side for mutual benefit; and there's surprising levels of uncertainty and ambivalence that come from both procurement and sales.

One important theme comes through in the replies and comments to the survey—procurement professionals contend that sales professionals can, and do, listen to the *voice of the customer*. Sales will proactively respond in a manner that complements the strategic expectations of procurement when procurement organizations demonstrate they are committed to the importance of strategy. Procurement expectations drive sales behaviors. Regrettably, tactical behaviors result in tactical reactions from both professional groups.

The demographics of the survey show there was solid participation from senior management in both professions. While the survey is an assessment of the current state, there is an old message that comes through. The message is represented by the following excerpt from Dr. Kraljic's 1983 article in *Harvard Business Review*, "No company can allow purchasing to lag behind other departments in acknowledging and adjusting to worldwide environmental and economic changes. Such an attitude is not only obsolete but also costly." This citation applies as much to sales as it does to procurement.

The survey points to obsolete attitudes. Activity is considered to be equivalent to productivity. Price trumps total cost. Relationships are a matter of time and place rather than the outcome of planned collaboration. In fact, only 7% of the sales respondents and 9% of procurement respondents consider themselves to currently have world-class processes with a strategic role in their company.

Sales and procurement executives who accept the reality of these perceptions should consider investing in assessing their levels of tactical versus strategic behavior; determine if making changes will improve their opportunity for success; and, if change is in order (as it would seem to be for most companies based on the survey results), develop a roadmap for transformation over both the short and long term.

Background

Sales believes, or suspects, certain things about procurement, and procurement believes, or suspects, certain things about sales. Supply chain organizations are investing to enhance the professionalism of their procurement practitioners as well as business processes. Sales organizations are faced with having to sell to teams and sourcing specialists. As the buying/selling model continues to evolve, the differences between perception and reality seem to be greater than ever before.

Credit for the genesis of this research goes to both procurement and sales professionals. Procurement professionals consistently inquire about the behaviors of sales professionals. "Why do salespeople always talk about partnership?" Others ask, "Why do salespeople backdoor sell?" These questions are evidence that procurement professionals are convinced that salespeople are trained to do whatever they can to limit involvement with procurement.

It's understandable to find sales professionals demonstrating the same suspicions about procurement. "Why won't buyers let us meet with end users?" On top of "We're sure that they have secret tricks. We just need a few tactics for dealing with them."

The prevailing question becomes: are these perceptions real and justified or are they imagined and groundless? To better understand current thinking and practices, Greybeard Advisors conducted a study to compare the perceptions of procurement and sales professionals.

Objectives

The intent of the survey was to collect, assess, and compare opinions held by both the procurement and sales disciplines based on the following:

- Knowledge and understanding of the marketplace
- The attention given to price, total cost of ownership (TCO) and total value (TV)
- Recognition and receptivity to developing and expecting offers based on TCO and TV
- The effectiveness of communication between sales and procurement professionals
- Roles and responsibilities of both professions
- The emphasis on tactics and/or strategy
- The use of cross-functional methods
- The significance of performance measurement
- Strategic engagement versus conventional engagement

Survey Methodology

Greybeard drew from its experience as practitioners and advisors to develop questions that could compare and contrast the perceptions of sales and procurement professionals. Appreciating that time comes at a premium, the questions were kept simple and limited to a total of thirty, including demographical inquiries. A five-point answer scale was applied to most questions for the purpose of assessing the respondent's emotion, or lack of it, for the item.

Greybeard sought support from online publishers and professional associations that represent both sales and supply chain. The links to the online surveys (one for sales and one for procurement) were distributed worldwide through announcements and e-mails, resulting in:

- One hundred six responses from sales professionals
- One hundred sixty-one responses from procurement professionals

Survey Elements

The survey was structured to assess perceptions—sales of procurement and procurement of sales—based on the following:

- Knowledge
- Understanding
- Methods
- Resourcefulness
- Performance
- Self assessment/our company

Key Questions and Results

In this section, the mirror-image questions are presented, followed by a short analysis of the survey results. In each case, we identify the statement that the procurement audience reacted to and the statement the sales audience reacted to. For example, in the first section the procurement representatives reacted to the statement: "Sales representatives are knowledgeable about the products and services offered by their company." That is followed by the statement that the sales representatives reacted to: "Procurement representatives are knowledgeable about the requirements of their company."

Section I: Knowledge

Procurement: Sales representatives are knowledgeable about the products and services offered by their company.

Sales: Procurement representatives are knowledgeable about the requirements of their company.

There is general agreement that both sides are knowledgeable of market and company requirements. This is an early indication of a mutual respect for each profession, but this does not hold up throughout the survey.

Procurement sees sales as knowing its products and services by a positive 79% (agree and strongly agree). Adding another 13% who are neutral on this question leaves only 9% (disagree and strongly disagree) of the procurement respondents as having a negative view of the knowledge of sales representatives. The answers may point to the likelihood that sales profession-als are either well trained or experienced, or both, making it possible for sales professionals to capably represent what their company offers.

While the sales responses point toward a respect for the procurement pro-fessional's awareness of the requirements of their company, the measure is not as strong. The sales position on procurement knowledge is 64% positive (agree and strongly agree) followed by 22% who are negative (disagree or strongly disagree) with 14% neutral (neither agree nor disagree).

Procurement: Sales representatives offer to share market knowledge, in-cluding information regarding current forecasts and trends in the marketplace.

Sales: Procurement representatives actively offer to share company require-ments, business plans, processes, and product usage, including information re-garding current forecasts/trends.

As early as this second question in the survey, there are signs of separation in the confidence that one side has for the other when it comes to the willing-ness to share information (Figure 20.1).

The responses continue to be somewhat favorable when procurement eval-uates sales with a 29% positive impression (frequently and always), 48% neu-tral (sometimes), and 23% negative (seldom and never).

It appears that sales professionals are not as complimentary as 9% (always and frequently) perceived procurement's willingness to share information, and

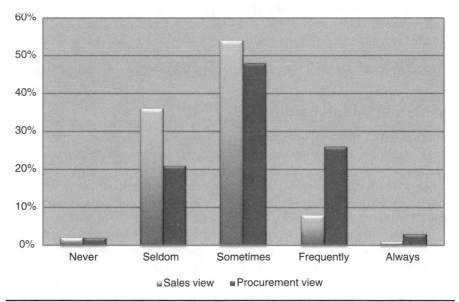

Figure 20.1 Actively sharing information

54% see this as happening only sometimes while 38% (seldom and never) countered that procurement professionals are not likely to share the requirements of their company.

It is possible that both sales and procurement are holding back—being cautious with what information is shared. Considering forecasts and trends typically represent data that can be found by doing some research, it's realistic to expect that both sides should be open to conveying this type of information. The variable may be that procurement is unwilling to share requirements or the business plans for their company. As for sales, openly providing details about the market could result in a competitive disadvantage.

Procurement: Sales representatives are knowledgeable of their competition and accurately understand how their products/services match up to competitive offerings.

Sales: Procurement representatives are knowledgeable of the marketplace and accurately understand how products/services compare.

This subject builds on the topic of understanding—of the marketplace, and of competition, along with understanding how products and services compare. Does sales understand its competition? Does procurement understand the differences in products and services being offered?

Procurement professionals show respect for the sales side, accepting that sales comprehends how their products and services match up as 46% (frequently and always) give sales professionals their due. Another 46% answered that sales understands some of the time. The remaining 8% contend that sales seldom knows its competition.

Sales responses are not as upbeat as 18% (frequently and always) rate procurement professionals as in tune with markets, 58% are neutral, and 25% seldom and never observe procurement favorably.

Section II: Understanding

Procurement: Sales representatives are well versed on *value-add offerings* including economic order quantities, consignment, payment terms, inventory management, and the impact on working capital/cash flow among others.

Sales: Procurement representatives are receptive to recommendations that have a positive impact on working capital/cash flow, including economic order quantities, consignment, payment terms, and inventory management.

Here there's a bona fide gap when it comes to the understanding of impact.

Sales views procurement as being receptive to recommendations that have a positive impact on working capital and/or cash flow, but it appears that procurement doesn't view sales as capable of delivering these types of proposals.

Procurement is receptive—64% of sales professionals (agree and strongly agree) that procurement is open to accepting recommendations that have a positive impact on working capital/cash flow for the areas identified. Only 18% are neutral, and another 18% are negative (disagree and strongly disagree) in finding procurement to be indifferent.

Procurement is split on whether sales professionals are well versed on the implications of *value-add* and are slightly more negative about this topic. In their responses to other knowledge questions, procurement gives credit to sales for knowing the marketplace, but for this one, they don't see sales as capable of putting their offerings into a meaningful context for the customer. Of the procurement replies, 26% are neutral on the question, 35% are positive (agree and strongly agree), and 39% are negative (disagree and strongly disagree).

Procurement: Sales representatives understand the fundamentals of TCO/TV.

Sales: Procurement representatives understand the fundamentals of TCO/TV.

Understanding of the fundamentals of TCO and TV are shown to be in question for both sales and procurement as seen by the other side. Looking at both sets of responses provides evidence that neither side has a favorable opinion of the other (Figure 20.2).

Sales replies are negative by more than 2 to 1 with 46% negative (disagree and strongly disagree), 21% positive (agree and strongly agree) when it comes to taking a position on whether or not procurement does or does not understand TCO, and 33% are neutral.

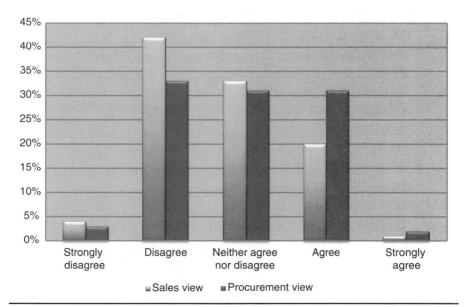

Figure 20.2 Understanding TCO and TV

Procurement professionals exhibit a similar neutral position at 31%. However, they are more positive with 33% (agreeing or strongly agreeing) saying that sales representatives understand TCO. The negatives come in at 35% (disagree or strongly disagree).

Procurement: Sales representatives' proposals address TCO or TV elements and are not based solely on price.

Sales: Procurement representatives request proposals that address TCO or TV elements and not just price.

Addressing TCO and TV appears to take a back seat to price. This is not an eye opener considering the survey was conducted during an economic downturn.

The results show procurement isn't persuaded that sales proposals are as attentive to TCO/TV as they should be. More than half of the responses (51%) point to a neutral (sometimes), 33% (seldom and never) show that it doesn't happen enough, and 17% (frequently and always) give credit to sales for going beyond price in what is proposed.

Sales asserts that procurement isn't interested in TCO with a significant 77% (disagree and strongly disagree) declaring that procurement is more interested in price than TCO and/or TV. Just 16% of the sales returns took the middle of the road, and 13% recognize procurement as interested in proposals that go beyond basic price.

Procurement: Sales representatives are effective at communicating the value of their product or service, emphasizing TV rather than price.

Sales: Procurement representatives understand and recognize the value of proposed products or services, distinguishing TV rather than price.

There is an apparent disconnect when it comes to communication of *value* by sales and acceptance of the message by procurement.

The predominance of procurement responses is neutral (defined as sometimes) when describing how effectively sales communicates value. Of the replies, 33% reflect that procurement has a positive feeling about the effectiveness with which sales emphasizes TV, and 14% come in at believing it seldom happens.

However, when it comes to receiving the message, sales disagrees (60%) that procurement is receptive to the message, 30% of the sales responses are neutral, and only 10% agree that procurement *gets it.*

Section III: Methods

Procurement: Sales professionals recognize and acknowledge procurement as the appropriate first point of contact for sales calls.

Sales: Procurement professionals are the appropriate first point of contact when selling to a company.

The *disconnect* continues when it comes to perceptions about the appropriate point of contact when selling into a company. Procurement professionals are mostly neutral (46%) in their take that sales professionals make procurement the first point of contact for a sales call while 29% (frequently and always) believe that sales first calls on procurement. The remainder, 24%, believe that it seldom or never happens.

In sharp contrast, 62% (disagree and strongly disagree) of sales professionals do not accept procurement as the *first point of contact*. Another 21% are neutral, and only 17% agree.

These numbers are evidence that while procurement believes that sales respects procurement as the *first point*, the sales numbers prove otherwise, pointing toward a belief that there are better places to start the selling process with a potential customer.

Procurement: Sales professionals view the role of the procurement professional as being primarily responsible for transaction management, with the perception that award decisions are made by others in our company.

Sales: Procurement professionals are primarily responsible for transactions and operations and should not be viewed as part of the *award decision-making* process.

For this question, procurement professionals take a strong position that they are viewed by sales, for the most part, as *transactional* rather than tasked with making awards decisions. This could be interpreted as—*to get the order*, you need to go to procurement.

Of the procurement responses, 56% weigh in with the position that sales views procurement as *transactional*, 26% are impartial, and the remaining 19% disagree contending that sales professionals give credit to procurement as having decision making responsibility.

Sales replies substantially defend procurement with 55% disagreeing that procurement should not be viewed as part of the *award making* process. 22% have no opinion one way or the other, and 24% suggest that procurement's only responsibility is operational.

Procurement: Sales professionals bypass procurement in order to sell, by contacting senior management or end users directly—that is, sales reps do *back door selling*.

Sales: Procurement professionals are reluctant to provide access to senior management or end users.

This topic is all about access—taking it or providing it. Sales professionals contend in 62% of their responses that procurement is unwilling to provide access to their senior management, 25% are neutral, and 12% offer that access is supported by procurement.

The procurement position affirms that sales engages in *back door selling* with 48% (frequently and always) observing that sales contacts are made directly to senior management or end users. Adding the 40% of sometimes answers, one can conclude that *back door selling* is a way of doing business in the minds of procurement professionals. Only 9% see it as happening seldom and 3% as never.

There is an intended direct connection between this question and the earlier question regarding the first point of contact. The correlation affirms that if sales can bypass procurement—it will. Along with the intended correlation, these questions were also intended to be simple. One could deduce that sales either does not respect procurement or sees procurement as an obstacle to go around.

Procurement: Sales professionals from nonincumbent suppliers *go through the motions* when submitting a bid, principally because they believe that the purpose of the bid is to satisfy a requirement, and there is no intention of awarding business to a new supplier.

Sales: Purchasing professionals take the *mechanical rabbit* approach—inviting new suppliers to bid, principally for the purpose of using that bid against the incumbent, with no intention of awarding business to a new supplier.

Sales professionals are faced with a difficult decision when it comes to responding or not responding to a request for proposal. Resources (defined as time and effort) for completing and submitting a response have an intrinsic worth and must be expended carefully.

There is an eye-opening degree of neutrality in the reaction of both procurement and sales. Procurement professionals took a sometimes position in 56% of their responses, and sales took a comparable 58%.

However, sales displayed their cynicism with 35% (frequently and always) believing that procurement takes a *mechanical rabbit* approach. Only 7% see this as a seldom occurrence.

Procurement was not nearly as disapproving with only 23% of their responses (frequently and always) facing up to the prospect that sales only goes through the motions due to lack of confidence in the bid process. In fact, procurement was positive to the extent of 21% (seldom and never) giving credit to sales for taking the bid process seriously.

Procurement: Sales professionals think that procurement uses *sharp practices* or *secret tactics* to *beat up* and undermine sales.

Sales: Procurement professionals use *sharp practices* or *secret tactics* to *beat up* and undermine sales professionals.

Tactics and practices are front and center with this question as sales professionals struggle uncertainly with mannerisms and bearing of procurement professionals.

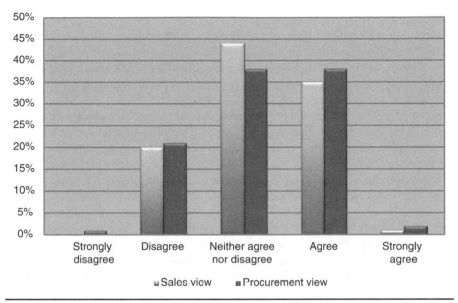

Figure 20.3 Sharp practices and *secret tactics*

Once again, a notable percentage of respondents from both procurement and sales took a neutral position on this question—sales at 44% and procurement at 38% (Figure 20.3).

As for the sales responses, 36% (agree and strongly agree) that procurement behaves in ways that undermine sales' efforts. Some 20% (disagree and strongly disagree) have confidence their procurement counterparts do not employ *secret practices*.

The procurement numbers are analogous and recognize the concerns of sales professionals, and 40% (agree and strongly agree) that sales is convinced that they (procurement) draw on *secrets* to *beat up* sales professionals. Another 22% (disagree and strongly disagree) take the position that sales professionals have confidence that they (sales) are dealt with properly.

Section IV: Resourcefulness

Procurement: Sales representatives use the term *partnership* and demonstrate that they are prepared to enter into a relationship based on the sharing of risk to achieve mutual benefits.

Sales: Procurement representatives are receptive to entering into a *partnership* based on the sharing of risk to achieve mutual benefits.

Partnership is generally acknowledged by customers to be a word that is used loosely by suppliers. Is the term *partner* being used appropriately as *sharing of risk* or just an overworked catchphrase?

Consistent with previous rejoinders, both procurement and sales professionals exhibit essentially the same measure of neutrality (meaning sometimes)—procurement perceptions are at 48%, and sales perceptions are at 47%.

Of procurement, 20% (frequently and always) buy into willingness of sales to share the risk for the purpose of achieving mutual benefit. But 34% (seldom and never) don't believe it.

As for receptivity for entering into a *partnership*, sales professionals don't see it with only 5% (frequently and always) convinced that procurement is willing, and a sizable 49% (seldom and never) just not seeing it at all.

Procurement: Sales organizations use cross-functional sales teams to respond to cross-functional sourcing teams.

Sales: Procurement organizations have increased their use of cross-functional sourcing teams and team negotiations to address their company's needs.

When it comes to applying a cross-functional approach to sourcing, there is a shift away from noncommittal sales responses to a marked recognition that procurement is moving in this direction. Procurement isn't sure or just doesn't see sales as embracing Newton's Law—for every action, there is an equal and opposite reaction—taking the same cross-functional approach to make the sale.

More than half of the sales professionals—52% (agree and strongly agree)—believe that procurement has increased its use of cross-functional teams and team negotiations, 35% are neutral (neither agree or disagree) and 13% (disagree) indicate that use of this approach is either nonexistent or isn't changing.

A notable 20% (always and frequently) of procurement professionals point out sales initiatives are cross functional. Many, 45% (sometimes) see it happening at times, and 35% (seldom and never) don't perceive it happening.

Procurement: If suppliers were to create cross-functional teams to respond to our team-based sourcing process, it is more likely that they would address our needs in their initial proposal.

Sales: When suppliers (sales) use a cross-functional team approach to respond to a customer's team-based sourcing process, it's more likely that sales will address the customer's needs with their initial proposal.

The affirmation for the effectiveness of *cross functional* from both contingents is one of the more remarkable messages to come through in the survey. It is one of the few times that both groups took a strongly agree, double digit position in answering the question with procurement at 12% and sales at 11% observing that cross-functional selling teams are likely to produce desired results.

Of sales professionals, 81% (agree and strongly agree) declare that when they apply cross-functional techniques within their own ranks, they are apt to deliver what the customer wants on the first try. Of the remainder, 15% are neutral, and only 4% disagree that the technique is productive.

Procurement comes across as encouraging sales to use cross-functional methods as 73% (agree and strongly agree) are in favor. They suggest that when sales professionals counteract with cross-functional teams then sales is likely to lead off with an offer that meets procurement's expectations. Of procurement, 22% is neutral on the point, and 5% disagree that cross functional teams get it right the first time.

Procurement: Selling teams invite procurement professionals from within their company to assist in the sales process.

Sales: In our company, sales personnel have the opportunity to request advice and assistance from their own procurement department to assist in the sales process.

While companies have both sales and procurement organizations under the same roof, it's not typical for either group to contact the other to draw from their resident expertise. The responses confirm that within a company, it's unlikely that one group will turn to the other as a resource. Given the relatively tactical nature of most sales and procurement departments, perhaps nothing is being lost by this attitude.

Sales responses are divided proportionally across *we do, we don't*, and *sometimes*. These professionals intimate that they are agreeable to turning to their own procurement group for advice and assistance—34% (frequently and always) come out as making this a practice. However, 30% (seldom and never) don't take advantage of the availability of in-house skills, and 36% (sometimes) are more casual in considering the possibility.

Even as selling teams purport to sometimes access their procurement counterparts, the responses of procurement professionals make it clear that it doesn't happen much. Overall, 64% are negative with a disquieting 23% pronouncing that it *never* happens, 41% showing it *seldom* happens, 29% say *sometimes*, and 9% (frequently and always) are invited to assist sales.

This question points out the strong possibility of a major disconnect in the perceptions of sales and procurement groups within the same company.

Section V: Performance

Procurement: Sales representatives support the use of *supplier scorecards* to measure performance (delivery, quality, service, cost reduction, cost avoidance, inventory reduction, etc.).

Sales: Procurement representatives convey the importance of using *supplier* scorecards to measure performance (delivery, quality, service, cost reduction, cost avoidance, inventory reduction, etc.).

Procurement has the responsibility to impart the seriousness of measuring supplier performance, and sales has the obligation to cooperate with the mutually beneficial evaluation of accomplishments, or lack thereof.

Of sales professionals, 46% hold back in declaring that procurement communicates the importance of scorecards saying it happens only sometimes, and 36% are positive (frequently and always), which is twice as many who say it seldom happens at 18%.

Procurement is much more willing to give credit to sales for backing the use of scorecards. Nearly one-third, 30% (always and frequently), accept that sales is supportive of scorecards, 35% (sometimes) point to inconsistency, and a matching 35% (seldom and never) report that sales doesn't subscribe to the usefulness of scorecards.

Procurement: Sales representatives demonstrate that they are serious about participating in *supplier scorecard* processes, including the development of action plans to address shortfalls.

Sales: Procurement representatives are diligent in the actual use and application of *supplier scorecard* processes, including the development of action plans to address shortfalls.

Implementation by procurement and cooperation from sales are the thrust behind this topic. How conscientious are procurement professionals in using and developing scorecards? Also, how serious are sales professionals about their involvement with adopting corrective actions?

Procurement is even keeled in their distribution of opinions about sales' gravitas for scorecards. Some 32% are neutral (neither agree nor disagree), 35% (disagree or strongly disagree) that sales is earnest about taking part, and 33% approve (agree and strongly agree) of sales' compliance.

Sales professionals aren't won over by procurement's propensity, or lack of it, for following the norms of using scorecards. They disagree by 43% (disagree and strongly disagree) while 30% are neutral, and 27% agree that procurement professionals are diligent in their discharge of these duties.

Procurement: Sales representatives understand the value of proposing *additional* or *ongoing* cost reductions that can be achieved through increased information sharing, process improvements, product substitutions, product modifications, etc.

Sales: Procurement representatives are receptive to unsolicited proposals for *additional* or *ongoing* cost reductions that can be achieved through increased information sharing, process improvements, product substitutions, product modifications, etc.

The word *cost* is pivotal to this question. The question asks about interest in cost reductions that are the result of sharing information and the receptivity to change—not just cutting the price—contingent on information sharing.

A substantial 46% (agree and strongly agree) of sales professionals credit procurement as being open to unsolicited bids that can impact cost, contingent upon information sharing. Another 39% came in as neutral (neither agree nor disagree), and 15% (disagree and strongly disagree) don't find procurement to be interested in such offers, or possibly in sharing information needed for such offers.

Procurement professionals acknowledge that sales comprehends the worth connected with offers that add to, or continue, cost reductions with 40% (agree and strongly agree) approving though 31% (disagree and strongly disagree) don't share this opinion, and 29% are impartial.

Procurement: Sales representatives embrace a collaborative approach to understanding our company's business requirements and how current market trends are affecting our requirements, and offer recommendations accordingly.

Sales: Procurement representatives are receptive to taking a collaborative approach to understanding how market trends are affecting their business requirements and how our company (the supplier) can assist them in addressing the affected requirements.

This question ties directly back to the question in the knowledge section that asked about willingness to share information. This question goes beyond sharing and attempts to establish the interest of each side for presenting or accepting offers prepared to deal with market conditions.

Of the sales responses, 39% (disagree and strongly disagree) maintain there is no interest from procurement for these kinds of recommendations, 23% give credit to procurement for wanting to know more, and 38% just can't say.

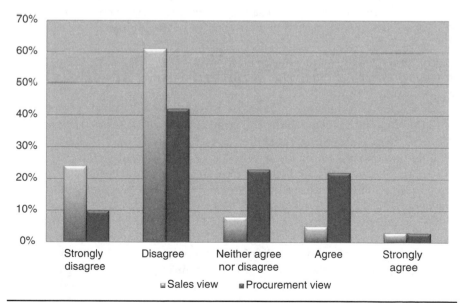

Figure 20.4   Does use of the internet make selling irrelevant?

Consistent with earlier responses, the majority of procurement upholds the willingness of sales to collaborate and deliver proposals accordingly—37% (agree and strongly agree) take the position that there is cooperation and interest though 28% don't believe so. Slightly more than one-third—34% don't have an opinion one way or the other.

Section VI: Self-assessment/Our Company

Due to the use of the Internet, long-term contracts, among other items, traditional *selling* is becoming irrelevant.

For the purpose of level setting—Section 6 starts with a basic question of whether or not the use of the Internet affects the underpinning of traditional *selling* (Figure 20.4). Before going into questions calling for a self-assessment of how involved procurement professionals are in strategic initiatives, it seemed appropriate to ask about the relevance of traditional selling.

There was substantial disagreement to this suggestion. More than half of procurement professionals, at 52% (disagree and strongly disagree), declared that the Internet overshadows traditional selling. A compelling 85% (disagree and strongly disagree) of sales responses pushed back on being displaced by the Internet.

Of procurement, 23% provided a neutral reply, and only 8% of sales abstained from taking a position.

It's noteworthy that 25% (agree and strongly agree) of procurement professionals answered that traditional selling is becoming extraneous whereas only 8% (agree and strongly agree) of sales consent to this thinking.

Procurement: In our company, procurement has a truly strategic role; we are involved early, and strategically, with revenue enhancement and new product development support.

Sales: Our customers invite our participation in their strategic procurement initiatives; we are involved early, and strategically, with revenue enhancement and new product development support.

This question asks procurement about its role in contributing to the top line of the company in the forms of revenue enhancement and new product development. This question is also specific about when procurement becomes engaged, with the emphasis on *early*.

Of procurement professionals, 51% (agree and strongly agree) responded that they are involved, 22% (disagree and strongly disagree) communicated they don't play a role, and 27% didn't make any statement about involvement.

As for sales being asked to help procurement in pursuing strategic revenue initiatives, it's a relatively balanced distribution of opinion. Sales professionals agree (agree and strongly agree) by 34%. For 36% (disagree and strongly disagree), the phone doesn't ring, and 30% are unmoved by the question.

This may be verification that if procurement is considered to be strategic, then procurement expects strategic support from their assigned sales professionals.

Procurement: In our company, procurement has a truly strategic role; we are involved early, and strategically, with all areas of cost management (i.e., there are no sacred cows).

Sales: Our customers invite our participation in their strategic procurement initiatives; we are involved early, and strategically, with all areas of cost management (i.e., there are no sacred cows).

When asked if procurement is involved early and strategically in all areas of cost management, without exclusion, there isn't quite as much certainty as 49% (agree and strongly agree) of procurement professionals take a position that they are engaged upfront in all areas of spend, and 22% are indifferent. Nearly one-third at 29% (disagree and strongly disagree) has some constraints on their involvement in cost management (i.e., there are *off limits* areas where procurement is not involved).

There is a corresponding reduction of confidence in the sales replies as 50% of the sales professionals disagree (disagree and strongly disagree) that procurement seeks a helping hand from sales, 29% aren't sure, and 21% (agree) believe they are called upon to play their part.

Procurement: In our company, procurement has a truly strategic role; we are involved early, and strategically, with working capital initiatives (payment terms, inventory).

Sales: Our customers invite our participation in their strategic procurement initiatives; we are involved early, and strategically, with working capital initiatives (payment terms, inventory).

As for working capital initiatives—defined for this survey as payment terms and inventory—procurement is convincingly positive about its acceptance in these strategic areas.

Of procurement professionals, 61% (agree and strongly agree) are likely to be called upon to contribute in this kind of activity. This is logical considering that payment terms, as well as inventory management, are supported by information technology.

The technology enables access to billing/spend detail and supplier inventory data, which are typically addressed early in the sell/buy process.

With the remainder, 21% stated they aren't sure, and 17% (disagree and strongly disagree) are on the outside of these working capital initiatives.

Of the sales responses, 38% were mixed on this question, and 32% (disagree and strongly disagree) of the sales professionals let it be known they aren't invited. The remaining 30% (agree and strongly agree) assure they are brought in to assist. Again, this makes sense considering the increased use of technology for spend and inventory management.

Procurement: In our company, procurement has a truly strategic role; we are involved early, and strategically, with *capital expenditures*.

Sales: Our customers invite our participation in their strategic procurement initiatives; we are involved early, and strategically, with *capital expenditures*.

Procurement professionals, based on 51% (agree and strongly agree) of the responses, again take a firm position that they participate strategically with capital spending though 22% (disagree and strongly disagree) tell that they are not involved, and approximately one-third didn't take a position on the question.

As for sales professionals—nearly half (disagree and strongly disagree) consider themselves left out of the loop on capital spending projects, 30% weren't specific, and 21% agree that their customers request their involvement.

Procurement: In our company, procurement is measured against strategic objectives (such as the areas in the preceding four topics), not merely price reduction.

Sales: In our company, sales is measured against strategic objectives, such as the number of new long-term relationships established, customer retention, etc., rather than just price metrics.

The sales responses disclose that more than half of the respondents contend that they are judged only on revenue, and 32% (agree and strongly agree) make it known that they are working toward strategic objectives. Only 16% had no strong opinion.

The opposite applies to procurement as 52% (agree and strongly agree) of the procurement professionals are confident that they are expected to meet strategic objectives, 23% (neither agree nor disagree) aren't sure, and 25% (disagree and strongly disagree) don't feel that they are measured against strategic objectives.

Section VII: Survey Demographics

Our Company: Current State of Procurement/Sales Practices

The responses from both procurement and sales present nearly a mirror image. Both groups see themselves as a mix of traditional and strategic with sales coming in at 75% and procurement at 70%.

Less than 10% of procurement responses and less than 10% of sales responses consider themselves to have a world-class process with a strategic role.

Our Company: Annual Revenues

The sales responses are evenly split with half representing companies that have a $1 billion plus in annual revenues and the other 50% coming from companies under $1 billion. The predominance of sales responses at 34% came from companies that generate between $1 billion and $10 billion (Figure 20.5).

Procurement replies show just about a 60/40 split with the bigger number coming from companies $1 billion and under. The largest representation of replies at 37% came from procurement professionals who represent companies with less than $100 million of annual revenues.

Our Company: Location

Procurement professionals weighed in on the questions from all over the world as 72% of the respondents were from North America, 11% from Asia, and Europe accounted for 7% of the responses. The remainder came in evenly from Africa, the Middle East, Oceana, and Latin America with 3% from each region.

Of the sales participation, 91% came from North America, 8% came from professionals based in Europe, and the remaining 1% came from Asia.

Job Title/Level

There was noteworthy involvement in the survey from top management in both procurement and sales. Of the procurement input, 60% came from the top end (top two levels) of the procurement organization with 38% from the top procurement or supply chain executive.

The same applies for sales as 71% of the professionals taking part in the survey represented senior management (top two levels of sales), with 42% from the top sales executive in the company.

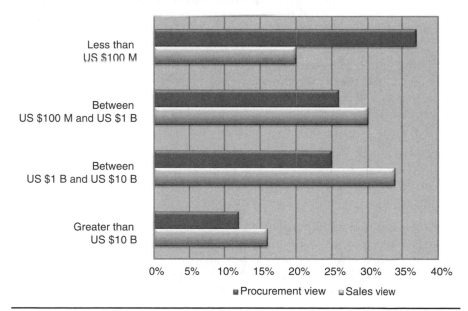

Figure 20.5 Annual revenue of company

Section VIII: Free Form Feedback

(From the Procurement Survey)

Procurement: Describe or list the characteristics of the most effective selling/sales process that you—as a purchasing professional—have ever encountered.

Note: The following are a selection from the free form responses (without edit):

- (1) Sales are completely informed about buying company's goals, objectives and daily concerns. (2) Extreme high level of communication on both bad and good events. (3) Continual communication with customers, users, and buyers.
- (1) Sales individuals that truly listen to the *voice of the customer* and proactively create proposals that respond to our business objectives. (2) Companies that are willing to challenge the *status quo* within our organization—assist us in identifying sources of competitiveness. (3) Ability to conduct open, honest communication—trust & credibility is everything.
- A supplier that understands elements of our business better than we do, and based on them, acts proactively to support us, is highly effective.
- Cross-functional team of knowledgeable associates who have a thorough understanding of what they're selling. Listens to the customer and answers questions directly. Responds to requests completely and in a timely fashion. Brings savings opportunities to the table before being asked to do so.
- Don't recall one.
- The sales professional has taken the time to research the company and become familiar with the operations, corporate mission statement, current annual report, and was prepared to clearly demonstrate their value proposition.

(From Sales Survey)

Sales: Describe or list the characteristics of the most effective sourcing/procurement process that you—as a sales professional—have ever encountered.

Note: The following are a selection from the free form responses (without edit):

- Goals stated up front: reduce the TCO by 20%; collaborative approach to understanding feature/benefit tradeoffs with price; engineering/manufacturing involved as well as procurement.
- Empowered and informed, understands the total cost of acquisition and looks beyond the price. Uses collaborations to achieve strategic ambitions. Invests in relationships.

- Using a collaborative approach to include new ideas and/or processes; willingness to entertain solutions outside of the specific parameters of an RFP; applying cost-of-ownership principles vs. pure lowest initial cost.
- Involvement was from the ground floor to the top floor with everyone's opinion carrying the same weight.
- The most effective sourcing process I was involved with did not involve the procurement group until the details and scope were defined and rough order of magnitude quotes were delivered. We sell custom developed solutions that can't be ported into a standard procurement process.
- The most effective relationships we have with customer procurement personnel is in organizations that are not procurement driven. Procurement is an important function in the organization, but sales, marketing, operations, etc. is heavily involved in technology and supplier selection.
- (1) They listened to our overall solution and realized the benefit in what was being presented. (2) Didn't treat our product as a commodity. (3) Shopped our total solution with like for like services. (4) Made a decision on value and solution not just on price.

Within-Survey Results

The primary purpose of the surveys was to compare the perspectives of sales and procurement professionals about each other. The survey data, however, also provided an opportunity for drawing conclusions *intra-survey*—that is, within each group of respondents. Those conclusions follow:

I. Procurement Respondents

a. Procurement respondents who characterized their company's procurement department as "World-class processes with a strategic role" were more likely to indicate that they see TV proposals or TCO proposals from sales reps.

b. On the other hand, respondents who characterized their company's procurement department as "Traditional purchasing consumed by daily tasks and fire drills" were less likely to indicate that they see TV proposals or TCO proposals from sales reps.

c. Procurement respondents were strongly of the impression that sales tries to by-pass procurement and *back door sell*—regardless of the state of the procurement organization.

d. Procurement respondents who characterized their company's procurement department as "World-class processes with a strategic role" were more likely to indicate that they see cross-functional sales teams from their suppliers.

e. On the other hand, respondents who characterized their company's procurement department as "Traditional purchasing consumed by daily tasks and fire drills" were less likely to indicate that they see cross-functional sales teams from their suppliers.

f. Procurement respondents were rarely invited to assist their company's own selling efforts—regardless of the state of the procurement organization.

g. Procurement respondents who characterized their company's procurement department as "World-class processes with a strategic role" were more likely to enjoy a *strategic role* in all areas that drive return on invested capital: revenues, costs, working capital, and capital expenditures.

II. Sales respondents

a. Sales respondents were equally divided in their view of whether procurement representatives understand—or do not understand—the fundamentals of TCO or TV. Furthermore, approximately 80% of sales respondents said that procurement does NOT request proposals based on TCO or TV. These results were consistent regardless of how the sales department characterized itself (e.g., world-class processes with a strategic role, traditional sales, etc.).

b. Nearly half of all sales respondents indicated that procurement has increased its use of cross-functional teams. Furthermore, approximately three-fourths of sales respondents said that sales is more likely to be successful addressing customer needs in its initial proposal by using a cross-functional team approach.

c. In companies that characterized their sales department as *world class*, nearly three-fourths indicated that the sales department has the opportunity to request advice and assistance from their own procurement department.

Some Final Thoughts

On the surface, the survey responses deliver what could have been anticipated. Procurement professionals are making some progress in performing strategically, but behaviors remain tactical. Outside the survey, there is compelling evidence that the role of procurement is growing in prominence within corporations. Senior management expects procurement to be more strategic. The survey confirms that procurement professionals also believe that they are being engaged more strategically by their internal customers. However, when procurement professionals were asked if they consider themselves to have a world-class process with a strategic role, only 9% said yes.

Senior management expects procurement to be more strategic and often believes that it's happening. Is it possible that procurement professionals aren't quite sure how they are to meet this expectation? Is the best available option to declare that your work is strategic when you recognize that something is missing—like a world-class process? The risk for procurement professionals is that the sales side is catching on to this disconnect. Sales professionals are now being schooled in developing *value-based* strategic solutions and recommendations.

To deliver these recommendations, the sales professionals can take one of three paths within a company—directly to the executive suite; directly to the stakeholders; or through procurement. Two of the paths aren't good for procurement. If the sales professional is not convinced that procurement will collaborate in the process, then the path of least resistance will be followed.

For the procurement organization that wants to achieve the next level, it's important to be part of the solution rather than part of the problem.

Chapter Notes

1. The original white paper from which this chapter was developed included graphs for each topic. Readers who want to access the research white paper can do so by visiting the resources section of the Greybeard Advisors website: http://www.greybeardadvisors.com/resources and selecting the White Papers option.
2. The authors acknowledge the important contributions of Jim Baehr to this chapter.

Index